# SOCIAL MEDIA MARKETING
# WORKBOOK
## 2020

2020 – Updated Version

by Jason McDonald, Ph.D.

© 2020, JM Internet Group

**https://www.jm-seo.org/**

Tel. 800-298-4065

"The perfect is the enemy of the good." – Voltaire

# TABLE OF CONTENTS

# 0
# INTRODUCTION

Welcome to the *Social Media Marketing Workbook 2020*! With a complete fact-checking of all available tips, tricks, and features, get ready to:

- Have some **fun**.

- **Learn how Social Media works.**

- Understand how to use **Social Media** to **market your business**.

- Create a step-by-step **Social Media Marketing plan**.

Fully revised and updated as of spring 2020, this workbook not only explains how to market on social media (from Facebook to LinkedIn, YouTube to Pinterest, Instagram to Twitter to Yelp and back again) but also provides access to **free social media marketing tools**. It provides overviews, detailed instructions, tips and secrets, resource notes and free tools for social media marketing, and access to step-by-step **worksheets** and **videos** that will help you market your product, service, or business on social media.

## Free Tools

Even better, if you register your copy, you also get access to my complete *Marketing Almanac* and *Social Media Dashboard*, with literally hundreds of **free social media marketing tools** to turbocharge your social media marketing not just on Facebook but also on LinkedIn, Twitter, YouTube, Pinterest, Instagram and other major social media platforms.

> *It slices, it dices. It explains how social media works. It gives you free tools. And it helps you build a social media marketing plan.*

## Why Market via Social Media?

If you own a business or work as a marketing manager at a business, you're probably intrigued by **social media** as a **marketing platform**. Hardly a day goes by that the "traditional" news media doesn't talk about Twitter, Instagram, Snapchat, Facebook, or YouTube, often in the context of some new way to reach customers and build buzz. Between TV shows like *Ellen* or radio shows like *Marketplace* encouraging you to "like" them on Facebook, or your next-door neighbor or perhaps a business competitor bragging about their latest tweet or "Stories" upload to Instagram, it seems like everyone is promoting their Facebook Page, their YouTube channel, their reviews on Yelp, or encouraging you to check them out on Snapchat. Now in 2020 everyone's buzzing about TikTok as the next new, new thing. What do they understand that you don't get? Or, even if you get a lot, what are secret tips and tricks that can improve your marketing even further? Social media is everywhere, and yet it can seem very confusing to the uninitiated. What is this *magical marketing* being conducted on *social media*, and how does it work?

## Let's Talk about You

Let's talk about you for a moment. Perhaps you own a small business, perhaps you're the marketing manager at a mid-size company producing ball bearings, or perhaps you are an ad agency guru charged with setting up a Facebook plan for a local non-profit. It's easy to be overwhelmed, and natural to feel like you're not sure how to market on social media. Perhaps you're just starting out with a **Facebook Page** for your **business**, or perhaps you've seen your teenager spend hours on **Instagram**, **TikTok**, or **Snapchat**, or you realize that the female, shopping demographic is "on" **Pinterest**. Perhaps the hip coworker dressed in black or one of his friends has looked down on you, condescendingly, when you don't understand the difference between a *hashtag* and a *retweet*. Or you've painfully learned that **Yelp** or **Google** reviews can make (or break) your business, only after an unhappy customer has trashed you online. Social media, after all, is all around us in today's 24/7 desktop, tablet, and mobile phone environment, and it does not seem to be simple!

Maybe you have already attempted a Facebook Page, a YouTube Channel, or a Pinterest board, but it hasn't really worked out. "How does social media really work?" you wonder. "What's all the fuss about, and can it really bring in customers and make sales?"

> *Don't worry. Enter the Social Media Marketing Workbook to the rescue, with step-by-step instructions on how to market on each social media network plus a conceptual framework, so you actually understand the nature of marketing itself.*

This book will explain the "how" – a step by step, systematic method to effective social media marketing. But before we dive into the "how," let's step back for a minute and ask the "why":

**Why market on social media?**

Here are some reasons why **social media marketing** is valuable:

- **Social media is big.** Facebook, the largest social media platform, has over two billion users worldwide and climbing; LinkedIn sports over 600 million members as "the" network for B2B marketers. Every day nearly 1 billion videos are watched on YouTube, and nearly everyone goes to Yelp or Google to check out reviews on local businesses.

- **Your customers are on social media.** Nearly everyone uses Facebook – from teenagers to grandmas, business executives to flight attendants. Most professionals have at least a LinkedIn profile. Everyone reads reviews online, many post pictures to Instagram, etc. *Fish where the fish are.* By participating in social media, you can reach your customers where they "hang out."

- **Social media is free**. Facebook, Yelp, Snapchat, YouTube, TikTok, Instagram, Pinterest... are, of course, free to use. Users love them because "for free" they get access to their friends and family, plus information on brands that they love. And in terms of marketing, there is a lot you can do, for free, to build your brand, spread eWOM (electronic word of mouth), help you stay top-of-mind with your customers, and even "get shares" or "go viral." (*Free, as we will learn, does not mean easy or no hard work involved – more on that later!*)

- **Social Media can reach not only existing but also new customers.** Between organic ("free") and paid reach on sites like Instagram, Facebook, YouTube or Twitter, you can not only stay in touch with your existing customers, you can also be discovered by new customers. Unlike on search engines like Google (where customers must proactively look for you), on social media, you can be discovered as customer No. 1 shares information with customer No 2. You can also be discovered not when a customer is proactively searching for you but when he just happens to be checking his Facebook news feed, or browsing photos on Instagram. Hashtags – the *#trendingtopics* that occur especially on Instagram and Twitter – are yet another way to reach people who aren't proactively looking for your product or service.

- **Social Media offers advertising opportunities.** While consumers may react negatively to advertising in the abstract, in the concrete, most will react positively to ads done well. Facebook, Instagram, Twitter, YouTube, LinkedIn, Pinterest – indeed every major social media platform offers targeted advertising that - when done right - can be an effective way to build your brand and sell more stuff. The reality, today, is that more and more networks are becoming "pay to play." Accordingly, the smart marketers have set a 2020 New Year's Resolution to become savvy social media advertisers.

## Social Media (Seems) Complicated

Social media, however, is also **complicated**. First of all, *using* social media is one thing, and *marketing* on social media is another. That snappy teenager might understand how to *use* Snapchat, but this doesn't mean she knows how to *market* on it. Even many experienced marketers are befuddled, as their knowledge of traditional marketing channels does not translate easily to social media networks like Instagram or Twitter. Indeed, many businesses simply fail at social media marketing, either doing nothing or spinning their wheels with endless busywork. They don't understand how social media functions and they fail to see the incredible marketing opportunities beneath the surface of this huge but messy brave new world of marketing. Quite simply, you have to invest some time to learn "how" to market on social media.

Even worse, many practitioners of social media mistakenly think that they understand it when all they are doing is spinning their wheels. They post, but no one listens, watches, or reads. They post, but few like, comment on, or share. And they post and even if they get engagement, their social media marketing strategy doesn't lead towards the ultimate marketing goals of building their brand and selling more stuff.

Or, in the new 2020 environment, many marketers whine about the demise of organic ("free") reach on Facebook, Instagram, and YouTube and avoid learning about and deploying the incredible advertising opportunities on each network. "If you can't beat 'em, join 'em," goes the old saw, but these marketers refuse to work with the gurus at Facebook, YouTube, or Pinterest who spend their days brainstorming how to make ads engaging and effective on their platforms. YouTube, Facebook, Pinterest, and the gang – after all – aren't charities. They're *for-profit businesses* based on *advertising*. So how do you advertise? How can you advertise effectively to build your brand and sell more stuff? It's complicated.

Fortunately, you hold in your hand (or at least hold it virtually in your Kindle or PC or in your ears if you're listening in audiobook format), the *Social Media Marketing Workbook*, a workbook that helps you understand the "how" of marketing your business on social media. You've joined that elite group of people who have taken the most important step: proactively seeking to educate themselves on how to market via this new world order.

## Who is This Workbook For?

This workbook is aimed primarily at **small business owners** and **marketing managers**. **Non-profits** will also find it useful. If you want to build buzz around your company or brand, increase your sales or sales leads, or expand your reach from your most loyal customers to their friends and family, and to the friends and family of those friends and family, this workbook is for you.

If you are a person whose job involves advertising, marketing, and/or branding, this workbook is for you. If you are a small business that sees a marketing opportunity in social media of any type, this workbook is for you. And if your job is to market a business or organization online in today's Internet economy, this book is for you. Anyone who wants to look behind the curtain and understand the mechanics of how to market on social media (from Facebook to LinkedIn, Twitter to Yelp, Pinterest to YouTube and beyond) will benefit from this book.

Anyone who sees – however dimly – that social media could help market their business will benefit from this hands-on workbook. And even if you are a skilled practitioner, this book will add value by helping you to think strategically about how to market via social media and as we go platform by platform, reviewing tips, tricks, and secrets that you might not know about.

Oh, and if you're a student or perhaps an *un-* or *under-*employed marketer, and you're building job skills, this Workbook will help you join the digital revolution by "going social." Marketing today has "gone digital," meaning that Search Engine Optimization (SEO), advertising, review marketing, and social media marketing are the skills you need to be a high-payed, high-power marketer in 2020. This Workbook teaches you the cornerstone skill of how to market on social media, but check out my other digital marketing books at **http://jmlinks.com/books** to educate yourself on SEO, Google Ads, or digital marketing more generally.

## How Does This Workbook Work?

This workbook starts first with an overview of **social media *marketing***. Beyond the positive "can do" attitude that you already have (if you've read this far, or purchased this book), the next most important asset is a "mental model" of what social media is, what social media marketing is, and the roles in this narrative between you as content producer and your customers as content consumers.

It's simple. If social media is a **party**, then **using social media** is akin to just *showing up at a party*. **Marketing** on social media, in contrast, isn't about showing up. It's about *throwing* the party!

Understanding this distinction between "attending" the social media party and "throwing" the social media party is the subject of **Chapter One**.

# SOCIAL MEDIA MARKETING = THROWING GREAT "ONLINE PARTIES"

**Chapter Two** is the next most important concept: **content marketing**. You need wonderful food and entertainment to keep your party going, and content is the "food and entertainment" of social media marketing. Accordingly, Chapter Two will explain to you how to set up and maintain a content production machine to feed all your social channels.

**Chapters Three** through **Ten** are deep dives into social media marketing, one medium at a time. We'll start, for example, with **Facebook**. First, we'll provide an overview of how Facebook works, explain everything from profiles to pages, likes to comments to shares, Edgerank to posting rhythm. It will all become much clearer, as we work through Facebook in plain English, written for "mere mortals." Along the way, I'll provide **videos** and **worksheets** that will act as "Jason as therapist," so you can fill them out and begin to outline your own unique Facebook marketing plan. Chapter **quizzes** help you test your knowledge and generate a nifty certificate suitable for framing and/or to place on your refrigerator. My goal is for you to not only *understand* Facebook marketing but actually to begin to *do* marketing on Facebook. Ditto for LinkedIn, Twitter, Instagram, YouTube, and the rest of the gang.

**Table of Contents**

4. **LinkedIn** – how to use the world's largest B2b network for your business, including advertising opportunities.

5. **Twitter** – an explanation of whether you should tweet, and if you do, how to use Twitter effectively for business marketing.

6. **Instagram** – how Instagram is like Twitter with pictures, how to market on Instagram, and even a brief comparison to **Snapchat**.

7. **YouTube** – a deep dive into the business side of YouTube, often hidden behind cat videos and Rihanna or Lady Gaga gyrations gone viral. Included is a discussion of how to leverage YouTube advertising opportunities for your video strategy.

8. **Pinterest** – the most effective social media for eCommerce stores and retailers, do-it-yourselfers, and those serving the female shopping demographic such as wedding photographers.

9. **Local SEO and Review Marketing** – how the "Review Revolution" is impacting local businesses, and how to use Yelp, Google My Business (Google's local service), and other review sites to promote your business via reviews.

10. **Email Marketing**. Email marketing is the "Rodney Dangerfield" of social media marketing. It don't get no respect. But it should, and so this Chapter explains why you should use email as part of your social media marketing system.

11. **Epilogue** – the "new" new kids on the block: Snapchat, Tumblr, TikTok, Medium, and new ways to go social and go marketing.

## » Meet the Author

My name is Jason McDonald, and I have been active on the Internet since 1994 (*having invented the Internet along with Al Gore*) and taught SEO, AdWords, and Social Media since 2009 – online, at Stanford University Continuing Studies, at both AcademyX and the Bay Area Video Coalition in San Francisco, at workshops, and in corporate trainings across these United States. I love figuring out how things work, and I love teaching others! Social media marketing is an endeavor that I understand, and I want to empower you to understand it as well.

Learn more about me at **https://www.jasonmcdonald.org/** or at my corporate website **https://www.jm-seo.org/**. Or just call 800-298-4065, say something flattering, and my secretary will put you through. (*Like I have a secretary! Just call if you have something to ask or say*). Visit the websites above to follow me on Twitter, connect with me on LinkedIn, or follow me on Facebook. *Sorry, my Snapchat feed and TikTok are so crazy, they're for friends and family, only.*

**Take My Classes**

I teach both online and face-to-face on the Stanford Campus. If you'd like to learn more or get an email alert when registrations are open, visit **http://jmlinks.com/classes**. The classes build on the books and focus on practical, hands-on knowledge of SEO and Social Media Marketing successes.

## >> SPREAD THE WORD: TAKE A SURVEY & GET $5!

If you like this workbook, please take a moment to take a short **survey**. The survey helps me find errors in the book, learn from student questions, and get feedback to improve future editions of the book. Plus, by taking the survey, I'll be able to reach out to you, and we can even become friends. Or, if not friends, at least friends on the Internet or Facebook which isn't quite the same thing, but still it's pretty good.

Here's how –

- Visit **http://jmlinks.com/survey**.
- Take a short **survey** about the book.
- I will rebate you $5.00 via Amazon gift eCard.

How's that for an offer you can't refuse?

This offer is limited to the first 100 participants, and only for participants who have purchased a paid copy of the 2020 edition of this book. You may be required to show proof of purchase and the birth certificate of your firstborn child, cat, or goldfish. If you don't have a child, cat, or goldfish, you may be required to prove telepathically that you bought the book.

## >> QUESTIONS AND MORE INFORMATION

I **encourage** my students to ask questions! If you have questions, submit them via **http://jmlinks.com/contact**. There are two sorts of questions: ones that I know instantly, for which I'll zip you an email answer right away, and ones I do not know instantly, in which case I will investigate, and we'll figure out the answer together.

As a teacher, I learn most from my students. So please don't be shy!

## ⏩ REGISTER YOUR BOOK

Finally, this workbook is meant to leverage the power of the Internet. Register your copy online to get a PDF copy of this book (with clickable links to make it easy to access online resources), and a complimentary copy of my *The Marketing Almanac*, a compilation of hundreds of social media tools not just for Facebook, LinkedIn, Twitter, etc., but for all the major platforms as well as pointers to learning resources for even more fun in the world of social media. You'll also get free access to my *Social Media Dashboard*, my absolute favorite free tools all set out for you to use in easy click-to-go format.

Here's how to **register** your copy of this workbook:

- Go to **http://jmlinks.com/social2020**

- Reenter this password: **social2020** at the welcome screen.

- Follow the instructions to enter your email.

- You're in. Simply click on the link for a PDF copy of *The Marketing Almanac* as well as access to the worksheets referenced herein.

Once you register, you get access to –

- **A PDF copy of this book**. Read it on your PC or tablet, and the links referenced in the book become clickable. This is a great way to extend the book into the myriad resources such as example websites or social media pages, FAQ's, support or help from the major vendors, and videos.

- **My social media marketing dashboard** – an easy-to-use, clickable list of the best tools for social media marketing by category (e.g., Facebook tools, Twitter tools, etc.).

- *The Marketing Almanac* – a collection of up-to-date social media tools in detail. While the *Dashboard* identifies my favorites, the *Toolbook* compiles the universe of free social media tools.

- **Videos** –an extensive collection of "how to" videos. You can browse them directly on my YouTube channel at **https://www.youtube.com/jmgrp**.

- **Quizzes** – an easy way to test your knowledge and reinforce what you're learning. The devil is in the details, and the quizzes test your devilish knowledge medium-by-medium.

## Jump Codes

Throughout the book, I reference the website **http://jmlinks.com/** plus various "jump codes." If you're reading in PDF format, the links are clickable. If you're reading in hard copy or on the Kindle, I advise you to fire up your Web browser, bookmark **http://jmlinks.com/** and then enter the codes.

Here's a screenshot:

For example, **http://jmlinks.com/16s** would mean first go to **http://jmlinks.com/** and enter "16s" in the jump code box. Your browser will then "jump" you to the referenced resource.

> **VIDEO.** Watch a video tutorial on how to use "jump" codes at **http://jmlinks.com/jump**.

OK, now that we know what this workbook is about, who it is for, and our plan of action...

**Let's get started!**

## >> COPYRIGHT AND DISCLAIMER

I knew you just couldn't wait for the legal stuff. *Calm yourself down, and get ready for some truly fun reading.*

Copyright © 2020, JM Internet Group and Excerpti Communications, Inc., All Rights Reserved. No reproduction or citation without written consent of the publisher. For details and to contact us, visit our website at **https://www.jm-seo.org/**.

This is a completely **unofficial** workbook to social media marketing. <u>No one</u> at Facebook, LinkedIn, Twitter, YouTube, Instagram, TikTok, Pinterest, Yelp, Google, Instagram, Snapchat, the White House or any other social media company has <u>endorsed this workbook</u>, nor has anyone affiliated with any of those companies been involved in the production of this workbook.

That's a *good thing*. This workbook is **independent**. My aim is to "tell it as I see it," giving you no-nonsense information on how to succeed at social media marketing.

In addition, please note the following:

- All trademarks are the property of their respective owners. I have no relationship with nor endorsement from the mark holders. Any use of their marks is so I can provide information to you. Don't confuse them with me, or me with them. I'm just a poor intellectual living in Oklahoma, and they are big, rich, powerful corporations with teams of money-grubbing lawyers.

- Any reference to or citation of third-party products or services whether for Facebook, LinkedIn, Twitter, Yelp, Google, TikTok, Yahoo, Bing, Pinterest, YouTube, Instagram, Snapchat, or other businesses, search engines, or social media platforms, should not be construed as an endorsement of those products or services tools, nor as a warranty as to their effectiveness or compliance with the terms of service with any search engine or social media platform.

The information used in this workbook was derived at the time of publication. However, social media marketing changes rapidly, so please be aware that scenarios, facts, and conclusions are subject to change without notice.

**Additional Disclaimer.** Internet marketing is an art, and not a science. Any changes to your Internet marketing strategy, including SEO, Social Media Marketing, and online advertising, are at your own risk. Neither Jason McDonald, Excerpti Communications, Inc., nor the JM Internet Group assumes any responsibility for the effect of any changes you may, or may not, make to your website or social media marketing based on the information in this workbook.

**Additional Additional Disclaimer.** Please keep your arms and legs in the vehicle at all times, be kind to one another, and do not cut other people off while driving. Please remember that everything you say and do, online, becomes part of your digital footprint, and when aliens download the digital records of earth in the year 2027, you'll either be remembered as a kind person or a jerk. Choose to be kind.

## » ACKNOWLEDGEMENTS

No man is an island. I would like to thank my beloved wife, Noelle Decambra, for helping me hand-in-hand managing our busy household and raising two wonderful girls, and as my personal cheerleader in the book industry. Gloria McNabb has done her usual tireless job as first assistant, including updating this edition as well *The Marketing Almanac*. I'd like to thank my two daughters, Hannah and Ava, and especially Ava who as a teenager in the trenches of today's "social media generation" has found the patience to explain Snapchat (and now, TikTok) to me at least three times. Last but not least, I would also like to thank my black Labrador retriever, Buddy, for countless walks and games of fetch, quizzical looks when I talked out loud to him about the vagaries of Pinterest or TikTok, during all of which I refined my ideas about marketing and about life. Those of you who own a dog will understand; those of you who don't, well, get a dog. It's "God" spelled backward for a reason.

And, again, a huge thank you to my students – online, in San Francisco, and at Stanford Continuing Studies. You challenge me, you inspire me, and you motivate me!

# 1
# PARTY ON - SOCIAL MEDIA MARKETING

Most books on **social media marketing** (or **SMM** for short) either focus on the high, high level of over-the-top hype or concentrate on the in-the-weeds level of micro technical details. It's either Gary Vaynerchuk's *Crushing It*, Mark Schaefer's *Marketing Rebellion*, Seth Godin's *This is Marketing*, David Meerman Scott's *The New Rules of Marketing and PR* – or it's *Social Media for Dummies*, *LinkedIn for Dummies*, or *Teach Yourself Facebook in Ten Minutes*.

**You're either up in the sky or lost in the weeds.**

This book is different: it focuses on the middle, productive ground – part **theory**, and part **practice**. It gives you a framework for how to "think" about social media marketing as well as concrete advice on how to "do" social media marketing on each particular network.

Throughout, it provides worksheets, videos, quizzes, **TO-DOS**, and deliverables, to help you create a step-by-step **social media marketing plan** as well as a step-by-step Facebook marketing plan, LinkedIn marketing plan, Twitter marketing plan, etc. Used in combination with the *Marketing Almanac* and *dashboard*, which identify hundreds of **free** tools for social media marketing in one convenient place, small business owners and marketers finally have a practical, hands-on method for social media marketing.

This first Chapter is about *how to think about social media marketing*. What is social media marketing? Why are you doing it? What should you do, step-by-step, to succeed?

**Let's get started!**

## TO-DO LIST:

» Understand that Social Media Marketing is Like Throwing a Party
» Recognize the Social Media Marketing Illusion

## » UNDERSTAND THAT SOCIAL MEDIA MARKETING IS LIKE THROWING A PARTY

Have you ever **attended** a party? You know, received an invitation, showed up, said hello and various meets and greets to other guests, ate the *yummy yummy* food, drank the liquor (or the diet soda), hobnobbed with other guests, ate some more food, danced the night away, thanked the hosts, and left?

*Attending a party is all about showing up, enjoying the entertainment and food, and leaving.*

Have you ever **used** Twitter? Facebook? Instagram? You know, logged in, checked out some funny accounts, read some posts, posted back and forth with friends and family, checked your updates, and then logged out?

That's *attending* a party. That's *using* social media.

*Using social media is all about logging in, enjoying what's new and exciting, and logging out.*

**Throwing** a party, however, is something entirely different from **attending** a party. Similarly, **marketing** via social media is something entirely different from **using** social media.

This Chapter explores the basics of social media *marketing*: of **throwing** the "social media party" vs. just **showing up**. That word *marketing* is very important: we're exploring how to use social media to build our brand, promote the visibility of our company, product or service, and even (gasp!) use social media to sell more stuff.

# BECOME A GREAT SOCIAL MEDIA PARTY-THROWER

Social media **marketing** is the art and science of **throwing** "great parties" on Twitter, Facebook, LinkedIn, Pinterest and the like in such a way that people not only show up to enjoy the party but also are primed to buy your product or service.

Let's explore this analogy further: how is social media *marketing* like *throwing a party*?

Here are three ways:

**Invitations = Promotion**. A great party needs great guests, and the first step to getting guests is to identify an attendee list and send out invitations. Who will be invited? How will we invite them – will it be face-to-face, by phone call, email, postal mail, etc.? For your social media marketing, you'll need to identify your target audience(s) and brainstorm how to get them to "show up" on your social media page via tactics like sending out emails, cross-posting your Facebook to your Twitter, or your LinkedIn to your blog, advertising, or even using "real world" face-to-face invitations like "Hey, follow us on Twitter to get coupons and insider deals."

*Social media marketing requires having a promotion strategy.*

**Food and Entertainment = Content.** Will your party have a band, a magician, a comedian, or just music? What is your entertainment strategy? What kind of food will you serve - Mexican, Chinese, Tapas, or something else? Similarly for your social media marketing: why will people "hang out" on your Facebook page or YouTube channel? Will it be to learn something? Will it be because it's fun or funny?

*Social media marketing requires having a content marketing strategy, a way to systematically produce yummy yummy content (blog posts, infographics, images, videos) that people will enjoy enough to "hang out" on your social media page or channel.*

**Hosting = Ongoing Management.** As the host of your party, you'll "hang out" at the party, but while the guests are busy enjoying themselves, you'll be busy, meeting and greeting, making sure everything is running smoothly, and doing other behind-the-scenes tasks. Similarly, in your social media marketing, you'll be busy coordinating content, interacting with guests and even policing the party to "kick out" rude or obnoxious attendees.

*Social media marketing requires on-going behind-the-scenes management, often on a day-to-day basis, to ensure that everything is running smoothly up to and including dealing with "rude" guests.*

# Social Media Marketing is Throwing a 24/7 Party Online

In addition, you want to think like a "party detective." Let's assume you're going to throw your spouse an amazing 40th birthday party. Before that party, you'll probably start attending other gatherings with a critical eye – noting what you like, and what you don't like, what you want to imitate, and even reaching out to the magicians, bands, and bartenders to find out what they cost and possibly hire them for your own party.

**Inventory Other Parties**

You'll "inventory" other parties and make a list of likes and dislikes, ideas and do-not-dos, and use that information to plan your own party systematically.

As a social media marketer, therefore, you should "attend" the parties of other brands online. Identify brands you like (REI, Whole Foods, Rustic Cuff, Author John Green, Bishop Robert Barron, CEO Jeff Bezos, fitness guru Shaun T), "follow" or "like" them, and keep a critical eye on what they're doing. **Inventory** your likes and dislikes, and **reverse engineer** what other marketers are up to. And in your industry, do the same. Follow companies in your own industry, again with the goal of "reverse engineering" their social media marketing strategy, successes, and failures.

For your first **To-do**, identify some brands or public figures you admire and "follow" them on Twitter, LinkedIn, Facebook, Pinterest, etc. Start making a list of what you like, or dislike, based on reverse engineering their online marketing strategy. Become a good user of social media, but with an eye to the marketing strategy "behind the scenes." Here are the steps:

1. **Log in** to one of your **social media accounts** (e.g., Twitter or Facebook).

2. Using the search function, **search for keywords** that are relevant to your business. If you are a wedding planner, for example, search for keywords such as 'wedding planning' or 'weddings' or 'party planners.'

   a. You can use a special Google search of *site:network* as in *site:facebook.com* "accounting firms" to use Google to find interesting items on any social media site rapidly. Note: there is NO SPACE between the : and the network. Visit **http://jmlinks.com/12v** to see this in action. You can also watch a **video** on this at **http://jmlinks.com/16g**.

b. Use the *Social Media Marketing dashboard > keyword tools* to research keyword "themes" around which your customers search and talk. Imagine a water cooler conversation by your customers on theme X or theme Y – identify which topics are relevant on social. Visit **http://jmlinks.com/smmdash** > keyword tools to begin.

3. Write down or **bookmark accounts that you find**. If you search for "hamburgers," and you find the Facebook page of the Palo Alto restaurant, "The Counter," then "like" that Page on Facebook and/or bookmark it. You'll need a list of five to ten companies that are like yours and/or that you can see are doing a good job on the platform.

4. Begin to **inventory** what you **like** and **dislike** about how they are running their social media effort. For Facebook, do you like their cover photo? Why or why not? Do you like their profile pictures? What about what they post, and how frequently? Imagine you are attending their party not "to have fun," but to "reverse engineer" how they are putting it on. Write this down on a spreadsheet or document.

We'll return to this process for each network, but for now and whether you're an experienced social media participant or not, start to look at social media as "parties" and start to step back and ponder what's going on on Twitter, Facebook, YouTube, etc., as the work of "party throwers" in interaction with "party attendees."

## A Party with a Purpose

Another fact to notice is that brands like Whole Foods or REI, or public personas like Khloe Kardashian or Shaun T – in contrast with the average John Doe or Sally Jones, well, these brands are on social media for an "ulterior motive," usually to "build their brand" and "sell more stuff." Social media marketing, in short, is like throwing a *party with a purpose*. While the birthday party you're throwing for your spouse on her 40th birthday is hopefully just a labor of love, corporate parties are not so benevolent. For example, the real-world corporate parties I've gone to in Silicon Valley have an ultimate purpose. You may show up at the Mentor Graphics' party at the *Design Automation Conference*, or the Analog Devices' event at the *Consumer Electronics Show*, eat their food, drink their liquor, and enjoy their entertainment, but they want something in return. They want you – as the partygoer – to listen to a spiel by their CEO or product marketing manager on their latest product, they want you to get a "warm and fuzzy feeling" about their brand, and they want you to think of them the next time you're ready to purchase something.

The same is true for corporate "parties" on social media marketing. These are parties with a purpose, which you can generally break down into two interrelated subgoals:

- Build **brand equity** among target customers, giving them a warm and fuzzy feeling that they "like" the brand so much they'll be favorably inclined to buy its product and/or service; and/or -

- **Get a sale**, by selling the product or service right then and there.
  - o Or, a few steps before the sale, a goal might be to get a sign up to an email newsletter, or a **sales lead / registration** from a free eBook or software download offer, etc. The "goal" of social media marketing can be to "acquire sales leads" in the form of names, company names, email addresses, phone numbers, etc., in exchange for "something free" like a software download, free eBook or free consultation.

Whether they're subtle about it (*just get that warm and fuzzy feeling*), or they're aggressive about it (*act now, and get a special discount for following us on Twitter*), social media "parties with a purpose" aren't exactly the same as a family party or gathering. Brands want something from their attendees: more money, more sales, and better brand equity.

As you begin to pay attention to competitors and brands that seem to "get" social media, I want you to be just a bit cynical, and look for the goals behind their "parties with a purpose" on Twitter, Facebook, LinkedIn, Snapchat, and the like. What's in it for them, and how do they blend this purpose into their "oh so fun" parties on social media? What's in it for their customers? And what's the *quid pro quo* of why users show up at the party, while the party producer goes to the trouble and expense of throwing the party? What's REI's goal for its Facebook page vs. what are the reasons why users show up at REI's Facebook "party?" Why do users watch Martha Stewart on YouTube, and why does Martha Stewart go to the trouble of creating a robust YouTube channel?

And as for you –

**Question:** What do you want to get out of your "party with a purpose?"

## A Brand Example: Rustic Cuff

For example, I love the brand Rustic Cuff, which is a Tulsa-based business that produces artisan-style bracelets. The brand is very active on social media and does a really good job at it. Take a look at their website at **https://www.rusticcuff.com/**, scroll down to the bottom and click over to their social icons. You'll see that they're active on Facebook, Twitter, Instagram, Pinterest, and YouTube.

Here's a screenshot of their Twitter account:

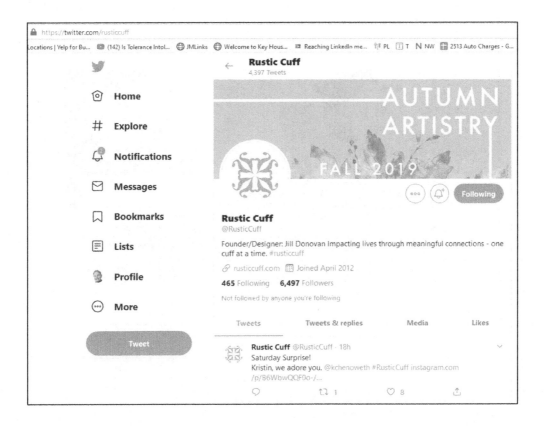

Next, step back, scroll down their account, and pay attention to what they're posting and be a bit cynical. Ask why? Rustic Cuff isn't a charity after all. This is a business, a business that wants to build its brand and sell more stuff. As you pay attention to Rustic Cuff's posts on Facebook, Twitter, and Instagram, you'll notice two types:

> **Fun Posts.** These are posts either by Rustic Cuff or by users that seemingly share their passion for beautiful jewelry and stylish stuff. These are probably more than 80% of their posts. **Purpose**: build positive brand equity.
>
> **Buy Our Stuff Posts.** These are posts which, much more shamelessly, connect the social media experience with an "act now!" feature to encourage a user to

skedaddle on over to RusticCuff.com and buy something. These are probably less than 20% of their posts. **Purpose**: get people to buy their stuff.

For example, here's a "buy our stuff" tweet from December 21, 2019:

Don't get me wrong. There's nothing unethical about this post; it's just a straightforward "buy our stuff post." But compared with many of their other posts (which focus on building up positive brand equity), this post is just a bit more *shameless* and direct towards a transactional plea.

Compare it with the following post, again from Rustic Cuff, but this time to Instagram on "Sunday Words of Wisdom:"

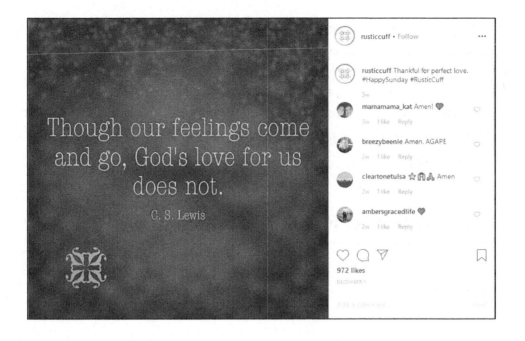

This post is inspirational. This post is religious. This post only tangentially builds their brand and "sells more stuff." It is not transactional. By looking at their posts, you'll realize that there's a mix of "buy our stuff" posts with other less transactional, more "feel good" posts such as the company's charismatic CEO sharing her words of wisdom, their customers having fun with their "cuffs," and even inspirational messages such as this one by C.S. Lewis.

Rustic Cuff is throwing a "party with a purpose," but doing so in such a wonderfully fun, engaging way that it's not in-your-face or obnoxious. The jewelry and photography of the bracelets are beautiful. The engagement with style is engaging. But it is there. They want you to buy more Rustic Cuff products, either *indirectly* because you "like" their brand and have positive feelings about them, or *directly* because you've seen a tweet, a Facebook post, or something on Instagram that pulls you directly into their eCommerce store.

In summary, Rustic Cuff isn't on Twitter, Facebook, Instagram, and Snapchat "just for fun." They have a marketing purpose: build their brand, and (ultimately) get people to buy their stuff. Once you understand this strategy, I assure you that you'll see it everywhere by every brand that does social media well. It's called **content marketing** and it's a key element to "parties with a purpose."

### Find and Reverse Engineer Companies that Do Social Media Well

How do you throw great parties? By attending them in "stealth mode," and paying attention to the details. So it goes with Social Media Marketing. How do you do it well? Your first task is to go on Twitter, Facebook, Instagram, LinkedIn, and other networks to identify companies that intrigue you. "Like" or "follow" them and start to think about their social media marketing "as if" you were attending their "party." Look for the "purpose" behind their parties, and how they blend this "purpose" into their content marketing strategy. And, in addition, you have an ulterior motive of your own: to "reverse engineer" how they are throwing such great parties, and how you can use that knowledge to improve your own "party with a purpose."

Welcome to *Spy vs. Spy*, social media edition.

## >> RECOGNIZE THE SOCIAL MEDIA MARKETING ILLUSION

As you begin to identify and monitor brands that you like on a given social media platform, you may be tempted to conclude that it's either really easy or they are just geniuses. Successful social media is based on **illusion**, however, just like successful parties are based on illusion.

How so?

Let's think for a second about an amazing party. Think back to a holiday party you attended, a great birthday or graduation party, or even a corporate event. Was it fun? Did it seem magical? It probably did.

Now, if you've ever had the (mis)fortune of planning such an event – what was that like? Was it fun? Was it magical? Yes and no, but it was also probably a lot of work, "in the background," to make sure that the party ran smoothly.

### The Party Illusion

Great parties have an element of **illusion** in them: they *seem* effortless, while *in reality* (behind the scenes) an incredible amount of strategy, planning, and hard work goes on. Similarly, great social media marketing efforts (*think Katy Perry or Lady Gaga on YouTube, think Whole Foods on Facebook or blogging, Airbnb or Aeromexico on Instagram, or REI, Zappos, Burt's Bees, or even Nutella on Twitter*), create an illusion. They (only) "seem" spontaneous, they (only) "seem" effortless. But in the background, a ton of work is going on to promote, manage, and grow these "social media parties."

# ILLUSION IS COMMON TO GREAT PARTIES AND GREAT SOCIAL MEDIA MARKETING

With respect to social media marketing, this **illusion phenomenon** often creates a weird problem for you vis-a-vis upper management or your boss. Upper management or your boss might mistakenly believe that "social media is easy," and/or "social media is free." You, as the marketer, might have to educate your boss that it only "looks" easy, or "seems" free. Social media marketing requires a ton of strategy, hard work, and (gasp!) even money or sweat equity to make it happen. Among your early tasks at social media marketing may be to explain the "social media marketing" illusion to your boss.

*It only seems easy. It only seems free.*

For your second **TO-DO**, organize a meeting with your boss and/or marketing team. Discuss all the things that have to get done to be successful at social media marketing, ranging from conducting an **inventory** of competitor efforts, to **setting up basic accounts** on Twitter, Facebook, Instagram, LinkedIn, etc., to **creating content** to share on social media (images, photos, blog posts, infographics, videos), to **monitoring** social media channels on an on-going basis, and finally to **measuring** your successes. Educate the team that although it might not take a lot of money, social media marketing does take a significant amount of work!

*We're planning an awesome party here, people. It's going to take a ton of work, it's going to be a ton of fun, and it's going to be incredibly successful!*

Now, *please don't get discouraged or overwhelmed.* It seems hard, and it seems like a ton of work, but once you know what to do, and you become systematic at doing it, you can do amazing social media marketing in just a few hours each week. Like preparing to get in shape, you'll need to commit to regular activities. But, like getting in the best shape of your life, thousands of people do it and do it well. It takes discipline, but YOU CAN DO IT!

*Imagine me greased up and sweating like Shaun T with my shirt off, jumping rope in front of you, yelling ARE YOU READY? Pop music is blaring, one of my groupies is saying, "It takes real work. It takes real effort, and guess what — that's just the warm-up!" Electrifying pop music is blaring over the loudspeakers. My ab muscles are jingling in front of your desk, and I'm leading you and year team (plus your boss) in a chant: WE CAN DO THIS WE CAN DO THIS.*

*Now, stop imagining me as Shaun T. It's getting weird.*

And here's a screenshot of the amazing, incredible, motivational Shaun T fitness guru Facebook Page (at 1.7 million followers) at **http://jmlinks.com/52v.**

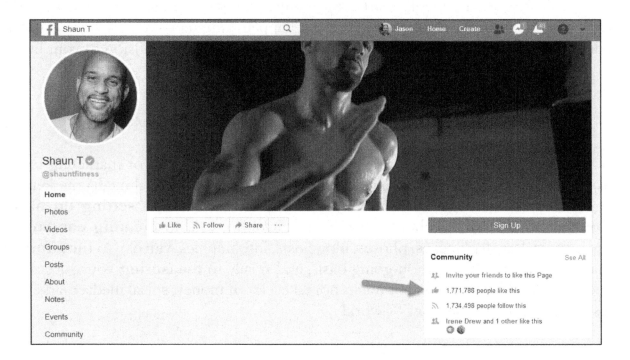

I'm not even a real Shaun T fan (I have 12 pack abs, meaning 2X the desired six-pack, after all). But I admire anyone with 1.7 million followers on Facebook, 942K followers on Instagram, 276K followers on Facebook, and 121K on YouTube. Plus an amazing can-do spirit, one that combines motivation with the technical knowledge of how to get in shape. Now, let's get back to our computers, potato chips, and iPhone cameras and make an incredible social media marketing strategy for your business! We can do this! Sitting down! Burning no calories! Munching on potato chips!

**Be Positive: It's Not the 1970s or 1980s**

Here's another motivational tidbit. As marketers, we are so **fortunate** to live in an amazing time with incredible new opportunities to reach our target customers. Can you imagine being a marketer in the sad decades of the 1970s or 1980s, when all they had was the Yellow Pages, trade shows, cold calling, and direct mail pieces? I mean, "Let your fingers do the walking," how pathetic was that? Feel sorry for those people in the past, as you and I are lucky to live during an **amazing marketing revolution**. We live in amazing times – Twitter, Facebook, Snapchat, Instagram, and even Google are just a few years or a few decades old (if that). It's like 1776 in the USA, 1917 in Russia, or 1789 in Paris, just no bloodshed!

Be **positive** about the present and the future. You are not only lucky enough to live during the *social media marketing revolution*. You are taking positive steps to become an expert at it!

### Know the Question and Find the Answer

Once you start to view social media marketing as a systematic process, a great thing will happen: you'll formulate concrete, *specific* questions. You'll formulate concrete, *specific* tasks, such as "how do I create an infographic?" or "what are the dimensions of a Facebook cover photo?," and "how do I schedule my posting to Twitter?"

I am going to share with you one of my best-kept secret websites. It's an amazing, powerful website that can literally answer almost any question. It's called, **Google**, and you can find it at **https://www.google.com/**. Bookmark this site. It's very useful.

Here's a screenshot:

OK, let me be serious. Once you formulate a specific question, such as "What is the character limit of a tweet?," you can Google it, to find the answer.

# IF YOU KNOW THE QUESTION, YOU CAN GOOGLE THE ANSWER

Once you realize, for example, that Facebook allows cover photos, and that smart Facebook marketers swap theirs out from time to time, you can create the "questions" of "How do you create a cover photo for Facebook?," "What are the dimensions of a

Facebook cover photo,?" etc. Now that Facebook allows videos as cover photos, you can Google "How do you set up a video as your Facebook cover?" You can type specific questions into Google to find the answers; Google will point you to the official Facebook help files as well as other helpful blog posts or answer sites on the Web. Indeed, people often make amazing "how to" videos on YouTube, and once you know a question, you'll almost always find someone who has made a YouTube of the answer. (YouTube is my second favorite top-secret site to find answers; check it out at **https://www.youtube.com/**).

*Yes, I know I'm being tongue in cheek, but you'd be amazed at how few people actually realize that they can Google their marketing questions about social media!*

In addition, all of the social media platforms have official help files such as **https://help.twitter.com** or **https://www.facebook.com/help**. You can Google your questions as well as go directly into the official help files. Ironically, the technical aspects of social media marketing such as "how to share a YouTube video" or "what are the character limits to a Tweet" are the easy ones, once you formulate them as questions and then just Google them or look them up in the help files.

## >> IDENTIFY RELEVANT DISCOVERY PATHS

Before we plunge into Facebook, LinkedIn, Twitter, and social media networks on a step-by-step basis, it's worthwhile to sit back and ponder the big questions of marketing.

*What do you sell?*

*Who wants it and why?*

*And, very directly: how do customers find you?*

This last one might seem like a simple question, but a great social marketer has a very specific understanding of the paths by which customers find her product, service, or company. This understanding then guides –

*How much should you focus on SEO (Search Engine Optimization)? How much should you focus on Google Ads? How much on Facebook? On LinkedIn? On Yelp? Or Twitter? Should you buy ads on Television, or (gasp!) send out unsolicited email (spam)? Is Pinterest worth the effort? What about ads on social media; should you advertise or focus solely on organic?*

It makes sense if you think like a fisherman, and you think of your customers like fish. If your "fish" tend to be on Facebook, then you need to prioritize Facebook in your marketing strategy; if your "fish" tend to be using LinkedIn, then you need to prioritize LinkedIn; if your "fish" tend to read reviews on Yelp, you need to prioritize Yelp. And if your fish are 13 years old and endlessly share their day-to-day hopes, dreams, and fantasies on Snapchat, well you better get snappin'.

**The Five Discovery Paths**

How do customers "**discover**" you? This is perhaps *the* most important question in marketing. Why? Because if a customer can't find you, if a customer doesn't learn about you, if a customer isn't jazzed about your brand, they can't buy your product or service. And if you don't have a firm grasp on how customers discover you, you don't know where to put your marketing efforts. You can't *fish for the fish* when you don't know *where the fish are*. You'll be advertising on billboards when they use Google. Or advertising on Google, when they use Facebook. Or focusing on organic posts on Instagram, when they use reviews on Yelp. Or doing the Internet when they're all in the real world. Or sending postcards through the US mail, or using the print Yellow Pages when you've been living in a cave for the last two decades and failed to realize that nearly everything (but not absolutely everything) is online.

In short, many businesses fail to understand *how customers discover them (Question #1)* and *how they, as marketers, can influence how customers find them (Question #2)*. How might customers find you? Let us count the ways.

**SEARCH.** The **search** path occurs when the customer is "searching" for a company, product, or service. For example, a customer is hungry. He types "pizza" into Google or Yelp. He browses available restaurants, chooses one, and shows up to get pizza. He *searched* for pizza. He *found* pizza. He *bought* pizza. The search path is the province of **SEO** (Search Engine Optimization), largely on Google but also on sites such as Yelp or Amazon that work via "keywords" to help customers find stuff that they want. **Google Ads** advertising (formerly called **AdWords**) is also helpful on this path.

The search path exists in the "real world" as well, as for example, when a customer goes to a mall and looks at the kiosk map to find out which stores sell gifts, or when a customer uses a directory of business accountants, or perhaps even when a customer asks friends or family if they "know any good painters." The key concept in search is that the customer knows what he wants and he pro-actively goes searching for it.

**REVIEW / RECOMMEND / TRUST.** The review / recommend / trust path is based on "trust indicators." In it, the customer already has created a list of vendors he might use, but he is researching "whom to trust." In this path, he might use the "reviews" and/or "stars" on Facebook, Yelp, Airbnb, TripAdvisor, or Google as "trust indicators" to predict which pizza restaurant is good (or bad). **Reviews** and **stars** are the most common trust indicators in social media marketing, but having a robust Facebook page, with many followers and interesting posts, can also be a "trust indicator." Having an expert-looking profile on LinkedIn can be a "trust indicator" for a CPA or an architect. A recommendation from a friend or colleague also plays into reviews and trust. The review / recommend / trust path is all about a customer "asking for help" from friends, family, business colleagues, or online review sites like Yelp, Amazon, TripAdvisor, etc. The key concept in review / recommend / trust is the reliance on *external validations* such as recommendations from friends or stars on Yelp.

**EWOM / SHARE / INFLUENCERS**. Wow! That pizza was great! Let me take a selfie of me chowing down on the pizza, and post it to Instagram. Or, wow, here is a cat video of cats at the pizza restaurant puzzled by the self-serve soda fountain. It's "gone viral" on TikTok and has sixteen million views! Or, oh my goodness, Oprah has just recommended we read the novel, *An American Marriage,* by Tayari Jones, so let's buy it on Amazon and get started.

The **share path** occurs when a customer loves the product, service, or experience with enough passion to "share" it on social media – be that via electronic word of mouth (eWOM), a share on his or her Facebook page, a "selfie" on Instagram, or a viral video on YouTube or TikTok. Others find out via shares from their friends or influencers, and suddenly yours is the most popular pizza joint in town. Indeed, **influencer marketing** is a type of marketing that straddles both the review / recommend / trust marketing and the share path; an "influencer" like Kim Kardashian recommends new jewelry, and then everyone goes out to buy it. The *influencer* is just a "trust indicator" *par excellence* with the push of *share* behind him or her.

In a sense, therefore, the "share" path is the flip side of the review path. The key concept in share is when a customer or influencer pro-actively "pushes" her love of your product or service to friends, family, or business colleagues. The "share" path is more pro-active, and the review / recommend / trust path is more passive, but they are closely related.

**INTERRUPT**. The interrupt path is the bad boy of marketing, both online and off. Interrupt marketing occurs when you want to watch a YouTube video, but before you can watch it, you have to view an annoying ad. Or it's the ads on TV that we "must" watch (at least had to watch before TIVO and DVRs came along) before we see the live sports event we want to enjoy. Or, it's when you get a "cold call" or "spam email" from a recruiter who's viewed your Profile on LinkedIn, or when you get a spam email on "amazing Viagra." Interrupt is largely **advertising**, and largely advertising to "push" products that people aren't proactively looking for. But just because people hate it doesn't mean it isn't useful. Spam works, and so do TV ads.

**BROWSE**. The browse path is all about getting your message *adjacent* to what a person is reading or viewing. In it, you're looking for something, reading something, or watching something, and alongside comes something else. For example, you go to YouTube to look up "how to tie a tie," and in the suggested videos at the end might be a video for Dollar Shave Club. Or you might see Dollar Shave Club videos suggested at the right of the screen. You're not proactively looking for Dollar Shave Club, but you see their information as you "browse" for related content on sites like YouTube, Facebook, or blogs. Or, you go to the mall "to shop" and happen to wander into a boutique, only to buy the newest dog toy - something that you really hadn't been considering buying in the first place. Or you read a newspaper or journal, or go to an industry trade show and just "happen" to notice a new product or service. The **browse path** is about getting your product or service *adjacent* to something the customer is looking at.

These are the five **discovery paths**, and as you look to your marketing, you'll see that everything in promotion can fit into one of these paths. There are both digital and non-digital examples of them. A door-to-door salesman, for example, is engaging in interrupt just as an unsolicited spam email or telemarketing call is, too. An ad on a billboard is "browse" just as an ad on the *New York Times* online is browse, too. Every promotional choice fits into one of the five discovery paths.

You'll also quickly realize that most marketing in the "real world" isn't pure. It has elements of more than one path. When you get an influencer to recommend your product, for example, you're using both the *share* path and the *review / recommend / trust* path. Or when you use SEO to propel a blog post to the top of Google, you're using both the *search* path and the *browse* path to get your product or service in front of potential customers. They find an interesting blog post through a Google search, they read it, and then they discover your product or service "adjacent" to the post. The marketing or promotional mix will often seek to engage customers across a range of paths, but it's useful to see them as distinct discovery methodologies.

All of these paths can come into play in an effective social media marketing strategy. Your job is to identify your customers, figure out where they hang out on social media, and position your message in front of their "eyeballs," to use the industry slang for getting *what you sell* in front of *how they see*.

## Outline Your Marketing "Big Picture"

For your third **TO-DO**, download the **Big Picture Marketing worksheet**. For the worksheet, go to **http://jmlinks.com/social2020** (then enter the code '**social2020**' to register your workbook), and click on the link to the "Big Picture Marketing."

In this worksheet, you'll write a "business value proposition" explaining what you sell, and who are the target customers. You'll also identify the most relevant "discovery paths" by which potential customers find your products. You will begin to realize that there is a "method" to the "madness," as you identify where your customers are and how best to reach them.

## » ESTABLISH GOALS AND KPIS (KEY PERFORMANCE INDICATORS)

Marketing is about measurement. Are we helping our brand image? Are we getting sales or sales leads? How do we know where we are succeeding, and where there is more work to be done? Why are we spending all this blood, sweat, and tears on social media marketing anyway? Is it paying off?

In today's overhyped social media environment, many marketers feel like they "must" be on Twitter, they had better get on Snapchat, or they "must" have a presence on Pinterest, etc. All of the social media companies – Facebook, Twitter, Pinterest, Snapchat, Yelp – have a vested interest in overhyping the importance of their platform, and using fear to compel marketers to "not miss out" by massively jumping on the latest and greatest social platform. **Social media guilt**, however, is to be avoided: if you define a clear business value proposition, know where your customers are, and establish clear goals and KPIs (Key Performance Indicators), you'll be able to focus on those social platforms that really help you and ignore the ones that are just hype.

# AVOID SOCIAL MEDIA GUILT: YOU CAN'T (AND SHOULDN'T) USE EVERY NETWORK

Let's identify some common **goals** for effective social media marketing. The boss might have an ultimate "hard" goal of getting sales leads or selling stuff online. Those are definitely important, but as marketers, we might look to intermediate or "soft goals" such as nurturing a positive brand image online or growing our online reviews.

Generally speaking, social media excels at the "soft goals" of growing brand awareness, nurturing customer conversations, encouraging reviews and the like and is not so good at immediate, direct goals like lead captures or sales. (Not surprisingly, this is why 90% of social media posts by brands are warm and fuzzy, and less than 10% are shameless plugs to buy more stuff).

In any case, having high-level yet soft goals is essential to being able to create a systematic, social media marketing strategy as well as a "drill down" strategy for an individual social medium, whether that be Twitter or LinkedIn, Instagram or YouTube.

Here are common goals for social media marketing:

**eWOM (electronic Word of Mouth).** Every brand wants people to talk about it in a positive way, and today a lot of that conversation occurs on social media. If you are a local pizza restaurant, you want people "talking" about you and your pizza on Yelp, on Facebook, on Twitter as a great place to get pizza, eat Italian food, cater a wedding, or host a birthday party for little Jimmy. As marketers, a common goal for social media is to grow and nurture positive eWOM, which might be positive conversations on Facebook, positive reviews on Yelp or Google My Business, relationships between customers and us and among customers, and the sharing of our brand across media.

**Customer Continuum.** *A prospect becomes a customer, a customer becomes a fan, and a fan becomes an evangelist.* For example, I'm hungry. I search for "great pizza" in Palo Alto, California, and I find your pizza restaurant. I try your pizza, thereby becoming a customer. It's good, and I'm a fan: if someone asks me, I'll recommend *Jason's Palo Alto Pizza.* And finally, I love your pizza so much, I wrote a positive review on Yelp, I created a YouTube video of me eating your pizza, I took a selfie for Instagram, and I have a new blog on Tumblr about your pizza. As marketers, we want to encourage customers to move to the right on the customer continuum: *from prospect to customer, customer to fan, and fan to evangelist.*

**Customer from Hell.** You also need to be aware of (and seek to mitigate) the "customer from hell" who can hate a brand so much that she writes a negative review on Yelp, posts negative comments on Facebook, or creates a viral YouTube video about your terrible pizza. (**Reputation management** is the industry term for being aware of both positive and negative social media discussions about your brand). Social media marketing is also about reputation management, and especially mitigating "customers from Hell."

**Trust Indicators.** Customers want pizza. Customers read reviews. Customers use reviews to decide which pizza restaurant is probably good. Similarly, when customers want to go to a theme park, they might check out the Facebook page. They like theme parks that have lively Facebook pages over those that have boring Facebook pages. **Trust indicators** are all about mental "shortcuts" that customers make to identify possible vendors, services, or products. A common goal of social media marketing, therefore, is to nurture positive trust indicators about our brand online: reviews, especially but not only.

Here's a screenshot of "Sushi" from Yelp. Ask yourself, which restaurant is probably better – the one with 169 reviews or the one with 88?

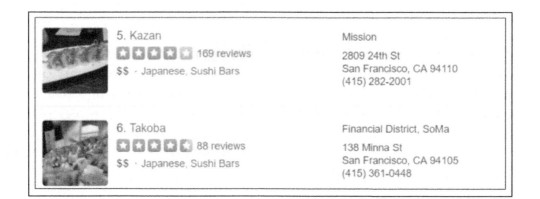

Similarly, the Sushi restaurant with tens of thousands of followers on Instagram must be better than the one with only a thousand, or the YouTube video with hundreds of thousands of views must be better than the YouTube video with just 100. Quantity matters as does the quality of star ratings, likes, and thumbs up or thumbs down. These create social trust.

**Stay Top of Mind.** You visit the pizza restaurant, one time. That encounter is an incredible marketing opportunity! As a marketer, I want to convert that "one touch" to "many," that single encounter to staying "top of mind" so I can remind you about my business, products, and/or services and entice you to come back. I want you to follow us on Twitter, so I can Tweet special deals, promotions, what's cooking, and stay "top of mind," so that when you're hungry again, you think, *Jason's Palo Alto Pizza*. I want you addicted to my fun Instagram feed, my clever Snapchat, and even to connect with us on LinkedIn for your business catering needs. Using social media to convert *one touch to many* and *stay top of mind* is an excellent goal.

**Promotion, promotion, promotion.** Social sharing – getting customers to market your brand to their friends, family, and colleagues – is probably the most common social media goal. You want your customers to Instagram their happy kids having a great pizza party at your pizza restaurant! You want your customers to share tweets about their amazing corporate catering event with their Facebook friends. And you want your customers to share your informative industry blog post on cybersecurity with their contacts on LinkedIn. *Encouraging social promotion is a huge, huge goal for SMM.*

Your **TO-DO** here begins by simply taking out a piece of paper, or opening up a Word document, and jotting down "soft" and "hard" goals for your social media marketing efforts. For extra credit, start to hypothesize which goals might be best accomplished on which social media network.

> **Question.** What are the marketing goals of your efforts at social media? (Write them down.)

## The Virtuous Circle

When you add up all of the goals listed above, and probably a few you may have identified that I've missed, you get to the **virtuous circle** of social media marketing. When your social media marketing efforts are working well, you can create a positive feedback loop.

> *The more positive reviews you have on Yelp, the most customers you get, the more customers you get, the more positive reviews. The more followers on Twitter you get, the more chances you have to get them to share your discounts, the more discounts they share, the more followers you get. The more people who like / share / comment on your Facebook page, the better your Edgerank (a measurement of how engaging one's content is), the better your Edgerank, the more people see your content, the more people see your content, the more shares you get on Facebook, the better your Edgerank….*

# NURTURE A VIRTUOUS CIRCLE

**Nurturing a virtuous circle** should be a major goal your social media marketing efforts. You want all of these "soft goals" to turn into "hard goals": a positive brand image to lead to more sales, and a stronger bottom line. All of this can be measured.

For your next **TO-DO**, download the **Marketing Goals Worksheet**. For the worksheet, go to **http://jmlinks.com/social2020** (then enter the code '**social2020**' to register your workbook), and click on the link to the "Marketing Goals Marketing."

In this worksheet, you'll identify your "hard" goals, whether you have something "free" to offer, and your "soft" goals on social media. Ultimately, these big-picture goals will be translated into much more specific goals, germane to a social medium such as YouTube, Twitter, or Facebook. Don't forget to conceptualize what a *virtuous marketing circle* would look like for your company. Visualize social media marketing success; you'll get there step-by-step.

## » REMEMBER THE BIG PICTURE

At this point, you've begun your social media marketing journey. You've understood that social media marketing is about "throwing" the party more than "attending the party." You've realized you need to start "paying attention" with regard to what other marketers are doing on social media, with an eye to "reverse engineering" their marketing strategy so that you have ideas of what you like, and do not like, in terms of social media. You've started to brainstorm "discovery paths" and "goals" for your SMM efforts.

And you've realized that once you've identified your goals, identified relevant social media, set up your social accounts, the really hard work will be a) promoting your social media channels, and b) creating the kind of content that makes them want to "like you," keep coming back for more, and share your message with their friends, family, and/or business colleagues.

You've understood that **promotion** and **content creation** are the big on-going tasks of successful social media marketing.

## »» CHECKLIST: SOCIAL MEDIA MARKETING ACTION ITEMS

Test your knowledge of the "Big Picture" of Social Media Marketing! Take the *Social media marketing quiz* at **http://jmlinks.com/qzsm**. Next, here are your "Big Picture" **Action Items**:

❑ **Research** whether your customers (and competitors) are on social media. If so, which networks? What are they doing? What interests them, and why?

> ❑ Use **keyword tools** to brainstorm **keyword "themes"** that interest your target customers. Research these keywords on Twitter, Instagram, LinkedIn, etc., to identify companies and customers to "watch."

> ❑ Identify a few *competitors* to reverse engineer, or **companies / brands / influencers to emulate**. "Like" their Facebook pages, "follow" them on Instagram, etc.

>> ❑ Begin to "reverse engineer" what they are doing on social media. What type of content are they posting – their own, other people's content, or UGC (User Generated Content)? What seems to be getting the most interaction, and why?

❑ **Identify** your **search discovery** paths. Which paths (*search, review (recommend, trust), eWom (share, viral), interrupt, browse*) are the most relevant to your business and customers?

❏ **Formulate** (and write down) your **KPIs** (*key performance indicators*) or social media marketing *goals* such as eWOM, movement along the customer continuum, prevent "customers from hell," grow trust indicators, stay top of mind, or leverage social media promotion not to mention "hard goals" such as eCommerce sales or sales inquiries.

## »» DELIVERABLE: OUTLINE A SOCIAL MEDIA MARKETING PLAN

Now that we've come to the end of Chapter 1, your first **DELIVERABLE** has arrived. For the worksheet, go to **http://jmlinks.com/social2020** (then enter the code '**social2020**' to register your workbook), and click on the link to the "Social Media Marketing Plan Big Picture Worksheet." By filling out this plan, you and your team will establish a vision of what you want to achieve via social media marketing.

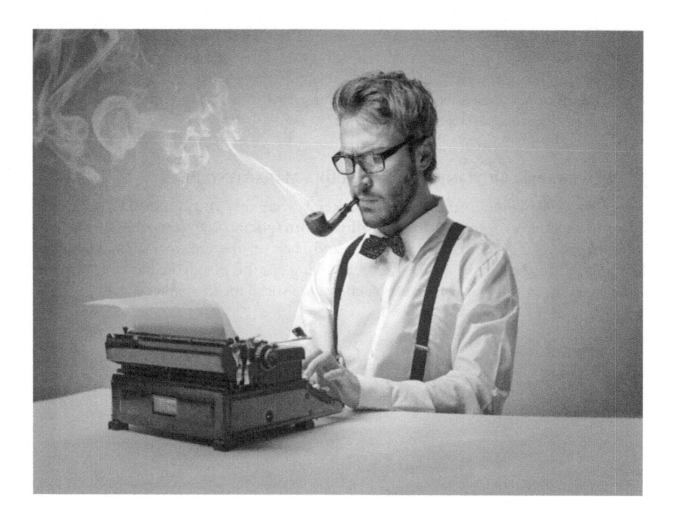

# 2
# CONTENT MARKETING

If social media *marketing* is throwing amazing Facebook fiestas, incredible Pinterest parties, and unbelievable YouTube soirees that not only attract and engage your potential customers but also lead them towards a better perception of your brand, and even result in real sales or sales leads ... well, "content," in short, is the "food and entertainment" of social media marketing. It's simple if you think about it. *No food, no party. No great food or entertainment, no great party.* You gotta have **content** just like you gotta have food and/or entertainment to get your party started (and keep it going).

Whether it's Instagram or Pinterest, Facebook or LinkedIn, YouTube or Twitter, you need to create and maintain a **content marketing machine** – a nearly endless series of blog posts, infographics, memes, photos, tweets, and/or videos that will feed the hunger for content of all your social channels.

In this Chapter, I'll overview the elements of your **content marketing machine**, and give you tips and tools to enable high speed and efficient production of content for social media.

**Let's get started!**

**TO-DO LIST:**

» Identify Content You Can Easily Produce

» Think Systematically About Content

» Identify Buyer Personas and Keyword Themes

» Produce Your Own Content on Schedule

» Blog, Blog, Blog: You Gotta Blog, Vlog, Phlog, and Post

» Curate Other People's Content

» Encourage User-Generated Content

» Interact with Interactive Content

» Remember the Big Picture

»» Checklist: Content Marketing Action Items

»» Deliverable: A Content Marketing Plan

## » Identify Content You Can Easily Produce

We're all good at something. Some of us can cook, some of us can't. Some of us can take photos, some of us can't. Some of us can write, and some of us can't. This is true for individuals, and it's true for companies as well. This is also true for companies as they work on their social media marketing.

Let's return to REI (**https://www.rei.com/**), for example. As a company that lives in the outdoor industry, REI is a company that is "good" at –

- **Taking photos and videos**. REI staffers take brilliant photos of the outdoors, photos that feature its products. Check out REI's Instagram at **https://www.instagram.com/rei/** to see for yourself.

- **Writing**. REI staffers write with passion about the environment, and about how much fun it is to "get outdoors." Check out REI's blog at **http://blog.rei.com/**.

- **Motivating customers to create content**. REI constantly encourages UGC or *user-generated content*, as its customers upload videos and stories about the outdoors, and interact on the company's social media channels. Check out the REI hashtag *#optoutside* on Twitter and Instagram. You can view it on Twitter at **http://jmlinks.com/52w** and Instagram at **http://jmlinks.com/52x**.

To see more of REI's content in action (posts, blog posts, videos, images), simply browse the company's Facebook Page at **https://www.facebook.com/REI/** and admire the remarkable content marketing machine of this online retailer.

### You, Too, Can Create Content

REI's content marketing machine may seem formidable, and it is. REI is a huge corporation in a very fun, very photogenic industry with many passionate outdoor men and women acting as fans. REI has tremendous advantages. But guess what? You, too, can create great content for your own social media marketing machine.

Before you feel daunted and give up, remember you probably aren't competing against the likes of REI, Disney, or Airbnb. You're competing against other companies in your own sad, pathetic industry, and they aren't any smarter or better than you. (*Ok, your industry isn't sad and pathetic, but you know what I mean. It's not inhabited by titans of industry or geniuses like Einstein.*). **You don't have to run faster than the bear; just faster than**

**your buddy**. So, with a little luck, some strategy, and some hard work, you can (and must) create a content marketing system to produce content to feed your social media needs.

Take Rustic Cuff, for example, which started as a small woman-owned business in Tulsa and grew into a powerhouse of fashion at **https://www.rusticcuff.com/**. Check out their Instagram, Facebook, Pinterest, and YouTube. Each social channel is amazing! Or check out Numi Organic Tea at **https://numitea.com/** and their social channels like Instagram or Facebook. Or, if you think social media is only for B2C (Business-to-Consumer) businesses, check out B2B (Business-to-Business) ThermoFisher Scientific at **https://www.thermofisher.com/**. With active channels on YouTube, Twitter, Facebook, and LinkedIn, each company shows you that businesses - small and large, consumer and B2B - have all plunged into social media and can (and are) succeeding. It takes effort, and the organic tea niche is different from the custom bracelet niche, and the B2B niche of selling high tech gadgets is different from the niche involved with what your business does and sells. Identify, research, and dominate your niche even as you look to best-in-class companies like Rustic Cuff, REI, Thermo Fisher, Numi Organic Tea or others that are great to *emulate* but should not *intimidate* you for your future success as a social media marketing maven.

**Remember**: you (and your company) are experts in something (hopefully, your products or services or at least something that relates to your products or services). You (and your company) are passionate about something (hopefully how your products or services are used). All you really have to do is use your iPhone to take pictures of this, your laptop to write about it, your Android phone to take videos, and some nifty online tools to create cheesy quotes about it, tweet about it, create infographics, about it, etc., etc.

> **Share your knowledge and your passion. Become a "helpful expert" to your customers.**

That's what content marketing is really all about.

Your first **TO-DO** is to inventory your own and your company's skill set. What type of content is going to be relatively easy for you, your company, and even your own customers to produce? If you're a pizza restaurant, for example, it's going to be pretty easy to whip out an iPhone and snap a photo of happy customers enjoying a birthday celebration, if you're a wedding planner, it's going to be pretty easy to take a quick video with the bride and groom on their special day, and if you're a CPA, it's going to be relatively easy to write a short blog post about upcoming changes to the federal tax code and how they impact married couples. Can you take photos? Can you shoot video? Can you write?

Or perhaps you love quotes. It's not going to be hard to go to a website such as Pablo (**http://jmlinks.com/29b**) and input a few motivational quotes that relate to your industry, pick an image, and generate a "quotable photo" for Facebook or Instagram. Perhaps you love data, and you can generate infographics using free tools such as Easely (**http://jmlinks.com/29c**), where you can input data and images and create eye-appealing infographics. And, finally, perhaps you're up for a more beefy type of writing, and you can conceptualize and write a free eBook. You can download templates from Hubspot (**http://jmlinks.com/29d**), or even go whole hog and write an eBook for Amazon using their free KDP services (**http://jmlinks.com/29e**).

Another point is whether you like **interaction**. Some people live on their phones; others live on Twitter or LinkedIn or Facebook, etc. They love interacting with others on social media. Appoint these folks to your social media content team, and have them find interesting content from others and like, comment on, and share it. Have them monitor your own brand content and, again, like, comment on, and share the comments of others. Interactive content is yet another type of content that needs to be part of your plan, just as "working the room" would be one of your tasks as a party host. Shake hands, say hello, ask about the wife or husband and kids, share the news of the day.

# WORK THE PARTY

The point of this exercise is to get you thinking about what type of written or visual content can you / your company produce easily and systematically to feed your social media channels. What are you good at, and what will come easily? Where are there easy opportunities to generate content, whether that be a photograph or a blog post?

## » THINK SYSTEMATICALLY ABOUT CONTENT

What kind of content do people generally want? What kind of content gets shared? Among the most popular and commonly shared items on social media are the following:

**Photos**. Photographs and images are the bread-and-butter of Facebook, Instagram, and even Twitter.

**Memes**. From *grumpy cat* to *success kid*, memes make the funny and memorable, sticky and shareable on social media. I love memes; here's a screenshot of one on "Social Media Marketing:"

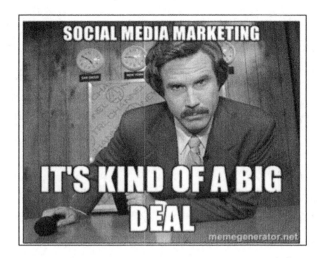

**Infographics and Instructographics**. From how to tie a tie to sixteen ways you can help stop global warming, people love to read and share pictures that tell a story, hopefully with facts.

**Blog Posts**. An oldie but goodie: an informative, witty, funny, informational, or fact-filled post about a topic that matters to your customers.

**Short Text Posts or Tweets**. Funny, important, moving, informative quotations. Cute and clever quips on industry events. Even within the 280 character limit of Twitter, you can share ideas that are short, sweet, and powerful. Here's a funny meme on that topic:

**Slideshows**. From Slideshare to just posting your PowerPoints online, slideshows are a hybrid visual and textual cornucopia of social sharing fun.

**Videos**. If a picture tells a thousand words, a video can tell ten thousand. YouTube is a social medium in its own right, but the videos themselves are content that can be enjoyed and shared on networks like Instagram, TikTok, and Facebook.

These are just the *archetypes* of content, the *genres* of information as it were. They're just empty shells. Your job is to identify which types will be the easiest for you and your company to produce, and to then, start your content production machine.

## » IDENTIFY BUYER PERSONAS AND KEYWORD THEMES

Social media marketing is a party, not a prison. If you don't produce content that your customers want to read or engage with, they'll leave. So, first up, educate your boss or CEO that the customers probably do not want to watch him or her reading the company's annual report. What may be interesting to your boss may not be what's interesting to the customers! **Don't be boring.**

Your second **TO-DO** is to brainstorm the **buyer personas** and **keyword themes** that customers care about, and the type of content that they'll be interested in and will find engaging.

### Build a Keyword or Social Media Theme Worksheet

While **keywords** do not play as tight a role in social media marketing, as they do in search engine optimization (SEO) or Google Ads, you still want to identify customer social media themes, whether these be "pain points" or "points of interest." What are people talking about on social media, what are they searching for on Google, and where does a topic that interests customers intersect with what you have to offer? You must get inside your customers' heads and brainstorm not only the types of content (images, blog posts, infographics) that interest them but also the content itself (i.e., What does it explain? What does it describe with passion? What does it convey as a photo?)

A good way to conceptualize this is to have a meeting with your marketing team and conceptualize **buyer personas** – stereotypical mockups of typical customers.

A Palo Alto pizza restaurant, for example, might brainstorm **buyer personas** like:

**The Hungry Worker Bee**. This is a man, aged 27-35, who works in downtown Palo Alto, and is looking for a quick bite-to-eat. He likes pizza and is value-conscious plus time-sensitive.

**The Office Manager**. She works in a nearby office and is charged with ordering the catering for office meetings. She's interested in fun, lively food that's easy to get and fits within her catering budget.

**The Busy Mom or Dad**. This person has a few young kids and lives close to Palo Alto. They're looking for either quick pizza delivery for a Thursday night, or perhaps a venue for their kid's birthday party.

Next, take each persona and brainstorm the types of content / themes that they'd be interested in. The *Worker Bee*, for example, would be interested in learning about coupons, discounts, and special offers of the "pizza of the day," for example. So you'd need to generate either coupon codes or perhaps short tweets about a "pizza of the day" that features *kale* and *pesto* and is on sale with a secret coupon code known only to your followers on Twitter.

The *Office Manager*, in contrast, might be interested in blog posts about how to throw better office parties, or catering ideas that are fun for yet another weekly sales meeting. And the *Busy Mom or Dad* might want to view (and share) photos of their kids (or the kids of their friends) having a blast on Birthday Night at the local pizza restaurant. Each buyer persona, in short, has certain thematic interests and needs.

> **Tool**. Hubspot produces a nifty buyer persona tool at
> **http://jmlinks.com/29s**. Answer a few questions, and the tool will literally create a buyer persona profile complete with photo.

## Tools to Research Keyword Themes

Once you've brainstormed a few buyer personas, role play "as if" you were that buyer persona and write down the keyword themes that might interest that person. To use a different example, let's say you're a wedding planner, you'd realize that the *bride-to-be* is an obvious buyer persona, and she'd be interested in topics such as "how to plan a wedding on a budget," or "tips on selecting the best wedding venue," or "how to deal with divorced parents and their new spouses at a wedding reception," etc. Or imagine your company sells insurance, you'd identify a buyer persona of the *busy thirty-year-old dad* with two kids, who wonders "what's the best way to set up a living trust," or "what's the difference between term life insurance and whole life insurance," and you'd write a nifty blog post or perhaps create an eBook. By role-playing, you get "inside the head" of each buyer persona and identify the topics that would interest them as a photo, as a blog post, as a tweet, as a video, etc.

Here are some fun tools that can help you brainstorm keyword themes for your social media content:

**SeedKeywords (http://jmlinks.com/29f).** Simply type in a scenario, and this tool generates a URL you can email out to your team members. Then, each can input the keyword themes that they think that "buyer persona" might be interested in.

**Hashtagify.me (http://jmlinks.com/27v).** Again, input a "starter" word or hashtag and this tool will show you related hashtags and metrics on popularity (shown visually by keyword size). It's based on Twitter but is really useful for any theme.

**Answer the Public (http://jmlinks.com/51e).** Ignore the creepy man. Enter some "seed keywords" that you think your target customers might talk about on social media. Browse suggestions. This is a really awesome tool to brainstorm keywords (after you get past the creepy man).

**Google AdWords Keyword Planner.** If you have a Google Ads account, and especially if you're spending a couple hundred dollars per month, you can use this Google tool to research keywords, related keywords, volumes, and value. The reality is that what people search for on Google is also often what they talk about on social. To access it, visit Google Ads at **https://ads.google.com/,** log in and then click on the "tools" icon at the top right, and then click on "Keyword Planner."

If you have a budget, I also highly recommend that you use Buzzsumo (**http://jmlinks.com/29j**). For $99 a month, this tool allows you to input a keyword and see the most shared content on Facebook, Twitter, Pinterest, Reddit, and Links. Here's a screenshot of the most shared content for the keyword *wedding*:

So your steps are:

1. Log in to Buzzsumo.com.

2. Enter a keyword such as "organic food" or "tax refund" and select a time horizon such as "past month" or "past year."

3. Sort by network such as Facebook or Pinterest.

4. Click to view the most shared content.

    a. Reverse engineer what it's about.

    b. Hypothesize why it received so many shares.

5. Click back and click on "View sharers" to see which influencers on Twitter shared the content.

The tool also allows you to enter the domain of a competitor or popular blog in your industry and see the most shared content as well. For example, enter *nytimes.com* to see the most popular content shared on the New York Times across social networks. You can also sort by network to see the most shared content on Facebook, Twitter, Pinterest, and blog links.

As you research keywords, look for themes that connect "what your customers want" with "what you offer." These are your primary themes; that is, themes that directly or very closely touch on what you offer. An example would be a Palo Alto pizza restaurant that would have themes like "pizza" or "Italian food."

Don't miss **adjacent keyword themes**. A Palo Alto Pizza Restaurant, for example, should realize that its customers will also be talking about, and interested in, keyword themes such as "places to eat in Palo Alto," "where to take a client to lunch," "things to do in Palo Alto, etc." Even themes like "birthdays" or "Columbus Day" would be relevant themes. You always want to "fish where the fish are," so look not only for keyword themes that are spot on to what your company offers but also for *adjacent* keyword themes. Aeromexico, to use a different example, is an airline that flies to Mexico, but it's social media keyword themes aren't just "airlines" or "cheap air tickets" but also keywords such *travel, best tourist destinations in Mexico, Latin America, things to do in Mexico City,* etc.

For your third **TO-DO**, download the **Keyword Worksheet** and the **Content Marketing worksheet**. For the worksheet, go to **http://jmlinks.com/social2020** (then enter the code '**social2020**' to register your workbook), and click on the link to the "Content Marketing." On the **keyword worksheet**, fill out the tab marked "Social Media Themes." On the **Content Marketing Worksheet**, fill out the sections on buyer personas and keyword themes.

## » PRODUCE YOUR OWN CONTENT ON SCHEDULE

Now that you have your buyer personas and keyword themes in hand, you can return to your list of content that's easy for you to produce, and look for opportunities. You're looking to marry "content that's easy to produce" with "content that your customers want." For example, our Palo Alto Pizza Restaurant would realize that customers like to see and share photos of themselves and their friends having a good time at the restaurant, especially pictures of family events such as birthdays. So your content production tasks become:

- **Birthday Customers.** Identify customers who are coming to the restaurant to celebrate a birthday. For example, have each waiter or waitress ask customers, "Is anyone celebrating a birthday today?" If so, ask if you can take a picture of their birthday party and share it to the company Facebook page. Get their emails and email them an alert that their party has been "shared" (*because they will likely then reshare it with their friends and photos*).

- **Incentivize.** Many restaurants already give the birthday customer a free dessert such as an ice cream sundae or brownie. Make sure that your restaurant has some incentive for customers who are celebrating a birthday to identify themselves. For example, "Check in on Facebook" and be entered to win a free pizza on your birthday!

- **Photo**. Take the photo. When the waiter or waitress brings out the birthday dessert, make sure that they have a mobile phone handy and ask the customers for consent to take a celebratory photo. Be on the lookout for other customer photo opportunities such as anniversaries, holidays like Valentine's Day or Cinco De Mayo, gatherings of friends, or even that group of business customers on a quick lunch.

- **Remind**. Get the email address, if possible, of one or all of the customers, or leave a card with the check that says "Check our Facebook Page and Instagram Page" for our birthday photos and birthday photo contest.

- **Promote**. Make sure that you have something like a "birthday photo contest" on Facebook or Instagram, whereby you upload the "birthday photos of the week" and then customers can vote by clicking the "like" button. The photo with the most "likes," wins, and its recipients can get a free pizza!

In this way, you have an easy-to-understand, content production system for your wait staff. Every time there's a birthday, they're going to ask for permission to take a photo and enter that photo in your Instagram / Facebook photo contest.

Next, let's look at **blog content**. You'll realize that one of your buyer personas is the busy office manager in Palo Alto who's looking for ideas for inexpensive, fun catering for the weekly sales meeting. You want your pizza restaurant to be discovered by her, and get in the rotation for caterers. She's probably looking for blog articles on human resources, catering, and employee morale as well as caterers in Palo Alto. So, in this case, you'd identify fun article topics for your blog on "how to boost employee morale with better office parties," or "tips on catering for employees who have diverse dietary needs," etc. In this case, you'd identify someone at the pizza restaurant who is a decent writer and assign that writing task of writing at least one blog post per month on the topic of "Palo Alto Catering" and related keywords.

Or, take your buyer persona of the Hungry Worker Bee. These people often go to Twitter or Instagram, searching for daily lunch specials, special deals, and information on "what's cooking." In this case, your content would be as simple as a daily tweet / photo with a discount code or hashtag such as *#PaloAltoPizza25* that they simply need to say upon ordering to get the discount. Or, perhaps you realize that *#tacotuesday* is a trending hashtag on Twitter every Tuesday, so your content production task it to piggyback on the buzz about *#tacotuesday* by having a taco-style pizza ready every Tuesday. You then tweet out a short tweet with picture on Twitter and Instagram and use the relevant hashtags.

In each case, you're identifying a type of content (*photo*, *blog post*, *video*, or *tweet*) that fits into the keyword themes that your target customers care about. You then figure out what content needs to be produced, who needs to produce it, and when it needs to be produced. Your **TO-DO**, here is to return to the **Content Marketing Worksheet** and populate the section on a Content Schedule. It should answer the following questions:

- What **type of content** needs to be produced, such as photos, videos, blog posts, tweets, etc.?

- What **keyword themes** does this content touch upon that matter to your target customers?

  - Don't miss **direct** themes (such as pizza or Italian food) vs. **indirect** themes (such as Italian-American holidays like Columbus Day, what to do in Palo Alto, or even themes like how to cater a great office party).

- **Who** is going to produce this content?

- **When** are they going to produce it? (Not just Tuesdays, but at what "event" or "moment," such as "Every time we have a birthday customer, we will offer to take a fun photo," or "Every Mother's Day we will have a customer contest asking customers for their favorite memory of their Moms.")

- **Where** will this content be **posted** on social media? Will it go to Facebook, Instagram, your blog, Twitter, YouTube, etc.?

Successful content marketing is about being very, very **systematic**.

## » BLOG, BLOG, BLOG, YOU GOTTA BLOG, VLOG, PHLOG, AND POST

Any business that's serious about social media marketing must have a blog if for no other reason than a blog gives you an easy place to put your articles, infographics, photos, and videos that you can then reference on Twitter, Facebook, Pinterest, etc.

**You gotta blog!**

If you don't have a blog on your website, ask your web designer to set one up immediately, preferably at your domain.com/blog. The easiest platform to use is WordPress. If you can't use WordPress or set one up on your own domain, I recommend Google's Blogger platform at **https://www.blogger.com/**. Tumblr (**https://www.tumblr.com/**) is another good one with the added benefit that it is a social media network in its own right.

**Blogs** are so important for social media content that I want to spend some time on blogging. I'm assuming you have set up a company blog, so structurally you're ready to write your first post. (If you've already written a few posts, you can also revisit and re-optimize them as indicated below).

Your blog and the blog posts on it can serve any or all of three purposes.

1. as a **trust indicator** to substantiate your company as a "helpful expert."

2. as an **SEO asset**, that is - as a way to get to the top of relevant Google, Yahoo, and Bing searches via basic SEO) (*This is covered in-depth in my SEO Fitness Workbook, so we will not cover it here*).

3. as **content** for posting and **sharing** to your social media networks.

4. as a **place to put** other content such as videos or photos.

Each of these, conceptually, are different things, but one blog post can be oriented towards one, or all, of them. For example, a blog post on "Seven Tax Tips for Expatriates Living in the USA," can be a *trust indicator* substantiating your CPA firm as experts in international tax issues, it can be an *SEO asset* helping get your company to the top of relevant Google searches, and it can be *content* that you can share on social media networks like LinkedIn to stay top of mind among potential customers and encourage social sharing.

## Identifying Keyword Themes for Your Blog

What should you blog about? What type of content should you create? The answer is to identify **keyword themes** that touch on what your target customers want to know about. Clients seeking international tax advice, for example, would be interested in reading blog posts on ways to minimize double taxation, or what types of behavior is most likely to provoke an IRS audit. Persons planning a wedding might be interested in comparing the merits of a "destination wedding" in Mexico, with an "at home" wedding in Los Angeles. And persons interested in cybersecurity for their corporations might be interested in a blog post with an infographic on the twelve most common security holes in a typical corporate network.

# A Strong Blog Touches on Keyword Themes that People Care About

### Emotion, Emotion, Emotion (and Some Utility)

In general, successful blog topics for social media will hit **emotional** themes such as usefulness, being counterintuitive or counterfactual, being shocking, provoking fear or outrage, or being funny. It's really all about utility or emotion; outside of LinkedIn (which is the most serious network), emotional triggers are by far the most common content!

Accordingly, if there is an "emotional" angle to your blog post, be sure to touch on it, and be sure to include it in your headline.

> *Once you have the keyword target, the next step is to write a catchy headline and write a catchy blog post that hits on either emotion or usefulness.*

Let's take the example of a Los Angeles CPA firm that has expertise in international taxation issues. Our keyword research has identified the FBAR requirements which require reporting of overseas assets as a "hot button" issue among our buyer personas. We might then take the topic of "FBAR compliance," and spin out blog headlines such as:

> *Why FBAR Matters to Your Clients (Even If They Don't Know It Yet) ("utility").*
>
> *Why What You as a CPA Don't Know About FBAR Is Going to Cost You ("fear").*
>
> *The FBAR: An Outrageous Intervention of the Government in our Lives ("shocking")*
>
> *An FBAR Tragedy: A Small Businessperson Forced into Bankruptcy ("Outrage or sentimentality")*

Fun tools that will help you "spin" blog topics and titles for social media are the Portent Idea Generator (**http://jmlinks.com/17g**) and Hubspot's topic generator (**http://jmlinks.com/9w**).

## Vlog, Phlog, and Post: Other Forms of Blogging

Blogging, of course, refers to the written word. A good blog post has a strong concept, catchy headline, and somewhere between two and five paragraphs. Pretty much every business needs to have a blog unless your business is just so visual that you can get by with just photos or videos. You should expand your definition of blogging, however, to include other forms of rapid-fire content. Let's discuss each type:

> **Vlog or video blogging.** You can blog with the printed word, but you can also "video" blog" or Vlog as on YouTube but also on native content on Facebook, Instagram, and LinkedIn. Indeed, with the rise of "stories" on Instagram and Snapchat, this is yet another type of "day in the life" video blogging. So think about short video content you can share across channels, and like blogging, this content can be very "spur of the moment."

> **Phlog or photo blogging.** Photos are the bread and butter of Instagram and Facebook, so think of being systematic as you produce photos of products, services, customers, events, etc.

> **Posting.** You can post straight text on Facebook, Twitter, or LinkedIn. These short posts (< 280 characters on Twitter) are like micro blog posts. Again, be systematic about the content that you'll share in text format. It can be as simple as posting "TGIF" on Friday, "I love Taco Tuesday!," or "The only thing we have to fear is fear itself" with some additional commentary about your industry or trends within it.

As with a more robust blog post, each type of "micro" blogging, "photo" blogging, or "video" blogging follows the same rules. Know what your audience wants and create content that touches on your keyword themes. Think interactively – what will your target customers like, comment on, or share? Give priority to emotions and counterintuitive content. Emotions work better than facts, and anything that's counterintuitive works better than things that are not. Think of content that is "man bites dog" not "dog bites man."

Think systematically. What can you produce easily and on schedule? It's easier if you think of content that's authentic and spontaneous vs. thinking that each piece of content needs to be a masterpiece that will stand for centuries.

**Share Systematically on Schedule with Hootsuite**

Finally, now that you have a well-written blog post (photo, video, etc.) that touches on trending industry themes of interest to key customer segments, it's time to share it. Post it to your blog, and then use a URL shortener like **http://bitly.com/** or **http://tinyurl.com/** to shorten your long blog URL. Then paste it into Hootsuite (**http://jmlinks.com/29k**), summarize the topic, and post it strategically to your Twitter, Facebook, LinkedIn, and wherever else appropriate. (Hootsuite has its own built-in link shortener as well; here's a screenshot:)

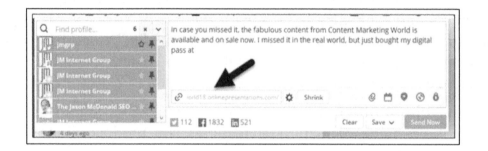

To sum up, once you know a keyword theme, the process of creating a blog post (or another type of blog-like content) is as follows:

1. **Identify the blog concept and relevant keywords**. These define what the blog post is about and which keywords people are likely to search for. Use a tool like Buzzsumo (**http://jmlinks.com/29j**) to see what's already being shared on social media sites.

2. **Outline the content and write a rough draft**. Just as in all writing, it's good to write out a rough draft. A good blog post should have about four to five paragraphs of text. "Less is more" when it comes to social media, so make the blog post pithy and informative.

3. **Identify a provocative image**. Whether it's on Instagram, Facebook, or LinkedIn, people respond to images. Use a royalty-free image site such as Foter (**http://foter.com/**) or Unsplash (**https://unsplash.com/**) and find an image that conveys the essence of your blog post.

4. **Write a catchy, keyword-heavy headline**. It's no accident that popular sites like *Buzzfeed* and *Huffington Post* use shocking or provocative headlines! *Dog bites man, Read Donald Trump's Latest Outrageous Tweet!, etc.* People react to, and share,

content that hits an emotional nerve and the headline is the first step toward a strong emotional reaction.

5. **Finalize the content**. Review your content and make sure it is easy-to-read, preferably with lists and bullets.

6. **Share the content**. Identify the appropriate social media platform such as LinkedIn, Twitter, Facebook, Instagram, etc., and share your post. Use a tool like Hootsuite to organize and schedule your shares.

VIDEO. Watch a video tutorial on how to write social media-friendly blog posts at **http://jmlinks.com/16p**.

## Your Blogging Objectives

In terms of social media marketing, your blog objectives are a) to stay "top of mind" among customers and their contacts, b) to substantiate your organization's brand image as a "helpful expert," and c) to encourage "social sharing" so that friends of friends, and colleagues of colleagues, can become aware of your company and its products or services. A strong blog post can be great as a trust indicator, great for SEO, or attractive for social media sharing, or all three! So, start blogging as well as vlogging, phlogging, and sharing short posts!

## » CURATE OTHER PEOPLE'S CONTENT

Effective content for social media comes in four main varieties: your own content, **other people's content**, user-generated content, and interactive content. We've discussed your own content, such as photos or blog posts that you will identify and systematically generate. But because you'll need a lot of content to feed your social media channels, you'll probably want to **curate** other people's content. So let's now turn to the second type of content – curated, or other people's content.

*Curate* is just a fancy word that means identifying useful content in your industry, summarizing it via a short headline or summary paragraph as in a tweet, and sharing this content on your social networks like Twitter, Facebook, LinkedIn, etc. I, for one, do a lot of content curation on Twitter and LinkedIn. You can check me out on Twitter at **http://jmlinks.com/37m**. Here's a screenshot of my sharing of a link to the Marketoonist:

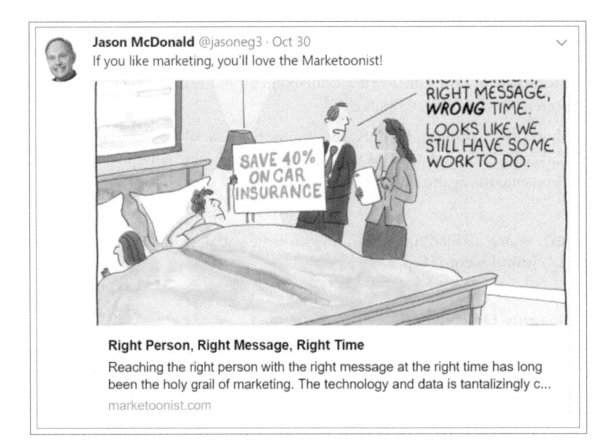

**Right Person, Right Message, Right Time**

Reaching the right person with the right message at the right time has long been the holy grail of marketing. The technology and data is tantalizingly c...

marketoonist.com

By diligently paying attention to blogs, publications, and trade shows on SEO, Social Media Marketing, and AdWords (via tools like *Feedly.com, Buzzsumo.com, Drumup.io*), I systematically identify, read, and "curate" the best content for my followers. I thus have other people's content to share on my own social media channels (Twitter, LinkedIn, Instagram, Facebook, etc.) and thereby work to stay top of mind with my target customers and position myself as a "helpful expert."

## Be a Helpful Expert

This idea of a "helpful expert" is a good way to wrap your head around content curation. You'll position your lead employees and/or your company as a whole as a "helpful expert" by looking through all the junk and noise in your industry, identifying the best / most useful content from industry blogs, gurus, and publications, and then sharing this content to your own social media channels. If producing your own content is all about being a good *photographer*, *writer*, or *videographer*, content *curation* is all about being a good *editor*.

The steps to content curation are:

1. Identify your **keyword themes** (which you have hopefully already identified above), including broader industry themes that you might not want to produce your own content, but you might want to monitor for relevant content.

2. Systematically **research and identify content**. Browse industry blogs, portals, websites, social media feeds, etc.. Separate the wheat from the chaff, meaning throw away the low-quality content and identify the truly interesting content that will interest your target customers.

3. **Summarize** this content in short format, ideally less than the 280 characters of Twitter, including a short URL to the full content using a URL shortener like bitly.com or tinyurl.com.

4. **Share** this content to your social media channels on a regular basis, using a scheduling software like Hootsuite (**http://jmlinks.com/29k**) or Buffer (**http://jmlinks.com/29m**).

## Advantages and Disadvantages

You might be tempted to ask why you should curate the content of others vs. using your own content. While it's certainly true that producing your own content is better (because you can control the message and directly promote your own company or product), few of us have the budget or resources to produce sufficient content on our own to fill our content pipeline. To stay top of mind with customers, you need a lot more content than you'll be able to produce yourself.

There are thus advantages and disadvantages to your own content vs. other people's content. The advantage of other people's content is that it is easy to get, while the advantage of your own content is that because it's yours, you can customize it to your desired message. The disadvantage of other people's content is that you do not control the message (and it thereby promotes them to some extent), while the disadvantage of your own content is that it takes time and effort to produce. It's a lot like the food at our party analogy. The advantage of other people's tacos is that they take less effort on your own part but (if they're good), they promote the actual producer of those tacos. The advantage of your own tacos is that they taste better (hopefully), and they promote you as the guru of tacos, but the disadvantage is that they are more work.

Going back to review the "types" of content you may want for your social media marketing content machine, you'll see that you have –

Your own blog post vs. the blog post of an industry guru

Your own photograph vs. the photograph of a great photographer

Your own quote vs. a famous quote by somebody else

Your own webinar vs. the webinar being put on by industry luminaries.

Go back and review some companies that are doing social media well (e.g., Whole Foods, REI, HP, Bishop Robert Barron, Seth Godin), and you'll see that many of them mix and match "their own content" and "other people's content" plus sometimes they commentate on the content of others (a "hybrid" model).

Let's drill down into other people's content.

## Finding Other People's Content to Share on Social Media

You want to start systematically identifying great content in your industry, and queuing this up to be shared on your social networks. Your goal is to be a "helpful expert," the person who tells others, "Hey! Did you know that so-and-so is having an amazing free webinar on Thursday?," or "Hey! Did you see that our industry journal just published an in-depth study on such-and-such topic?" Other People's Content or OPC is easy to find, easy to share, and helps to position you as the person or company that really has their ear to the industry pulse.

How do you find quality content produced by other people? How do you do this in an easy and systematic way?

Fortunately, there are tools to help you systematically identify and share other people's content. (All are listed in *The Marketing Almanac, content marketing section* and on my *Social Media Marketing Dashboard*). Here are some of my favorites:

**Bookmark / Read Industry Blogs.** Identify the top industry blogs in your industry, bookmark them (and/or input them to Feedly), plus follow them on social media as on Facebook, LinkedIn, Twitter. You can share their content with your followers, plus commentate on content that they're producing. To find blogs in the first place, go to Google and type in a keyword relevant to your company's industry and the word blog. For example, visit **http://jmlinks.com/12w** which is a sample search for blogs on *proteomics*

**Google Searches.** Enter your keyword themes into Google. Click on the *Tools Menu > Past Month*. Alternatively, click on the *News* tab. This is a good way to find timely blog post and articles on your keyword themes for sharing. See it in action for "organic food" at **http://jmlinks.com/37n**. You can input these "saved searches" to your Start.me page as well.

**Google News.** Google News is one of the best free tools to aggregate information. Log in to your Google / Gmail account, and visit **https://news.google.com/**. Once you do so, you'll get an email alert when Google finds new news and this content will appear in Google News on the left under "saved searches." You can also manage your feed by clicking on "For you" on the left and adding keywords or topics. Watch a video on how to use Google News for social media marketing at **http://jmlinks.com/46y**.

**DrumUp (https://drumpup.io).** DrumUp integrates easily with most social media platforms and helps you curate and share content that is useful to your followers.

**Feedly (http://feedly.com)** - Feedly is a newsreader integrated with Google or Facebook login. It's useful for social media because you can follow important blogs or other content and share it with your followers. It can also spur great blog ideas.

**Easely (http://easel.ly)** - Use thousands of templates and design objects to easily create infographics for your blog. A competitor is Piktochart (**http://piktochart.com**).

**Buzzsumo (http://buzzsumo.com)** - Buzzsumo is a 'buzz' monitoring tool for social media. Input a keyword, select a date range like "last week," and this tool will show you what is being most shared across Facebook, Twitter, LinkedIn, etc. You can also input a domain such as *nytimes.com* or one of your industry blogs and also see what is being most shared from that domain.

**Google Alerts (https://www.google.com/alerts)** - Google alerts allow you to input keywords and then receive daily or weekly alerts of new items that the Google search engine finds on those keywords. It's useful, but I like Google news better.

A final nifty tool is Start.me (**https://start.me/**). Sign up for this free service, and you can build a personalized dashboard with links to all your favorite industry blogs, key tools like Feedly or Buzzsumo, canned searches on Google, etc. You can even share these dashboards with your team. Imagine having a Monday afternoon assignment of launching your Start.me personalized dashboard, browsing Feedly and key industry blogs, checking your Google alerts, and then quickly identifying interesting content, summarizing it, and sharing it to your social media networks by scheduling it to Hootsuite. *We're talking about the systematic production of content marketing here, factory edition.* By being systematic, you can fill your social media content pipeline in just a couple hours a week.

"I want to be a machine." ~ the artist, Andy Warhol

## Keep Your Secrets Secret

And, as part of the social media illusion, you don't have to share the amazing tools above with your customers. They'll just think you are gung-ho awesome. The "illusion" of effective social media marketing will work in your favor; you will be perceived as the industry guru that somehow, never sleeps, and is aware of every important industry trend, "how to" video on YouTube, and key article that's up for debate in the industry blogosphere.

> **VIDEO.** Watch a video tutorial on using Buzzsumo, Feedly, and Hootsuite to identify and share "other people's content" for social media marketing at **http://jmlinks.com/16j**.

## » ENCOURAGE USER GENERATED CONTENT (UGC)

Never forget the *social* element of social media. Don't think of this as a project you'll do by yourself; you need employees in your company to help, and you need the participation of your customers and fans. You'll want to enlist the support of other employees in your company, especially the frontline, customer-facing staff, to look for content opportunities. If at all possible, you also want to encourage user-generated content or UGC. UGC is both cheap (your users will be doing the heavy lifting) and engaging, as users love to share and see their own content.

Here are some ways to encourage UGC:

> **Ask**. Simply ask for feedback. Don't just post a photo to Instagram or Facebook. Post a photo with a query. Post a picture of your latest "Taco Pizza" concoction and ask users if they think they'll like it. Don't post a photo that says "Happy Mother's Day" to Facebook, but rather post a photo of a mom and child and ask users to share their favorite memory of their own mom.

> **Have Contests.** Within reason, contests are a great way to solicit UGC. Don't just post a picture of a cute kid at his birthday party eating pizza in your restaurant. Post the photo of the kid, and ask them to enroll in your "cutest kid of the month" contest as measured by Facebook and Instagram likes. Want to see what contests are up and out on Instagram? Check out the hashtag *#contest* at **http://jmlinks.com/52y**.

**Conduct Surveys.** Use your blog, your Twitter, or Facebook to engage in customer surveys. Twitter, for example, has made the app easy to use; simply select the "Add Poll" icon on a Tweet. For Facebook, merely Google "Facebook Poll App" and you'll find an assortment of free and paid apps for Facebook. SurveyMonkey and Google also offer free / paid versions of survey software.

**Use Hashtags.** Especially on Instagram, but also on Twitter, you can set up a special hashtag just for your customers to share posts about your products or services. Airbnb does this on Instagram with *#airbnb* (**http://jmlinks.com/29p**) as do vendors like REI with *#optoutside* (**http://jmlinks.com/29q**). If you're in a fun industry where people like to "show off," you may not even have to incentivize people with a contest to get them to generate photos, tweets, or other content that promotes your brand!

You can also commission content, for example, by sending bloggers free product samples and asking them to blog or video blog about your products or services. (If you do so, you'll need to have them identify per FTC regulations that they were given free stuff). Search YouTube for *unboxing* (**http://jmlinks.com/29r**), for example, and you'll discover there's a whole genre of unboxing or haul videos in which people showcase and talk about products.

**Influencer marketing** is yet another buzzword for UGC. It has come to mean paid or at least promoted content. So for influencer marketing, you:

1. Identify influencers who reach the types of customers you want to reach.

2. Reach out to them via email, their agents, or emerging marketplaces such as Upfluence (**https://www.upfluence.com/**). Most influencers require at least free product if not a paid promotion fee.

3. The influencer then shares to his or her social following some type of content about your product or service. It could be a product review, a coupon or special deal, a contest, etc.

UGC is all about encouraging customers, fans, superfans, and even (paid) influencers to take about and "spontaneously" share to their social channels content that casts your product or service in a positive light. Your **TO-DO** here is to brainstorm which users are most likely to spontaneously create positive content about your company, product, or service. How do you identify them? How do you motivate them? How can you nurture them?

## » INTERACT WITH INTERACTIVE CONTENT

Finally, as you are working on your own content, content curation, and UGC, don't forget that social media is really all about **engagement** and **interactivity**. All of the algorithms favor content that engages people as measured by likes, comments, and shares. A YouTube video that "goes viral" usually does so because people like it, comment on it, and share it. Ditto for a Facebook post that gets a lot of traction, or a tweet that shows up prominently in Twitter moments. As you create content, curate content, or catalyze UGC, always think:

1. **What's in it for them?** Why would a user even want to passively read or consume this piece of content in the first place?

2. **Why would they like it?** What will cause them to hit the "like" button, and why?

3. **Why would they comment on it?** What prompt can you devise that will engage them in a conversation around this piece of content?

4. **Why will they share it?** Content that gets shared extends your reach, and saying that something "went viral" really means that people engaged with it so fervently that they massively liked it, commented on it, and shared it. But why?

Next, flip this around and realize that you as a content producer and brand need to interact with the content of others. If someone comments on your YouTube video, respond back in the comments. Do the same if someone comments on your Facebook or LinkedIn post, tweet, etc. If someone reviews you on Yelp, respond to the review and say thanks. If they engage with you, engage back with them. Have conversations with your fans and superfans across all channels.

**Be Interactive.** Set a goal of a daily or weekly log in to each and every one of your social channels. Scan for user comments, and comment back. Thank people for reviews on Facebook, Google, or Yelp. "Tag" people in photos on Instagram or Facebook. Follow the followers of your competitors. Reach out to influencers, superfans, and prominent people on Twitter and talk "to" them about your keyword themes. Be interactive both with people who have commented on your content; be pro-actively interactive with new people especially on platforms like Twitter or LinkedIn where it's considered OK for people to strike up online conversations with strangers.

## Look for Content and Engage with It

Moreover, look for content by your users, by potential users, and by influencers. Find their content and engage with it by liking, commenting on, and sharing it. Here's just one example, based on LinkedIn.

1. Sign in to your LinkedIn account.

2. In the search bar, type in a keyword theme that matters to your company and/or customers.

3. Click the button marked content.

4. Scroll through content posted by others to LinkedIn and like, comment on, and share content that's relevant to you and your brand.

Here's a screenshot:

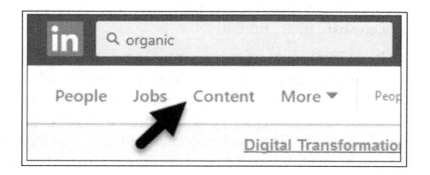

Do the same with hashtags across Facebook, LinkedIn, Twitter, and Instagram. Identify key hashtags and engage with the content being shared across them. Here's a screenshot for the hashtag *#organic* on Instagram at 31 million posts:

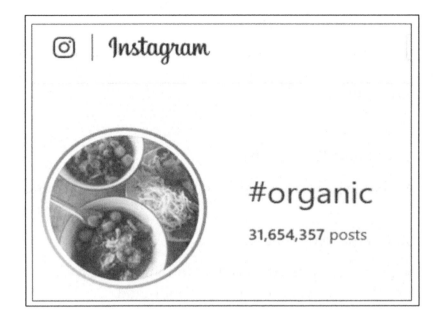

In this way, across all the networks, you can quickly identify content put up by others on themes that matter to your business. You can then like, comment on, and share that content. Indeed, people respond to the "flattery" that you took the time to read, like, comment on, and even share their content.

It's not just LinkedIn or Instagram, of course. You can do the same process on all of the networks. Find posts on Facebook that matter to your brand and comment on them, find tweets on Twitter that matter to your brand and like or comment on them, find videos on YouTube that matter to your brand, and thumb up / thumb down, comment on, and share them. Interactive content means making this process of searching for and engaging with others a key part of your content marketing strategy.

## INTERACTIVITY IS WHERE "IT'S AT" ON SOCIAL MEDIA

Interactivity can be as simple as following, liking, commenting on, and sharing the content of other brands or individuals in your industry. Or it can be as complicated as identifying "influencers" more powerful than you and systematically drawing them into a conversation or interaction. By engaging with this content, you'll draw the attention of others and become part of the conversation. No one likes people who just talk. Any good conversation is about talking and listening, listening and reacting, sharing and bringing others into it. Social media, in summary, is a *conversational* platform, not a *broadcast* medium.

## » REMEMBER THE BIG PICTURE

At this point, you've begun your social media marketing journey. You've understood that social media marketing is about "throwing" the party more than "attending the party." You've realized you need to start "paying attention" with regard to what other marketers are doing on social media, with an eye to "reverse engineering" their marketing strategy so that you have ideas of what you like, and do not like, in terms of social media. You've started to brainstorm "discovery paths" and "goals" for your SMM efforts.

And you've realized that once you've identified your goals, identified relevant social media, set up your social accounts, the really hard work will be creating the kind of **content** that makes them want to "like you," keep coming back for more, and share your message with their friends, family, and/or business colleagues.

Setting up social accounts on Facebook, Twitter, Instagram, YouTube, LinkedIn, etc., is the easy part. You should now understand that **content creation** and **promotion** are the big on-going tasks of successful social media marketing.

## »» CHECKLIST: CONTENT MARKETING ACTION ITEMS

Test your knowledge of Content Marketing! Take the *Content marketing quiz* at **http://jmlinks.com/qzcm**. Next, here are your Content Marketing **Action Items**:

❑ **Brainstorm** the types of content that your company can easily produce such as photos, memes, infographics, blogs, quotes, slide shows, videos, etc.

❑ Identify **buyer personas** and **keyword themes**. Create a *Keyword Worksheet* identifying your keywords on a continuum from "adjacent" or "educational" to late-stage or "transactional" keywords.

❑ **Research** content by **competitors** using a tool like Buzzsumo to identify the *most shared content* and reverse engineer why. Brainstorm how you, too, can create highly interactive or shareable content.

❑ Identify the **four types of content**: your own content, other people's content, UGC (User Generated Content), and interactive content. What will be your easiest and most effective mix of content?

   ❑ Create a **content map** for your own content to be produced.

   ❑ Set up **tools** like Google News, Feedly, DrumUp or Buzzsumo to pre-identify the content of others.

❑ Brainstorm **UGC content opportunities** and, if possible, set up the "systems" to begin encouraging UGC.

❑ Set aside a specific time each day or week to identify and find **interactive content**, whether as posted by customers or fans to your own brand channels or by customers or fans across hashtags and relevant content themes.

❑ Create a **content calendar** identifying the type of content you will produce, when it will be produced, and who will produce it. *Set up a **blog** and begin blogging, for example. Set up a calendar of who will check Feedly and share content (and when), for example. Set up a calendar of who will check hashtags and interact with content that's trending, etc.*

❑ **Share your content** in a systematic way using a scheduling tool such as Hootsuite or Buffer.

Check out the **free tools**! Go to my *Social Media Marketing Dashboard > Content Marketing* for my favorite free tools on content marketing. Just visit **http://jmlinks.com/smmdash**.

## »» DELIVERABLE: A CONTENT MARKETING PLAN

Now that we've come to the end of Chapter 2, your **DELIVERABLE** has arrived. For the worksheet, go to **http://jmlinks.com/social2020** (then enter the code '**social2020**' to register your workbook), and click on the link to the "Content Marketing Worksheet." By filling out this plan, you and your team will create a plan for all the yummy yummy content, both yours and that of other people, that you'll need to fill your social media pipeline.

# 3
# FACEBOOK

**Facebook** is a great place to begin your Social Media Marketing journey! Let me give you five good reasons.

First, Facebook is – by far – the **largest social media platform**, with over two billion active users and countless profiles, Pages, and groups. Nearly everyone who matters to your business has a Facebook profile, and survey after survey ranks Facebook as the most used social media platform.

Second, once you **understand the dynamics of Facebook** – *Profiles and Pages, Timelines and Posts, Likes, Comments, and Shares...* you'll more easily **understand the dynamics of other social media** like LinkedIn, Twitter, or Instagram.

Third, Facebook has a component in its **algorithm** (called colloquially *Edgerank*), which essentially **rewards** you for posting items that users interact with (as measured by *likes*, *comments*, and *shares*). Understanding what *Edgerank* is, and how to improve your *Edgerank* will help you be a better marketer on Facebook. Understanding *Edgerank* will also help you market better on the other platforms, as all of them use something similar in their own proprietary algorithms.

Fourth, because of its extensive **reach** and its nuanced **targeting** options, Facebook is an incredible **advertising** platform. Throw in the fact that Facebook owns Instagram, and Facebook advertising options are second to none in social media!

Fifth and finally, Facebook is **fun**! Social media marketing should not be thought of as a chore, but as a way to get closer to your customers and build a community of evangelists around your company, product, or service.

The question is not whether your customers are on Facebook, but rather what they are doing, and how you can brainstorm a social media strategy to reach them.

**Let's get started!**

**TO-DO LIST:**

» Explore how Facebook Works

» Inventory Companies on Facebook

» Understand the Importance of Like & Edgerank

» Set up and Optimize Your Facebook Page

» Brainstorm and Execute a Posting Strategy

» Promote Your Facebook Page and Posts for Free

» Odds & Ends: Groups, Events, Facebook Live, etc.

» Advertise on Facebook: Basics

» Advanced Facebook Targeting

» Advertise on Facebook: the Superfan Strategy

» Measure Your Results

»» Checklist: Facebook Action Items

»» Deliverable: a Facebook Marketing Plan


## » EXPLORE HOW FACEBOOK WORKS

To understand Facebook as a marketer is to understand the "F's": friends, family, fun, photos, and "fake." Before you set up (or optimize) a Facebook Page for your business, before you start posting, before you start advertising, and before you start measuring your successes and failures, take some time to research how Facebook works. Throughout this Chapter, we'll use Facebook on the desktop (not the mobile phone) as for research and marketing purposes it's easier to manipulate Facebook on a big screen. But if you're a mobile-first sort of person, be aware that you can manage everything via your phone as well.

First, I'm assuming you have a personal Facebook profile; *if not,* simply go to **https://www.facebook.com/,** or download the mobile app for your phone, and sign up. Facebook has a wonderful help section at **https://www.facebook.com/help/** - just click on "get started on Facebook." Once you sign up – as an individual – you'll have a **profile.**

Next, I'm assuming you have a few friends and family. Send them "friend requests," and vice-versa. (Hopefully, they like you enough to accept and vice-versa). Facebook, like LinkedIn but not like Instagram, Twitter, or Pinterest, requires that users "be friends" in order for the interactive magic to occur. OK, with some friend requests sent, requested, and accepted, now post some photos of your family, your dog, your trip to

Las Vegas or whatever, to your "timeline." When you log in to Facebook on your desktop or your phone, look at your "news feed." Your *news feed* will show you the posts of the friends and family with whom you are connected; when they post to their *timeline*, it will show in your *news feed* (with some caveats about *Edgerank*, more about this later). Similarly, when you post to your timeline, those posts will show on the news feed of your friends when / if they log into Facebook whether on their computers or their phones.

The timeline and news feed are interrelated symbiotically:

> Hannah and I are **friends** on Facebook. One of us has pro-actively accepted the other's "friend request."
>
> Hannah **posts** a picture of something she finds interesting to her Facebook **timeline**.
>
> I see that picture when I log in to my Facebook **news feed**.

Here's a screenshot showing this two-way relationship, with the first arrow pointing to my "timeline," where I can share a status update with text and/or photos with my friends, and the second arrow pointing to a post by Hannah to her timeline and hence my "news feed," where I see what my friends or contacts (such as Hannah) have shared:

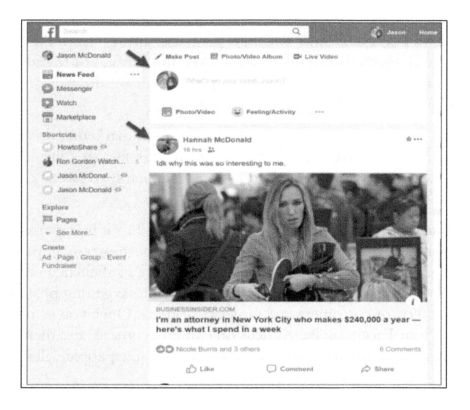

The reverse is also true. If I post something on my timeline, such as my latest fun photo of my dog Buddy or a selfie of my wife and me at the movies, then Hannah can see these posts when she logs into Facebook and views her own news feed. In summary:

Posts to *my timeline* show up in Hannah's *news feed*.

Posts by Hannah to her *timeline* show up in my *news feed*.

Why? Because we're not only father and daughter, endless supplier of money and endless taker of money, but also "friends" on Facebook. 99% of the activity on Facebook, both on the desktop and on the phone, occurs in the news feed.

Now, this doesn't just happen between two people like Hannah and me. Rather it occurs in a multidimensional way. When I post to my timeline, that post has the chance to be shown in the news feed of *everyone* with whom I am friends on Facebook; when *anyone* with whom I am a friend on Facebook posts to his or her timeline, that post has an opportunity to appear on my news feed. And vice-versa, all day long 24/7 until the end of time.

Here are the important takeaways for marketers about the basics of how Facebook works:

1. **The News Feed is Dominant.** Few people, if any, go from the news feed and click over to the Pages of businesses or even the Profiles of friends. It's all about posts to the timeline and the readership that lives on the news feed. The news feed is "where it's at."

2. **Content**. You need a lot of content to succeed at marketing on Facebook! The news feed is cluttered, very cluttered, and moves fast. It's like a swift river of content, so you – as a marketer – must post frequently to have a chance of being noticed.

3. **Your Facebook Page isn't That Important.** While it is important to optimize your business Page on Facebook, precious few customers will pro-actively visit your Page directly. Most will only see your posts in their news feed. So spend most of your time and effort on where the action is: getting posts to appear on the news feed of customers and target customers. Once you've done the basics to set up your Facebook Page, focus on content, content, and then more content rather than tweaking the look-and-feel of a Page few people will see.

4. **Create Content that is Truly Engaging.** Because of how crowded (and competitive) the news feed is, you MUST create fun, informative, engaging and interactive content. Boring, "buy my stuff" content won't work on Facebook. Interactive and engaging content – content that is counterintuitive, fun, engaging, and over-the-top, "you gotta see this" – is "where it's at" on Facebook. Engaging content is king, queen, and jack on Facebook.

**The Five F's: Friends, Family, Fun, Photos, and Fake**

With the basics under your belt, spend some quality time as a "user" just bopping around Facebook. Connect with friends and family, reach out to old girlfriends and boyfriends (if you so desire, or maybe they'll reach out to you…), "like" some business pages that interest you. Get into the vibe of it as a user, and then sit back and ask yourself:

What's going on here? What's really going on Facebook? What are people posting (and why), and what are people engaging with (and why)?

Pay attention to what people are sharing on Facebook. Generally, you'll see it falls into the themes of friends, family, fun, photos, and fake plus some other themes:

- **Friends, Fun, Family.** Whether shared in photo format, as an image, as a video, or just as plain text, Facebook is a place where people share stuff about their friends and family. Notice how many likes, comments, and shares fun photos of friends and family garner on Facebook. Facebook is a giant, collective social scrapbook.

- **What I'm Doing Today.** Alongside photos and texts of friends, family, and fun, people share text, photos, and even videos of what they're doing today. Posts of the peach cobbler they just made, their beautiful garden tomatoes, or perhaps their dog doing a weird trick – these "here's my life" type of fun photos are a huge theme in Facebook content as well.

- **Photos.** Photos dominate Facebook! Photos of friends at the beach, at Disneyland, High School graduations, Bar Mitzvahs, new babies. People are constantly posting photos with short commentaries, generally about friends, family, and fun. Video content, while less common, is even more engaging. *Facebook Live* allows people to stream content in real-time.

- **Fake.** As we will discuss in a moment in more detail, Facebook is often "fake." People share the happy and successful moments of their lives, but not so much the sad and unsuccessful events. Facebook is how we project our lives as we wish them to be, not 100% as they truly are.

- **Politics and Outrage.** Yes, sadly, there are the political folks on Facebook, and they have their place. They're like Uncle Harry at the family picnic who can't stop talking about how much he loves the President and the Republicans, and Aunt Martha who wants to bend your ear about how plastics in the ocean are devastating the planet. Political conversation and outrage has its place on Facebook, though many people don't like it, and respond to it negatively if at all. But some folks live and breathe it.

And –

- **Games, Social Contests, Groups.** For some people, Facebook is a place for social games. There are also groups on Facebook which allow people to collaborate and communicate, as for example a "group" of people taking a High School class in US History or a "group" of people who share a passion for duck hunting.

- **News & Commentary.** Increasingly, Facebook is becoming a major source of news. Thus, people log in, and see news posts (often by the media, often shared by friends), and "like," "comment," or "share" these news items. Note that this is controversial. Facebook CEO, Mark Zuckerberg, has indicated that he clearly wants to de-emphasize Facebook as a source of news.

Notice as well a theme that we'll come back to on other social platforms like Instagram: **narcissism.** We live in the age of the selfie, and people love to share content that positions themselves as AWESOME.

*Look at our happy family at Disneyland! Look at me and my date at the Cheesecake Factory! Wow, look at these cool photos of me when I went skydiving in Peru over Machu Pichu with my girlfriend and pet cat and took a selfie to memorialize it so you can (enviously) see how incredible my life is.*

Facebook, you see, is full of **fake**, of how life ought to be or at least of how life might be if everyone was really as "into" everyone else's narcissistic lifestyle as it might seem. To listen to an informative podcast on how the "fake" of Facebook can impact your own psychology, check out **http://jmlinks.com/29v**. (On a side note, once you realize that your own life will never live up to the fake happiness you see on Facebook, you'll be better adjusted, happier, and more realistic about your own mortality).

## Facebook Through the Eyes of a Marketer

Be that as it may, the marketing goal is to understand the *vibe* or *culture*, of Facebook so that your company's marketing message can blend in and build on this culture to nurture your brand image, grow your customer connections, and ultimately sell more stuff. The content you post on Facebook must mesh with the culture on Facebook which is friends, family, fun, photos, and fake.

As you research Facebook, ask yourself these questions:

1. Are your **customers** on Facebook?

2. If so, what are they posting and interacting with? What's really **engaging** to them?

3. How can you **tailor your marketing message** so that it seems "natural" given Facebook's focus on friends, family, and fun? Either –

   a. **Directly**, showcasing your company's fun product or service; or

   b. **Indirectly**, showcasing an activity adjacent to your company's product or service (more about this in a moment).

## Searching Facebook for Posts

Return to your content marketing plan and get out your keyword themes or targets. Research whether people are posting and talking about your keywords on Facebook, or if not your primary themes, perhaps themes adjacent to what your company sells or does.

To search Facebook, log in to Facebook and look for the search bar at the top. You'll see *Search* in gray text. Enter a keyword. Here's a screenshot searching for stuff about "organic food" on Facebook:

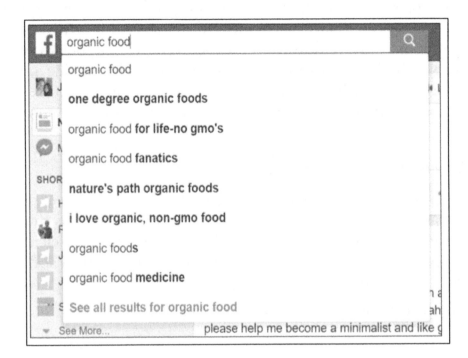

Next look at the **tabs** across the top of the search screen. You can search Facebook by keyword for:

**Posts** – these are posts by people about the keyword you just entered.

**People** – these are people who have this keyword in their bio and/or posts.

**Photos** – these are photos posted to Facebook on the keyword.

**Videos** – these are videos posted to Facebook on the keyword.

**Pages** – these are business pages that have the keyword in their bio and/or posts.

**Places** – these are local businesses and hangouts in the "real world."

**Groups** – these are groups on Facebook that touch on the keyword.

**Apps** – these are apps promoted or used on Facebook around this keyword.

**Events** – these are events being talked about on Facebook on this keyword.

**Links** – these are links to websites and blogs being shared on Facebook about this keyword. You can also enter a domain such as "nytimes.com" in the search box and find which links are being shared the most (about your own domain, or that of a competitor).

Let's focus on Posts, which gets to what people are posting and interacting with on this keyword theme. Click on *Posts* from among the tabs across the top. Scroll down, and you'll see posts by friends as well as public posts on these keywords. Here's a screenshot:

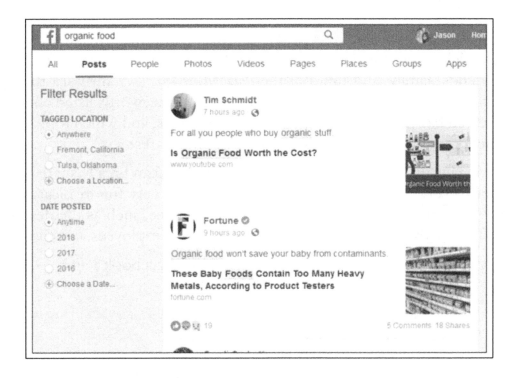

In this way, you can research if people are posting either on keywords *directly* relevant to your business or on keyword *adjacent* to your business. You're looking for both types of keyword themes – *direct* or *indirect / adjacent*. Why? Because there's no point in posting content that people aren't already interested in, and engaging with, on Facebook.

Let's look at airlines as examples of keyword themes on Facebook. Air travel is anything but fun. We're stuck in cramped quarters with total strangers, fed peanuts and soft drinks, suffer through terrible WiFi and are subject to TSA searches and endless flight delays. I don't know of many people, even those who fly first class, who truly love the air travel itself. But the *destinations* are another story. Who doesn't want to go to Cancun or Paris? Who isn't interested in visiting the Pyramids or Beijing? So in terms of keyword themes possible on Facebook we have:

*air travel*

*airlines*

*airfares*

vs.

*Cancun*

*Beijing*

*The Pyramids*

You can see right away that the *primary* keyword themes don't really fit Facebook's culture of friends, family, and fun, but the *adjacent* or *secondary* keyword themes do. A little research will confirm this; try entering a few of the keywords listed above into the Facebook search bar. Which topics are getting more posts, and which topics are getting more interaction as measured in likes, comments, and shares?

This insight means that if you're an airline, therefore, you can't really share content that *directly* relates to your product or service because it's not very fun or pleasant. But you can share content that's *adjacent* to your product or service, such as the destinations to which you fly or perhaps the great people who are your employees and customers.

For example, check out this post by Aeromexico to its Facebook Page:

The post emphasizes the adjacent theme on a destination that is fun (*Belize*) and not the much less fun aspect of the travel to/from the destination on a crowded airline.

Returning to your own business, research your keyword themes that are directly related to your business vs. those that are adjacent to your business. Start asking yourself, "What is this conversation about?" and "How could your company participate in this conversation in a meaningful way that also showcases your brand?" You'll see a lot of posts by businesses on Facebook, but pay attention to the likes, comments, and shares of individual posts to gauge whether real customers are actually engaged in this conversation. So your questions are:

1. Are customers posting on keyword themes that matter to your business, either *directly* or *indirectly* (*adjacently*)?

2. Are these themes getting a lot of interaction as measured by likes, comments, and shares?

3. How can you (as the marketer) create content that will interact with customer-based content yet be authentic and non-obnoxious?

4. Will your content focus on directly relevant themes, adjacent themes, or perhaps both?

## Are You a Fun Company or Not Fun Company?

At an abstract level, look deep into your company's soul, and ask yourself which Facebook strategy makes the most conceptual sense:

Are you a **fun company** in a **fun** and **photogenic industry**? If so, post fun photos or photos of your product or service directly. (Example: REI at **https://www.facebook.com/REI/**).

Or, are you a **not-fun company** *adjacent* to a fun and photogenic industry? If so, post photos of "fun" things adjacent to your product or service. (Example: AeroMexico airlines at **https://www.facebook.com/AeromexicoNA/** – in which the service itself (*air travel*) isn't nearly as much fun as the adjacent activity (*tourism*)).

Or, are you a **not-fun company** in a **not-fun industry**? If so, you'll have to think out of the box on content creation for Facebook. (Example: Progressive

Insurance at **https://www.facebook.com/progressive/,** which posts lots and lots of content that has little to do with insurance, directly).

Not all products or services will work on Facebook; that's OK, too, as your mission is to identify which social media networks work most easily for your company and focus on those.

As you build out your Facebook content and posting strategy, continually measure based on likes, comments, and shares:

- What types of posts are your Facebook fans posting, liking, commenting on, and sharing? Which ones seem to be the most successful in generating interaction, and which the least?

- What are your competitors doing that seems to be working as measured by likes, comments, and shares? (*Be careful with competitors – if they are posting a lot but getting little engagement, that's a sign that their strategy is NOT working and you shouldn't copy it*).

- What are other companies that are not competitors yet might act as models for your Facebook strategy doing, and what is working for them? Why or why not?

Conceptually, here are the possibilities (answer yes or no, after you do some research):

1. Your customers are on Facebook. Yes or no?

2. Your customers are engaging with content on Facebook. Yes or no?

    a. Your customers are engaging with content themes that are *directly* relevant to your business. Yes or no?

    b. Your customers are engaging with content themes that are only *indirectly* or adjacently relevant to your business. Yes or no?

3. Your competitors are on Facebook. Yes or no?

    a. Your competitors seem to be having success on Facebook as measured by the quantity of likes to their Facebook Pages plus the engagement with their content. Yes or no?

    b. You see other companies to emulate on Facebook. Yes or no?

4. You see a path forward to a successful Facebook content strategy. Yes or no?

At this point, don't worry about all the technical details. We'll get into the details in a moment, but your first task is to research or re-research whether Facebook actually shows potential as a way to reach your customers, build your brand, and ultimately, sell more stuff. If you're already active on Facebook as a company, this is a good opportunity to re-evaluate whether it's working and/or whether you see a way to make it work at all.

## » INVENTORY COMPANIES ON FACEBOOK

Assuming you see potential on Facebook, it's time to dig deeper. But before you dig further into the technical details of setting up your own Facebook Page and optimizing your posts, it's incredibly important to make a list of companies (whether competitors or more general consumer brands) that you admire on Facebook. You want to monitor them, and reverse engineer what they're doing that's working.

> *Imitation is the highest form of flattery, and identifying successful brands to reverse engineer is the easiest way to master marketing on Facebook.*

So, now we are going to shift gears from **profiles** (individuals) to **Pages** (companies). You'll want to identify companies that are on Facebook and reverse engineer their marketing strategy.

### Ways to Search Facebook

First, return to your **keyword themes** that matter to you and your potential customers. For example, if you are a maker of organic baby food, you would use the key phrases "organic food" and "baby food" to identify companies that are already on Facebook. If you are a company that organizes bird-watching tours, then you'll be searching Facebook for keywords like "birding," "birding tourism," or perhaps "ecotourism." As you find companies that seem to be doing a good job with Facebook marketing, you'll be making an inventory of what you like / dislike about their Facebook marketing in terms of their cover photo, profile picture, tabs, and their posting strategy above all else.

Your **TO-DOS** here are to identify companies that seem to "get" Facebook, and to inventory what you like or dislike about how they have set up their Facebook Page, and how they are posting content to Facebook.

Returning to the first step, here are the two best ways to find commercial Pages to inventory for your Facebook marketing plan.

**Method #1 - Search Facebook Directly.** Simply type into the search box your keyword as in "organic food." Next, at the top tab click on "Pages." Here is a screenshot:

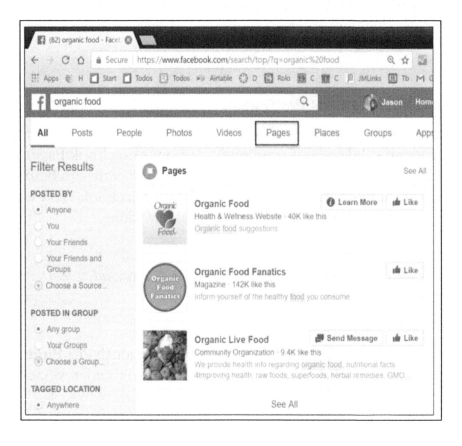

And then after you click "Pages," you'll see:

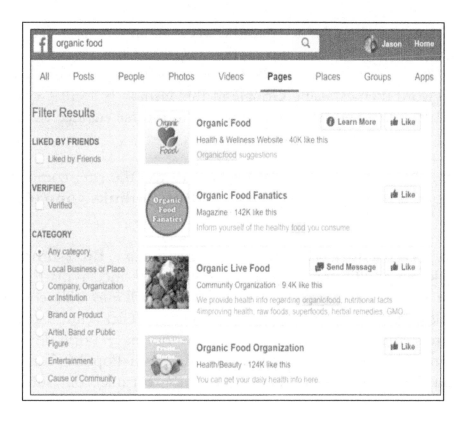

You'll see a list of relevant commercial Pages. You can click on each one, identify companies that seem to "get" Facebook, like them in your personal profile (so you can keep an eye on them), and begin to inventory your likes / dislikes.

**Method #2 - Identify Facebook Pages via Google Search**. Go to Google. Type into the Google search box *site:facebook.com* "organic food." (Note: use quotation marks around multi-word phrases for best results). Google will then return to you a list of commercial Pages on Facebook with that term in it. To see this in action, go to **http://jmlinks.com/2i**. Here's a screenshot:

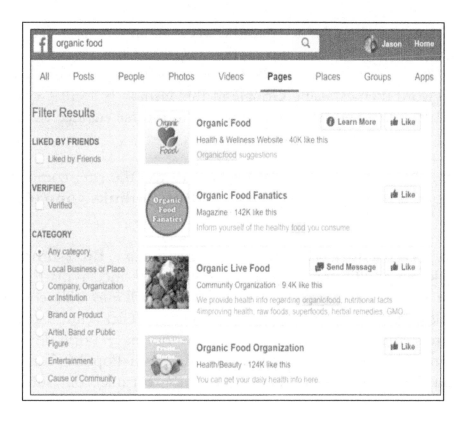

It's very important that there be no space between *site* and *the colon*. It's *site:facebook.com* not *site: facebook.com*. You can use this tactic on Google for any social media; as for example, *site:yelp.com massage therapists Boston*, or *site:twitter.com industrial fans*. Once you know your keyword themes, using Google in this fashion is a great way to browse a social media platform to find relevant companies to reverse engineer.

**VIDEO.** Watch a video tutorial on how to use the site: command to search Facebook for social media marketing at **http://jmlinks.com/16g**.

**Method #3 - Identify Facebook Pages via Buzzsumo.** Buzzsumo (**http://jmlinks.com/29j**) tracks shares across social media platforms, including Facebook. For $99 / month, you can use this tool to drill into what content is getting engagement vis-à-vis your keyword themes, and then click "up" to the Pages and Profiles that are sharing this content. Even better, they have a drill-down tool just for Facebook. Sign up for an account, click into "Research Popular Content," click on Facebook, and then enter a seed keyword such as "organic" or "surfing." Here's a screenshot:

In this way, you go from *keyword > most popular content > pages and profiles that have shared that content > ideas for your own content strategy on Facebook*.

If you don't want to spring for Buzzsumo, you can also search Facebook by keyword, drill into posts, and then click up from popular posts to the Pages or Profiles that shared that content. Just use the left-hand column to filter posts to "Public" and then by date such as the current year. Here's a screenshot for a search of Facebook posts on "organic":

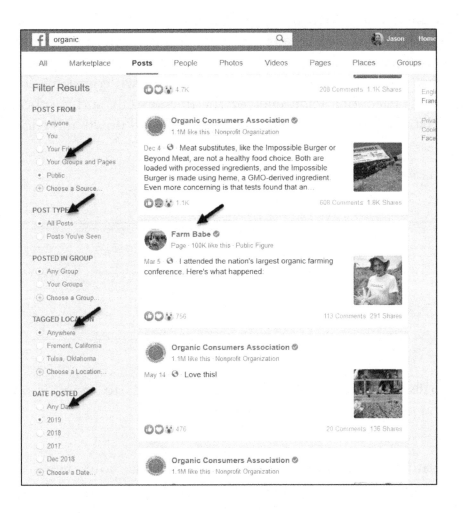

In this way, I can search Facebook for posts on "organic," and set my post type to "Public," "All Posts," "Any Group," "Anywhere," and Date Posted to 2019. Then I can drill into the Farm Babe post and see that this page made a post called "I attended the nation's largest organic farming conference. Here's what happened" that garnered 113 comments and 291 shares. You can also do this for a URL such as "nytimes.com" or "rei.com" to see the most popular shared content via a competitor's domain.

# IDENTIFY COMPANIES WHO DO FACEBOOK WELL AND INVENTORY THEM

Don't be afraid to like companies on Facebook (even your competitors) in your individual account. In fact, I strongly encourage it. By "liking" companies you actually "like," you'll experience them marketing to you, and you can then reverse engineer this for your own company. Indeed, Facebook itself encourages companies to "spy" on other companies. Once you've set up a Page for your own company, for example, log in to your business Facebook Page, click on the Insights tab, and Facebook will suggest companies similar to your own to monitor. Simply scroll down and click on "Pages to watch."

Here's a screenshot:

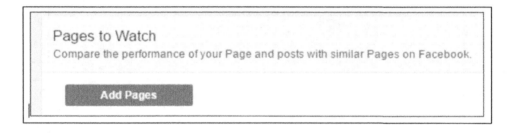

Identify a shortlist of between three and ten companies to monitor on Facebook. I recommend you identify two different types:

> **Competitors.** Companies that are very much like your own company, that is direct competitors and companies that are closely like your own.

> **Companies to Emulate.** These can be companies like REI, Geico, or Navy Federal Credit Union that really seem to understand social media marketing and do a good job on Facebook.

You don't only want to research and follow competitors because in many cases they won't be doing a very good job at Facebook marketing and you'll be learning from the dullards. By adding in some larger consumer companies that are doing a great job, you'll be learning from the best of the best. You can then take that knowledge back to your own sad, pathetic industry and crush it. I'm being a bit facetious, but my point is that if you want to learn how to play basketball, watch Michael Jordan and LeBron James, not the High Schoolers playing at your neighborhood court. Identify, monitor, and reverse engineer the best. A company like REI has a lot to teach us all about how to do Facebook marketing.

**Analyze Posts by Competitors and Other Companies**

Returning to the regular Facebook interface, once you like a company, its posts have the opportunity to show up in your news feed. We'll dive into why, or why not, in a moment. But for now, let me share with you a trick so that you can easily find the posts by Pages you've decided to monitor.

Log in to your Facebook personal account, then scan down the left column and look for a link under *Explore > Pages*. Click on that, and you'll see posts from companies that you have liked. Here's a screenshot:

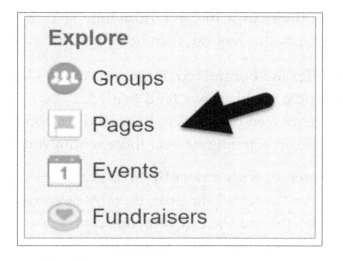

You can also click on *Explore > Pages Feed* to go directly to posts by Pages that you have liked. If you are logged into Facebook, you can also click on this link - **http://jmlinks.com/29w** - to go directly there. Pay attention to what they're posting and what's getting a lot of interaction. Look at their Pages and deconstruct their cover photos, profile photos, tabs, and other items.

For your second **To-do**, download the **Facebook Research Worksheet**. For the worksheet, go to **http://jmlinks.com/social2020** (then re-enter the password **'social2020'** to register your workbook), and click on the link to the "Facebook Research Worksheet." You'll answer questions as to whether your potential customers are on Facebook, identify brands to follow, and inventory what you like and dislike about their Facebook set up and marketing strategy.

## » UNDERSTAND THE IMPORTANCE OF LIKE AND EDGERANK

To market successfully on Facebook, you need a detailed understanding of its **structure** and how it works. Most importantly, you need to understand the difference between a profile and a Page, and what "like" means vis-a-vis a Page and/or a post, as well as *comment* and *share*.

For your inventory, you'll need to know some vocabulary about what is what on Facebook.

Let's review this:

- **People have "profiles."** This is *Jason McDonald*, a real person, for example. I have a *profile* (not a *Page*) on Facebook.

- **When two people "friend" each other by exchanging a "friend request,"
Facebook puts them in a like relationship.** If I "friend" my friend, Tom Jones, and he accepts this request, then he and I are connected via Facebook.

- **When two profiles are connected, if person A posts to his timeline, person B will see that post on his news feed** (with the *Edgerank* or *Facebook algorithm* caveat that the news feed can be very busy, and Facebook prioritizes the posts of friends with whom you interact over those whom you ignore).

    - **People interact with a post** by "liking" the post, "commenting" on the post, and/or "sharing" the post, thereby essentially re-posting it to their own timeline so that their own friends can see / interact with the post. In the background, Facebook **Edgerank** keeps track of which profiles, Pages, and posts are the most interactive, and favors them in the news feed across the social network.

- **Companies have Pages, not profiles.** A *profile* (person) creates a *Page* (company) and then manages it as an Admin.

- Companies can (and should) have more than one Admin. The *Page* for the JM Internet Group (**https://www.facebook.com/jm.internet**) is managed by me (a *profile*) for example.

    - Pages can NOT exist without sponsorship by at least one profile!

    - Any Admin can delete / change / post to a Page!

- **When a person ("profile") "likes" a business "Page," this creates a Facebook relationship between the "profile" and the "Page."** When I like Safeway (**https://www.facebook.com/Safeway**), that means that when Safeway posts to its timeline, it might show on my news feed. By "liking" Safeway, I have given it permission to talk to me via Facebook.

    o **People interact with a post** by a Page by "liking" the post, "commenting" on the post, and/or "sharing" the post, thereby essentially re-posting it to their own timeline so that their own friends can see / interact with the post. In the background, Facebook *Edgerank* keeps track of which posts are the most interactive, and favors them in the news feed across the social network.

To read the Facebook help files on setting up a business Page, go to **http://jmlinks.com/1c**. Note that you can technically create not just "Pages" for local businesses or places, companies, organizations, institutions, brands or products. You can also create "public figure Pages" for artists, bands, or public figures (think CEO of your company, a la Martha Stewart), or even Pages for causes or communities. For most companies, you'll choose either the local business option, the company option, or the brand / product option. To see the options, go to **http://jmlinks.com/29x**.

## It Gets Complicated

Here's where it gets complicated. Remember our Social Media Marketing goals? Among them: staying top of mind and encouraging social sharing? *Edgerank*, which is part of the Facebook algorithm, intervenes at this point. When a Page posts to its timeline, that post will show up on the news feed of "profiles" (people) who have liked it based on several factors:

- The individual (a.k.a., "the profile") must have liked the Page in advance.

- If the individual previously liked the Page, and generally liked posts by the Page and/or commented on them and/or shared them, then the *Edgerank* of that Page is improved. The higher the *Edgerank* (based on more interaction between that Page and the individual), the more likely it is that the post by the Page will show in the particular individual's news feed.

- A real-time analysis of the post: the faster and wider a post gets interactivity (likes, comments, and shares), the more powerful its Edgerank and it, therefore, gets even more publicity.

In essence, Facebook monitors whether users interact with the posts of a Page: the more users who interact with the posts of a Page, the higher the Edgerank of that Page and its posts, and the more likely users are to continue to see posts by the Page in their news feed.

If this sounds confusing, just remember that Facebook heavily favors posts that get engagement as measured by likes, comments, and shares. Facebook wants users to "stay engaged" and "stay on Facebook," so it heavily favors content that is highly engaging.

## Edgerank is Dead. Long Live Edgerank!

You are going to read on the blogosphere that Edgerank is "dead," that Facebook replaced it with a machine learning algorithm in about 2011 (See **http://jmlinks.com/29z**). Technically, that's true. But – and it's a very big but – Facebook continues to use its algorithm to "score" the relationship between a Page and a Profile, that is between a brand and a person, down to the level of a given post.

### That Which You Call a Rose…

*Whatever you call it, Edgerank or the Facebook algorithm, Facebook clearly scores your Page and its Posts. The more interactive those two are, the more likely it is that users will see your posts in their news feeds. The point is to realize that the Facebook algorithm is there, in the background, using AI (Artificial Intelligence) to promote what's engaging to users and bury what's not.*

If you as a Page post something to your timeline, how likely is it that a fan of your page, or Profile, is going to see it in his or her news feed? The likelihood that a person will see your post is the result of a basic structural factor (i.e., *that the person already likes your Page*), and some dynamic factors, such as –

- Content that generates a lot of likes…

- Content that generates a lot of comments…

- Content that generates a lot of shares…

o   Etc. See **http://jmlinks.com/29y**.

The long and short of the Facebook algorithm as a marketer is the *more interactive* a post is, *the more* it will show in the news feeds of your fans. Hence:

**Encouraging interactivity is the #1 goal of your Facebook marketing!**

To use an example, let's look at the Mayo Clinic and me on Facebook.

1. I like the Mayo Clinic business Page on Facebook (**https://www.facebook.com/MayoClinic**), giving it permission to talk to me via Facebook.

2. The Mayo Clinic posts images, photos, blog post summaries, etc., to its Facebook Page timeline, such as tips on how to live healthy, information on diseases, and even information on how to keep your pets healthy.

3. I like these posts, I "comment" on these posts (*"Oh, yes, I am going to eat more kale!"*), and even better I "share" these posts on my own timeline by clicking the share button.

Here's a screenshot of a recent post by the Mayo Clinic:

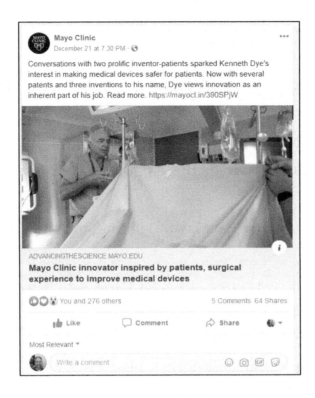

If you look closely, you can see that this post has 276 likes, 5 comments, and 64 shares. You can see that I've also liked it, and that Facebook is encouraging me to "write a comment." The post has done very well on engagement!

Behind the scenes, therefore, Facebook is more likely to push this post in front of Mayo Clinic fans because the more engagement a post gets the more predictive that is that it will get still more engagement. Facebook lives off of this "virtuous circle," and again and again across all social networks you'll see that driving engagement is the Holy Grail of success at social media marketing.

Engagement, however, is relative and every brand on Facebook is engaged in a competitive struggle to keep their fans engaged with content. Compare this post to a post by REI on the need to build more wildlife-friendly crossings across our highways and byways:

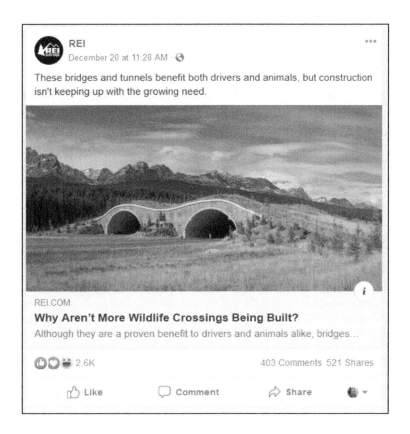

This post has 2,600 likes, 403 comments, and 521 shares. It's in a different league, entirely, from the Mayo Clinic post. Notice that it is a highly emotional appeal based on our "outrage" that we're not doing enough to save animals.

In both cases, **social resonance** encourages likes, comments, and shares. And notice how in both cases the posts have interesting text, provocative photographs, and links to a blog post or video. By *design,* the posts are meant to engage the audience.

Returning to my relationship with the Mayo Clinic post, by "liking," "commenting," or "sharing" this post, I, too, am telling Facebook I am engaged with the Mayo Clinic Page.

*The more I do this, the more I will see its posts in my news feed.*

Now, flip this around as marketers, your goals become:

- To increase your *Edgerank,* or your *Facebook algorithm score* to be more semantically correct, (and the probability that people will see your posts in their news feed), you MUST get more likes, comments, and shares of your posts!

- To increase your *Edgerank*, you must get **interactivity**!

Encouraging **interactivity** (or as it is sometimes called **engagement**) is the name of the game when it comes to Facebook marketing. Oh, and if you're asking whether people can do more than just "like" your posts by clicking not just "like" but the new emoticons on Facebook – of course, you want that, even more. A "share" is the best of all, followed by a "comment," and then by a "like," in terms of interactivity.

# ENGAGEMENT IS GOAL #1 FOR YOUR FACEBOOK POSTS

Let's dig deeper here.

**Posting strategy** is all about what you post, and using those posts to drive up interactivity, and improve your Edgerank. So, first you've used content marketing to identify the types of content that interests your target customers, second, you've created photos, videos, and written blog posts that connect "what you have" with "what they're interested in." Now you want to think about packaging that content in such a way that it spurs them to like, comment, and/or share that content on Facebook.

What drives people to interactivity? The answer is, first and foremost, **emotion**. Anything that sparks an emotional reaction of "how shocking," or "Oh my gosh I didn't know that," or "I heartily agree with that idea," or "*Aw, shucks, I love puppies and babies and mommies and I want to support our troops too, and I hate pollution and bad people and criminals and scams…*" Anything that provokes an emotional reaction, especially one that inclines a person to click "YES! I agree," is what you're after. Oh, and **utility** is good, too, like "the secret to poaching eggs" (*Don't use vinegar despite what you see on YouTube, seriously*)… or something **counterintuitive** (like, *check out the trend for flaming hot Cheetos turkey for Thanksgiving*)… is also likely to work.

Here's a post from Buzzfeed which got 9,800 "likes," 19,000 "comments," and 5,600 "shares:"

BuzzFeed Food
November 17, 2017

In the year of our Lord 2017, you can now cook your turkey with this Hot Cheetos recipe .

BUZZFEED.COM
Flamin' Hot Cheetos Turkey Is The New Trend For Thanksgiving Dinner, Apparently

9.8K                     19K Comments  5.6K Shares

Like          Comment          Share

That's one flaming hot turkey, isn't it? It just begs to be liked, commented upon, and shared with friends and family.

The point, as a marketer, is to realize that our posts – not just on Facebook but to all social media marketing – need to be emotional, useful, and/or counterintuitive. People interact with and share "man bites dog" not "dog bites man."

Here are example categories of posts that are likely to spur customer interactions:

- **Sentimental Posts**. Posts of kittens and puppies, posts of kids, posts of moms and dads, posts of moms and dads holding kittens and puppies. Posts about the 4th of July, posts about how much you love a cause... Brands on Facebook often post "sentimentality bait": posts that people click like on to indicate that they "agree" with the cause. So every Mother's Day, you can see brands posting pictures of mothers and their kids, and people clicking like on these posts because they like their mothers... which is increasing the Edgerank of these Pages.

- **Utility**. Posts that explain "how to do" stuff, especially things that are counterintuitive or funny. Such as "Ten Ways Not to Ask a Girl Out," or "Five New Ways to Lose Weight While on a Vacation."

- **Counterintuitive**. Posts that take things you "think" you know, and explain that they don't really work like you think they do. Especially common are things that people "think" are safe, but in fact are dangerous such as rawhide dog chews (*who knew that they were dangerous?*).

- **Funny**. Humor is big on Facebook. Posting jokes, funny quotes, videos, images (memes), etc. Things that make people laugh, get them to click like, comment, or share. Queue the funny babies, babies with dogs, and of course cat videos.

- **Surveys, Polls, Contests**. Asking your audience a question, and getting them to use the comments as a way to interact with that. *Take this quiz and learn which Star Trek character best describes your love life.*

- **Quotes**. Sentimental, humorous, make-you-think quotes, especially when hoisted on top of picturesque and contemplative scenery like mountains or fuzzified people. *Do or do not. There is no try – Yoda from Star Wars.*

- **Outrage**. Things that make people mad, mad enough to comment, like in the sense of opposing the thing that outrages them, and even share. Outrage is very big on Facebook, and brands (rather cynically) leverage this outrage to increase their Edgerank. *Click "like" if you think dolphins shouldn't die in Tuna nets, animals shouldn't be abused, etc., for example.*

- **Controversy**. Controversy, but in a good way, can be very good for your posts to Facebook. For example, avoid posting touchy subjects like abortion or gun control, but do post on "fun" controversies such as *"Is a bikini or a one-piece a better bathing suit?" "Is it OK not to serve turkey on Thanksgiving?," or "Which is better a cat or a dog?"*

In all cases, a good-looking photo or video is a must. To really dive into what's getting shared on Facebook visit Buzzsumo at **http://jmlinks.com/29j** and enter your keywords. This tool will show you what's getting the most interaction not just on Facebook but also on Twitter, LinkedIn, and Pinterest. There's both a free and a paid version of the tool. I guarantee you'll see that content that touches on some, or all, of the themes listed above, is what's "getting shared" and "going viral" on Facebook.

How can brands use this insight? Well, in terms of **posting strategy**, brands will post items that are specifically engineered to increase engagement and thereby increase their *Edgerank*. Look back at the brands you like, and begin to notice how they are using strategies like emotion, fun, outrage, humor or other ways to spur interactivity.

# FACEBOOK REWARDS YOU FOR INTERACTIVE POSTS

Here are some brands that I admire in terms of their Facebook marketing, all of which build Edgerank by sharing interactive content on a regular basis:

**Bishop Robert Barron (https://www.facebook.com/BishopRobertBarron)** – known as the Catholic social media superstar, Bishop Barron shares history and theological insights, and shows how something as ancient as Catholicism can leverage new media to grow its reach and build its brand.

**Navy Federal Credit Union (https://www.facebook.com/NavyFederal)** – if you monitor its Page, you'll see a steady dose of sentimentality, especially pictures of military men with babies (a double whammy: *yes, I support our troops, and, yes, I like babies!*).

**The Super Dentists (https://www.facebook.com/TheSuperDentists)** – similarly to Metamucil, this San Diego kids dentists takes something not-so-fun (dentistry) and effectively builds eWom, one-touch-to-many, and even social sharing via pictures, contests, sentimentality posts and the like.

**REI (https://www.facebook.com/REI).** REI is an outdoor, sports retailer and uses Facebook to share "how to" information about hiking, campaign, and other outdoor sports, promote its products, and build a community around people who like the outdoors (and love its products).

**Taco Bell (https://www.facebook.com/tacobell)** – the edgy, youth brand is a master at building awareness, creating the "fourth meal" (just what obese America needed), and making factory food fun.

**Metamucil (https://www.facebook.com/Metamucil/)** – there, I admit it. I use Metamucil! Any brand that can take something so private, and grow a Facebook page to 236,000 fans, has got to be doing something right. "Reverse engineer" how a product you probably didn't think of as friends, family, and fun uses social media on a regular basis (pun intended).

Make a list of your own favorite brands, like them on Facebook, and constantly "reverse engineer" their content and posting strategy. Imitation, after all, is the highest form of flattery.

## Posting Rhythm

Now the point of all this, as marketers, isn't that we really love babies and military personnel (although we probably do). It's to:

- Improve our *Edgerank* to increase the probability that our Facebook fans will see our posts.

- Use our built-up *Edgerank* to propel posts that market our products or services into the news feeds of our fans, for free.

This gets to **posting rhythm**. Smart marketers will post ten or twenty "fun, fun, fun" posts to drive UP their Edgerank, and then one "buy my stuff" post that has a good chance of showing in the news feed. So your posting rhythm should be something like 80% fun stuff and 20% or less "buy my stuff" posts:

*Fun, Fun, Fun, Fun, Fun, Fun, Fun, Fun, Fun, Buy My Stuff, Buy My Stuff Fun, Fun, Fun, Fun, Fun, Fun, Fun, Fun, Fun,*

In other words, smart marketers build up their Edgerank by posting lots of fun, interactive content, and then "spend" their Edgerank with a "buy my stuff" post. Rinse and repeat as needed.

## Get Your Fans to Share

Even better, business Pages on Facebook will post items that their fans are likely to share with their own friends. If you post something to your Facebook Page (e.g., a contest to win a free week's supply of your products or a quote that is inspiring), and your Facebook fans share it with their friends and family, well, you've hit a home run.

Why? Because Facebook (and people) pay a heck of a lot more attention to posts by people than to posts by Pages. So by all means, post stuff to your business Page that excites your fans so much that they do the sharing! (We'll return to the importance of fans and superfans at the end of this Chapter).

**Give away Free Tacos to Encourage Massive Viral Shares**

As an example, here's a post by Taco Bell promoting "free" Tacos because of "stolen bases" during the 2017 World Series – 16,000 likes and 8,697 shares! Taco Bell announced that every time a base was stolen, they would give away free tacos.

Hence:

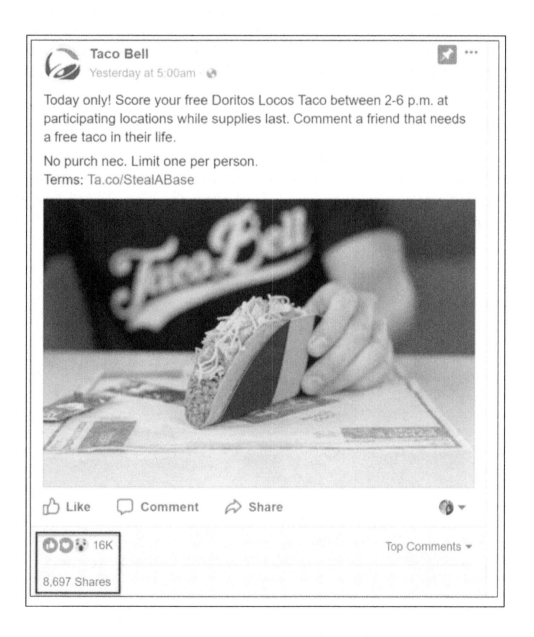

Now, that's a lot of shares! Admittedly, Taco Bell has an enormous budget, but the point is that this "free" promotion was used to create tons of "spontaneous" shares by fans of Taco Bell, thereby leveraging the "superfans" of Taco Bell to create viral buzz on Facebook. So ask yourself what is your "free Taco promotion" that your fans will take over the finish line (to mix sports metaphors)?

## Facebook Rewards Posts by People over Posts by Pages

The reason for this tactic is that the *Edgerank* of people is much, much higher than the *Edgerank* of company Pages. So, to the extent that you can create a post that will be shared on Facebook, you can get your fans to market your company's products. Don't think in terms of only the *Edgerank* of your Page but in the *Edgerank* of your customer evangelists or superfans (those people who not only like your Page, but interact heavily with your posts by liking them, commenting on them, and even sharing them to their own friends and family).

Let me repeat that:

> The *Edgerank* of people is much higher than the Edgerank of company Pages. **So getting your customers, fans, and superfans, to share your posts is a fundamental component of an effective Facebook marketing strategy.**

Here's another example. Here's a post of a military dad with a baby by Navy Federal Credit Union that got 854 "likes," 15 "comments," and 43 "shares":

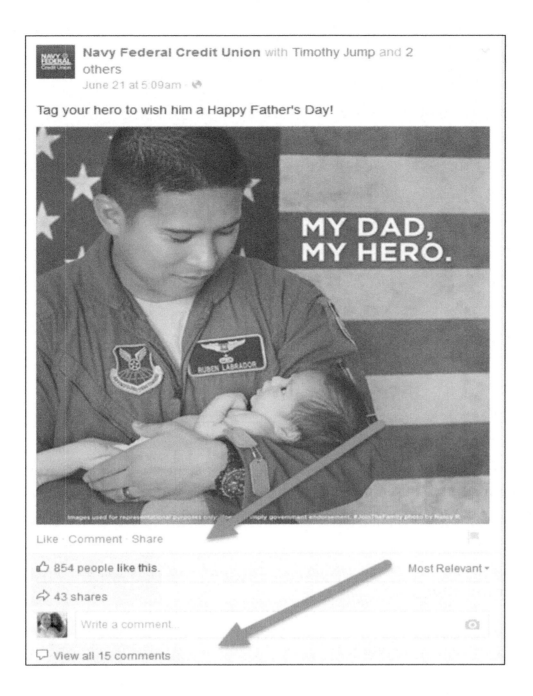

And here's a shameless "buy our stuff" post. Notice how few likes, comments, and shares it garnered:

If you reverse engineer what Navy Federal Credit Union is doing on Facebook, it's posting items to drive up interactivity (fun stuff), and then occasionally posting items that are aimed to sell its products or services (serious stuff). So their posting rhythm is:

*fun, fun, fun, fun, fun, fun, fun, fun, fun,* **buy our stuff***, fun, fun, fun, fun, fun, fun, fun,* **buy our stuff***, fun, fun, fun, etc*

.

There are two factors at work here:

*Edgerank*: improving the *Edgerank* of posts by a Page, improves the *Edgerank* of all its posts to some degree. (Note: this is also a reason to pay attention to the time of day, because *Edgerank* is determined "on the fly," and if a post does well "out of the gate," it will tend to do better over time).

**Social Sharing**: getting the fans of a Page to share the posts with their own friends and family.

Generally speaking, posts that are highly interactive get boosts on both measures. As you reverse engineer the posting strategy of competitors and/or brands you admire on Facebook, notice how they try to spur either one or both of the above.

> **VIDEO.** Watch a video tutorial on how to identify and inventory competitors and companies to emulate on Facebook at **http://jmlinks.com/16q**.

## » SET UP AND OPTIMIZE YOUR FACEBOOK PAGE

Now that you've got the basics of Facebook down, it's time to set up or optimize your own company Page. A good way to do this is to compare / contrast Pages that you like and use your inventory list to identify to-dos. Let's go down item by item to see things you need to do in terms of Facebook Page Setup.

Log in to your Facebook Page, and then use the top *settings* menu.

- **Page Roles > Admins**. Your Page needs at least one Admin (you), but I recommend more than one. Realize that anyone who is an Admin can post to the Page, and also delete any other Admin. Your Admins should be reliable, and if you ever part ways (e.g., fire them), be sure to remove them as an Admin. *Located under Settings > Page Roles*

- **General Settings** (*Located under Settings > General*)

  o **Visitor Posts**. This setting allows users to post to the Page as well as add photos or videos. Note that Taco Bell and The Super Dentists have this "on" (anyone can post to the Page) vs. the White House, which has this "off." If you trust your fans, turn it on. If you're concerned about spam and controversy, turn it off.

  o **Tagging Ability**. Similar to the above, allows users to "tag" others in photos.

  o **Page Moderation and Profanity Filter**. You can turn on filters that block naughty words like the "f" word, and/or enter specific words. If a user attempts to post or comment using these words, they will be blocked from your Page.

- o **Other items**. Scroll through the list, and you can find other miscellaneous items such as banned users, post attribution, and notifications. For most of these, the default settings are fine.

- **About Your Page**. *Click on the About Tab*. Fill out this information in detail. If you are a local business and want to allow "check-ins," be sure to click "Edit Page info" and then click "Has a street address" and fill that out. Also add an email address, phone, and website as well as your "Story," which explains what your business does.

- **Enable the Review Tab**. Local businesses, in particular, should enable the review tab and solicit reviews from happy customers on Facebook. To do so, go to *Settings > Templates and Tabs > Add a Tab > Reviews*.

- **CTA / Call-to-Action Button**. Your Facebook Page can have a CTA button. Click into your Page and find the button on the far right. If you don't see it, click down underneath your Page's cover photo. Click the blue "edit" button. Available options are "Book with you," "Contact you," "Learn more about your business," "Shop with you," or "Download your app." Learn more at **http://jmlinks.com/53c**.

- **Facebook Shop**. Facebook is now "shop" friendly. To enable it, change your Page template to the "shopping" template. Fill out the details and get started selling directly on Facebook. Alternatively, you can link directly to your own e-commerce website or store off of Facebook. Learn more at **http://jmlinks.com/53d**.

- **Tabs**. You can reorganize your "tabs" by clicking *Settings > Templates and Tabs* and then you will see "Tabs" in the center. You can then drag and drop tabs to move them around, or create new ones. **Note**: you can use this feature to turn on the important Review Tab (allowing customers to review your business). Just scroll to the bottom and click "Add a tab."

Here are a few more important setup issues:

- **Visitor Posts**. As already mentioned, if you are confident that your user community will help your brand, I recommend turning this "on," as this allows users to post information to your Page, and thereby encourages social sharing and spread. If you are worried about hostile or naughty users, turn this off.

- **Local Business Address**. If you enter a physical address (on the "about" tab) and your Page type is local business, then the **Review Tab** will be automatically enabled; if you don't see it, go to *Settings > Templates and Tabs > Tabs* and then "Add a Tab." This allows users to review your Page and/or business. Turn it "on," if you think reviews will help you. If mobile users are important, this will also enable them to "**check in**" when they are at your business – and remember, when they "check-in," Facebook will alert their friends (social sharing). (The Super Dentists (**https://www.facebook.com/TheSuperDentists**) has this on).

- **Call to Action Button**. This allows you to promote an action such as sign up for our newsletter, watch a video, etc. For an explanation, visit **http://jmlinks.com/1d**. Taco Bell has this set up for "use app." Available actions are: *Book Now, Contact Us, Use App, Play Game, Shop Now, Sign Up, or Watch Video.*

**VIDEO.** Watch a video tutorial on how to optimize your Facebook Page settings at **http://jmlinks.com/16k**.

**Set up Your Cover Photo and Profile Picture**

Now that you've completed the basic structural set up for your Page, it's time to think about the graphic elements: the **cover photo** and the **profile picture**. The cover photo, of course, is the long horizontal photo that visitors see when they visit your Page. The profile picture is the square box that identifies your Page, both when they visit your Page and as a small icon when you post something that shows in their news feed. If you pay attention to companies like Taco Bell, the White House, Navy Federal Credit Union and the like, you'll see that they systematically rotate their cover photos. When a new cover photo is uploaded, that creates a post and an opportunity to alert your fans. Any change in the cover photo in particular "broadcasts" that change to people who like the Page.

Facebook is all about photos, so it's worth putting an effort into having photogenic themes for your profile picture and cover photos (as well as, of course, your actual posts). Hire a good photographer, encourage your staff to take authentic photos of your product or service and happy customers, and take other steps to get engaging art for your cover photo and profile picture. Rotate them often. Make an effort to have photos that engage your audience, not photos that are cheesy or boring.

For the technical specifications on changing your cover photo and/or profile picture, visit **http://jmlinks.com/1e**. The cover photo, in particular, is an opportunity for fun, high-quality photos and for seasonal rotations. Follow a vendor like REI (**https://www.facebook.com/REI**), and you'll see not only seasonal rotation but also thematic unity among their cover photos on Twitter (**https://twitter.com/rei**), Facebook, Instagram (**https://instagram.com/rei/**), etc. The coolest Pages now sport not just photos but videos as their Facebook covers.

For your third **TO-DO**, download the **Facebook Setup Worksheet**. For the worksheet, go to **http://jmlinks.com/social2020** (then re-enter the password '**social2020**' to register your workbook), and click on the link to the "Facebook Setup Worksheet." You'll answer and outline the basic setup issues for your Facebook Page.

## » BRAINSTORM AND EXECUTE A POSTING STRATEGY

Now that you've set up your Facebook Page, you need to think about **content marketing** and your **posting strategy**. Remember that social media marketing stands or falls ultimately on the success of your content. You must systematically produce and share a ton of content to your Facebook page! A good goal is at least one post per day to your Facebook Page, if not two or even three.

### Choose a Strategy for Your Post

When you first log in to your Page, you'll see a blank box that says "Write a post." Click on the three dots in the lower right corner to expand all the options. Here's a screenshot:

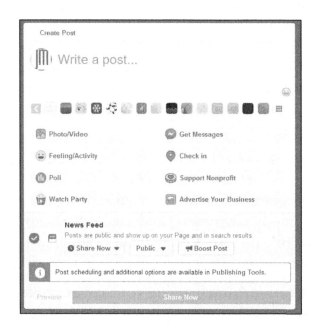

The most common option is to write some text and click on Photo/Video. Then upload a photo or video for your post and click "Share now. However, there are other options such as "Poll" to create a poll. Within Photo/Video, you can also experiment with photo albums, photo carousels, slideshows, and "instance experiences" which combine photos and videos. You can do this either on the desktop or on your mobile phone; you just have to be an Admin to your Page and make sure you've clicked over to your Page from your Profile.

You can also "**pin**" a post to the top of your Facebook Page. To do this, first post your content to Facebook. Then click on the "three dots" on the top right and select "Pin to Top of Page." Here's a screenshot:

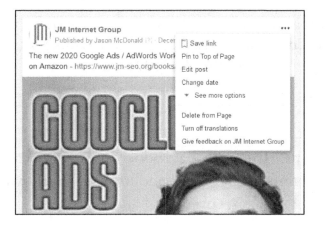

You can also **schedule your posts** by clicking into "Publishing Tools" at the top. Then click "Scheduled Posts" at the left, and then the blue "Create" button. At the bottom where it says "Share Now," click down and select "schedule." Here's a screenshot:

In this way, you can log on once a week and schedule out your Page's posts for the week. You can also schedule far in advance, planning your posts for major holidays like Christmas, New Year's, Martin Luther King Day, etc.

Common things to post are:

- **Photographs and Images**. Facebook is very visual, and you'll need to systematically identify photographs and images that fit with your brand message and ideally encourage likes, comments, and shares.

- **Video**. Facebook allows both "Facebook Live" (live video) and "Facebook Native" (recorded video). Brainstorm video ideas and begin posting these to your Page. Indeed, the Facebook algorithm clearly favors native video content over YouTube content or text, so video is a strong organic opportunity on Facebook.

- **Blog Post Summaries**. To the extent that you have an active blog and are posting items that fit with friends, family, and fun, post headlines, short summaries and links to your blog.
  - Be aware of a little HTML on your blog here. Generally speaking, the first or "featured" image in the HTML code will become the shareable image and the META DESCRIPTION tag in HTML will become the default description when sharing a blog post to Facebook. Thus, whenever you write a post for your blog be sure to write a pithy title, META DESCRIPTION, and put a fun image on the post.

- **Quotes**. People love quotes, and taking memorable quotes and pasting them on graphics is a win/win.

- **Infographics and Instructographics**. Factoids, how to articles, especially ones that are fun, are excellent for Facebook.

- **Quizzes, Polls, and Response-provoking posts**. Ask a question, and get an answer or more. These are great for encouraging interactivity.

Turn to the content marketing section of the *Marketing Almanac* for a list of tools that will help you find other people's content and create your own. I recommend Hootsuite (**http://jmlinks.com/29k**) to manage all your social postings across platforms, but I also recommend that you vary your posting strategy so that you have some posts that go live instantly, some that are "natively" scheduled inside of Facebook, and still others that are posted by a third-party app like Hootsuite or Buffer. This is so as to cover all your bases vis-à-vis the Facebook algorithm.

## Four Types of Content for Facebook

Remember the four types of content and flesh out what type(s) will make the most sense for you on Facebook:

**Your Own Content**. This is creating blog posts, photos, videos, infographics, and other fun and engaging content yourself. Note that the format that gets the highest engagement is generally native video (videos that are uploaded directly to Facebook), and the content with the highest engagement is always built on emotion.

**Other People's Content or Content Curation**. This is using tools like Feedly or Buzzsumo to identify fun and engaging content by others and share this on your Facebook Page as a "helpful expert."

**UGC / User Generated Content**. This is creating opportunities like Facebook contests or hashtags that encourage users spontaneously to create content and share it either to your Page or about your brand on Facebook.

**Interactive Content**. This is logging in as your Page and commenting on the posts made to your Page, plus identifying and interacting with the contents of fans and superfans.

Throughout, remember that ALL content you post on Facebook needs to be focused on friends, family, and fun with a good dose of emotions and counterintuitiveness to encourage social sharing. The only exception is the 10-20% of your posts that will be "buy my stuff" type, but even for those, try to tilt your message towards friends, family, and fun.

For your fourth **To-do**, download the **Facebook Posting Worksheet**. For the worksheet, go to **http://jmlinks.com/social2020** (then re-enter the password **'social2020'** to register your workbook), and click on the link to the "Facebook Posting Worksheet." You'll systematically build out a posting strategy based on the four types of content.

Once you get this done, it's time to post. Remember that Facebook marketing requires a commitment of time and resources. You can even create an editorial calendar and assigned **To-dos** for your team so that every day you are posting to Facebook on a regular basis.

**How frequently should you post?**

Because the Facebook news feed is very crowded, you can safely post quite frequently; even several times a day. But this differs with your audience, so pay attention using the Insights tab as to what posts get the best response, and whether the time of day matters. Pay attention as well to your Page likes and unlikes, to see if your posts are delighting or annoying your followers.

Experiment and measure, and you'll figure out a posting rhythm that works for you.

# POST 80% OR MORE ABOUT "FUN," AND 20% OR LESS ABOUT "BUY MY STUFF"

Don't forget that most of your posts (80% or more) should be about friends, family, and fun, and only a few (20% or less) should be direct pitches to buy your stuff. If you oversell your stuff, your fans will ignore your posts, unlike your Page, and your *Edgerank* will suffer.

## » PROMOTE YOUR FACEBOOK PAGE AND POSTS FOR FREE

Once you've set up your Page, and begun to populate it with posts on a regular basis, you've essentially "set up" your "party." You've created a good-looking Facebook Page for your business, and you're posting so frequently that when someone lands on the

Page, they'll see there's a lot of fresh, fun, and engaging content. These "trust indicators" will encourage them to like your Page, thereby allowing you to post to your timeline and (hopefully) reach them when they check their news feed.

Now it's time to send out the "invitations," that is, to promote your Facebook Page to users. In and of itself, a Facebook Page will not be self-promoting!

Remember: social media is a party. You must have yummy yummy food and entertainment for people to show up, and stick around – that is, great and engaging content. So as you promote your Facebook Page, always keep front and center "what's in it for them?" – what will they get by "liking" your Facebook Page, and checking it out on a regular basis? What content will they find on your Page that will excite and engage them?

Let's focus first on free ways to promote your Page and its posts. Here are some strategies:

- **Real World to Facebook.** Ask customers face-to-face to like your Facebook Page. If you are a museum store, for example, be sure that the cashiers recommend to customers that they like your Facebook Page? *Why? Because they'll get insider tips, fun do-it-yourself posts, announcements on upcoming museum and museum store events, etc.* If you are a dentist office, ask them to like your Facebook Page perhaps to be entered in a contest for a discount or gift certificate. Have all customer-facing employees ask customers to like your Facebook Page, and train them with a ready answer as to why "liking" your Facebook Page is worth it.

- **Hashtags and Trending Topic.** While not as important on Facebook as on Instagram, Twitter, and LinkedIn, hashtags do exist on Facebook. Create a "custom hashtag" for your brand and/or research hashtags on Facebook and include them in your posts. See **http://jmlinks.com/43e** for an example, and see **http://jmlinks.com/43g** for more information.

- **Cross-Promotion**. Link your website to your Facebook Page, your blog posts to your Facebook Page, your Twitter to your Facebook Page, etc. Notice how big brands like REI do this: one digital property promotes another digital property.

- **Facebook Messenger for Business.** Facebook Messenger is a text message app owned and operated by Facebook. It is highly popular, especially outside of the USA. To enable messenger on your Facebook Page, click "Settings" at the top of the Page, then from "General" click "Messenger Platform," and then check the box to allow people to contact your Page. Learn more at **http://jmlinks.com/43p**. Commercial products are also available called "chatbots" which use Artificial Intelligence (AI) to automate this process; simply Google "Facebook Chatbot" to find an array of vendors who offer these services.

- **Email**. Email your customer list and ask them to like your Page. Again, you must have a reason why they'll like it: what's in it for them? Have a contest, give away something for free, or otherwise motivate them to click from the email to your Page, and then like the Page. You can even upload a customer email list, and Facebook will use it to "suggest" your Page to matches. See **http://jmlinks.com/37r**.

- **Interact with Other Pages**. Interact with other Pages, share their content, comment on timely topics using #hashtags, and reach out to complementary Pages to work with you on co-promotion. Use the Facebook search feature to find other Pages that are interested in your keyword themes and comment upon them while logged in as your Page. To learn how to do this, visit **http://jmlinks.com/43h**.

- **Use Facebook Plugins**. Facebook has numerous plugins that allow you to "embed" your Facebook Page on your website, and thereby nurture cross-promotion. To learn more about plugins, visit **http://jmlinks.com/31a**. Another good plugin is the Facebook button for WordPress at **http://jmlinks.com/44b**. In this way, your blog can promote your Facebook Page, and your Facebook Page can promote your blog. Similarly, your YouTube videos can promote your Facebook Page, and your Facebook Page can promote your YouTube Videos.

- **Leverage your Fans and Superfans**. People who like your Page are your best promoters. When they first like your Page, when they comment on a post, when they "check in" to your local business on Facebook, and especially when they share your posts, their friends see this. Remember, it's *social* (!) media, and encouraging your customers to share your content is the name of the game. Create content that your users will pro-actively want to share such as funny memes, contests with giveaways, scholarship opportunities, coupons, useful "how to" articles, etc.

- **Interact with Your Fans and Others**. Your Facebook Page shouldn't just be one-way. When a fan likes, comments, or shares your post, respond to them in the comments section. Empower your employees as individuals and your brand as a Facebook Page to talk with customers on Facebook. Respond to reviews posted by customers to your Facebook Page as well.

- **Identify Influencers**. Find people on Facebook who have a lot of personal followers and who are willing to work with your brand. Some may want to charge money; some may be free. But regardless, identify and reach out to high profile individuals who can share your Page content to their followers. Always remember to explain to any influencer what's in it for them: it may be a direct payment, it may be a free product sample, it may be co-op promotion, but there has to be something "in it" for them (or they won't do it).

## Local Businesses: Reviews and Check-ins

Local businesses have two promotional tactics that are very important. First, there are customer **reviews** on Facebook (now, formally called "Recommendations"). A "local business" that enters a physical address into Facebook enables the "review this business" feature. Once the feature is enabled, you can then ask customers to review you on Facebook (by email, face-to-face, etc.); and then, when they write a review, Facebook may alert their friends and family, thereby leveraging one happy customer to reach new customers. To learn more about reviews on Facebook, visit the help file at **http://jmlinks.com/43f**.

Here's a screenshot of the "Review Tab" for the Mecca Coffee Company, my favorite coffee and spice store in Tulsa:

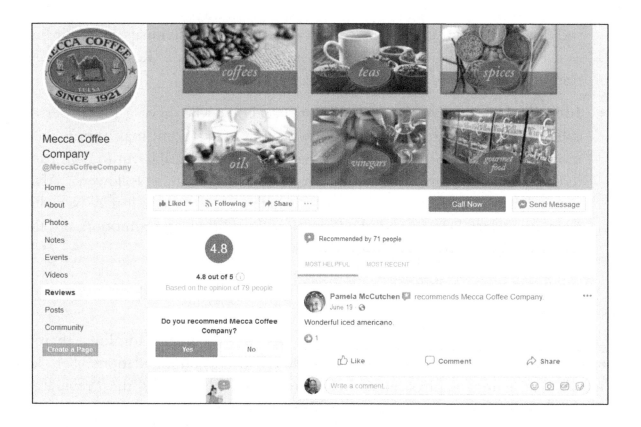

You can see that Mecca Coffee has a 4.8 out of 5 star rating and has been reviewed by 79 people, including Pamela McCutchen who loves their iced Americano. If you drill into their reviews, you'll notice that not all of them are positive; you – as the brand – can't control which reviews are posted, so be ready for good or bad reviews if you enable this feature.

Mecca Coffee has overwhelmingly positive reviews as a whole. Reviews give Mecca Coffee "trust indicators" so that with an aggregate score of 4.8/5, the company is perceived as a great spot for coffee, tea, and spices in Tulsa. Reviews also encourage "social spread," since when a customer writes a review, the Facebook algorithm can highlight this to friends and family. Study after study shows that people are most likely to believe friends and family when making a purchase decision.

We'll discuss the challenges of review marketing in more detail in Chapter 9. Suffice it to say at this point that if you enable reviews on Facebook, you want to encourage happy customers to write reviews and be ready to deal with unhappy customers, attempting to assuage their concerns to the greatest extent possible.

**Check-ins on Facebook**

The second benefit to being a local business on Facebook is "Check-ins." "Check-ins" allow customers who are at a physical brick-and-mortar store to "check in" via Facebook on their phones. This means that their friends and family can see that they've checked in, thus giving social credence and social spread to your business. Any local business should make sure that they are correctly set up as a local business on Facebook and have enabled the check-in feature. Then, encourage customers face-to-face to check in to the business. Perhaps, for example, have a weekly contest among customers who check in to win something like a $50 gift certificate. You can even use "check in" at a trade show or real-world event by temporarily making your business address the same as the convention center, and have people "check in" at your trade show booth. To learn more about Facebook check-ins, visit **http://jmlinks.com/37q**.

Whether you're local or not, a vibrant Facebook Page isn't built in a day. It's built on a foundation of good content posted to your Page, and then using the tactics listed above to promote awareness of your Page and grow interaction.

## » ODDS & ENDS: GROUPS, EVENTS, FACEBOOK LIVE, ETC.

While posts by Facebook Pages constitute the lion's share of marketing on Facebook, there are other opportunities. Let's run through those now.

> **Facebook Groups.** One of the best ways to work with fans and superfans is to create a group for your brand. A group means that anyone can post, however, so you do not have the kind of control that you do with a Facebook Page. But Facebook Groups are definitely worth checking out if you have a core of devoted fans and superfans. You can use a group to discuss upcoming new products or services, discuss industry events, comment about ideas that surround your brand, etc. Think of a group as you would think of an informal customer meeting at your brick-and-mortar store.
>
> > **Search Groups.** You can search groups in your industry by using the search bar in Facebook and typing in a keyword such as "organic" or "weddings." Then click "Groups" to browse groups. You can also type in the name of a competitor or company to emulate such as "Airbnb" to see if there's a "branded group" created by a competitor or company to emulate. Check out AirBnB's branded group at

http://jmlinks.com/52z to see a best-in-class example of group focused on superfans of Airbnb, specifically hosts and superhosts.

**Group Marketing (Direct).** If you decide a branded group focused on your company, products, or services is for you, here are some things to think about. First and foremost, what's the point of the group? Why will customers want to join it? After all a group is, by definition, interactive. Anyone can post, and anyone can chime in. So your best group is one that is customer-focused and almost "runs by itself." You, as the group manager, should really take a back seat and let the customers lead the way. Second, you can take the lead in some instances by sharing inside stories, tips, secrets, tricks, etc., about your company or product / service. The best groups are really for "superfans." Third, you can make a group private or public and adjust the settings to give you control over who gets in and how. You can also moderate the comments (or choose not to). Learn more about the technical issues of Facebook Groups at **http://jmlinks.com/43j**.

**Group Marketing (Indirect).** Another way to market via Facebook groups is to join them, as an individual, and promote your own company by being a "helpful expert." A photographer, for example, might join groups focused on weddings and then share her expertise on how to take great photos. A company that sells crafting and quilting products might have its CEO join and contribute to Facebook groups the focus on arts and crafts. Or a company that sells birding tours, might join groups on birding and contribute useful content, photos, and posts to enthusiasts for birds. The point here is to be useful, relevant, and an expert and let the publicity flow back to your brand in a low key way.

**Facebook Events.** If your company can host real-world events, or even live or virtual events on Facebook, you can set up an event. Just as in the real world, an event lives on a calendar and is an opportunity for people to learn more, purchase tickets., etc. Think of an event like a book reading, poetry slam, or perhaps a fashion show at your store just in digital format. Learn more at **http://jmlinks.com/43k**.

**Facebook Live.** Persons and Pages can now stream live video on Facebook. Learn more about Facebook Live at **http://jmlinks.com/43m**. The trick here is to figure out what type of video content your fans would like to see (and participate in) live. It's great for product demos, lectures, book readings, and other types of content that might exist "in the real world" but translate easily into video. To see examples of what's being streamed right now live on Facebook, visit **http://jmlinks.com/43n**.

**Facebook Appointments.** You can use Appointments on Facebook to let customers book services with your business from your Facebook Page. Click into your Facebook Page and then the blue CTA (Call to Action) button on the right underneath your cover photo. Select the "Book with you" option and follow the instructions.

**Facebook Stories.** Brands can create "stories" which are short video vignettes of a "day in the life" of your business. Originally started on Snapchat and Instagram, these are yet another way to stay in touch with your superfans. Learn more at **http://jmlinks.com/53a**. For story ideas from brand pages that you follow, you can go to *facebook.com/stories* or visit **http://jmlinks.com/53b**. The best stories share fun, interactive, and "insider" information about a "day in the life" of your brand.

Each of the above is a special use of Facebook. They're not for every business. The main questions to ask yourself are:

1. Will your customers be interested in using this feature? Why or why not?

2. What will your share / talk about / post to the feature? If it's an event, for instance, what kind of event will it be? What will happen at the event? If it's a group, what will be the reason for the group and what will you (and others) share on the group that will be interesting? If it's live, what will happen during the live broadcast?

3. How much time will it take for you as a business to engage via the platform?

4. How will you promote it? A Facebook group, Facebook live, or Facebook event will not promote itself. You have to promote it, just as you'd promote the real-world equivalent.

## » ADVERTISE ON FACEBOOK: BASICS

With the decline of organic reach, you pretty much have to advertise on Facebook to succeed. The fact of the matter is that the Facebook news feed has become very, very crowded and that people are generally much more interested in the posts of their friends and families than in posts by brands. Add into this the shellacking that Zuckerberg and Facebook took from the US Congress on "fake news," and it's no surprise that Facebook has severely tilted its algorithm to *suppress* posts by organizations and brands and *promote* posts by friends and family. The result is that nine times out of ten you have to spend money to advertise on Facebook in order to succeed. Let me emphasize this:

> *For all intents and purposes, you MUST spend money on Facebook advertising to succeed at Facebook. Despite what Facebook tells you, the days of a truly "free" organic strategy on Facebook are over.*

Like your website, your Facebook Page doesn't promote itself. You have to have a promotion strategy that combines free efforts, paid efforts, and hybrid pay-to-free efforts to get the word out. You can browse Facebook's official information on advertising at **http://jmlinks.com/31c**, but let me walk you through the basic opportunities here.

## Promote Your Page or Other Elements

When you log in as a Page administrator, you'll see a blue button in the left column called "Promote." Click on that blue button. Next, you should see options similar to these:

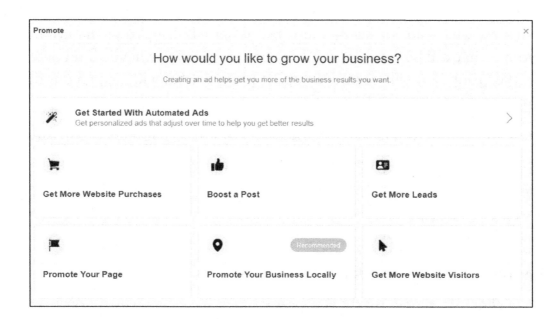

You can also scroll down to see more options. Among the available options are:

**Get Started with Automated Ads** – i.e., answer some Facebook questions and get their algorithm to suggest an advertising strategy. *This is not very useful, and overly complicated.*

**Get More Website Purchases / Get More Website Visitors** – i.e., advertise a link to an external e-commerce store or website. *This is using Facebook not to promote your Facebook Page but rather to advertise your website. It is most useful if you have an e-commerce website, or have a consumer-friendly business that can benefit from sales leads (like a realtor business, massage therapist, plumber, etc.)*

**Boost a Post** – i.e., boost your posts to fans of your Page as well as other demographic targets. *This is a strategy to get people to actually see your posts in their news feed and is highly recommended.*

**Get More Leads** – i.e., advertise something "good" via a feedback form, and in exchange get customers names, emails, and other contact information. *This is a way to collect leads from customers for follow up, directly on Facebook.*

**Promote your Page** – i.e., advertise your Page and grow its "likes" to demographic targets. *This is a strategy to grow your Page likes if you are international or national as opposed to just a local business.*

**Promote your Business Locally** – i.e., showcase your Facebook Page to a local target audience. *This is a strategy to grow your Page likes and is useful to build your Page audience.*

## The Most Common Strategy: Boost a Post

For now, let's assume you want to do the simplest thing, which is to boost a post of yours on Facebook. Boosting a post means paying Facebook to put your post to the top of the news feed; it's paying Facebook to preference your post in its algorithm so that customers and potential customers are likely to see it.

You can start the boost process in two ways:

1. Log in to your Facebook Page. Then click the blue "Promote" button on the bottom left. Select "Boost a Post." Next, find the post you want to boost and select the blue "Boost Post" button.

2. Alternatively, just log in to your Facebook Page. Scroll down until you find the post you want to promote and then click the blue "Boost Post" button on the

far lower right corner. You can also do this as you create the post itself. This is the easiest way to boost a post.

Once you've clicked on the blue "Boost Post" button, you should see something like this:

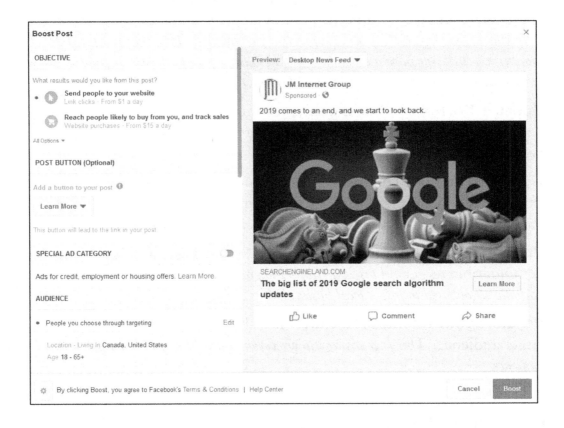

## Targeting: Choose Who Will See Your Post

Who will see your post? You have to define the audience under the section called AUDIENCE. Let me show you two easy selections.

First, there is "**People who like your Page**." You've invested time, effort, and even possibly money building "likes" for your Page. Now you want folks who have expressed an interest in your business actually to see your posts. To do this, under AUDIENCE, select the option: "People who like your Page." This means that people who have already liked your Page will be more likely to see your Post in their news feed. You are essentially paying Facebook to boost your Post into their feed. You set a budget and a time horizon. This is the most effective method to get people who have already liked your Page actually to see your posts.

You can also boost to "People who like your Page and their friends," which is a good strategy for social spread.

Second, another good option is "**People you choose through targeting**." This is how you can use Facebook to reach not only people who like your Page but people who have not, that is potentially new Facebook fans and potential new customers.

To do this, select "People you choose through targeting" and then hit the "Edit" in blue. Here's a screenshot:

Next, under "INCLUDE people who match at least ONE of the following" type in keywords that match customer interests. If you are selling wedding dresses, for example, you can type in "Weddings" or "Bridal." If you are selling purses, you can type in "purses" or "fashion," etc. This is very powerful as Facebook knows a lot about its audience, so you can target people by keyword interests, really on nearly any topic.

Here's a screenshot for "Weddings":

Imagine any interest that people have in their leisure lives, and that's a good target on Facebook. What's not so easy to target is non-leisure activities, such as people who are researching nuclear physics or business managers who are looking for web design services. Facebook is very "B2C" (business to consumer), so the best interest targets reflect the friends, family, and fun culture of Facebook.

In this way, you can boost a post and focus it at people who meet your demographic targets. These are not people who like your Page, but rather potential targets. These people can interact with your Post, click over to your website, and like your Page as well. Your ads can be shown not only on Facebook but also on Messenger and Instagram; just scroll down and check or uncheck those boxes as desired. This second type of targeting is a good way to use Facebook as an advertising medium to reach people you target by demographic characteristics.

Don't miss the fact that you can also geotarget, target by age, and target by sex. For geotargeting, click "edit" in blue. Then click the "x" to the right of United States and/or Canada if selected (as these are the defaults). Then type in a city such as "Tulsa, Oklahoma" to target only people who live in Tulsa. The default is a 25-mile radius. Here's a screenshot:

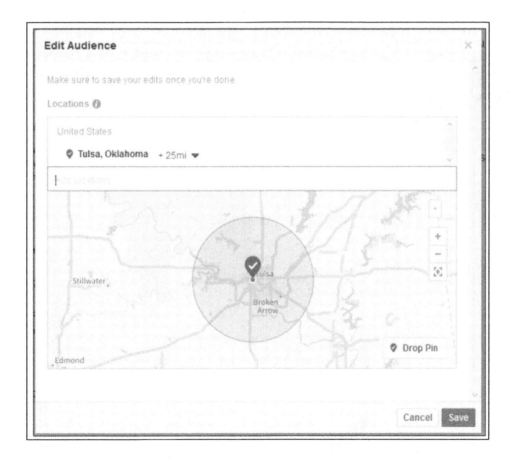

You can also target zip codes and combinations. To target men or women, you must select the "People you choose through targeting" option. You can also target an age range.

**Audiences**

Once you create an audience, you can save it as an "audience" for future use. You can view audiences you've created by clicking on "Manage Promotions" while logged into your Facebook Page and then selecting "Audiences" on the far left. You can also get there by clicking "Ad Center," and then "Audiences." Or when logged into Facebook, just go to **http://jmlinks.com/43x**. (Facebook is not going to win any user interface design awards, that's for sure).

Once you've found where Facebook hides your audiences, you can also create new audiences here, and they will appear as an option when you boost a post. This is a time-saving way to create an audience, once, and then re-use it again and again as you boost posts.

To do that, click on the blue "Create Audience" button and select "Saved Audience." Then follow the steps outlined above to define your audience. In this way, you can build out a library of targeted audiences for your posts and easily access them. Once created, you should see your audiences when you boost any post under AUDIENCE. If you've created more than a few audiences, you may need to click the "See All" link that appears in blue. Here's a screenshot:

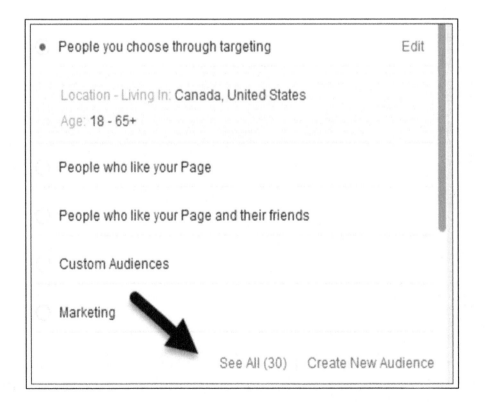

**Summary: Boosting a Post and Targeting It**

In summary, here's are the steps to the most basic way to promote your Facebook content through advertising:

1. **Create a post** that has a brief headline or summary, a compelling image, and – if desired – a link to your website, blog, YouTube channel, e-commerce store, etc.

    a. Be sure that this post fits into the culture of friends, family, photos, and fun.

    b. If possible, make the post something that people are likely to engage with and even like, comment, or share with their own friends and family.

2. **Boost this post** on Facebook, to any combination of:

    a. People who like your Page;

    b. People who like your Page and their friends (useful when friend recommendations are likely to improve your marketing);

    c. People who live within 25 miles of a city or zip code or another geographic target

3. Or, **boost this post** on Facebook to any combination of:

    a. People who show an interest in relevant keyword themes such as "weddings" or "bridal."

    b. People who live within 25 miles of a city or zip code or another geographic target.

    c. Sex: men, women, or both.

    d. Age: select an age range.

Nowadays, you can't succeed on Facebook without an ad budget. I recommend a minimum budget of $300 / month for your average small business, and for a larger business, the sky's the limit.


## » ADVANCED FACEBOOK TARGETING

Let's dive into more advanced targeting tactics on Facebook. Recall that Facebook advertising allows you three important options:

1. Promote your Page to grow likes.

2. Promote a post by boosting it.

3. Promote a website URL to grow web traffic.

You can also advertise an app on Facebook, create a lead generation form, promote yourself on messenger, etc. But the three options listed above are the most common. To get started, just log in to your Facebook Page and then click the blue "Promote" button at the bottom left.

We'll assume you have something to advertise and have created a photo or video plus some text to describe your offer. Next, let me share with you three advanced **targeting** strategies for advertising on Facebook.

**Method #1 – Advanced Demographic Targeting**

We've already seen that Facebook can target your advertising to people who like your Page, people who like your Page and their friends, or demographic targets such as people who show an interest in weddings, live in Tulsa, Oklahoma, are women, and are aged 21 to 40. But Facebook demographic targeting can be much more sophisticated than that.

Facebook has a feature called "Audiences," and you can create and save an audience that matches demographic characteristics that you want. First, log in to your Facebook Page and then click on "Manage Promotion" on the far left, and then on Audiences. Next, click the "Create Audience" button at the top right.

Give your audience a name that summarizes the target such as "Potential Brides" or "Women 62-75 Near Retirement." I recommend you ignore selecting the Gender, Age, or Location until you select the detailed targeting. The interface is very buggy, and I have better luck setting the demographic targets first and then returning to these aspects. So scroll past these options, ignore the warning in red that you must select a location, and scroll down to "Detailed Targeting" until you see "INCLUDE people who match at least ONE of the following:"

Here are some strategies:

> **Keywords.** Simply type keywords that describe what your target customers are interested in or are like. For example, type "weddings," "bridal," or "retirement." As you do this, pay attention to which words show up on the list. You can choose more than one; even better, look for more narrow, "nichey" keywords that really

speak to your best customers. Understand, however, that if you choose more than one it's an "or" statement – if you choose "Weddings" and "Jet Skis" then it's anyone whose interest either match weddings OR jet skis.

**Competitors**. If a competitor has a Facebook Page and if that competitor's Page has over around 5,000 followers, then it is likely that they'll show up when you type the name of their Facebook Page. For instance, try typing in "Whole Foods Market," and you'll see it listed as an "interest." What this means is that you – perhaps a smaller, newer competitor in the organic food marketplace – can target those people who have liked the Whole Foods Page on Facebook. Your to-do here is to type in the names of competitor Facebook Pages and see if they appear; you can even set up an audience and call it "competitors," populating it with all your competitors in one mega audience. With the exact names of similar Pages in hand, then use these names to input into Facebook ad targeting and create a "custom audience" of people who follow Pages similar to yours.

**Employees**. You can target people who work at a competitor. So, again, try typing in "Whole Foods Market," and pay attention to the right. You should see "Employers" listed, which means these are not people who like the Facebook Page but rather people who work at Whole Foods. A good target can be journalists, so for instance, you could target people who work at the New York Times. Again, they have to be a pretty big company for this to work. You can also do this by clicking "Browse" and then *Demographics > Work > Employers* and, again, typing in the company name.

**Browse**. You can click on the "Browse" tab and browse by category. This gives you three broad categories – *Demographics*, *Interests*, and *Behaviors*. Drill into each and you'll see subcategories, such as:

Demographics

> Education

> Life Events

> Parents

> Politics (US)

> Relationship

> Work

Interests

> Business and industry

Entertainment

Family and relationships

Fitness and wellness

Food and drink

Hobbies and activities

Shopping and fashion

Sports and outdoors

Technology

Behaviors

Mobile Device User

Anniversary

Consumer Classification

Digital activities

Expats

Mobile Device User

Mobile Device User / Device Use Time

More Categories

Multicultural Affinity

Purchase Behavior

Soccer (So important it gets its own category, haha!)

Travel

Facebook clearly knows a lot about the demographics, interests, and behaviors of its audience. It's very willing to sell you access to its audience by slicing and dicing these attributes so that your ad – whether it's a promotion for your business Page as a whole, a boosted post, or an ad from Facebook to your website or e-commerce store – will succeed at reaching the right people.

Note that you can also get to audiences by going to Ad Manager. Click the downward chevron at the top right, then "Manage ads," then drill into your "Ads Manager," then "All Tools" at the bottom left (as you hover on the Ads Manager) menu, then *Assets > Audiences*. Wasn't that easy? Or when logged into Facebook, just go to http://jmlinks.com/43x or visit **https://www.facebook.com/adsmanager/** then click on the Menu (Top Left), and then *All Tools > Assets > Audiences*.

In any case, you can create and save a very defined audience for use as a targeting method for any and all advertising on Facebook.

**Method #2 – The Facebook Pixel**

The **Facebook Pixel** is a tracking system deployed by Facebook across the Internet. Basically, Facebook encourages website owners to add the Facebook Pixel to their websites. Then Facebook can combine the data it already knows about a person via Facebook with the data it collects on websites. You, as the marketer, can participate in this massive invasion of consumer privacy (*oops, I mean this wonderful method of targeting ads to your customers*) by adding the Facebook Pixel to your website. (See http://jmlinks.com/43c for full information on the Facebook Pixel). If you're running WordPress on your website, you can download and install the "Pixel Cat" plugin which makes it relatively easy to install the Facebook Pixel on your website. Just search for "Pixel Cat" as a plugin when logged in to your WordPress website or visit **http://jmlinks.com/43s**.

Once installed, the Facebook Pixel can be used to create a **custom audience**. Broadly, you can create an audience of everyone who hit your website; more narrowly, you can create sub audiences, such as an audience of persons who hit your website but did not convert or persons who hit specific pages or sections (such as men's clothes, women's clothes, or teenagers' clothes if you were an e-commerce clothing vendor, for instance). You can then use these audiences and subaudiences to target your ads on Facebook. An e-commerce site that sold jet skis, for example, could target all website visitors with ads on Facebook or, more cleverly, target only those visitors who did not convert and buy a jet ski. A clothing store could target ads to men, women, and teenagers separately, and so on and so forth. You can also assume that folks who hit your website are good prospects to like your Facebook Page, so you can use the Facebook Pixel to grow likes to your Facebook Page, and then boost posts and set up other types of Facebook ads so that your website grows your Facebook Page, and your Facebook Page grows your website and desired actions such as selling stuff on an e-commerce store or driving web feedback forms.

The Pixel, in short, unifies your website with your Facebook Page. It's awesome!

Installing and setting up the Facebook Pixel, however, is not easy. It's sort of something designed by computer geeks, for computer geeks. You may need to reach out to a technical webmaster for help with the installation and conversion issues. You can also go to Fiverr.com and just search "Facebook Pixel" to find experts who can install the Pixel technology for you.

Once the Facebook Pixel is installed, it may take about 14 days to collect enough data. If you have a big website with lots of traffic, it can be faster. If your website doesn't have a lot of traffic, however, the Pixel might not work at all. You need about 20,000 visits a month to your website for it to function. We'll assume you've installed the Pixel and have enough website visitors for it to work.

It's going to get complicated at this point. Bear with me and be patient. Facebook's advertising platform is very complicated, the support files are sparse, and there is no phone support. But it's worth slogging through the pixel installation and then creating custom audiences to take advantage of this incredible way to target customers.

Here's how to create a Custom Audience using the Facebook Pixel:

1. Log in to your Facebook business page, by first logging into your personal Facebook account, and then clicking on Pages on the left. It can also be found at **http://jmlinks.com/43y**.

2. Get to "Ads Manager" by clicking on the downward chevron in the top right of Facebook. Select "Manage Ads" or just go to **http://jmlinks.com/43z**. Be sure to click into your Ads Manager (if, for some reason, you have more than one account). This step may not be necessary in all cases.

3. On the top left, click the Menu and then All Tools in blue. This is very hidden and just a little piece of text. Here's a screenshot:

4. Click over to *Assets > Audiences*, which should get you to **http://jmlinks.com/44a**.

5. Click the blue "Create Audience," and select "Custom Audience."

6. Click "Website."

7. Follow the steps there, as you should see your website visitors and options such as visits to a specific page or conversions. Here's a screenshot:

And once you've installed and set up the Facebook Pixel, you can further drill down to create sub-audiences. Here's a screenshot:

Once you've done this, you should start to see your Pixel audience available when you boost a post, advertise your page, or promote your website via Facebook advertising.

In summary, your steps are:

1. Install the Facebook Pixel on your website.

2. If desired, modify the Pixel so that you can track visits to key web pages and/or conversions on an e-commerce or lead generation site.

3. Log in to Facebook and get to the "Audiences" section in Facebook Ads Manager.

4. Define a "custom audience" based on your Facebook Pixel (all website visitors) or a sub audiences (non-converters, visitors to key pages, etc.).

Once defined, you can then use and reuse your Facebook Pixel as a "custom audience" to boost a post, advertise your page, or advertise a link to your website. You may have to click into "Custom Audiences" to see it. Here's a screenshot:

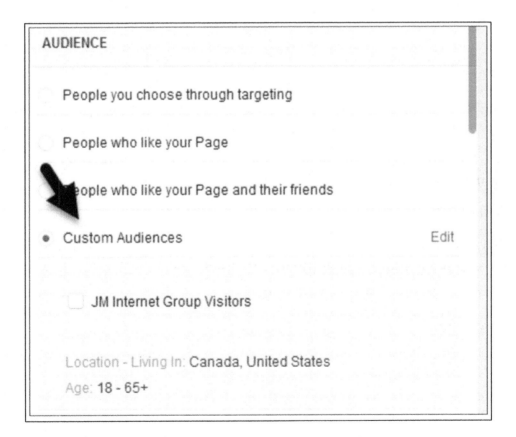

**Method #3 – Custom Audiences**

A third advanced targeting technique is to create a "custom audience." (To learn more about "Custom Audiences" on Facebook, see **http://jmlinks.com/43r**). First, let's explain the confusing Facebook terminology. Facebook has:

> **Saved Audiences**. These are sets of people you create by making demographic choices (such as *women, interested in weddings, living in 90210*).
>
> **Custom Audiences**. These are sets of people you create by uploading or sharing data with Facebook such as using the Facebook Pixel or uploading customer emails.

Ultimately all of them live under the "Audience Tab" in Facebook Ad manager at **http://jmlinks.com/44a** so it seems a distinction without a difference. Just be aware that Facebook refers to them as *audiences*, *saved audiences*, and *custom audiences*.

After the Facebook Pixel, the most common type of custom audience is to upload a list of customer email addresses, which Facebook will attempt to match with the customer emails that it has. Here's how.

1. Log in to your *Facebook Page > Ads Manager > All Tools > Assets > Audience*.

   a. Be sure to click over to *Assets > Audiences*, which should get you to **http://jmlinks.com/44a**.

2. Click the blue "Create Audience," and select "Custom Audience." (You may be prompted to upgrade to Facebook Business Manager).

3. Select "Customer List."

4. Then either Add customers by uploading a customer email list directly or if you are using MailChimp follow the instructions there.

Here's a screenshot:

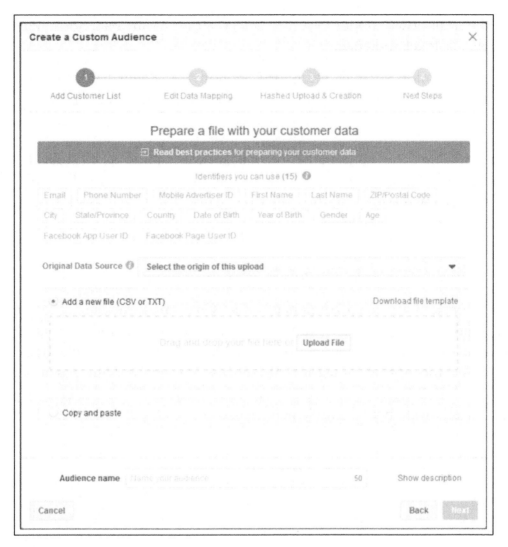

At this point, you upload a CSV or TXT file of customer email addresses. This will build a "custom audience" based on email addresses as Facebook matches the emails you uploaded with the emails customers have entered into its system. Once created, this new audience will show as a "custom audience," and you can use it to target advertising.

## Method #4 – Lookalike Audiences

Finally, you can create a "Lookalike Audience," which means Facebook will look at your Facebook Page or Facebook Pixel data and attempt, through the miracle of artificial intelligence, to create an audience of similarly minded people. To create a "Lookalike Audience," get to Audience Manager as described above. Then,

1.  Click the blue "Create Audience" button and then "Lookalike Audience."

2. In the pull-down under Source, select either your Facebook Page or your Facebook Pixel audience.

3. Select a location such as Texas or Oklahoma. It needs to be pretty big, as this won't generally work for a city or a zipcode. But you can experiment.

Once created, your Lookalike audience will appear named as "Lookalike – People who…" when you target an ad. A "Lookalike audience" is essentially using Facebook to mimic the characteristics of those people who either visit your website or have already liked your Facebook Page.

## » ADVERTISE ON FACEBOOK THE SUPERFAN STRATEGY

Once you've created a "Saved Audience" or a "Custom Audience," you can return to advertising and use these defined audiences as a targeting method. For example, if you return to your Facebook Page, find a post you want to boost, and select "Boost Post," you should see the option "Custom Audiences" to access your Facebook Pixel or uploaded email audience or the option "Saved audiences. If you've created more than a couple "Saved Audiences," you'll need to select "See All" to select from all your "Saved Audiences." Here's a screenshot:

Custom Audiences

Marketing

See All (30)    Create New Audience

Click on "See All" and then select whichever "Saved Audience" you want to use to target this individual boosted post. If you'd like to advertise your Facebook Page or a link to your website rather than boosting a post, log in to your Facebook page, and click on "Promote" in blue at the bottom left corner and then select your desired option. Again, you'll see under AUDIENCE new options such as "Custom Audience" and then a list of "Saved Audiences," plus a link to "See All" if there are more than just a few.

In this way, after you've created "Saved Audiences" or "Custom Audiences," you can quickly target any advertising on Facebook to a defined audience.

## The Superfan Strategy

Remember, however, that the Edgerank of your Facebook Page isn't very strong as compared with the Edgerank of fans and superfans. Facebook heavily favors posts by people and posts by friends and family over posts by brands. The reality is that your organic reach as a Page will be pretty abysmal.

However, by using advertising to reach your fans and superfans, you can ignite sharing among them. In this way, you can "use" your fans and superfans to broaden your reach on Facebook. Fans, of course, are people who have liked your Page, and superfans are those who have liked your Page and are highly engaged with your brand. Influencers are those who have a really broad and engaged audience themselves.

Think of targeting fans, superfans, and even influencers with your content via advertising, and then make this content so engaging that they want to share it with their audience. You're getting advertising to work with organic on Facebook, or rather advertising to ignite organic. It's pretty cool.

Here's how to do this:

1. Create a piece of compelling content, such as a post that is highly emotional, has a great image, and a message that fits your brand such as a contest, giveaway, sentimental or shocking message, something counterintuitive, etc.

2. Boost this post.

3. Select the option "People who like your Page."

Because people who already like your Page are – by definition – fans and superfans, you can use advertising to reach them, and then because you've created compelling and shareable content, get them to share this content with their friends and family You can also think of creating a "saved audience" such as people who work at the New York Times, Huffington Post, and Newsweek – that is influencers like journalists and bloggers.

Your ads are being targeted at people who, by definition, are likely to engage with it and share it.

This is how content gets started in the sharing process on Facebook, and indeed, how a lot of content "goes viral." It's boosted through advertising to fans and superfans at the get-go.

For example, here's a post by REI entitled "Meet 4 Women Who Broke Barriers in the Outdoors:"

Notice how this has 3900 likes, 121 comments, and 1,000 shares. You can bet that behind the scenes there was an initial advertising push to get this post out in front of REI's fans and superfans. Plus, it's clear that the content fits their brand themes of the outdoors plus leverages a social cause ("women's rights") that many people want to learn about and support. If you're cynical, you could even say that many people will "virtue signal" their support of women's rights by liking, commenting, and even sharing this type of content.

REI is using great content that supports its brand and is highly shareable in combination with advertising to create a post that "goes viral." REI is leveraging fans and superfans (plus their motivation to "support" a cause) to promote its message through Facebook.

So it's not advertising OR organic reach on Facebook, it's advertising AND organic reach by using the latter to ignite the former.

> **VIDEO.** Watch a video on Facebook advertising and superfans at **http://jmlinks.com/43t**.

## » MEASURE YOUR RESULTS

Facebook offers good measurement for your organic and advertising efforts. Log in to your Facebook Page, and then click on the **Insights** tab at the top tabs. Here you'll find an overview of your Facebook activity, and a post-by-post breakdown of the reach of a post and the engagement. A graph will tell you when your fans are most engaged. You can select "Pages to watch," and keep an eye on your competitors – even down to which posts of theirs were the most interactive.

For any of your posts, click on the post, and a popup window will give you drill-down information. Here's a screenshot of a post to the JM Internet Group Facebook Page:

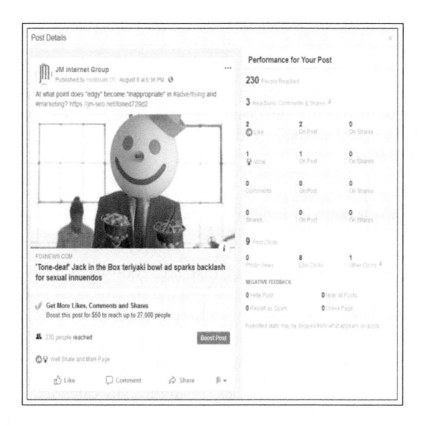

If you look closely, you'll see that it reached 230 people, got 2 likes and 8 links clicks but no comments or shares.

And here's a screenshot of a post of our own content (i.e., a link to a blog post) that was boosted for $200.00

Pay attention to the *reach*, *likes*, *comments*, *shares*, and *clicks* of all your posts (both organic and advertised). All of this is influencing *Edgerank*. The *more interactive* your Page and posts are, the *higher* your Edgerank, and the *higher* your Edgerank, the *more* people will see your posts and Page.

Remember: **Interactivity** is where it's "at" on Facebook!

You'll also very clearly see that posts that are "boosted," that is supported by advertising, have a much bigger reach and therefore a bigger opportunity for likes, comments, and shares vs. posts that rely on free, organic reach.

You can also hover with your mouse over the comments and shares to see who did what, and even "invite them" to like your Facebook Page.

Back to the tabs on the left, you can click down into any category. For instance, you can click on "Followers" to see data about who is following your page. Click on "People" to see demographic data about who is following your page.

All in all, Facebook provides excellent insights into who is interacting with your posts and Page. Use this information to make your Page better and better as measured in posts that garner more likes, comments, and shares!

## Google Analytics

Many of us want to drive traffic from Facebook to our website, even to our e-commerce store or to download a free eBook or software package to get a sales lead. Sign up for Google Analytics (**https://analytics.google.com/**) and install the required tracking code. Inside of your Google Analytics account on the left column, drill down by clicking on *Acquisition > Social > Overview*. Then on the right-hand side of the screen, you'll see a list of Social Networks. Find Facebook on that list, and click on that. Google Analytics will tell you what URLs people clicked to from Facebook to your Website, giving you insights into what types of web content people find attractive.

You can also create a custom **segment** to look at only Facebook traffic and its behavior once someone clicks from Facebook to your website. For information on how to create segments in Google Analytics, visit the videos at **http://jmlinks.com/43u** and **http://jmlinks.com/43v**. For the complete Google help files on understanding and building segments visit **http://jmlinks.com/43w**.

In summary, inside of Facebook, you can see how people interact with your Page and posts. Inside of Google Analytics, you can see where they land on your website and what they do after they arrive.

> **VIDEO.** Watch a video tutorial on how to use Google Analytics to track clicks from social media sites like Facebook to your website at **http://jmlinks.com/16n**.

## »» CHECKLIST: FACEBOOK ACTION ITEMS

Test your knowledge of Facebook! Take the *Facebook marketing quiz* at **http://jmlinks.com/qzfb**. (Before or after you do, check out the free, official Facebook learning site called "Blueprint" at **http://jmlinks.com/53e**.) Next, here are your Facebook **Action Items**:

❏ **Research** Facebook to find out whether your customers are on it and what they are doing. Identify **keyword themes** that are either directly relevant to your brand or adjacent to it.

❏ **Identify** both **competitors** and **companies to emulate**; "reverse engineer" their Page set up and posting strategies.

❏ **Investigate** which types of **posts** are getting the most **interaction** from fans and why. Pay attention to whether these are in keyword themes directly related to your products or services, or just adjacent to them (or both).

❑ **Set up and Optimize your Facebook Page.** Identify profile and cover photo art. Select the appropriate tabs, including whether to enable the "review" tab or not and whether to allow posts to the Page by fans.

❑ **Brainstorm a Posting Strategy.** Begin to systematically create blog posts, photos, videos, etc., that match your marketing strategy to the interests of your target fans. Seek to encourage likes, comments, and shares. Consider doing Facebook live broadcasts or setting up a company-specific branded hashtag or Facebook group.

❑ **Promote your Facebook page** via the real world, cross-promotion among Internet properties, and other free promotional tactics. Grow your Page likes.

❑ **Set up Facebook Audiences.** Set up and save custom audiences to Facebook, such as the Facebook Pixel audiences, demographically defined audiences, and audiences from email lists.

❑ **Advertise on Facebook.** Allocate at least a basic budget to boost posts on Facebook to your own fans, and consider more aggressive advertising tactics like boosting posts to fans and superfans that are likely to get shared as well as using Facebook advertising to reach potential new customers who are not already fans of your Page.

❑ **Measure your Facebook results** using KPIs such as the growth of Page likes, the volume of interactivity of individual posts (e.g., likes, comments, and shares), and whether Facebook is generating traffic to your website up to and including sales or sales leads.

Check out the **free tools**! Go to my *Social Media Marketing Dashboard > Facebook* for my favorite free tools on Facebook. Just visit **http://jmlinks.com/smmdash**.

### »» DELIVERABLE: A FACEBOOK MARKETING PLAN

We've come to the end of our chapter on Facebook, and your **DELIVERABLE** has arrived. For the worksheet, go to **http://jmlinks.com/social2020** (then re-enter the password '**social2020**' to register your workbook), and click on the link to the "Facebook Marketing Plan." By filling out this plan, you and your team will establish a vision of what you want to achieve via Facebook.

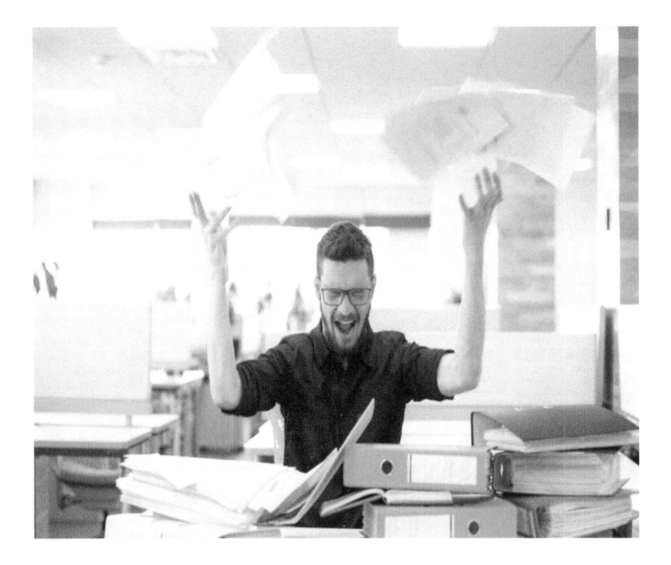

# 4
# LINKEDIN

If **Facebook** is all about *friends, family,* and *fun* – a kind of 24/7 *company picnic*, **LinkedIn** is all about *business networking* – a kind of 24/7 online *corporate party*. Indeed, if you've ever been to a big trade show such as the *Consumer Electronics Show* in Las Vegas, you've likely attended corporate *meet-and-greets, wine and cheese* events, or *breakout learning sessions* on important industry topics. These industry conference "parties" feature free food and entertainment, a speech or two by the CEO, and lots of *business networking* between vendors and potential customers. Dressed in business casual, people listen attentively, are in "learning" mode, and are also ready to introduce themselves and their products to you and others.

**Business networking,** in short, is the No. 1 activity via LinkedIn marketing!

Although LinkedIn is used heavily for job search, this Chapter will focus exclusively on **how to market a business on LinkedIn**, specifically the three big marketing opportunities for businesses: 1) helping employees to optimize their **profiles** (as well as encouraging employees to promote your business on LinkedIn) 2) using LinkedIn to **network** with customers and prospects, and 3) leveraging a **company page** for your business. We'll also discuss the basics of advertising on LinkedIn.

**Let's get started!**

**TO-DO LIST:**

» Explore How LinkedIn Works

» Optimize Your LinkedIn Profile (and Your Employees', Too)

» Schmooze on LinkedIn: Your Social Rolodex

» Be Active on LinkedIn: Posts, Articles, and Video

» Be Active on LinkedIn: Connections, Comments, and Groups

» Use LinkedIn Company Pages

» Promote Your LinkedIn Profile, Posts, and Pages

» Advertise on LinkedIn

» Measure Your Results

## » EXPLORE HOW LINKEDIN WORKS

Let's review the basic structure of LinkedIn:

- **Individuals have LinkedIn profiles**, which function as online resumes listing skills, education, and interests. Profiles allow one individual to "connect" with another individual; once connected, any post by individual No. 1 will show in the news feed of individual No. 2. In this sense, LinkedIn profiles function structurally in exactly the same way as Facebook profiles: you send *connection requests* (the same as *friend requests* on Facebook), and once accepted and connected, you and the other individual can directly check each other out, communicate via LinkedIn messaging, and see posts to each other's news feed.

- **Individuals can join groups.** While groups on Facebook are of limited business interest, groups on LinkedIn are very important. As at a major trade show, LinkedIn has "break out" groups by topic (from petroleum engineering to marketing to advertising to WordPress web design and beyond), that bring like-minded people together in a professional way. Note, however, that it is *people* (and not business *Pages*) that participate in groups.

- **Companies can have LinkedIn Pages.** As on Facebook, companies can create business Pages on LinkedIn. Individuals can follow companies, and by doing so, give permission for that company to communicate with them. Posts by the company have a chance to show in the news feed of individuals who have "followed" a particular company. Company Pages can also advertise on LinkedIn.

- **Posts and the News Feed.** When an individual shares a post or article to his or her LinkedIn profile, or a company shares a post on its LinkedIn Page, those posts show up in the news feed of connected individuals. LinkedIn, like Facebook, therefore has a posting rhythm in which individuals and businesses compete for eyeballs and attention.

Structurally, therefore, LinkedIn is very similar to Facebook. *Profiles and connection requests, Pages and following, posts and news feeds.* It is also similar in content: people posts just text, text with a photo or image, text with a link to a blog or website, and/or native video.

### A More Business-Oriented Culture

The **culture** of LinkedIn, however, is far more serious and business-oriented than Facebook. On LinkedIn, people are in "learning" and "business mode," sharing information and posts about business trends and topics, not the latest photo of their baby, cat video, or SNL skit that has gone viral. Common LinkedIn posts are about industry news, a job promotion, a corporate webinar, or perhaps commentary on business and national news. LinkedIn's content is far more serious and business-oriented than that shared on Facebook. Content marketing for your business on LinkedIn thus needs to fit the business- and career-oriented themes of the network.

In addition, the **structural** similarities between LinkedIn and Facebook hide a very different **pattern of interaction**. Whereas on Facebook, the center of marketing is the business *Page*, on LinkedIn, the center of gravity lies with the personal *profiles* of employees. Whereas on Facebook, you primarily interact with business Pages in terms of marketing, on LinkedIn you primarily interact with the *employees* of various businesses. Ironically, marketing on LinkedIn centers on persons (i.e., your employees), while marketing on Facebook centers on brands (i.e., your company page).

# LinkedIn's Center of Gravity is the Personal Profile

LinkedIn's center of gravity, in summary, is *person-to-person interaction.* This makes sense if you compare a company picnic (Facebook) with a business networking event (LinkedIn). Whereas at the former, you interact with the company (who brings the food and entertainment, and pays for the party), at the latter, you interact with the employees of the company, talking about industry events and schmoozing about shared interests. In a business environment, you don't network with *companies*, after all. You network with the *individual employees* of a given company. Ironically, marketing on LinkedIn is thus focused on person-to-person activities vs. on Facebook, where it is more brand-to-person in nature.

### Don't Talk to Strangers?

Whereas on Facebook most of us are suspicious of friend requests from people we don't know, or only barely know, on LinkedIn, it is much more common to send a connection request "out of the blue" or to a person you just met. Ironically, talking to strangers is more difficult on Facebook than it is on LinkedIn! And, whereas on Facebook, it's impolite to ask what one "does for a living" or to "pitch business ideas," on LinkedIn this is so important as to be a core function. With even the most tangential of connections on LinkedIn, you can easily reach out and ask for a relationship. For example, here's a screenshot of me reaching out to *New York Times* journalist Nellie Bowles, with whom I am a second-level connection:

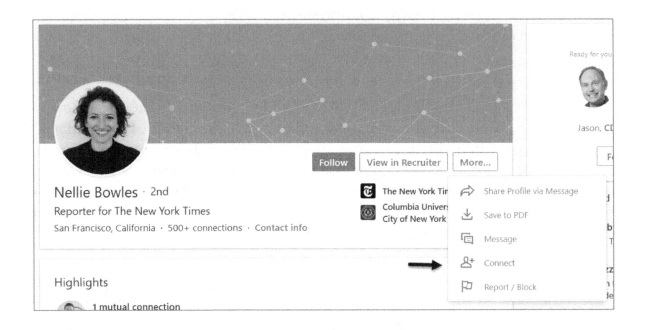

By clicking the three dots and then "connect," I can ask to be her "LinkedIn connection," as it were. People on LinkedIn, in short, are in **business networking mode** and it's OK to connect to strangers, and talk about and talk up your business, up to and including sales pitches (within polite reason). This makes it a fantastic social medium for business-to-business marketing!

## LINKEDIN IS THE 24/7 BUSINESS NETWORKING EVENT

In addition, LinkedIn **groups** are rather robust, especially in technical areas. For a technical sector such as oil and gas, for example, people increasingly use LinkedIn groups as a way to keep informed about their industry. LinkedIn's robust technical groups are thus one example of LinkedIn's focus on "lifelong learning." Another is LinkedIn's acquisition of Lynda.com and its transformation into **"LinkedIn Learning" (https://www.linkedin.com/learning/)**. This acquisition brought a robust learning platform to the network, emphasizing the growing trend to use LinkedIn as a way to stay up-to-date with industry trends and technical skills. Finally, although business Pages do exist on LinkedIn and are increasingly important for business-to-business companies, their utility is much weaker than on Facebook for business-to-consumer companies. On the other hand, the organic reach of business Pages on LinkedIn is much better as compared to Facebook.

## LinkedIn is a Team Sport

Perhaps the most important distinction is to think of Facebook as a *company-first* marketing platform and LinkedIn as an *employee-first* marketing platform. Whereas on Facebook, you can manage your marketing "top down," using your company Page as your primary customer interaction vehicle, on LinkedIn you must rely heavily on your employees. Every customer-facing employee needs to be "on board" with your LinkedIn marketing. He or she needs a robust LinkedIn profile and a passionate commitment to schmooze with other LinkedIn members through outreach, posting, and group participation. To succeed at LinkedIn as a business, each and every customer-facing employee must actively participate as an individual, and your company should manage its own LinkedIn business page in tandem. LinkedIn, in sum, is an **employee team sport**.

> ***Employee participation*** + *an active* **LinkedIn business page** = *LinkedIn marketing* **success**.

In fact, LinkedIn even has a paid service called "Elevate," that enables employee co-promotion with your business at **http://jmlinks.com/31f**.

## You = You and Your Employees on LinkedIn

Throughout this Chapter, I will often refer to an individual "you" as participating in LinkedIn, but remember when I say "you," I mean "you" as an individual as well as "you" as a team of like-minded, enthusiastic employees. If your company is one employee, five employees, or five hundred employees, the real key to LinkedIn success is to get everyone "on board" and participating! Go team!

### Search LinkedIn

First, you'll need to research LinkedIn to estimate its value to your business marketing efforts. (We'll assume you've already set up a basic personal profile on LinkedIn. If not, visit LinkedIn and sign up either via their website or their app). For your first **TO-DO**, log on to LinkedIn, and search by keywords that are relevant to your company or industry. Identify persons, groups, and companies that are active on these topics.

Simply type a keyword of interest into the search bar at the top of the LinkedIn page (e.g., "organic food" if your company is involved in the organic industry, or "oil and gas," if your company works in the petroleum industry). Then, in the scroll window select "See all results." Here's a screenshot for keyword, "petroleum:"

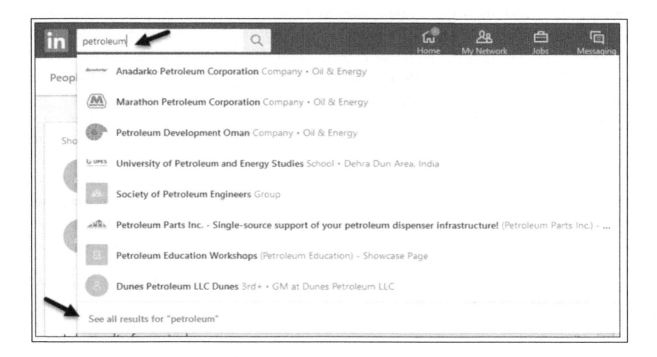

Next, across the top, you should see "People, Jobs, Content, More..." To search for people, click "people." This will get you people whose profiles and/or activity contain the target word (in this case "petroleum"). Here's a screenshot for keyword "petroleum" and then "people:"

You can then click on any person and see his or her activity. By selecting "Connections" you can narrow this down to 1st, 2nd, or 3rd level connections, and you see more information for 1st level connections, of course. (1st level connections are people who have already accepted your connection request or vice-versa, whereas 2nd level connections are connections of connections, and 3rd level are connections of connections of connections). You can also select "companies" to see companies who have the keyword in their LinkedIn Page. You can then "follow" these companies much as you would on Facebook, and you can drill into their employees as well.

Next, you can search for "posts" that contain the keyword by clicking "Content." Here's a screenshot searching for "oil and gas" content:

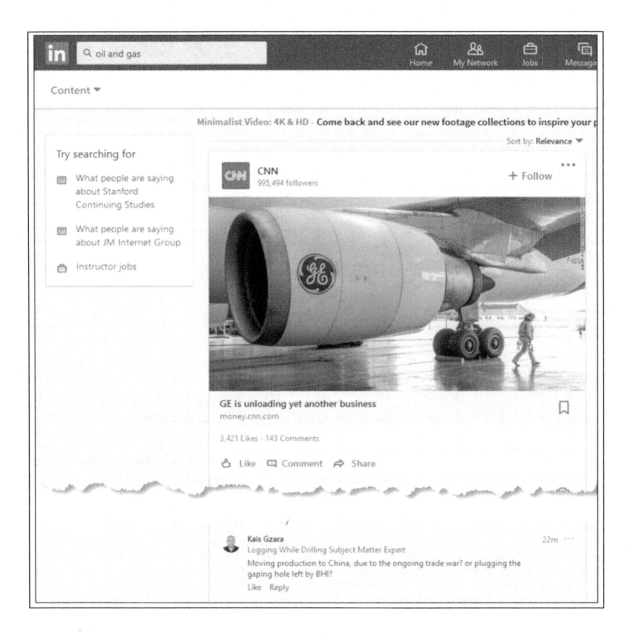

In this way, you can quickly scan who's posting what about a keyword such as "oil and gas." Pay special attention to video content, as video is the fastest-growing type of content on LinkedIn. You can also select "Groups" to see what groups exist and, again, see how active people are on a content theme.

Remember as you research LinkedIn that the center of gravity is personal profiles and posts, not so much company Pages. Don't fall into the trap of thinking it's all about company pages, even though LinkedIn advertising is (mistakenly) company-focused (because that's how they sell ads). For reference, check out the LinkedIn help center at **http://jmlinks.com/45y**.

For your first **TO-DO**, download the **LinkedIn Research Worksheet**. For the worksheet, go to **http://jmlinks.com/social2020** (then reenter the code 'social2020' to register your workbook), and click on the link to the "LinkedIn Research Worksheet." You'll answer questions as to whether your potential customers are on LinkedIn, identify individuals and companies to follow, and inventory what you like and dislike about their LinkedIn set up and marketing strategy.

## » OPTIMIZE YOUR LINKEDIN PROFILE (AND YOUR EMPLOYEES', TOO)

The **personal profile** is the foundation of LinkedIn. Just as on Facebook, an individual needs to set up a LinkedIn profile and populate it with information about him or herself. Unlike on Facebook, however, this personal profile is highly visible and acts as a kind of "public resume." As a business owner or marketer, you'll want your own well-optimized profile, but you'll also want to motivate your CEO, other key executives, and any employees that are customer-facing to set up and optimize their LinkedIn profiles. Make sure that each and every "customer-facing" employee has an optimized LinkedIn profile.

The **TO-DOS** here are:

1. **Sign up** for LinkedIn as a personal profile (and encourage everyone else in the company to sign up as well!)

2. Identify the **keywords** that represent your business value to other people, that is keywords that "describe you" as a businessperson and/or a company or non-profit, such as "WordPress web designer," "CPA," or "Business Coach for startups," or "Apple iPhone App development firm."

3. **Optimize** your personal profile so that it –

    a. Clearly and quickly represents your **personal business value proposition** as well as that of your **company**.

    b. Is **findable** via LinkedIn search by **keywords**.

    c. Establishes **trust** in you and your company as an authority and someone who is worthy of a business partnership.

First and foremost, think of **search** and **trust**. By search, we mean that people will go to Google and/or LinkedIn after they have met you or a key employee. They'll *search* you on the Internet with an eye to deciding whether you have any skeletons in your closet, whether you seem knowledgeable about your subject, and whether you seem like a good person to do business with. This trust will *flow up* to the company as well.

Nowadays, people go to networking events such as trade shows and return with business cards and email addresses. They then *vet* these people and their companies by searching for them on Google and on LinkedIn. Indeed, you can optimize your LinkedIn profile to show high on Google or Bing searches for your own name plus keywords.

> Think of your LinkedIn **profile** as your **public resume**. Think of your employees' profiles' as their **business cards** to exchange at an industry trade show.

To see my LinkedIn profile via Google search, for example, just search for "Jason McDonald social media" on Google and look for the link to LinkedIn; or simply visit **http://jmlinks.com/3g** where I have pre-built this search for you. Note that my LinkedIn profile appears in about position four on a Google search for *Jason McDonald SEO*. Here's a screenshot:

Jason McDonald - Senior SEO / Social Media Director - JM Internet ...
https://www.linkedin.com/in/jasoneg3 ▾
View Jason McDonald's profile on LinkedIn, the world's largest professional ... SEO, AdWords & Social Media Consultant & Expert Witness - San Francisco Bay ...

The concept here is when someone meets me (*or meets you, or meets a key employee*), they'll often go back to their office and "Google" you or look you up on LinkedIn before they'll reach out for a business relationship. As a marketer, you want to use LinkedIn to show prominently in a search for your name plus keywords, plus you want your LinkedIn profile to show off your expertise and talents. Just like a real (paper) resume, your LinkedIn resume (profile) should be optimized to be found and to put your best foot forward. It should also be publicly viewable without the necessity of being logged into LinkedIn.

> **Think your name plus keywords**. There are 33,000,000 results on Google for *Jason McDonald*. So people would search not just for *Jason McDonald* but for *Jason McDonald* plus keywords to check me out. *Jason McDonald SEO, Jason McDonald Social Media,* or *Jason McDonald AdWords*. Do likewise for yourself and key employees. What keywords best describe your utility to customers? Are you *Aileen Smith the Accountant, Jake Harris the Javascript Programmer,* or *Jeevan Lakshmi the Environmental Architect?*

## Optimize Everyone's LinkedIn Profiles

Now it's time to call a "group meeting" of your employee team. Have them each optimize their LinkedIn profiles vis-à-vis your target keywords and target customers. It is essential that **all** key, customer-facing employees optimize their LinkedIn profiles.

> **Remember**: *LinkedIn is a team sport: you need every employee "on board" with full and eager participation! If they're ho-hum about this, explain that this new, optimized profile will be very useful to them after they get fired for lack of enthusiasm, and they're out looking for a job! (Just kidding – now smile for your new profile picture).*

As you work with key employees, let's turn to the steps to **optimize** a LinkedIn profile for search and trust.

> **A "Helpful Expert" via Keywords.** What value do you provide for others in a business relationship? Remember: you are NOT looking for a job. Generally, you are positioning yourself as a "helpful expert" in a defined area. Are you a WordPress expert? An expert CPA for small business? An architect with a focus on eco-friendly design? Brainstorm and define the logical keywords that someone would append to your name. There are, for example, many "Jason McDonalds" in this world. But I want to rank and be trusted as the Jason McDonald that can help you with **SEO**, **Social Media**, and **Google Ads**. Thus, I embed those keywords in my profile and write it well enough to convey my value as a helpful expert in those endeavors.

> **Once you have identified your keywords, weave them strategically into your LinkedIn profile starting with the LinkedIn professional headline.**

To access these features, click on *LinkedIn > Me > View Profile* while logged in to LinkedIn. Then click on *View Profile*. Here's a screenshot:

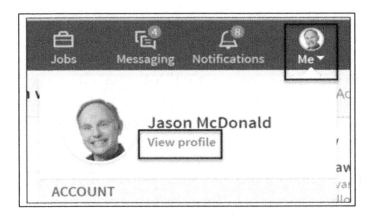

Next, hover over an area, and click on the pencil icon to edit. Here's a screenshot:

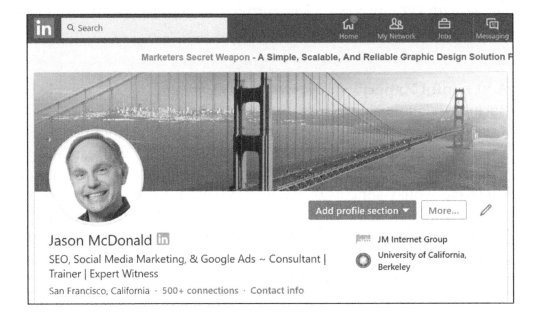

At this point, you should be in the "edit profile" section of LinkedIn. Let's go through the optimization step-by-step. (Note: some of these features may appear in a different order in your Profile than as listed below).

> **Headline.** This is the most important text on your LinkedIn profile for discoverability via search and as a quick statement of your value as a "helpful expert." It should answer the question, "What can you do for me?" Here's a screenshot of mine:

**Current (Position)**. This is your current job, so state it well.

**Country, Zip Code, Locations within this area, and Industry**. Fill out as appropriate.

**About**. Like a real resume, this describes your skills and experience. *Do NOT write this like you are looking for a job if you are NOT looking for a job!* Instead, use ALL CAPS and other ways to break up the content. Populate it with relevant keywords that people might search on LinkedIn, and make it easy to read. It should state your business value proposition succinctly. Write this "as if" you were explaining to someone at a business networking event what you do, and how this is relevant to what they might need.

**Media**. Add links to external documents, including SlideShares or YouTube videos.

*(Note: You may have to click out of "edit intro" and back into the more general "edit profile" section to access the next items).*

**Experience**. Here's where you input your current and past employment. If your company is on LinkedIn with a company page (and, of course, it should be), a logo will be available. Again, write succinct summaries of current and past employment that contain logical keywords (do not overdo this), and explain how you can help an interested party to accomplish something of business value.

**Licenses & Certifications**. List any professional certifications here. I am officially certified in Google Ads, for example, so I list that in this section.

**Education.** Don't be shy. Populate your education section with your educational achievements, not only degrees but any awards or extra-curricular activities.

**Accomplishments.** Input any languages you speak as well as certifications. I speak Klingon, fluently, so I put that here. (Humor is part of my brand, get it?)

**Interests.** LinkedIn will populate this with companies and groups you follow. So find some, and follow them.

**Add New Profile Section.** If you like, you can beef up your profile even further by adding publications, skills, honors, patents, etc. This is located on the top right in blue.

VIDEO. Watch a video tutorial on how to optimize your LinkedIn Profile (as well as that of key employees) at **http://jmlinks.com/16r.**

## A Word about Interests

At this point, we are optimizing your LinkedIn profile for **search** and **trust**. In terms of interest and groups (which you can see at the very bottom of your LinkedIn profile), therefore, you might consider joining groups not because you plan to participate in them actively but because they convey your interests and skills. For example, I am a member of both the Harvard and UC Berkeley alumni associations really just to convey that I am smart, and attended these prestigious institutions. Similarly, I am a member of Ad Age and WordPress experts groups to convey my interest and expertise in those topics. (I don't actually participate in these groups in any serious way – I'm too busy!) Think of groups like you would think of college extracurricular activities on your resume: to convey interests and skill.

Here's a screenshot of my LinkedIn "Interests," which is people I follow and groups I belong to:

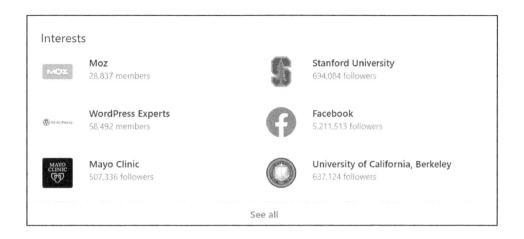

Don't I look impressive? That's the point of my personal profile – to wow potential customers that I'm smart, I'm skilled in technical things like SEO, social media marketing, and Google Ads, that I went to prestigious schools, teach for Stanford, and participate in lively groups on my areas of core competency. Is this a bit hyped up? Yes, that's the point. Explain to every employee in your company that if they don't toot their own horn, no one else will.

## Contact and Personal Info

You want to make it easy for people to contact you via LinkedIn. At this point, stay logged in to "edit profile," and click up to the very top of the page. Find the "Contact info" link and click on that. Here's a screenshot:

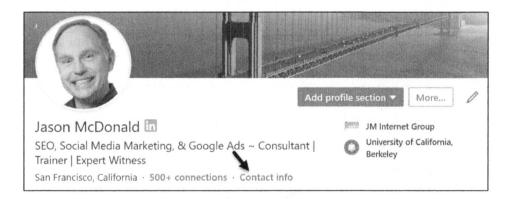

Once you click the "Contact info" link, you can then edit how to contact you. This is important as it allows connections to contact you. Click the pencil icon and edit these sections.

Here's a screenshot:

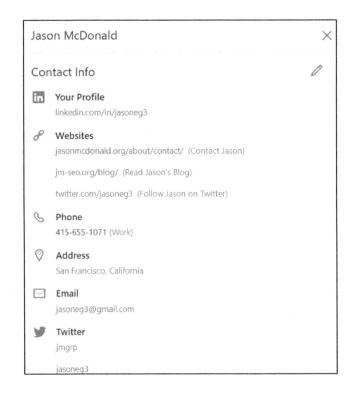

A tip here is if you select "Other" under websites, then you can write a custom caption. You can see that I've selected "Other" and then written "Contact Jason," which is a direct link to my blog's contact page. This then appears to potential contacts like this:

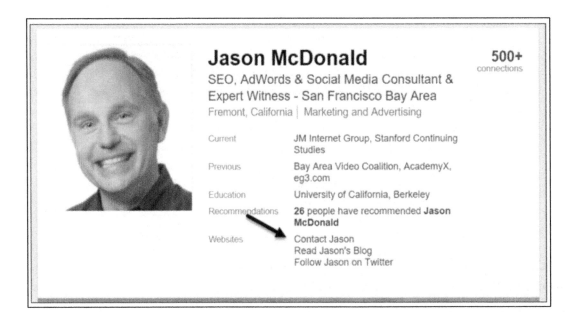

In this way, I make it easy for anyone to contact me via LinkedIn even if they are not yet a connection. Note: I would not put my physical address on LinkedIn; there's really no purpose, and there are too many crazies on the Internet. You can (and should) enter your city if you're interested in local connections. But other than that, I recommend you fill out each section.

Next, optimize your public profile and URL. To do this, click out of "edit contact info" and back up. Then on the right side, find "Edit public profile and URL." Click on that. Then click on Edit URL to edit your public URL (visible to Google). Choose something short, sweet, and stable. You do not want to change this after you select a public URL.

Next, edit your visibility settings. Generally speaking, you want to be 100% public on LinkedIn, but people often configure their visibility settings incorrectly. Click *Me > View Profile* and then on the far right, click "Edit public profile & URL" and scroll way to the very bottom until you see "Edit Visibility."

Here's a screenshot:

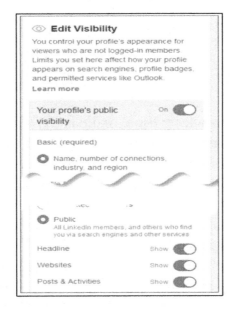

Mine is set to **Public**, meaning outsiders can see my information. I also have selected "show" for all the features. Generally, most of us want to be highly visible on LinkedIn, so I recommend setting ALL these elements to "show." An exception might be a very prestigious CEO or venture capitalist, who only wants to be visible to their LinkedIn connections. But most customer-facing employees should be visible to everyone. Note, however, that only 1st degree connections can see your contact information such as your email address or phone number, which is why under "contact info," I recommend you include links to your public blog, website, or contact page as well as your Twitter handle, as these are visible to all people on LinkedIn, regardless of their connection level.

Finally, if you scroll to the very bottom and click on "Public Profile Badge," LinkedIn will give you the HTML code so that you can put a direct link on your personal blog, company website, etc., to your LinkedIn profile. This is great for cross-fertilization, and to establish yourself as a "helpful expert" on other venues. Here's a screenshot:

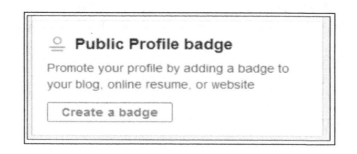

**A word about privacy.** For most of us, we want to be highly **visible** *(non-private)* on LinkedIn. We want potential customers, friends, and business associates to find us easily. Therefore, set your public profile as "visible to everyone," and check all of the boxes below. *If, for some reason, you do NOT want to be publicly visible on LinkedIn, then set the visibility and checkboxes accordingly.*

One of the more common mistakes people make is to think of the LinkedIn profile like the Facebook profile. Whereas on Facebook, you often want to be *invisible / private* to strangers, on LinkedIn you often want to be *visible / public* to strangers. Accordingly, setting your LinkedIn to *private* defeats the purposes of search and trust as part of your LinkedIn marketing.

For most people, therefore, I recommend that they set LinkedIn to fully *visible / public*.

# GENERALLY, LINKEDIN IS *PUBLIC* PROFILE & *PUBLIC* COMPANY, WHILE FACEBOOK IS *PRIVATE* PROFILE & *PUBLIC* COMPANY

At that point, you're done with populating and optimizing your LinkedIn profile for **search** and **trust**. Congratulate yourself and your employee team: you've optimized your LinkedIn public resumes!

For your second **To-do**, download the **LinkedIn Profile Worksheet**. For the worksheet, go to **http://jmlinks.com/social2020** (then reenter the code 'social2020' to register your workbook), and click on the link to the "LinkedIn Profile Worksheet." You'll answer questions to help you set up and optimize your LinkedIn Profile.

## Skills, Endorsements, and Recommendations

While building out your profile, you'll notice that some people have many **skills, endorsements**, and **recommendations** on LinkedIn. Like references for a resume, these are generally all positive. Here's a screenshot of my skills and endorsements:

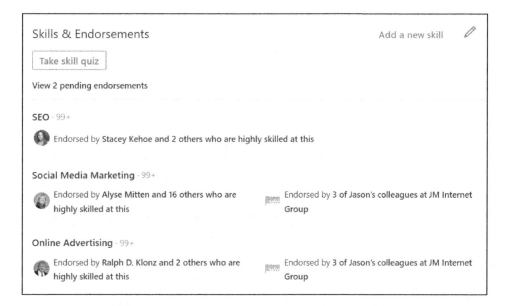

If you want to be endorsed for a new skill, click "Add a new skill." LinkedIn will prompt your connections to endorse you for this and all your skills, so over time, you'll build up a bunch of endorsements. Note: new for 2020, LinkedIn has added "Take skill quiz" as an option. In certain technical areas, you can take a test, pass it, and then show a badge on your profile.

Next, take a look at **recommendations**. Here's a screenshot:

*Note: you control whether recommendations show on your public profile; you can suppress any you do not like.* In both cases, your LinkedIn connections are endorsing or recommending you, thus giving you social clout that you're an expert in a given area.

## Solicit Recommendations and Endorsements

Your **TO-DO** here is to ask for recommendations and endorsements from friends, coworkers, and business colleagues. One of the best ways to get them is to do them for other people pro-actively. After completing a project with an outside vendor, for example, connect to that person on LinkedIn and write him or her a glowing recommendation and endorsement. Often, they will reciprocate. *(This is called "pre-emptive" recommendations in LinkedIn lingo.)* You can also click on the "Ask for a recommendation" and follow the prompts to ask a LinkedIn connection for a recommendation. And if you click the "pencil" icon, you can reorganize how your recommendations appear.

Regardless of how you solicit them, getting many positive recommendations and endorsements will make your LinkedIn profile shine.

## » SCHMOOZING ON LINKEDIN: YOUR SOCIAL ROLODEX

Nearly everyone needs an optimized personal profile on LinkedIn, if for no other purpose than job search. For those whose job is "client or customer-facing," meaning identifying, interacting, and schmoozing with potential clients, the primary purpose of LinkedIn is to *schmooze*. (Schmoozing, of course, is another word for business networking: expanding your circle of business contacts, nurturing their respect for you, and keeping top of mind so that when they have a business opportunity, they think of you).

By nurturing your 1ˢᵗ level contacts and being active on LinkedIn, you can use LinkedIn as your online social rolodex, extending beyond just people you actually know to people you'd like to know for your business needs. Let's investigate schmoozing on LinkedIn, namely:

**1ˢᵗ level contacts**: these are people who have accepted your connection requests.

**2ⁿᵈ level contacts**: these are 1ˢᵗ level contacts of your 1ˢᵗ level contacts (*friends of friends*, as it were).

**3ʳᵈ level contacts:** these are contacts of contacts of contacts.

### LinkedIn Connections: What's Your Bacon Number?

Your "Bacon number" is a term coined to humorously point out that nearly everyone on the planet is connected to actor Kevin Bacon. Cher, for example, has a Bacon number of two because she and Jack Nicholson appeared in *The Witches of Eastwick*, and Jack Nicholson and Kevin Bacon appeared in *A Few Good Men*.

So Cher is a 1ˢᵗ level connection with Jack Nicholson and a 2ⁿᵈ level connection with Kevin Bacon. (*Which means that my Bacon Number is a four because my Mom knows Cher, Cher knows Jack Nicholson, and Jack Nicholson knows Kevin Bacon*).

How does the Bacon number concept relate to LinkedIn? LinkedIn uses the same system universally: you can *direct message* or *see the email* of your 1ˢᵗ level connections, and you can see through your 1ˢᵗ level connections to your 2ⁿᵈ level, for example:

Cher can message via LinkedIn or email Jack Nicholson, directly. (1ˢᵗ level).

Cher can "see" that Jack Nicholson is connected to Kevin Bacon, and ask Jack to "introduce" her to Kevin, or at least mention that she "knows" Jack Nicholson (2ⁿᵈ level).

Unlike on Facebook, you can easily see your 2ⁿᵈ or 3ʳᵈ level connections on LinkedIn. To see your 1ˢᵗ or 2ⁿᵈ level connections, just hit the search bar with a "blank search." Then select "People" and then 1ˢᵗ or 2ⁿᵈ to see your connections by level. In this way, I can see that I have 4,540 first level connections, and 1.7 million (!) 2ⁿᵈ level connections (connections of connections). To browse 3ʳᵈ level connections, the easiest thing to do is to type a keyword into the search bar such as "accounting" or "WordPress," click search, then *People > 3rd+*. You can communicate with each level in different ways.

## 1st Level Connections

1st level connections are the best. You can directly message / find the email of anyone who is your 1st level connection. To do so, simply search on LinkedIn for the name of someone with whom you are already connected. Then:

> Click on the **blue** "Message" box. This sends them a message via LinkedIn, and in most cases, will also send them an email alert that they have a message waiting on LinkedIn.
>
> or –
>
> Click into an individual person and then click on the "**Contact info**" tab, and you can view their email address, phone number, and address.

Or, let's assume you're trying to find a connection that has a particular interest or skill. Rather than typing a person's name into the search box, type a keyword / keyphrase such as "WordPress," or "Joomla," or "Accountant for small business" and hit search. Across the top, click on "People." Then on the far right, you can filter by 1st, 2nd, or 3rd level connection plus additional keywords. Filter for 1st level connections.

Here's a screenshot:

Check the box marked "1ˢᵗ," and then you can search your 1ˢᵗ level LinkedIn connections by keywords, as in this example for those 1ˢᵗ level connections I have who indicate "WordPress" in their profiles. LinkedIn also has more advanced filters, which you can get to by clicking the "All filters" button at the top right.

Essentially, you are able to use LinkedIn as a searchable rolodex of 1ˢᵗ level business contacts: define what type of person you want to contact (or prospect), search for them, and reach out directly. In this way, LinkedIn is like a huge virtual rolodex to organize and manage your business contacts.

# HAVE A REASON OR "CARROT" TO CONNECT

Just as you would in the real world, remember that you need a reason to be contacting them, some type of "carrot" or "bait" to start a conversation. Perhaps your business has a new webinar or eBook, perhaps you're going to be at a real-world trade show and want to invite them to a wine and cheese event, perhaps you're going to be in their city and want to stop by and say hello. You need a reason why you're reaching out, and that reason shouldn't be a shameless just "by your stuff" type of reason.

### Working with 2ⁿᵈ Level Connections

While you can direct message (send emails or see the email addresses of) 1ˢᵗ level connections, this is not true of 2ⁿᵈ level connections (who are the 1ˢᵗ level connections of your 1ˢᵗ level connections). You can find 2ⁿᵈ level connections by the same process of search (either by name or by keyword). You can then view their profile and click the "connect" button to ask for a connection. For example, here's a screenshot of a 2ⁿᵈ level connection for me, Catherine Stewart who works at WordPress.com:

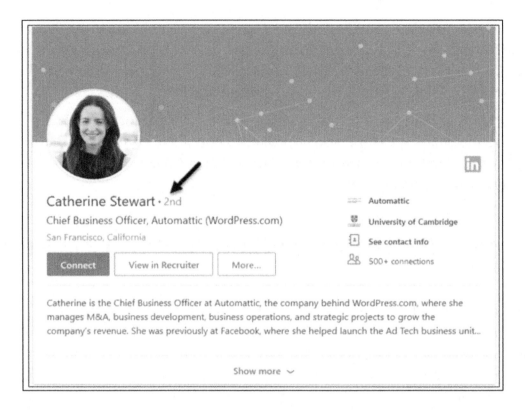

I can also see just below this my 1$^{st}$ level connections that know Catherine. So, if – for point of argument – I know John Doe, who knows Catherine, then I could reach out to John, first, and ask him if he is OK with me mentioning his name, and then I can message Catherine and mention I know John. To do that, I click on the blue "Connect" button, and then the "Add a note" feature to send a custom message:

In this way, Catherine is more likely to accept my request to connect. Alternatively, of course, I could just mention that I met Catherine at a trade conference or have some other reason why we should connect. She'll also be able to see that we're connected through 1$^{st}$ level connections, so she's pretty likely to accept. Indeed, most people are on LinkedIn to network, so they're likely to accept connection requests if they seem professional and relevant. Just don't spam out connection requests or you'll get banned from the platform.

Another technique to grow your connections is to:

1. Search LinkedIn by keyword, such as "marketing managers" or "WordPress designers" or "small business owners."

2. Identify 2nd level connections, and request connections based on some type of relevancy.

3. Be sure to have a "reason" for the connection such as a shared interest, or perhaps a content "carrot" such as an upcoming webinar, new book, participation at a trade show, etc.

Note if you use this process, you'll be able to see 1st level connections (of course), and for 2nd level connections, you'll be able to see and use the blue "Connect" button. For 3rd level (or greater than 3rd) connections, LinkedIn removes the blue "Connect" button, and you have to click into the three dots and then connect. Here's a screenshot:

You can try a connection request (though since you have no connections in common, they might be suspicious). Just be sure to have a reason why you are relevant to them as a connection. In some cases you'll be required to know the email of the person with whom you want to connect; thus, always be on the lookout for the emails of potential clients. Many people list their email addresses on their business cards, so business cards retain a lot of usefulness.

Sometimes you will NOT see the "connect" option, so you have to try some non-LinkedIn method to get to this person. In this scenario, then, you can:

1. Upgrade your LinkedIn account to a paid account and use InMail to reach out to this person.

2. Click on their "contact info," and if they have a Twitter account, you can reach out via Twitter.

3. Take their name and some pertinent information, Google them and reach out via their blog or website.

For example, here's a screenshot of a 3<sup>rd</sup> level, person who has inputted his contact info:

Remy DeCausemaker                                    ✕

Contact Info

🔗 Remy's Profile
   linkedin.com/in/decause

🔗 Websites
   opensource.com/users/remyd  (Opensource.com)

   foss.rit.edu  (FOSS at RIT)

   decausemaker.org  (Blog)

🐦 Twitter
   Remy_D

In this way, I can start the relationship "off" of LinkedIn and then once we know each other in some fashion, send a connection request which is more likely to be accepted. Most people are pretty open, however, and in my experience generally accept connection request even if they are "out of the blue."

You can mix and match job titles and keywords. I often search for "professor" (a job title) and then "social media marketing" (a keyword phrase) to identify professors who may be teaching marketing courses and are interested in assigning my book. Then, I look for 1ˢᵗ, 2ⁿᵈ, and 3ʳᵈ level connections. If we're not connected, then I send a custom message such as this:

You can customize this invitation ✕

Include a personal message (optional):

Hi Ms. Lee,
I noticed you are a professor teaching social media marketing. I have a very popular book on it called the Social Media Marketing Workbook, and I am promoting "review copies," so I'd love to connect. If you want a review copy, message me back. ~ Jason McDonald                                          28

Cancel    Send invitation

In your case, then you have these steps:

1. Identify by searching by keyword and/or job title, potential LinkedIn connections.

2. Click the "connect" button (if available).

3. Have a reason why they should connect to you for your personalized note.

**Working with Connections**

As you build up your connections, you want to think about reasons why they would like to connect to you. "What's in it for them" is always the question to ask when reaching out on social media.

Here's a typical LinkedIn scenario for 1ˢᵗ and 2ⁿᵈ level connections.

Let's suppose you are the sale manager for a company in the Proteomics industry. (*Proteomics is the large-scale study of proteins and is used heavily in industry to analyze organic materials*). You're going to "Proteomics World" in Boston, and you'll be introducing your new "Proteomics 2020 widget" product to the industry. You are planning on having one of those fun-filled wine and cheese parties, where your company will roll out the red carpet with free food and wine, and in exchange, attendees will be updated on your new "Proteomics 2020 widget." It's a business meeting with a little fun, a little free food and drink, and some salesy information about your new widget.

Your job is to get people to attend. You go to LinkedIn and search for:

*Proteomics*

*Check: People*

*Check: 1ˢᵗ level*

*(You also select Locations > Greater Boston area, as the show is in Boston).*

You can direct message all of these 1ˢᵗ level people and invite them to the wine and cheese event. Remember: social media is a *party*, not a *prison*, and in terms of content you have something *fun* and *interesting*: your *wine and cheese event.*

Next, do your search by keyword, filter for 2ⁿᵈ level connections. Find a connection that interests you, and click on his or her name. When LinkedIn asks you for a custom note, explain that you'll be at Proteomics world in Boston and you'd like to invite them to your wine and cheese event. They'll be likely to accept because it's relevant and sounds fun. You can do this as well for 3ʳᵈ level connections.

Once your 2ⁿᵈ or 3ʳᵈ levels accept your connection request, then they become 1ˢᵗ level connections, and you can directly message them via LinkedIn. Thus the circle of schmoozing continues…

Alternatively, you can send an InMail (see **http://jmlinks.com/3m**) with a paid account, but it's probably more effective to reach out for connections directly. After all, people trust people they know more than a "cold" call or a "cold" InMail / email.

*It's not what you know (in business). It's who you know.*

The bottom line, therefore, is to use your 1ˢᵗ level connections to get to your 2ⁿᵈ levels, and the **TO-DO** for LinkedIn is to be expanding your 1st level network constantly, but how?

**VIDEO.** Watch a video tutorial on how to work with 1ˢᵗ and 2ⁿᵈ level connections on LinkedIn at **http://jmlinks.com/16s**.

## How to Expand Your LinkedIn Connections

If having many connections is the name of the game on LinkedIn, how do you grow your connections? Here are some strategies:

**Ask.** Continually ask every business person you meet for their email, and then look them up on LinkedIn. Next, click the Connect button and then fill out the information as indicated (you'll need their email and then write a note as to how you met them). I recommend customizing your personal notes, such as *"Hi Sallie! You and I met at Proteomics world last week, and I'd like to connect with you on LinkedIn."* If she accepts, she becomes a 1ˢᵗ level connection.

> **No Spamming.** Do not overly aggressively contact people you do not know because spamming LinkedIn can lead your account to be deactivated.
>
> **Lifetime Limit.** Be aware of the lifetime limit of 3000 invitation requests and 30,000 total connections, designed to prevent connection spamming.

**Reach out to People Who Viewed Your Profile.** Over time, people will "check you out" on LinkedIn. LinkedIn monitors who viewed your profile. Even at the free account level, and even more with a premium account, you can see who looked at your profile and then reach out to them with a connection request, explaining, "Hey, I see you looked at my profile. Let's connect!" To see who viewed your profile, go to *LinkedIn > Me > Who Viewed Your Profile*. If you don't see it there, go home to your LinkedIn feed and then on the far left look for "Who's viewed your profile" or just visit **http://jmlinks.com/46d**.

**Get People to Ask You.** Even better than asking people to connect to you, is to get them to ask you. Ideas for this would be:

- **Real World to LinkedIn**. If you give a presentation at a trade show, ask attendees to connect with you on LinkedIn. Include LinkedIn on your business cards, and literally mention LinkedIn when you meet business associates in real life.

- **Your Website or Blog**. Place the LinkedIn icon on your website or blog, and encourage visitors to connect. (To generate a personalized

LinkedIn badge, click on *Me > View Profile > Edit public profile & URL* and scroll to the very bottom ).

- **Other Social Media**. Connect your LinkedIn to your Twitter, Facebook, blog, etc., and encourage people who already follow you on Twitter, for example, to connect with you on LinkedIn. If you have an email list, ask people to connect with you by emailing them.

**Uploading Your Contacts**. LinkedIn is happy to scour your email connections directly. To do this, click on *My Network*, and then on the left, find the icon that says, "Some of your contacts aren't connected with you on LinkedIn - Connect with them and never lose touch." If you also have the email address of potential connections, you can allow LinkedIn to look at your email contacts and then match you with potential connections.

To do this:

1. Click on "My Network."

2. On the left, click under "more options" under "your connections."

3. It will then prompt you with icons for Gmail, Yahoo, Outlook etc., or you can upload an email address file (such as a customer list).

    i. You'll then get a visual prompt of potential connections, and you can check or uncheck the persons you want to send connections requests to. Again, be careful not to be spammy with this.

You can read the help file on importing email addresses into LinkedIn at **http://jmlinks.com/53h**.

The bottom line for you and your team is to do everything you can to encourage business contacts to connect with you on LinkedIn, because the more you grow your 1st level contacts, the more you can directly connect to them, and the more you can use them as introductions to their 1st level contacts, i.e., your 2nd level contacts. *Schmooze, schmooze, schmooze* to grow your LinkedIn network!

**With Whom Should You Connect?**

There are different strategies in terms of reaching out, or accepting, the connection requests of others on LinkedIn. There is no right answer. For someone who is customer-facing (e.g., sales), he or she should probably accept every inbound request. For someone who is a venture capitalist, he or she might accept requests only from people they really know. Another strategy is only to accept requests from people for whom you'd actually do a favor in real life. I generally accept everyone who wants to connect with me, and then if they start spamming me with messages, I disconnect from them. Typical connection strategies are thus:

- Connect with everyone who sends you a connection request, regardless of whether you know them or not. Then unconnect if they spam you.

- Connect only with people you actually have met in real life or some capacity, as for example, people you've met at a trade show or know via a LinkedIn group.

- Connect only with people you actually know in real life, like coworkers, people at customer companies you've done projects with, etc.

- Connect very selectively, like only with people who are very close business connections. (A venture capitalist or CEO might use this strategy).

- Connect only with people who would help you move, or connect only with people who will help you move bodies. I'm just kidding of course, but you can be very selective if you "have the money" or "have the influence" and are more the recipient of requests than the sender. A famous venture capitalist with a  bag of money, for example, can be very choosy. A newly hired sales guy at a tech firm, not so much.

There's no right or wrong answer.

## Are Paid LinkedIn Accounts Worth It?

Unless you are an active recruiter, an active job seeker, or an outbound salesperson actively "cold calling" or prospecting, I do not generally recommend paid LinkedIn accounts. The main advantages of a paid LinkedIn account (of which there are several types) are:

- Enhanced cosmetics for your profile, such as a larger photo and the prestige of a "premium" account;

- Ability to turn on "LinkedIn Open Profile," which allows ANYONE to message you via LinkedIn regardless of whether they are 1st, 2nd, or 3rd level connections. To learn more, visit **http://jmlinks.com/53f**.

- Better positioning when applying for a job;

- Access to everyone who's viewed your profile in the last 90 days;

- Ability to see 3rd degree profiles;

- Additional search filters, and the ability to filter and save search results (great for sales prospectors);

- Learning Resources via LinkedIn learning.

- Up to 15-30 InMails per month to directly contact anyone on LinkedIn, even if you are not connected; and/or (depending on the package you get)

- More detailed analytics.

To learn more about LinkedIn Premium, visit **https://premium.linkedin.com/**.

Your **TO-DO** here is to brainstorm a logical connection philosophy. If your purpose on LinkedIn is to use it for customer outreach and heavy schmoozing, then connecting with anyone or everyone makes sense. If your purpose is more passive or more secretive, perhaps just using LinkedIn as a public resume, and/or to keep up-to-date on industry trends, then connecting only with real-world connections makes sense. Remember: once you accept a connection request, you become a 1st level connection, meaning that person can directly contact you via LinkedIn and email, as well as see your contact information. Similarly, he or she can see your 2nd level connections (unless you block that in settings). So, if you need to be more secretive, then be more judicious about with whom you connect. If not, not. There is no right or wrong connection strategy: just pre-think a strategy that makes sense for your marketing objectives.

And, remember, it's not just about "you," it's about "you" and "your team." LinkedIn is a team networking sport at the corporate or business level!

### Brainstorming a Schmoozing Strategy

For your third **TO-DO**, download the **LinkedIn Schmoozing Worksheet**. For the worksheet, go to **http://jmlinks.com/social2020** (then reenter the code '**social2020**' to register your workbook), and click on the link to the "LinkedIn Schmoozing

Worksheet." You'll brainstorm your strategy for growing your LinkedIn connections. (Remember to do this with each and every customer-facing employee).

## » BE ACTIVE ON LINKEDIN: POSTS, ARTICLES, AND VIDEO

In the real world of business, it's a truism of marketing that you need to "look active." People respect people who are involved and engaged and look down on people who seem to be doing nothing. Similarly, on LinkedIn, it is important to present at least the appearance of activity. By being active, you "look active" (a **trust** indicator) plus you have new ways to reach out to prospects and customers to stay top-of-mind and generate business inquiries.

Posting frequently – posts, articles, and video – as well as being active in LinkedIn groups, in short: a) makes you seem active (and therefore trustworthy), and b) gives you more opportunities to be top of mind among prospects, thereby increasing opportunities for connections and business engagements. Just as at a business networking event, be active and engaged in a serious way. Participation is important!

**Remember**: LinkedIn is a team sport, and only individuals can post to their own accounts. Getting employees to post and be active is yet another example of why getting all your customer-facing employees "on board" is a key element of LinkedIn success.

### LinkedIn Content

You want to distinguish the possible pieces of content you can post to your profile on LinkedIn (we'll cover company Pages in a moment). These are:

**Text**. As on Facebook, you can literally just log in to LinkedIn and share an idea or thought, such as, "It's Monday! And I am super psyched because Monday means the start of my work week!"

**Photos**. You can upload a photo with or without some text. Imagine taking a picture of your lead salesperson at your booth at the Consumer Electronics Show.

**Videos**. LinkedIn has gone "all in" on video and is favoring "native" video uploaded to the platform. You can also post a link and summary to a YouTube or Vimeo video.

**Articles**. Formerly called LinkedIn *Pulse*, you can write a long-form piece to LinkedIn's native blog platform.

As on Facebook and other networks, you can (and should) include *#hashtags* in your post. LinkedIn has worked hard to increase the use of hashtags on the network, as it tries to be not just the place to search for jobs but the place for industry updates and continuing education.

Let's review LinkedIn Content one-by-one.

## Texts and Photos

This is the easiest to understand. When you log in to LinkedIn, you'll see a box with "Start a post," and to the right of that, icons for a photo, a video, or a document (which allows you to upload a PDF, for instance.). Just start typing and share a thought. If you want to include an image, just click the image box / camera icon and upload a photo from your phone or desktop. Here's a screenshot:

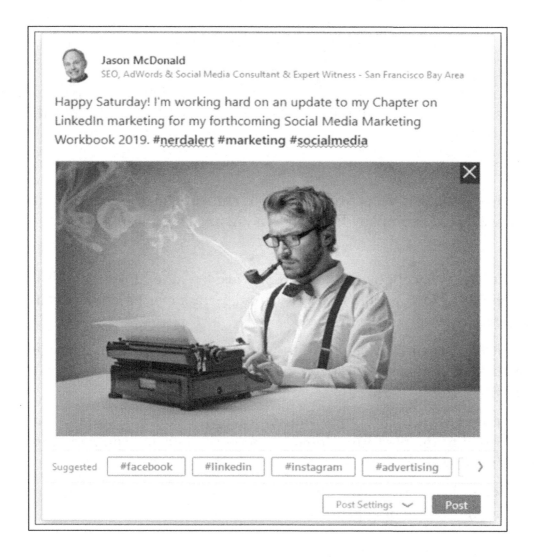

At the top, click on the downwards icon under "Anyone," and LinkedIn gives you options such as to share to the public, to only people connected to you, and to public + Twitter (if you attached Twitter to your account). The hashtags then become clickable and discoverable across LinkedIn.

You can also include a **link** to an external resource (such as your blog, your book on Amazon, or a landing page on your website). LinkedIn will automatically shorten the URL for you, which is pretty neat. Once you make a post, you can then click to *Me > Post and Activities*, and you can get data on how many likes, comments, and shares your posts are getting. Here's a screenshot of a post by me with some data:

This means it got 131 views, 7 likes, and 1 comment. Thus you can measure your posts (and the posts of your employee team members) to see what type of content is being favored by the LinkedIn algorithm and getting the most engagement. Remember: just as on Facebook, if you share a *post* to your profile and I am a 1ˢᵗ level connection, then that *post* has a good chance of showing in my *news feed*. The news feed on LinkedIn is the first content that greets a person when he or she logs in.

**Content** is king, and queen, and jack on LinkedIn as on all social media. Turn back to your Content Marketing plan, and remember you'll need both other people's content and your own content to share on LinkedIn as *posts* or as *articles* to LinkedIn (more on articles in a moment). But first, here are some ideas of what you can share as *posts* to LinkedIn:

- **Blog Post Summaries**. To the extent that you have an active blog and are posting items that fit with LinkedIn's professional focus, post headlines, short summaries and links to your blog.

  o Note that the first or "featured" image will become the shareable image and that the META DESCRIPTION will become the default description when sharing. Choose striking, fun images for your blog posts!

- **Quotes**. People love quotes, and taking memorable quotes (on business themes) and pasting them on graphics is a win/win.

- **Comments and Engagements on Industry Items**. Identify, comment, and share items that are relevant to your industry, and especially to the interests of your target customers. Be that "helpful expert" on LinkedIn that people turn to for what's happening.

- **Infographics and Instructographics**. Factoids, how to articles, top ten lists, 7 things you didn't know lists, especially ones that are fun yet useful, are excellent for LinkedIn.

- **Quizzes, Surveys, and Response-provoking posts**. Ask a question, and get an answer or more. Great for encouraging interactivity, especially when the interaction is business-oriented. A great idea is to mention a project you are working on, and ask for feedback before, during, or after.

Turn to the content marketing section of the *Marketing Almanac* for a list of tools that will help you find other people's content and create your own. I recommend Hootsuite (**https://www.hootsuite.com/**) to manage all your social postings across platforms. I recommend Feedly (**http://www.feedly.com/**) as a way to organize industry blogs and the content of other people so that you can be a useful sharer of third-party information on LinkedIn.

## Articles

One opportunity not to be missed on LinkedIn in terms of posting is articles on LinkedIn, formerly called *Pulse*. LinkedIn is aggressively trying to grow its role not only for job seekers but for the fully employed. (Check out LinkedIn learning at **https://www.linkedin.com/learning/**, and you can even apply to be an instructor at **http://jmlinks.com/46f**, which is a great way to showcase your talents as a "helpful expert" on LinkedIn.)

Let's return, however, to articles. *Articles* post to LinkedIn's internal blog, and anyone (including you) can easily post an *article*. Be sure to get the LinkedIn lingo: a *post* is when you share something external to LinkedIn such as a link to a blog post on your company blog, whereas an *article* is when you write (and share) something to LinkedIn's *internal* blogging platform.

To get started, search for articles posted to LinkedIn that are relevant to your social media keywords and themes. LinkedIn, unfortunately, doesn't have a very good way to search for articles. So go to Google and type in:

*site:linkedin.com/pulse {keyword}*

as for example:

*site:linkedin.com/pulse petroleum*

You can also use the "Tools" menu on Google at the far right and filter for articles posted in the last year or month. To check out a sample search, visit **http://jmlinks.com/45z.**

In this way, you can find native articles to LinkedIn posted by persons in your industry. For example, here's a post entitled, "Swimming upstream in a down market: tips for new petroleum engineers" at **http://jmlinks.com/46a.** And here's a screenshot showing it received 225 thumbs up, 12 comments, and 54 shares:

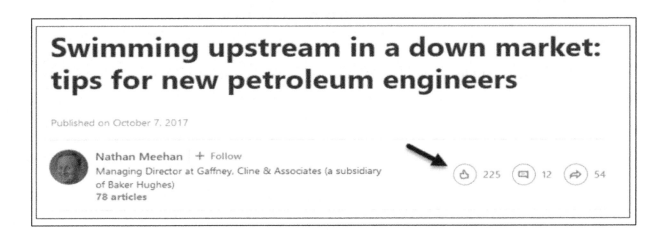

You can also click on the author's name (Nathan Meehan) and even "follow" him, which is not the same as connecting. You can now "follow" people on LinkedIn in a public way, which is akin to following them on Twitter or on Medium (**https://medium.com/**) which are 100% public platforms. The difference between following and connecting is that in the former, you see their posts in your newsfeed but they do not see yours; in the latter, both of you see each other's posts.

In this way you can research what's being published on LinkedIn that's getting engagement in your industry, follow "competitive" people on LinkedIn, and stay competitive yourself.

As you brainstorm topics to write your own *articles* for LinkedIn, here are the steps:

1. **Identify a topic** that will interest your prospects and customers, such as an industry trend or a common "pain point" in your industry or more generally in business. Pay attention to trending topics that appear at the far right when you log in to LinkedIn, or search by keyword in your industry. The "trend is your friend," so to speak.

2. **Brainstorm and identify keywords** using tools like Google suggest, Ubersuggest, or Answer the Public. (See **http://jmlinks.com/smmdash**, keyword search for these tools). Pay attention to what's trending on LinkedIn and which authors are getting engagement in your industry and why.

3. **Write a strong article with a great headline**, catchy first paragraph, and some substantial content that will be useful to readers and position you as a "helpful expert."

4. **Tag your article with relevant tags and use hashtags** – these influence whether your article will show in their news feed and/or relevant searches.

Inside of LinkedIn, articles live under the icon "Write an article." Here's a screenshot:

To write an article, just click on the "Write an article" and start writing. LinkedIn is very keen to promote articles. What with its acquisition of Lynda.com and now being owned by Microsoft, LinkedIn is trying to grow beyond job search to be more a site for "lifetime professional learning." Piggyback on this trend, and LinkedIn will promote your articles not only to your own connections but even to people you do not know. For this reason, articles on LinkedIn is a great promotion strategy!

For example, you can see a LinkedIn article by me on "United Breaks Noses: What United's Latest Really, Bad Day Teaches about Social Media Marketing" at **http://jmlinks.com/31h**. If you are the article owner, LinkedIn will also show you nifty metrics on who viewed the article and what types of people they were. Here's a screenshot:

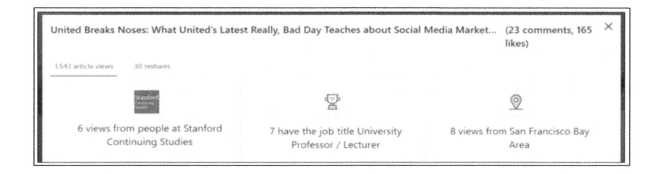

This means that it got 1,543 views, 23 comments, 165 likes, and 30 shares – proof that if you hit a good trending topic, LinkedIn will promote your articles pretty wide and far.

## Articles Reach Beyond Your Connections

LinkedIn articles also allow individuals with whom you are NOT 1st level connections on LinkedIn to "follow you." Even better, when you share your LinkedIn article on other social networks (e.g., Twitter, Facebook, Pinterest) and encourage people to cross over to LinkedIn, LinkedIn monitors this activity. If you get enough momentum, an article can "go viral," and really supercharge your LinkedIn connections.

LinkedIn's own marketing team is keen to promote articles, so if you've written something substantial, be sure to tweet your articles to LinkedIn Marketing at **https://twitter.com/LinkedInMktg**. In summary, mix posts to LinkedIn from your own blog, content from others, and native articles on your LinkedIn timeline.

## Video

LinkedIn has gone all-in on video and now allows native video by both profiles and pages. In fact, rumor has it that their algorithm favors "native" video over posts that link to competitors YouTube, Vimeo, or Facebook.

It's not hard to post a video, either on the phone or by uploading on your computer. The hard part is creating the video. Just as with any content, brainstorm:

- **Your target audience**. What do they want to watch and why?

- **The content itself**. For a video, storyboard or at least outline what you're going to talk about in your video.

- **The technical aspects**. Fortunately, LinkedIn video need not be technologically spectacular. It's more important that it be authentic and useful to your audience than slick and Hollywoodesque.

Many videos on LinkedIn are commentary on industry events; a common type is a person at an industry show, sharing his or her perspective on "goings-on" at the show. To upload a video, just click on "video" on either the mobile app or desktop and upload. Note that the upload can be very slow, so do not close the browser window before it's uploaded. To view the help file about LinkedIn video visit **http://jmlinks.com/46b**.

**Tip**: once you post a video to LinkedIn, find it in your feed and click the three dots top right and find the "share link:"

Copy that link and save it somewhere because once your feed ages, it can be very difficult to find your video posts. You can also embed the post on your website or blog as you do with a YouTube video. To see an example, check out this video from leading LinkedIn guru Viveka von Rosen at **http://jmlinks.com/46c**. As far as I know, there is no way to search for "native videos" on LinkedIn, but you can try search content for "video" plus your keywords as in "video organic" and then browsing to see which video is native.

### How frequently should you post?

Now that the LinkedIn news feed is very crowded (and the reality is that only a few people outside of job seekers and outbound marketers check their feed daily), you can safely share posts and/or articles quite frequently, even several times a day. But this differs with your audience, so pay attention to your shares, by monitoring thumbs up and comments (*for LinkedIn posts*) and stats (*for articles*). Your goal is to be interesting, informative, useful, and friendly as trust indicators and hopefully get social spread among your LinkedIn connections, especially via articles. Note that you can see who responded to your posts, and this gives you an opportunity to connect with them. Finally, an *article* should be a more thoughtful, in-depth piece of content vs. a *post* to LinkedIn which can be short and simple, as simple as just your thoughts on something trending in your industry or a short headline and link to an interesting article written by someone else.

## Create a LinkedIn Posting Plan

For your fourth **TO-DO**, download the **LinkedIn Posting Worksheet**. Sit down with your team and work together for a plan, as a company, and a plan, for each key employee. For the worksheet, go to **http://jmlinks.com/social2020** (then reenter the code '**social2020**' to register your workbook), and click on the link to the "LinkedIn Posting Worksheet." You'll create a systematic plan for posts to LinkedIn, both your own content and the content of others.

As much as it is fun and easy to post, the reality of LinkedIn today is that outside of job seekers, not everybody checks LinkedIn on a daily or even weekly basis. So while frequently posting to LinkedIn is a good idea, recognize that LinkedIn does not have the sheer volume of Facebook in terms of active engagement. Keep that in mind when you measure the ROI of posting to LinkedIn.

> **VIDEO.** Watch a video tutorial on how to share posts and articles on LinkedIn at **http://jmlinks.com/16t**.

## ≫ BE ACTIVE ON LINKEDIN: CONNECTIONS, COMMENTS, AND GROUPS

Interactivity is where it's "at" on LinkedIn, so get your team to interact with their connections and followers on LinkedIn. Let's review some of the interactive opportunities on LinkedIn to stay top of mind with customers and prospects.

## Connections and Comments

When you log in to LinkedIn, you'll see your news feed. LinkedIn prioritizes content by your connections, so you'll generally see content posted by connections first. This is a good opportunity to scan new content quickly and then like, comment, and share.

Note that when you do, LinkedIn will notify the person who created this content. For example, here's a post by Christian Terry about Facebook memes and he's asking for comments. When I wrote mine, this means that he'll get a notification as well as will people to whom I am connected. My interactivity pays off by helping me to stay top of mind with everyone I'm connected to on LinkedIn:

Note as well that when you comment on something it shows in your "posts and activity" which you can get to by *LinkedIn > Me > Posts & activity*. Another good idea is when you log in to LinkedIn, look at the far right of the screen under "Todays' news and views." Here's a screenshot

:

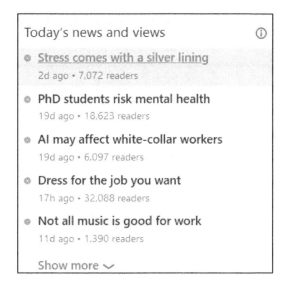

This means, for example, that 7,072 persons are engaging with the article entitled "Stress comes with a silver lining." You can then click into this trending article, see posts on it, and chime in with your own two cents. Using **interactive content** is a great way to schmooze yourself into the hearts and minds of other folks on LinkedIn. Here are your steps:

1. Research content on LinkedIn by looking at hashtags, trending topics, or doing keyword-focused searches for "content" in the top bar.

2. Peruse content on that theme that is of interest to you and your target customers.

3. Like, comment, or share the content of others. Note that when you comment on their content, they get a notification (!).

4. As people react to your comments, reach out to them with connection requests.

Let's explore this method via search. As opposed to just viewing your news feed, go up to search, click on the blank search bar, and just click "content" at the bottom without typing anything in. Here's a screenshot:

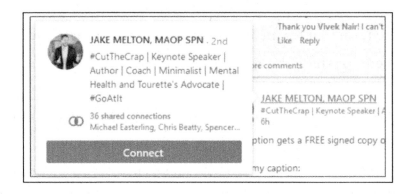

This gives another view of content related to you that is different than the news feed, prioritized by your 1ˢᵗ and 2ⁿᵈ level connections. Using the pull-down menus, you can filter by date, by connection level, and by industry.

Then, scroll through it and comment on relevant articles by folks in your industry. For any person, you can hover by their name and see whether they are a 1ˢᵗ, 2ⁿᵈ, or 3ʳᵈ level contact. Here's a screenshot:

Notice how Jake is a 2ⁿᵈ level contact, which means I can then comment on his post or article, get his attention, and possibly begin a relationship. Identifying and interacting with relevant contact by 2ⁿᵈ or 3ʳᵈ level contacts is yet another great way to schmooze and grow your network on LinkedIn.

**Search by Keyword for Content**

You can also search LinkedIn for content by keyword. Just go back to the search bar and follow these steps:

1. Click on the search bar.

2. Type your keyword into the search bar.

3. Click "see all results" at the bottom.

4. Click "Content" in the gray at the top.

It's a little hard to do, so play around with it. Just be sure you are both entering a keyword and searching ONLY content. Then scroll down the results and find interesting content and people and like, comment, or share their posts or articles. This is a fantastic way to identify relevant content and people quickly, and schmooze. Here's a screenshot for a search for "petroleum" content:

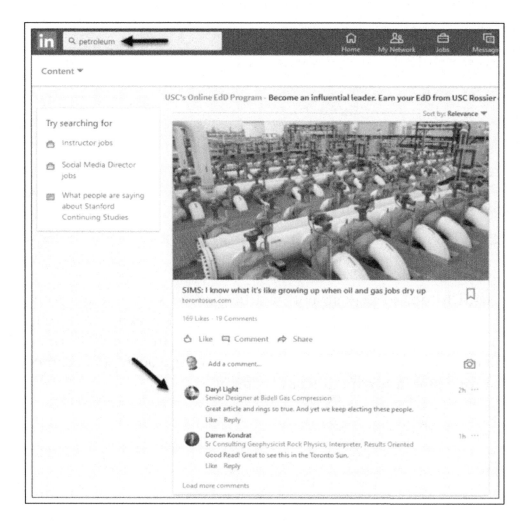

I can either add a comment, or I can reply to the comments of others. Again, each time I comment or reply LinkedIn will notify the recipient, thus building buzz around me on LinkedIn and giving me opportunities to schmooze with more people. Obviously, do not spam people – be useful and engaging, so focus on content in which you actually have something useful to contribute!

## Groups

With LinkedIn's growing emphasis on "professional learning," it should come as no surprise that LinkedIn has a growing ecosystem of groups on every topic imaginable. Compare LinkedIn groups to the "break out" sessions at your industry trade show: interested parties show up, listen to each other, participate in discussions, and showcase their questions (and answers) on professional topics. Oh, and occasionally, they use groups as yet another opportunity to **schmooze** *(surprise!)*. By participating tactfully in LinkedIn groups, you can grow your prestige (and that of your company). It's a soft sell environment, however; anyone who is a member of a group that you are a member of is a good prospect to become a LinkedIn 1<sup>st</sup> level connection.

To find relevant groups, simply search LinkedIn by keyword, click on "See all results," then "More," and then "Groups." Groups can be standard, open, or closed, meaning for some groups you have to ask to join, and for others you just join up. By clicking "ask to join," you are requesting the group moderator to approve your membership.

Once you've joined a group, you may see posts from group members in your news feed or you can click to groups by going to *My Network > Groups*. You can also visit **http://jmlinks.com/46e** which is **https://www.linkedin.com/groups/** as LinkedIn strangely makes it hard to find your groups. To learn more about LinkedIn groups, read the official help file at **http://jmlinks.com/31j**.

## Group Promotion Strategy

LinkedIn is a serious social media platform; so please don't "spam" groups with self-serving "buy my stuff" messages. Instead, join relevant groups, pay attention to the on-going discussions, and post informative and useful content. It's a soft sell environment. Let group members realize how smart and useful you are, and then reach out to you directly.

As you research (or join) groups, pay attention to the quality of the discussions. Some groups are fantastic: full of motivated, informed, honest people. Other groups are quite spammy with everyone talking, and few people listening. Just as at a professional trade show, be choosy with your time and efforts. Not all groups are created equally.

Your **TO-DO** for groups is simple:

- **Log on** to your LinkedIn account.

- **Search for relevant groups** by keyword.

- **Identify** interesting and useful **groups**, and join them (or apply to join if it's a closed group).

- **Monitor** and begin to **participate**.

- Diplomatically position yourself (and your company) as a **helpful expert**.

## Join the Groups of Your Customers

Here's a tip for marketers. Don't just join groups that are relevant to your professional interests; join groups that your interest your target *customers*. A WordPress web designer, for example, would join groups on WordPress to boost her professional skills but also join (and participate in) groups for small business owners, where she could contribute to the discussion and in a very "soft sell" way, showcase her skills on WordPress.

Your to-do's here are thus:

1. Identify keywords that are *relevant to your customers* (i.e., pain points or desires that they have and might be joining LinkedIn groups to explore).

2. Identify LinkedIn groups that your customers are joining.

3. Joining those groups yourself.

4. Participating in a useful way on these groups. Don't be spammy!

5. Interacting with and connecting with potential customers as you participate in these group as a "helpful expert."

By joining groups that are *relevant to your customers* and being a "helpful expert" in those customer-facing groups, you can build your brand and leverages LinkedIn far more effectively than by joining groups *of your peers (and competitors)*.

## » USE LINKEDIN COMPANY PAGES

Like Facebook, LinkedIn offers company Pages. And like Facebook, you must first have an individual profile to create (or manage) a company page. To view the official LinkedIn information on company pages, visit **http://jmlinks.com/3h**. The steps to create a business Page on LinkedIn are:

1. Sign in to your personal profile.

2. Click on Work at the far right, top, and then "Create a company page" at the bottom or just go to **http://jmlinks.com/3j**.

3. Add your company name, and your email address, matching the company website domain.

4. Enter your company name.

5. Enter your designated Admins.

Now that you have created a company Page, it's time to optimize it. Log in, first, to your personal profile. Next click on Me, and the pull-down arrow. Find your company on the list as indicated by *Company Page*. You can also just search for your company by name and click "Manage Page." Next, when you're on your Company Page, then click on the various "pencil" icons you'll see throughout. These allow you to update your background photo, company description, and specialties. Here's a screenshot:

Click on the "pencil" at the far right to edit your Page, including your tabs. There's not much to a LinkedIn Company Page. You can only optimize:

- **Page Info**. Enter or adjust your company name, accordingly.

- **Buttons**. Add specific buttons with links.

- **About**. Enter a keyword-heavy yet relevant description of your company. Explain your value proposition: what can you do for LinkedIn members?

  o **Description**. Describe what your company does; focus on what you do for customers.

  o **Other Items**. Enter your website URL, phone, industry, company size, company type, years founded, etc.

  o **Specialties**. Enter keywords that match what your company does.

  o **Hashtags**. Enter hashtags that match your business focus.

- o **Featured Groups**. Enter groups that match what your company does.

- **Designated Admins**. Located under *Admin Tools > Manage*, here, you can add or remove Admins. Any Admin has full `control of the page; so if you terminate an employee, remove them first!

- **Cover Photo**. Similar to the Facebook cover photo, you can change your LinkedIn (cover) image.

- **Company Logo**. Similar to the Facebook profile picture, you can change your LinkedIn Profile picture.

For a fee, you can add a "career" tab to your LinkedIn Company Page as well as a "Life" tab. These are useful really only if your company is using LinkedIn to recruit employees, not for marketing to customers. Learn more at **http://jmlinks.com/53j**.

The reality is that few people "search" LinkedIn to find companies. So the bread-and-butter of your company page is to post interesting items (both your own content and that of other people) to people who follow your page because externally they have already decided to follow you. For example, existing customers or people who find your blog interesting might "follow" your company on LinkedIn to stay updated.

For tips from LinkedIn on how to nurture effective company Pages, please visit **http://jmlinks.com/3k**.

## Page Posting Strategy

Although most of the action on LinkedIn is at the profile to profile level, you can post via your company Page as well. Just as with a profile, the trick is to identify interesting, engaging content (both your own and that of others) to post to the Page. In reality, you can cross-post content on both employee profiles and the company page. For example, if the director of marketing writes an informative piece for LinkedIn articles, you can "cross post" this to your LinkedIn company feed. Similarly, you can identify interesting industry-related articles on Feedly, and share this content at both the profile and Page level.

To share a *post*, just log in to your Company Page, and click on "Start a post" link. Just as with a personal profile you can share either just text, text with a photo, video, or link to an external website, or native video. **Note**: Company Pages cannot post articles, however; only individuals can.

Essentially, you are trying to position your company as a "helpful expert" on a relevant topic, by posting:

- **Your own content** such as your company's blog posts, videos either on YouTube or native to LinkedIn, infographics / instructographics, reports, eBooks, industry studies that deal with industry issues in an informative way;

- **Other people's content** similar to the above. Remember to post the content of your own employees!

- **Self-promotional content** like announcements of free Webinars, eBooks, upcoming trade shows, new products, etc.

Note that your **posting rhythm** of *fun, fun, fun, fun, buy my stuff* on Facebook translates on LinkedIn to:

*useful, useful, useful, useful, useful, useful, useful, attend our webinar, useful, useful, useful, useful, useful, useful, useful, download our free eBook, useful, useful, useful, useful, useful, useful, visit us at the trade show...*

**Get Employees to Post Your Content as Well as Your Company Page**

And remember, LinkedIn marketing is a **team sport**: if you have a great blog post, video, or infographic, have it posted not only to your company LinkedIn page but have key employees share it as an update on their own LinkedIn profiles as well!

In other words, make 80% or more of your posts useful, and only 20% or less, shameless, self-promotional announcements. If you like, you can "pin" a company update to the top of your company Page. Simply find the update, and click the "three dots" and then "Pin to top."

Here are some examples of effective LinkedIn company pages:

- Thermo Fischer Scientific at **http://jmlinks.com/36k**.

- Intel Corporation at **http://jmlinks.com/36m**.

- Bayer at **http://jmlinks.com/53k**.

- Social Media Examiner **http://jmlinks.com/36p**.

To find companies to emulate, either search LinkedIn directly by keywords or use this Google trick. Go to **https://www.google.com/** and enter:

*site:linkedin.com/company {keyword}*

*site:linkedin.com/company {company name}*

*as for example:*

*site:linkedin.com/company "organic food"* at **http://jmlinks.com/12t**.

You'll find that LinkedIn is fast becoming a better home for more "serious" or even "boring" companies than Facebook; companies whose business value proposition is more *business-to-business* rather than *business-to-consumer*, and whose customers engage when they are in their work / professional / business mode. Find and follow competitors and companies you admire on LinkedIn. You'll also find that the organic reach of business Pages on LinkedIn dwarfs that of business Pages on Facebook.

In sum, if your business is *business-to-business* such as professional services like Web design, accounting, business attorneys, computer services, SEO, social media marketing, marketing services... any business-to-business, professional service, then a company Page on LinkedIn can be a very effective marketing tool.

## » PROMOTING YOUR LINKEDIN PROFILES, POSTS, AND PAGES

Once you and your employees have established their individual profiles, begun to share posts or articles, set up a company Page, and begun to populate it with posts on a regular basis, you've essentially "set up" your social media party on LinkedIn. Now it's time to send out the invitations. In and of itself, nothing on LinkedIn is truly self-promotional.

Remember: social media is a **party**. You must have yummy yummy food and entertainment for people to show up, and stick around. So as you promote your LinkedIn **content**, always keep front and center "what's in it for them" – what will they get by connecting with your employees on LinkedIn or following your company LinkedIn page?

Generally speaking, people on LinkedIn are looking for informative, educational, useful, professional content relevant to their industry and job, so that they can stay informed and educated. If on Facebook the name of the game is *fun*, on LinkedIn the name of the game is *useful*.

# FACEBOOK IS ABOUT FUN; LINKEDIN IS ABOUT USEFUL

Assuming your profiles and Page have lots of useful content, here are some common ways to promote your LinkedIn accounts:

- **Real World to Social.** Don't forget the real world! If you are a serious technology vendor of single board computers, and you're at the industry trade show, be sure that the folks manning the booth, recommend to booth visitors that they "connect" with your employees and "follow" your business LinkedIn Page. *Why? Because they'll get insider tips, industry news, free eBooks and webinars – stuff that will keep them abreast of the industry, and better informed at their jobs.*

- **Cross-Promotion**. Link your website to your LinkedIn profiles and Page, your blog posts to your profiles and Page, your Twitter to your profiles and Page, etc. Notice how big brands like Intel (**http://www.intel.com/**) do this: one digital property promotes another digital property.

- **Content**. Don't think of content on LinkedIn as post it and forget about it. Rather think about content as a promotion strategy. Post interesting and engaging content, and then as people respond, respond back to them. Also, work on interactive content: search LinkedIn weekly or even daily for discussions going on on topics that matter to you and your business. Chime in with your two cents. Being interactive with content on LinkedIn is a promotion strategy as much as a content strategy.

- **Hashtags**. LinkedIn is increasingly promoting hashtags, so include relevant #hashtags in your posts. To find them, search the existing posts of others by keyword and look for the "#" symbol, guess at them (e.g., #organic), or you can use this link for the most popular #hashtags on LinkedIn: **http://jmlinks.com/46z**.

- **Email**. Email your customer list and ask them to "connect" with key employees and/or "follow" your Page. Again, you must have a reason why they'll do so: what's in it for them? Have a contest, give away something for free, or otherwise motivate them to click from the email to your profiles or Page, and then connect.

- **LinkedIn Internal**. More at the profile level than on the Page level, participation on LinkedIn in an authentic way can grow one's follower base. LinkedIn articles are especially useful for this, as are LinkedIn groups. Internal promotion is not particularly strong on LinkedIn, but it should still be in the mix.

- **Use LinkedIn Plugins**. LinkedIn has numerous plugins that allow you to "embed" your LinkedIn content on your website, and thereby nurture cross-promotion. To learn more about plugins, visit **http://jmlinks.com/31k**. In this way, your blog can promote your LinkedIn content, and your LinkedIn content can promote your blog. Similarly, your YouTube videos can promote your LinkedIn Page, and your LinkedIn posts and articles can promote your YouTube Videos and vice-versa.

- **Leverage your Customers**. People who already have connected with you and your company are your best promoters. Remember, it's *social* (!) media, and encouraging your customers to share your content is the name of the game. You want to leverage your connections as much as possible to share your content. On LinkedIn, it's all about being useful! Indeed, a timely article to LinkedIn can be picked up by key influencers, go viral, and exponentially increase your personal and company reach.

# GET YOUR CUSTOMERS TO HELP PROMOTE YOUR LINKEDIN CONTENT

## » ADVERTISE ON LINKEDIN

One of the best ways to promote your LinkedIn content is through **advertising**. LinkedIn offers highly focused targeting options for its ads. Here are the basic options:

**Sponsored Content**. On your LinkedIn company page, find a post. At the top of the post, click on the gray "Sponsor Now" button and follow the instructions. This is similar to "boosting" a post on Facebook.

**Message Ads (formerly Sponsored InMail)**. LinkedIn allows you to send "Sponsored InMail," which is a type of email marketing. Yes, it's a bit spammy, but you can essentially use LinkedIn to send out targeted (unsolicited) emails to prospects.

**Text Ads**. These ads appear at the far right of the LinkedIn screen and in the app and are links to external websites. This is a great way to promote a business webinar, eBook or some type of lead generation form.

**Video Ads**. With the migration to video, you can now advertise native video on LinkedIn.

**Follower Ads**. These are ads used to promote a Company Page and thus grow its follower base.

We'll discuss LinkedIn targeting in a moment, but let's look at these options not from the perspective of the format but rather from the perspective of your advertising objective:

**Objective #1: Use LinkedIn to Promote Your Website**. Like most social networks, LinkedIn makes it easy for you to set up an ad that goes FROM LinkedIn TO your website. An example might be setting up an ad on LinkedIn to promote a webinar on a new product. You'd set up a demographic target (such as people in the Proteomics industry), set up a "text ad" on LinkedIn, and then pay by click. LinkedIn would show your text-based ad to people who are in the Proteomics industry, they'd click over to your website, and register for your webinar. Ads appear at the top and top right on LinkedIn.

**Objective #2: Use LinkedIn to Promote Your Posts and Company Page**. Here, you're using LinkedIn advertising to grow the follower base of your Company Page and/or to boost the reach of posts by your Page. You'd set up a demographic target (such as people in the Proteomics industry), boost the post (or choose a Follower ad), and LinkedIn would promote the Post and/or your Page to persons who would see (and hopefully engage with) your content. Note: within a Post, click on the "Sponsor now" link at the top to "boost" a post (that is, advertise it).

**Objective #3: Use LinkedIn to Generate Highly Targeted Leads**. Here, your objective is a little spammy. LinkedIn will allow you to send "unsolicited InMails" to members via "Message ads" (formerly called "Sponsored InMails). These ads can only be sent in the name of a *person* (not a *Page*), so you'd choose a person such as your CEO or Business Development Manager, and then follow the steps after "Lead Generation" in LinkedIn ads to send a "Message ad." These ads can be personalized to include the name of each person sent, company name, job title, and/or industry, and appear in their InMail InBox. An example would be sending a sponsored InMail from the CEO to invite an individual to attend a real-world event at Proteomics world or perhaps a targeted webinar online.

Sponsored InMail ads, in my experience, are the most effective form of advertising on LinkedIn. They're unique in the social media landscape in that they are essentially like unsolicited email advertising. Here's a screenshot of what it looks like inside LinkedIn when someone clicks into their messages:

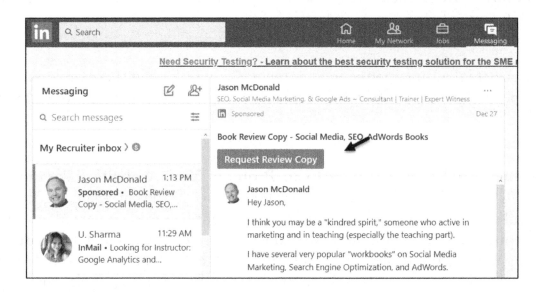

If you look closely, you'll see that it's marked "Sponsored" in the top left. You can turn "on" or "off" the clickable blue box in your ad. I have it turned on and formatted to say "Request review copy" as this "Message ad" is used to promote my books. This third option is thus a little like ads in Gmail, Google's free email platform. Be aware that because this is very much like unsolicited email it is both highly effective and highly obnoxious. Use "Message ads" with discretion.

Visit LinkedIn's information center at **http://jmlinks.com/31m** to access more detailed official information on LinkedIn's advertising opportunities.

## Demographic Targeting

As on Facebook, you can **demographically target people** on LinkedIn based on their interests. Whether you're promoting a Page post, advertising an offlink to your website, or using Message Ads, LinkedIn allows you to demographically target:

By **geography**. Target by country, state, city, or town.

By **followers**. Target only to people who already follow your Company Page or exclude your followers.

By **targeting criteria**. Target people specifically by:

*Company name*

*Company industry*

*Company size*

*Job title*

*Job function*

*Job seniority*

*etc.*

In this way, you can take a piece of content and laser-target it to LinkedIn users based on who they are down to very specific attributes. The big challenge, however, is that aside from job seekers, many people do not frequently check their LinkedIn news feed. So, whereas Facebook reaches nearly everyone *frequently* (but they're in friends, family, fun mode), LinkedIn tends to reach people outside of job search only *sporadically* (when they're in business learn mode). Therefore, the *reach* of LinkedIn advertising is a bit of a challenge, and the cost per click can be pretty high as well.

## Use Your Company Page and Employee Profiles in Tandem

LinkedIn does not currently allow you to directly promote individual profiles or the posts / articles of individuals via advertising. Only *Pages* (not *Profiles*) can advertise. How can you thus use your company, LinkedIn Page, to assist your employee posts and articles? Here's how:

1. Have the employee **post** to his or her **blog**; and/or
   - Have the employee create an **article** for LinkedIn.
   - Find the link to that article by clicking on the top right, three dots.
2. **Pay to advertise** this content via your Company Account by following the steps at LinkedIn Campaign Manager (**http://jmlinks.com/53g**).

In this way, you can use your company Page to grow the following of individual key employees as well as advertise their content for thought-leadership and brand purposes.

You can thus use your Company Page to help promote your employee profiles and your employee profiles to help promote your Company Page. It's a team sport.

## » MEASURING YOUR RESULTS

LinkedIn offers more metrics at the company level than at the personal profile level.

### LinkedIn Profiles

First, let's look at the profile level. Log in to LinkedIn. Then, on the far left find "Who's viewed your profile" and click into it. Here's a screenshot:

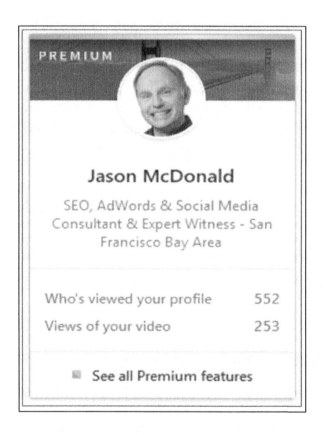

This will show you data on who's viewed your profile. Depending on whether you have a free or premium account, you can see who's viewed your profile and then reach out to them with a connection request.

You can also see at the top left your follower count. Click on "Posts and Activities," and then on "Followers." Here's a screenshot:

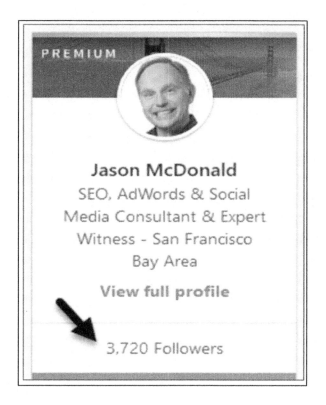

Right underneath that click on "your followers" and you can see who's following you. You can then follow them back. To see your connections, go to *LinkedIn > Me > View Profile > Connections.* Here's a screenshot:

## LinkedIn Posts

You can also see data at the post level. For example, here's a screenshot of a post with data:

You can see that this post had 132 views, 8 likes, and 1 comment, for example. You can also toggle between articles and posts at the top; just remember that an article is a post to LinkedIn's internal blog system. As with posts, you can see views, likes, comments, and shares.

If you post an article to LinkedIn, stats on its performance will also be visible. Go to *LinkedIn > Me > Posts and Activity > Articles* to see this data. There isn't yet a video tab, so you have to scroll through "All activity" to find any native videos you uploaded. For any piece of content, you can see likes, comments, and shares. Your objective is to figure out what your audience likes and give them more of it.

## LinkedIn Pages

LinkedIn Page data is more robust. If you are logged in as the company, simply click on the "Analytics" tab and LinkedIn provides lots of graphical data about your Page and its reach. Click on "Notifications," and you can see likes, comments, shares, and mentions in more detail.

## Google Analytics

For many of us, we want to drive traffic from LinkedIn to our website, even to our e-commerce store or to download a free eBook or software package to get a sales lead. Sign up for Google Analytics (**https://analytics.google.com**) and install the required tracking code. Inside of your Google Analytics account on the left column, drill down by clicking on *Acquisition > Social > Overview*. Then on the right-hand side of the screen, you'll see a list of Social Networks. Find LinkedIn on that list, and click on that. Google Analytics will tell you what URLs people clicked to from LinkedIn to your Website, giving you insights into what types of web content people find attractive.

You can also create a custom **segment** to look at only LinkedIn traffic and its behavior. For information on how to create custom segments in Google Analytics, go to **http://jmlinks.com/1f**. For the Google help files on segments go to **http://jmlinks.com/1g**.

In sum, inside of LinkedIn, you can see how people interact with your Page and updates as well as those made by individual profiles. Inside of Google Analytics, you can see where they land on your website and what they do after they arrive.

### »» CHECKLIST: LINKEDIN ACTION ITEMS

Test your knowledge of LinkedIn! Take the *LinkedIn marketing quiz* at **http://jmlinks.com/qzli**. Next, here are your LinkedIn **Action Items**:

❑ **Research** whether your customers (and competitors) are on LinkedIn. What are they doing? What interests them, and Why?

  ❑ Identify a few ***customer profiles*** that match your *buyer personas*, and determine how active they are.

  ❑ Identify **companies** to "reverse engineer" who are doing a good job on LinkedIn. Remember to look at the company employees' profiles as well as the company Page.

❑ **Optimize the LinkedIn Profiles** of key employees vs. target keywords; be sure that each Profile clearly explains the "value proposition" to a target customer.

❑ Strategize how to **grow the 1st level connections** of key employees, including recommendations and endorsements.

❑ Brainstorm **content ideas** that give you something enticing to "offer" to 1st and 2nd level connections (e.g., free eBooks, webinars, interesting articles to LinkedIn, wine and cheese events at industry trade shows, etc.).

> ❑ Begin sharing useful posts to LinkedIn aimed at your target customers.

> ❑ Begin occasionally posting useful articles to LinkedIn aimed at your target customers.

> ❑ If possible, consider doing "native video" on LinkedIn.

❑ Identify, join, and participate in **customer groups** on LinkedIn; do not spam!

❑ Set up a **LinkedIn Company Page** and begin posting useful content.

> ❑ Strategize how to grow / promote your Company Page, including **advertising** to promote your Page content as well as the posts of key employees.

❑ Evaluate whether **LinkedIn advertising** such as boosted content or "Message ads" to targeted prospects might help your LinkedIn efforts for a decent ROI.

❑ **Measure** your **KPIs** on LinkedIn for both Profiles and Pages such as the growth of your connections and the interactivity of your posts and articles.

Check out the **free tools**! Go to my *Social Media Marketing Dashboard > LinkedIn* for my favorite free tools on LinkedIn. Just visit **http://jmlinks.com/smmdash**.

## »» DELIVERABLE: A LINKEDIN MARKETING PLAN

Now that we've come to the end of our chapter on LinkedIn, your **DELIVERABLE** has arrived. For your final **TO-DO**, download the **LinkedIn Marketing Plan Worksheet**. For the worksheet, go to **http://jmlinks.com/social2020** (then reenter the code 'social2020' to register your workbook), and click on the link to the "LinkedIn Marketing Plan Worksheet." You'll brainstorm your strategy for LinkedIn at both the employee (profile) and company (Page) level.

# 5
# TWITTER

Do you Tweet? Should you? Twitter is among the most misunderstood of all the social media. On the one hand, it dominates news and pop culture, giving Twitter a brand presence second only to Facebook. *Ellen DeGeneres tweets. Donald Trump tweets. CBS News tweets.* And so the logic goes, *you better tweet, too.* But, on the other hand, Twitter is so full of noise, news, and craziness that it isn't necessarily a good marketing venue for many businesses. In fact, many businesses tweet and no one is really listening, so Twitter becomes a complete zero in terms of return on investment.

In short, Twitter can be an **effective marketing channel** for your business or Twitter can be a **huge waste of time**. Which is it? Should you use Twitter, and if so, how? The answer, of course, is "it depends." It depends on whether your customers are on Twitter, and whether you can systematically implement a Twitter marketing strategy.

In this Chapter, you'll learn how Twitter works, how to figure out if Twitter is a good opportunity for your business, how to set up your Twitter account, and – most importantly – how to tweet effectively. Throughout, I will point you to free tools and resources for more information as well as worksheets to guide you step-by-step. Even if you are already tweeting, you'll learn how to use Twitter for marketing as opposed to just pecking endlessly at 280 characters.

**Let's get started!**

**TO-DO LIST:**

» Explore How Twitter Works

» Inventory Likes and Dislikes on Twitter

» Create Twitter-friendly Content

» Tweet to Journalists, Bloggers, and Influencers

» Brainstorm and Execute a Tweeting Strategy

» Promote Your Twitter Account and Tweets

» Advertise on Twitter

» Measure your Results

## » EXPLORE HOW TWITTER WORKS

One easy way to understand Twitter is to think of it as a **microblogging** platform. Blogs are all about having an inspiration for a blog post, composing a strong headline, and writing some detailed paragraphs about the topic. Twitter is very similar, just a lot shorter - 280 characters, to be exact. (*Twitter used to limit you to just 140 characters, but that's now been doubled due to twitflation*).

Let's compare writing a blog post and composing a tweet.

When you write a blog post, you a) conceptualize a **topic** (*hopefully of interest to your target audience*), b) write a **headline** and the **blog post** itself, c) append an **image** or perhaps embed a **video** as an optional feature, and d) **promote** the post. Similarly, within the constraints of a 280 character tweet, you a) conceptualize a **topic** of interest to your (potential) followers, b) write a **headline / tweet** (they're basically one-and-the-same on Twitter), c) append an **image** or **video** as an optional element, and d) **promote** your tweet.

# TWITTER IS MICROBLOGGING

One difference, between Twitter and blogging, is that a tweet often points *outward* to an in-depth blog post, a video, an infographic, or an image. A tweet can be just a "headline" pointing out to the "rest of the story;" think of Twitter as a "headline" service pointing to your blog, offer on your e-commerce website, YouTube videos, etc. But, tweets can be self-standing as well. And tweets can be conversational as when one person responds to others, and whole groups of people tweet into a conversation.

As for content, tweets can be:

- **Just text**. Start typing a thought, idea, reaction, news announcement or whatever up to 280 characters.

- **A photo or image**. You can upload a photo on your computer or via your phone and the Twitter app.

- **A video**. Twitter, like all the platforms, has gone gaga for video. Upload a short video of less than 2 minutes and 20 seconds. You can also "go live" with live video on Twitter.

Check out the official tutorial on how to use Twitter at **http://jmlinks.com/46h**.

**Twitter is Like Facebook (and Instagram, LinkedIn, and Pinterest…)**

Structurally speaking, Twitter also shares many similarities with other social media. Like Facebook, LinkedIn, Pinterest and other social media, your Twitter account (a.k.a., "Page") can be "followed" ("liked") by others, who are alerted in their news feeds when you tweet new items. In addition, tweets can be discovered through *#hashtags* plus people can *retweet* (share) your tweets, respond to them, or favorite them, thereby drawing the attention of their followers to you.

In fact, as Twitter becomes more visual and Instagram becomes more textual, these two are on a "collision course," and the world may not be big enough for the both of them!

The names may have changed, but the basic structure of Twitter works pretty much like that of other social media platforms:

- Individuals have *accounts* on Twitter ("Profiles" on Facebook).

    o Companies also have *accounts* on Twitter ("Pages" on Facebook).

- If an individual *follows* your account on Twitter ("likes" your Page on Facebook), then when your company tweets it will show up in the *news feed* of that individual (technically their Twitter *timeline*).

- Individuals can

    o *like* a tweet – "like" a post on Facebook;

    o *respond* to a tweet – "comment" on Facebook; and/or

    o *re-tweet* a tweet to their followers (reshare posts on Facebook).

- They can also create *lists* and *moments*, which are compendia of tweets.

The structure of Twitter is thus quite similar to that of Facebook; the big differences are that Twitter is shorter, faster, and noisier than Facebook.

### What's Unique about Twitter?

Twitter is the most open of all the social media. Anyone can set up a Twitter account in literally minutes, and start tweeting – there's no required authentication. And anyone can listen in. There's no required friending or connecting as on Facebook or LinkedIn. Indeed, even people who do not follow you can easily find and read your tweets. They can even contact you without your pre-approval. Let me repeat these important Twitter facts:

> **Anyone** can instantly set up a Twitter account and start tweeting: no authentication required;
>
> **Anyone** can listen in to anyone on Twitter: no friending required; and
>
> **Anyone** can message **anyone** via Twitter: it's completely open.

# TWITTER IS OPEN

So anyone can talk on Twitter, a fact that, in combination with its focus on news and pop culture, may explain why Twitter is the most "no holds barred" of all the social media. Because it is so open, however, Twitter also offers unique marketing opportunities oriented on precisely this openness; you can tweet to journalists, the President (or not), the followers of your competitors, anyone and everyone – and everyone can listen in and discover new and engaging content. Twitter's openness gives it reach unrivaled by networks like Facebook or LinkedIn.

Lots of folks are tweeting and talking on Twitter (including bots, which are automated robots pretending to be people), but is *anyone really listening*? That's a different question, and the answer varies a great deal based on your industry, your status, and your skill at building an audience on Twitter. As with all social media, your first to-do is to investigate whether your target audience is on Twitter and, if so, how you can reach them as a marketer.

### Twitter is Noisy, Really Noisy

Because of its openness and because of its focus on short, newsy content, Twitter is a blizzard of information with lots and lots of noise obfuscating the interesting stuff. Whereas Facebook is all about friends, family, and fun "as if" you are at a company picnic or family reunion, Twitter is "as if" you were listening to all talk radio stations and all cable TV stations at the same time.

To get started, search for competitors and brands to emulate. On the desktop and on the app, just click on the "magnifying glass" and start a search. For instance, type in "organic" and then click over to people. Here's a screenshot:

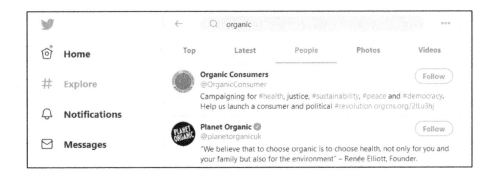

In this way, you can find companies or brands on Twitter that focus on "organic." Then click into a company such as *@OrganicConsumer* and click the "follow" button to "follow" them.

You can also browse Twitter for trends. On the app, click on the magnifying glass and then click "trending," "news," "sports," "fun," or "entertainment." The Twitter algorithm will give you the most popular, trending content by genre. On the desktop, click on the *#Explore* icon on the left and then you'll see "For You," "News," "Sports," etc. Here's a screenshot:

Rather than paying attention to massive pop culture or news trends, I recommend you drill down by search. Look for persons to follow, companies or brands to emulate, influencers, superfans, and others who are focused on your industry. The trick is to drill down into the niches in your industry and realize that if all you see are the rather silly or outrageous headlines on Twitter, you're missing its opportunities. "Riches are in the niches" on Twitter, very much so.

## Twitter's Culture

Twitter's culture is fast-paced and used primarily to share news (about everything) and/or to share gossip (about pop culture and politics). It's also rather rude and even full of cyberbullying. Inappropriate, mean-spirited comments are rife on Twitter. Twitter is where pop culture is discussed, Twitter is where politics is argued over, Twitter is the 24/7 news cycle on steroids, Twitter is full of crazy, fun, over-the-top, inappropriate, crude, and inappropriate hashtags and conversations. Twitter is ground zero for political correctness. Twitter is ground zero for Donald Trump and the Alt Right. Twitter is home to insanity, but Twitter is also powerful because of its incredible reach into every nook and cranny of the culture.

Twitter is a complete, insane mess. Twitter makes you believe we are living in the end times. Twitter has been responsible for revolutions and cat videos gone viral.

*I love Twitter!*

*I hate Twitter!*

In fact, Twitter is even home to *Twitter mobs*, which are crowds that attack people who are "beyond the pale," with "pale" being the other side of whatever the frenzied mob doesn't seem to like. See **http://jmlinks.com/46j**.

## Is Twitter for You? Tuning In and Tuning Out

With all these pros and cons, the question becomes whether or not Twitter is for you, whether or not your customers are on Twitter, and – if so, whether you can use it to market to them. If, for example, your business lives in an industry that thrives on news, Twitter may be great for you. If, for example, your business is connected to politics, news, or pop culture, Twitter may be essential to your marketing efforts. If you are a nonprofit that advocates into the public square, Twitter is definitely a must. If you are a politician, you gotta be on Twitter. If your business is about coupons, special deals, and foodie events, Twitter may be an amazing marketing opportunity. If you attend industry trade shows or want to reach specific journalists hungry for story ideas, Twitter can be your secret marketing weapon.

Throughout, keep your eye on how to *tune in* to the appropriate conversations on Twitter and *tune out* the blizzard of useless Twitter noise. Like talk radio or the 365 channels on cable TV, it's all about *tuning in* to an audience to succeed at Twitter marketing.

*Tune in to Twitter conversations that matter to your business, and tune out of Twitter conversations that don't.*

While Twitter is not for the faint-hearted, with some skill and knowledge, you can "tune in" to relevant content and conversations for your brand and "tune out" of the over-the-top insanity that gives Twitter a bad name.

## Sign up for Twitter

If you haven't already signed up for Twitter, simply go to **http://jmlinks.com/1h**. For complete information on setting up your business, go to **http://jmlinks.com/1i**.

The basics of a setting up a business Twitter account are as follows:

- **Your Account / Your Username / Twitter Handle**. A username such as **@jmgrp** becomes your Twitter handle or URL (**https://twitter.com/jmgrp**) and shows up in your tweets. Choose a short username that reflects your brand identity. **Shorter names are better** because although they no longer count in the character count, tweets are limited to 280 characters and long usernames look somewhat stupid. As with most social media, you need an email address to sign up, or you can use a mobile phone number; unlike Facebook pages, you can only have one email address / password / user – or you can use third-party apps like Hootsuite (**http://www.hootsuite.com/**) or Tweetdeck (**https://tweetdeck.twitter.com/**) to let multiple people access your account.

- **Profile Photo**. This is essentially the same as a profile photo on Facebook. The recommend images size is 400x400 pixels. It shows on your Tweets when viewed in a follower's news feed.

- **Bio**. You have 160 characters to explain your company brand, products, and/or services. Be sure to include an http:// URL link to your company website. You can insert *#hashtags* and *@mentions* in your bio, and these are now clickable. Branded hashtags have thus come to Twitter bios just as on Instagram.

- **Header Image**. Similar to the Facebook cover photo, you get 1500x500 pixels to run as a banner across your account page.

- **Pinned Tweet**. You can "pin" a tweet to the top of your Twitter account so that it shows first when users click up to your Twitter page. For example, compose a tweet that promotes your email newsletter, and then "pin" this to the top of your Twitter account.

Here's a screenshot of how to "pin" a Tweet:

Essentially, find the tweet you want to pin, click on the downward arrow, and then click on "pin to your profile page."

To access any of the other settings and features, go to your page on Twitter (as for example, **http://twitter.com/jmgrp**), be sure you are logged in, click on the small profile picture at the top right, click "profile," and finally click on the "edit profile" button in the far right of the screen. If you're logged in you can also just go to **http://jmlinks.com/31v** or **https://twitter.com/settings/account** when logged in.

Not much can be customized, but in this day of Internet hacking and piracy, I recommend that you turn on **login verification**, which will require a mobile phone code for any new login.

## Following and Followers

Now that you've set up your account, you can "follow" people or brands on Twitter by finding their Twitter accounts and clicking on the "follow" link. Similarly, people can follow you on Twitter by doing the same. No approval is necessary – just find people or accounts that interest you and click "follow." Twitter is like YouTube or Instagram (and not Facebook or LinkedIn) in that there is no real distinction between a "brand"

and a "person" on Twitter. Everyone just has an account or handle, so it's *@jasoneg3* (for me as a person) and *@jmgrp* (for the JM Internet Group as a brand), and they function the same.

As you are logged in to your account (either personal or business, it doesn't matter), start searching for and following persons and brands that interest you. Just remember that outsiders can see whom you follow, so if you're going to follow competitors, I'd follow them with your personal account not your business account.

For example, to follow the outdoor retailer, REI, you'd search for REI on Twitter to find their account, or visit **https://twitter.com/REI** and click the blue "Follow" button. Here's a screenshot:

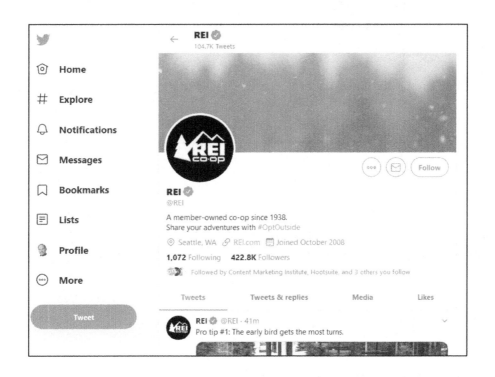

Note as well how after you click "follow," Twitter suggests other, similar accounts such as *@Patagonia*. You can see that REI has 422.8K followers, and is following 1,072 accounts. At the very top you can see that they have made 104.7K tweets. The blue check indicates it is a Twitter-verified account (something necessary for big brands or famous people to preclude fraud).

The more followers an account has, the more powerful it is. The more people follow it and the fewer people it follows, the more powerful it is. If you see an account that has about the same number of followers as it is following, then many of its relationships are "follow for follow," which is indicative of weakness.

Just as in High School, the most powerful people are followed by "everyone," while they tend only to follow other high profile people. Here's a screenshot of Oprah's account on Twitter, showing she is followed by 42.7 million people yet follows only 309:

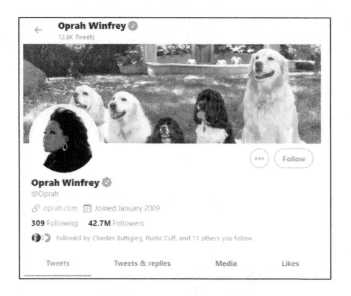

The same goes for anyone on Twitter. The more followers they have, the more important they are. The fewer people they follow, the more important they are. Pay attention as well to the content areas that they play in. Oprah is an expert on pop culture for example, not on auto repair. REI is an expert on outdoor activities not cooking, and so on and so forth. Look for "powerful" influencers or superfans in your industry as measured by what they tweet about and how many followers follow them. *#HighSchoolNeverEnded*.

## Following Content Marketing on Twitter

In terms of content, Twitter works the same as Facebook or LinkedIn. When people follow you on Twitter, they see your tweets in their news feed (Twitter *timeline*) subject to the clutter of the rapidly-moving Twitter news feed and a secret algorithm in Twitter that attempts to prioritize interactive Tweets (e.g., similar to Facebook *Edgerank*). Similarly, you can share the tweets of others (called *retweeting* or *RT*) to your own followers and others can share your tweets to their followers. It's *social* media after all.

As you're researching Twitter look for a) accounts of competitors, and/or b) accounts of people or brands to emulate. Here's a pro tip. You can create a "list" on Twitter by clicking on the "lists" tab to the left. Then name it by topic such as "organic" for people in the organic industry, "outdoors" for companies like REI or Bass Pro Shops, or perhaps "competitors" for people that you compete against. You can make your list public or private. Then when you're logged into Twitter you can click into your list to filter out all the noise and filter in just the accounts you've put into your list. To see an example, check out my list of movers and shakers in the SEO industry at **http://jmlinks.com/53m**. Here's a screenshot:

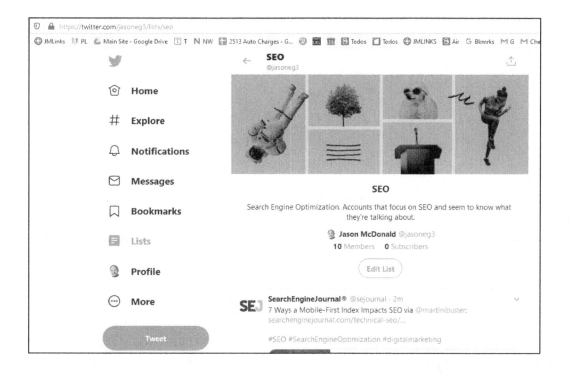

## Understand a Tweet

*Tweets* are the heart and soul of Twitter and correspond to *posts* on Facebook. A tweet is limited to 280 characters. If you use an app like Hootsuite, that app will also give you a character count. Or you can use a service like **http://www.lettercount.com/** and pre-count your characters. As you compose a tweet, you can also string together more than one tweet in a thread. Here's a screenshot:

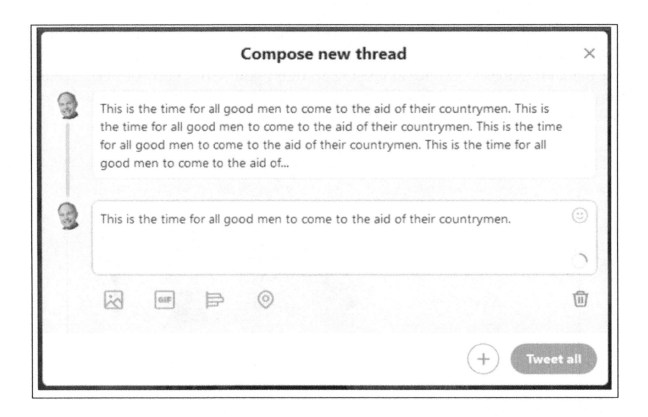

Think of a tweet as a news headline or very short microblog post with just a little supporting information. If you tweet a link to a blog post or other Web page, use a URL shortener like **http://bitly.com/**, **http://tinyurl.com/**, or the "short link" feature in WordPress, so as not to waste characters. Twitter has a built-in shortener as well. You can create a self-standing tweet, or you can tweet "outlinks" to blog posts, videos, or images. You can tweet either on the phone, on your computer, or through a third-party app like Hootsuite.

Most tweets these days combine elements. They have text with a link to an external blog or video, and then a photo or video underneath. Here's an example:

This tweet by *@terrywhalin* has a short "headline" plus a "mention" plus an outward bit.ly link plus an image.

Notice that if your tweet references an external URL, and that URL has a featured image, Twitter will display the image from the website. For example, here's a screenshot of a tweet by me to a blog post I wrote about technical tips for Instagram marketing with the image and headline being pulled from my blog:

Thus, if you don't manually add an image to Twitter, it will pull the image from the blog post or website. As a marketer, this speaks to having coherent titles and featured images on any and all website content.

You can also post a "native" video to Twitter, and then the video itself becomes the image:

And on any tweet, you can see at the bottom replies (comments), retweets (shares), and likes. For instance, on the tweet above, you can see it had 5 comments, 21 retweets, and 29 likes.

The goal is obviously to get your fans to reply, retweet, and like your company's tweets!

If you click on a tweet (just click somewhere in the middle of the text), you can view the conversation going on around that tweet. For example, if you click on the tweet above, you'll be shown the comments and conversation around that tweet. Here's a screenshot:

Note that you're not in control of the conversation! Twitter is open, meaning fans, friends, haters, hecklers, and just plain crazies can chime in on any tweet. This is something President Trump might need to learn, as click into any tweet by the President, and you'll see a firestorm of content – much of it negative. For example, President Trump tweeted:

> **Donald J. Trump** @realDonaldTrump · 7h
>
> Our Steel Industry is the talk of the World. It has been given new life, and is thriving. Billions of Dollars is being spent on new plants all around the country!
>
> 15K   12K   47K

And, as you can see, there are 15,000 replies. Among them:

In other words, it's social media, so be aware that anyone, anywhere can tweet right back at you – in agreement, in disagreement, good, bad, ugly, or just plain crazy. More than any other social media, Twitter conversations can be rather rough and rather rude (*that's the downside*). More than any other social media, with the possible exceptions of YouTube and Instagram, however, Twitter allows people to discover new content that is not "in" their circle of friends (*that's the upside*).

And each reply can garner more replies, retweets, and likes. Twitter is the 24/7 social conversation going on around everything.

## Understand Hashtags

A **hashtag** (#) in a tweet indicates a keyword or theme and is clickable in a tweet. Think of a hashtag as a keyword / subject / theme about which people are talking: *sports, the Oakland A's, global warming, the 2020 presidential campaign, the Academy Awards*. Hashtags should be short, and can NOT include spaces. Anyone can create one, and the success, or failure, of a hashtag is a function of whether many or just a few, people use them. And, yes because Twitter is totally open there is no control: anyone can use them for any purpose, and a hashtag can overlap two discussions.

> **Nota Bene**: *Anyone can create a hashtag! Anyone can chime in on a hashtag! No one controls a hashtag!*

How a hashtag is used, however, is a function of the crowd: the crowd decides what the hashtag really means.

To find existing hashtags, use **http://hashtagify.me** or simply search Twitter using the # hashtag in front of a topic such as *#organicfood* or *#free*. Note that hashtags can NOT include spaces. So it's *#organicfood,* not *#organic food*. Or just search Twitter by keyword and look for the # hashtag symbol. For example, here's a screenshot of a tweet with hashtags *#natural, #organic, #mommyandme,* and *#gifts*:

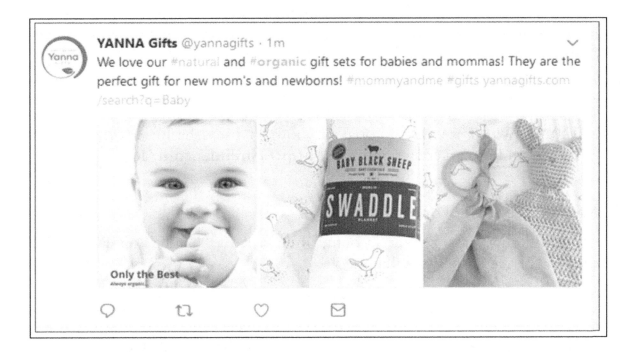

You can click into any one of these hashtags to discover more tweets and thus more hashtags. Hashtags, after all, are "conversations" around a topic and are clickable in a tweet to discover more tweets on that topic. To see the "conversation" on Twitter on *#organic* visit **http://jmlinks.com/31p**. I recommend that you research, identify, and maintain a running list of *hashtags* that are important to your company.

# #HASHTAGS DESIGNATE CONVERSATIONS ON TWITTER

In the tweet above, the hashtags *#organic* and *#natural* are "themes" around which people converse on Twitter. By including hashtags in your Tweets, you can be found by non-followers who are interested in and following, that topic on Twitter. For example, if you are a seller of organic baby food and have a new flavor out, you might tweet with hashtags as follows:

Hey followers! Our super baby plum recipe is out. **#babyfood #organic #natural #food**. *http://bit.ly/1234*

These hashtags become clickable in a tweet, and for people who are interested in that topic, your tweet becomes part of an enormous conversation around that theme. So, finding popular, relevant hashtags and tweeting on them is a good promotion strategy on Twitter. Remember, however, that you have to stand out and get attention amidst all the noise!

VIDEO. Watch a video tutorial on how to use #hashtags on Twitter and Instagram for marketing purposes at **http://jmlinks.com/16u**.

## Understand the @ Sign or Handle

The @ sign designates a Twitter account, often called a "handle" on Twitter. When included in a tweet, it does two things:

- It becomes **clickable**. Anyone who sees this tweet can click on the @handle and go up to that account to view the account and possibly follow that person on Twitter; and

- It **shows up in the news feed of that person** and **sends an email alert** to him or her that they have been mentioned. This is called a "mention." A *mention* means essentially that: someone has mentioned you (your Twitter account) in a Tweet. Nowadays, people also use the word "tag" to mean including the @*account* in a tweet or a post to Instagram, though technically "tag" is more photo-centric.

Here's a screenshot:

Raw Halo @RawHaloUK · Sep 13
It's #OrganicSeptember so we're celebrating with a truly delicious #Competition. Simply RT and follow @RawHaloUK and @SoilAssociation to be in with a chance of winning a bundle of #organic chocolate. 1 x winner to be announced 30/09/18. #Win #Giveaway #Prizedraw

Raw Halo (@*RawHaloUK*) has tweeted to its followers an announcement about a competition and, inside that, has included @*SoilAssociation*. Anyone seeing this tweet can click "up" to @*SoilAssociation*'s account, and @*SoilAssociation* would have received a "mention" notification in their account news feed.

In fact, anyone can tweet to anyone. Just search for the account and then on the far left click on the "Tweet" to button. For example, if I want to tweet to @*Peetscoffee*, the Bay Area's best coffee chain, I visit their account and then look for the "Tweet" button on the left:

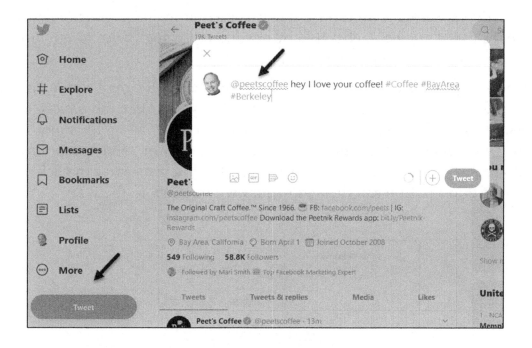

When I click on the "Tweet" link, Twitter then pre-populates my tweet as indicated above. It begins with @*peetscoffee* which is both a "mention" and a way to tweet "to" a person or account. Now here's the deal. Twitter is totally open; you can find anyone on it, and tweet to anyone (except the very weird minority that has made their accounts private). When you include their handle as in @*peetscoffee* in your tweet, this "mention" triggers an alert to them in their feed. This means that you can tweet to anyone on Twitter regardless of whether you follow them, or they follow you. It's completely open.

# USING THE @ SIGN, YOU CAN TWEET TO ANYONE

Unlike Facebook or LinkedIn – you do not need "pre-approval" to converse with someone via Twitter. Again, when your Tweet contains the @*handle* of someone else, that generates an alert in their news feed and often via email. **Via Twitter, you can tweet to anyone!** (*More on this in a moment*).

> **VIDEO.** Watch a video tutorial on how to use the "@" sign or "handle" on Twitter for marketing purposes at **http://jmlinks.com/16y**.

**Understand Mentions and Retweets**

We've already explained a **mention**. When someone includes your @*handle* in their Tweet, that's called a *mention*: clickable by anyone following them, to go "up" to your account and learn about you or your business.

A **retweet** is a special type of mention and designated by *RT* on Twitter. In it, person *A* retweets the tweet of person *B*. Meaning, he takes your tweet and tweets it out to his followers. Imagine if Ellen DeGeneres recapped your joke on her TV show, or imagine if one of your vendor partners tweeted out your product or service announcement to their followers. To retweet a tweet, find a tweet that interests you can click on the two arrows at the bottom. You can then add your own message to the RT:

And then if you click "Retweet with comment:"

You can **retweet** tweets that interest you, and more importantly, your own followers can retweet your tweets to their followers, thus expanding your reach. Getting retweets should be a prime objective of your Twitter marketing. A mention or "retweet" of your tweets would spur followers of followers to learn about you and might result in a massive increase in your follower count. Retweets also show as "mentions" in the account of the person or brand that originally composed the tweet.

You can also of course **comment** on the tweets of others; they get notified that you've commented on their tweet, and this also tends to show in the newsfeed of people who follow you. Interactivity is important for content marketing on Twitter, so follow, like, comment, and retweet the accounts of people in your industry whether they be competitors, industry luminaries, or even customers.

Here's a screenshot of a retweet, designated in Twitter lingo by *RT*:

@*Robots_and_Ais* is retweeting @*Yale* (Yale University) which tweeted about a data science and neuroscience grant which includes a "mention" of @*NSF* (the National Science Foundation). In this way, the followers of @*Robots_and_Ais* learn about the tweet by @*Yale*. This is how information can spread from one account to another on Twitter.

*You don't have to be a Hollywood star to do this: identify important people in your industry and converse with them via the @sign (handles). Your followers can see this conversation, and their followers can see it too (if the person responds to you) — thereby cross-pollinating your accounts. (See technical details below).*

## Tweet (Privately) To Someone

Here are some esoterica about mentions or retweets. When you tweet directly to someone (by including their account (@ sign) <u>at the very beginning</u> of your tweet), that tweet is visible to **only** those folks who follow **both** accounts. If you put a dot "." before the @ sign, your tweet shows up in the news feed (officially called your "timeline" on Twitter, but not to be confused with the "timeline" of Facebook) of all of your followers, even if they do not follow the mentioned account. For example, if I tweet:

*@katyperry love your music, give me free concert tickets!*

> (This tweet shows to ONLY those people who follow @jasoneg3 AND @katyperry) and it shows in Katy Perry's own timeline (if she actually checks it)).

vs.

*.@katyperry loved your concert, give me free concert tickets!*

> (This tweet shows to ALL people who follow @jasoneg3, AND it shows in Katy Perry's own timeline (if she actually checks it)).

And, if Katy responded, then she and I would be having a public conversation viewable to her fans, and to my fans. In other words, if I can provoke a person "more important" than me to engage in a public Twitter conversation, I have the opportunity to get her followers to follow me. (Unfortunately, Katy never responded).

Note: there has been some controversy about how all this works; I've tested it again and again and, despite what Twitter officially says, and despite what the cognoscenti of the blogosphere say, the "old rules" seem to still apply. If you want your tweet to show in your feed to everyone, start it with a "dot." If you want it to be more private, start it with the @ sign. In both cases, realize that nothing is really private on Twitter. You can also DM (Direct Message) a person on Twitter which is a step more private. However, **never** fall into the trap of thinking anything on the Internet is truly private. For both yourself and your brand, think of all your social media content (and emails for that matter) as something that might ultimately come out to haunt you later. Be on your best behavior.

To read more about the "dot" in front of the "@" sign in more detail, visit **http://jmlinks.com/2k**. For the official Twitter guide to Twitter for Business, visit **https://business.twitter.com/** and for the official Twitter help files, visit **https://support.twitter.com/**.

## » INVENTORY OF LIKES & DISLIKES ON TWITTER

Now that you understand the basics of how Twitter works, it's time to research whether your customers are on Twitter and identify competitors in your industry who are on Twitter and/or successful businesses on Twitter to make an inventory of your likes and dislikes.

### Find Accounts on Twitter

Stay signed into your Twitter account. There are several ways to find accounts to follow on Twitter:

- **Visit their Websites**. Most big brands will have a prominent link to Twitter, right on their Website. For example, go to **http://www.rei.com/** or **http://www.wholefoods.com/**, find the Twitter link, click on it, and hit follow. Go to your competitor websites and do the same.

- **Search on Twitter**. While logged in to your account, go to the top right of the screen and in the "Search Twitter" box, enter the names of competitors, businesses you like, or keywords. To find stuff on Twitter about organic food, just type in "organic food" into the search box. Then, when you find an account you like, just click "follow" and you will now see its tweets in your news feed.

- **Advanced Search on Twitter**. You can find Twitter Advanced Search by first doing a search, then clicking on "Search filters" on the left, and then "Advanced Search" at the bottom. Or, just visit **http://jmlinks.com/46k**.

### Use Google to Find Twitter Accounts

Outside of Twitter, go to Google and type in *site:twitter.com* and your keywords. For example, on Google, type in *site:twitter.com "organic food"* and the trusty search engine will identify Twitter accounts with that keyword. Google is often a better way to find Twitter *accounts*, whereas Twitter search is a better way to browse individual *tweets*. Remember: there is no space between site: and twitter – it's *site:twitter.com* not *site: twitter.com*. To see this in action, go to **http://jmlinks.com/2j**.

Once you follow companies, you can browse their Twitter pages easily by clicking on the "following" link at the top left of the page while you are logged in to your Twitter account. In this way, you can see who they follow. Here's a screenshot –

Jason McDonald
@jasoneg3

So if you click on "following", you can see the accounts and persons I follow. If you click on "follower", you can see who follows me. Now, think like a marketer. You can identify competitors, click on folks following them (a.k.a., their customers) and follow them, or even tweet to them. There are no secrets really on Twitter, including the customer lists of your competitors.

For example, I can be an up-and-coming organic grocer in Austin, Texas, and I can research and identify accounts on Twitter that are competitors to me, such as Farmhouse delivery (@*texasfarmhouse*). Then I can click on their followers, and reach out to them. Here's a screenshot of the followers of @*texasfarmhouse*:

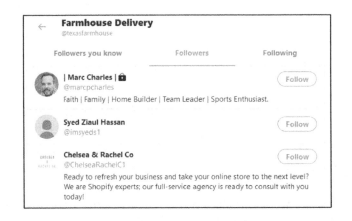

I can not only identify, but also follow and tweet to their followers or customers. I can also review their tweets to see which ones have the most interaction, participate in those conversations, and even follow or tweet directly to those people who make comments. Indeed, I can even create Twitter ads that specifically target the followers of my competitors.

You can also easily find influencers on Twitter. Here's how:

- Use Google and other tools like LinkedIn or Buzzsumo.com to identify Twitter accounts of key influencers, competitors, journalists, etc.

- Search Twitter for "journalist" or "blogger" and your target keywords.

- Tweet "to" these key influencers with a free offer like your latest eBook or a free product sample.

- Look at who they follow (and tweet to those people).

- Look at who follows them (and tweet to those people).

Even if you aren't using Twitter to connect with your customers directly, you can use this "tweet to anyone" strategy in combination with Google and/or LinkedIn to literally communicate with anyone via Twitter! This feature of "Tweet to anyone" is unique to Twitter and is, in my opinion, its coolest feature for marketers.

Returning to company set up issues, your **TO-DO** here is to identify companies on Twitter, both in and outside of your industry, so that you can inventory what you like and dislike. Here are some inventory questions:

- **Username**. Usernames should be short yet convey the brand. Do you like / dislike the usernames of brands that you see?

- **Profile Picture**. As is true in all social media, the profile picture shows when viewed on someone else's timeline. Do you like / dislike the profile pictures of various companies on Twitter? Why or why not?

- **Header Photo**. Similar to the Facebook cover photo, this wide banner dominates the account visuals. How are competitors and other businesses using the header photo on Twitter?

- **Pinned Tweets**. Are any brands using the pinned tweet feature? If so, how?

- **Account Bio**. How are brands using their bio to market via Twitter? Do you see any opportunities or pitfalls here?

- **Following and Followers**. Whom are they following and who follows them? What does this tell you about their effectiveness on Twitter? Are there opportunities to steal their followers? Why and how?

- **Lists**. Have they created lists? Are they on the lists of others? What does this tell you about bookmarking vis-à-vis this company and/or its themes?

## Posting or Tweeting Strategy

You'll quickly realize that Twitter offers little customization and that most of the action on Twitter has to do with *posting strategy* or *tweeting strategy*. What are businesses tweeting, and why? What is their *tweeting rhythm*? Similar to all social media, the idea is to spur interactivity, get replies, retweets, and likes, and drive traffic to desired actions such as website visits or visits to your eCommerce store.

Pay attention to companies in your industry as well as hashtags (see below) in your industry, all the while asking the question: are our customers on Twitter? If so, what are they tweeting about? What are they interacting with, and why?

Let's review some accounts on Twitter and reverse-engineer their posting strategies. Do the same for businesses that you like and/or competitors in your industry.

## Twitter Marketing: Common Uses

Here are common uses for Twitter and example accounts:

- **Celebrities**. Examples are Katy Perry (**https://twitter.com/katyperry**) , Justin Bieber (**https://twitter.com/justinbieber**), Ellen Degeneres (**https://twitter.com/TheEllenShow**).
    - o **Marketing Goals**: stay top of mind, get social shares, use Twitter to cross-promote their concerts and TV shows, **posting rhythm** of *fun, fun, fun, fun, buy my concert tickets,* etc.

- **Politicians**. Examples are Hillary Clinton (**https://twitter.com/hillaryclinton**), Donald Trump (**https://twitter.com/potus**), Bill de Blasio (**https://twitter.com/billdeblasio**).
    - o **Marketing Goals**: stay top of mind, get social shares, use Twitter to motivate followers to take political action. **Posting rhythm** of newsworthy, newsworthy, newsworthy, take political action or donate...

- **Political Causes and Non-Profits**. Examples are Greenpeace (**https://twitter.com/greenpeace**), Red Cross

(**https://twitter.com/redcross**), Catholic Charities
(**https://twitter.com/ccharitiesusa**).

- o **Marketing Goals:** stay top of mind, get social shares, use Twitter followers to take political action or make donations. Posting rhythm is similar to politicians.

- **Brands.** Examples are REI (**https://twitter.com/rei**), Gucci (**https://twitter.com/gucci**), Martha Stewart Living (**https://twitter.com/marthaliving**).

  - o **Marketing Goals:** stay top of mind, get social shares, use Twitter followers to connect to buy actions, also use Twitter as an "insider" or "best customer" channel for secret coupons, inside deals and information. **Posting rhythm** is fun, fun, fun, fun, buy my stuff.

- **Restaurants and Food Trucks.** Examples are Kogi BBQ (**https://twitter.com/kogibbq**), Ricky's Fish Tacos (**https://twitter.com/rickysfishtacos**), Newark Natural Foods (**https://twitter.com/newarkfoods**).

  - o **Marketing Goals.** stay top of mind, get social shares, use Twitter to drive real-world traffic to a store or restaurant, usually looking for insider information or special deals / coupons.

For most for-profit businesses, common marketing goals for Twitter are:

- **Stay top of mind / one touch to many.** To the extent that your users are on Twitter (usually to follow up-to-the-minute news), you can use Twitter to continually remind users about your company, product, and/or service.

- **Insider / loyalty programs.** If you are a brand with a core group of loyal customers (e.g., REI's loyal group of outdoor fanatics, or Gucci's loyal group of fashion addicts), you can use Twitter to stay in touch with this elite group and reward them with insider information, tips, special deals, and even coupons.

- **Coupons / bargains.** If you use coupons or discounts, especially in retail, customers commonly scan Twitter for coupons and special deals.

- **Foodies / coupons / bargains / what's cookin'.** Especially in the food truck industry, but in any big downtown area with a lunch scene, foodies look to Twitter to identify special deals, coupons, and what's cookin'.

- **On-going Discussions**. By using #hashtags (e.g., *#AIDS, #globalwarming, #obamacare*), you can participate in an on-going global discussion and thereby market your products. A special case of this is trade shows, which often use a hashtag (*#CES* for Consumer Electronics Show, for example) to allow participants to converse via Twitter.

- **News Alerts**. To the extent that you generate and/or participate in news, Twitter is the go-to service for breaking news (especially vis hashtags and trending searches).

- **Political Action**. For non-profits and political groups, Twitter is the go-to place to organize politically and discuss politics. If you or your organization is into politics, you gotta be on Twitter!

- **Twitter Chats**. You can have a public chat on Twitter, usually using a custom hashtag. In this way, you can engage and interact with your super fans. See SproutSocial's guide to Twitter chats at **http://jmlinks.com/31q**.

# IDENTIFY COMPANIES WHO DO TWITTER WELL, AND REVERSE ENGINEER THEM

For your next **TO-DO**, download the **Twitter Research Worksheet**. For the worksheet, go to **http://jmlinks.com/social2020** (then reenter the code '**social2020**' to register your workbook), and click on the link to the "Twitter Research Worksheet." You'll answer questions as to whether your potential customers are on Twitter, identify brands to follow, and inventory what you like and dislike about their Twitter set up and marketing strategy.

## » CREATE TWITTER-FRIENDLY CONTENT

Content is king on Twitter, just as it is on all social media. We've already covered the basics, but let's review them:

- Each tweet is limited to **280 characters**, though you can string tweets together.

- **Hashtags**, designated by the # symbol as in *#organic* or *#organicfood* designate conversational themes and are clickable in tweets.

- The **"@" sign** designates a handle and is clickable in a tweet; even when you are not following or followed by a person, using their handle (as for example *@jasoneg3*) is a "mention" and generates an alert to that person.

- **Followers** can view, like, comment on, and share or retweet content on Twitter.

No one is in control of anything on Twitter, and the pace is very fast. In terms of content, you can:

- Tweet just **text**.

- Tweet **text** with **@ signs and #hashtags** to reach out to persons and/or conversational themes.

- Tweet text and **images / photos**.

- Tweet **links** to external websites like blogs.

- Tweet **short-form video** that is "native" on Twitter.

In terms of actual content, you want to tweet things that are of interest to your customers. If you're a brand, you want to tweet news announcements, new products or services, links to new blog posts or YouTube videos, etc. You also want to tweet and comment on industry news.

## TWEET INTERESTING STUFF #DUH #DONTBEBORING

Take a look at a big brand account like REI (*@REI*) and "reverse engineer" their content strategy. You'll see: a) tweets about the outdoors, b) tweets with links to their blogs and YouTube videos, c) contests, d) special deals or coupons as well as "insider" alerts on new products, e) new product alerts, and f) surveys. Compare that with an author or public figure such as the author *@StephenKing*, who tweets out a lot of social commentary as well as interesting stuff relating to his novels. (*Whether his political or social commentary helps or hurts his brand is a question for his marketing team*). Or take a look at @*kogibbq*, the Korean / Mexican fusion barbeque chain in Los Angeles. They tweet 80% the location of their trucks in LA, and 20% is fun photos, what's cooking, and some interaction with their fans.

Each account is filling a content marketing pipeline with tweets that are relevant to its brand, and alternate on a continuum between commentary on industry events or news up to in-your-face, "buy my stuff" content. As with all social media content, it should be 80% or more, *fun fun fun fun fun fun fun fun* and 20% or less *buy my stuff buy my stuff buy my stuff*.

## Twitter Content is What You Make of It

Twitter content, in short, is what you make of it. It's the kind of content that is engaging to your fans and can be as simple as a coupon code, as complex as a link to a blog post on climate change or as silly as your response to #*mondaymadness*.

Do not miss the importance of **interactive** content on Twitter. Twitter is conversational. For example, here's a screenshot of some of the conversation around just one of REI's tweets on the national parks:

REI does a great job with content, but where is the brand participation here? What is the brand's reaction? Sometimes it's as if the brand, public persona, or other person is conspicuous by their absence in interactive content on Twitter. That's a mistake.

Interacting with your fans and others is a key content opportunity on Twitter. So join in the conversation as a brand!

Your to-dos with respect to Twitter content are to identify:

- **hashtags** or topics that you want your brand's message to be part of the conversation;

- **text, images, photo**s, and even **videos** that you can post natively to Twitter on these themes;

- **external links** to your blog or website with summaries posted to Twitter;

- **interactive conversations** between your brand and customers that are relevant and positive for your brand; and,

- an awareness of and readiness for **pushback** from customers and hecklers, as no one is in control of Twitter.

Always look at the problem from the perspective of your target customers. Why will they want to follow you on Twitter? What will they get out of your content? What's in it for them? Is it as simple as a coupon or special deal? Is it participation in an insider or superfan event? Is it a sense of belonging to a "cool club?" Is it a conversation with you and others on Twitter about the news of the day?

The *why* is as important as the *what* when it comes to a Twitter content marketing plan.

## Think Before You Tweet

On a cautionary note, make your team aware that Twitter (and the Internet) is like an elephant. *It never forgets.* Because Twitter is so immediate, people often shoot off their mouths or their tweets without thinking worse than they do on any other social media platform. As the Russians say:

*"A word is not a bird; once it flies out, you can't get it back."*

If you don't have something nice to say (even on Twitter), it's probably better not to say it at all. Stay positive and stay classy. If you're a big brand, have a policy that more than one person needs to look at and approve each and every tweet before it goes out. It's easy to click and tweet, and it's very, very hard to call back a tweet you wish you hadn't sent in the first place.

Just ask the TV star Roseanne (@*therealroseanne*) whose racist tweet ended up getting her TV show canceled in May 2018 after a firestorm of social media outrage (See: **http://jmlinks.com/46m**). One has to wonder where her sanity was, and where her marketing team was *before* she tweeted. If you have a hot-blooded CEO or executive, ask yourself this question *before* an inappropriate tweet causes a social media train wreck for your brand.

## » TWEET TO JOURNALISTS, BLOGGERS, AND INFLUENCERS

One of the uniquely valuable uses of Twitter is a "deep dive" into using this ability to tweet to anyone. Using Twitter's openness, you can identify journalists, bloggers, or other influencers in your industry and tweet to them. They don't have to pre-approve, or "like" you. Twitter is 110% open.

In fact, because Twitter is where news breaks first, it is probably the favorite social media channel of journalists. Thus, since journalists and bloggers actively monitor Twitter for news, they are "hungry" for you to "pitch" them story ideas.

**Journalists and bloggers love Twitter, so tweet your news directly @ them.**

Let's say, for example, that I want to send a free review copy of my *Social Media Marketing Workbook* to journalists and bloggers who write on small business. First, I'd go to Twitter and identify journalists and bloggers through Twitter and Google searches (*site:twitter.com*) for keywords like *small business journalist*, or *small business blogger*. Then, I'd go to each Twitter account, click on the "Tweet to" icon located just below their profile picture, and copy/paste the following message:

> *Hey! I see you write on #smallbusiness. Are you interested in a free review copy of my Social Media Marketing Workbook 2020?*

Here's a screenshot of my tweet to journalist Kai Ryssdal (@kairyssdal) for the 2019 edition:

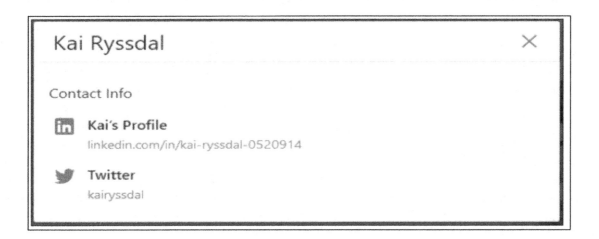

**Tweet to Kai Ryssdal**     ✕

@kairyssdal Hey! I see you write on #smallbusiness. Are you interested in a free review copy of my book, the Social Media Marketing Workbook 2019? Message me back if so.

⊚ Austin, TX

Tweet

Remember that when you use the "Tweet to" feature your tweet is generally not broadcast to your own followers (though it is still public and discoverable) unless you put the period "." in front of the @handle. *In this way, you can use Twitter to send "unsolicited tweets" to journalists and bloggers, without annoying your own followers.* It's not unlike the way you use LinkedIn to reach out to 1st and 2nd level contacts.

## Using LinkedIn and Twitter in Combination

Indeed, you can even use LinkedIn in combination with Twitter. First, search LinkedIn by keywords, click on *People*, and then browse any level (1st, 2nd, or 3rd), click into a person in the search results, and then click on *See contact info* to find their Twitter account (if they inputted it to LinkedIn). Here's a screenshot of Kai Ryssdal on LinkedIn (with whom I am NOT connected), showing that you can use LinkedIn to "find him," click on contact info to find his Twitter account, and then use Twitter to tweet to him.

**Kai Ryssdal**     ✕

Contact Info

**Kai's Profile**
linkedin.com/in/kai-ryssdal-0520914

**Twitter**
kairyssdal

In this way, you can combine the power of LinkedIn's social rolodex to identify journalists, bloggers, and influencers, and the openness of Twitter to reach out to them via "unsolicited" tweets. Here are the steps:

1. Research journalists, bloggers, and other influencers in your industry via Twitter and LinkedIn.

2. Have a "carrot" ready such as a free eBook, webinar, wine-and-cheese event at an industry trade show, etc.

3. Tweet to them a solicitation essentially saying, "*@journalist* Hey I see that you are a journalist / blogger / influencer interested in {*keyword*} and I have this {*carrot*}. Are you interested?"

As is always true on social media, however, don't be spammy. Have a legitimate and interesting reason why you are reaching out to them and be respectful. If they do not show interest, move on to the next target.

## » BRAINSTORM AND EXECUTE A TWEETING STRATEGY

Optimizing your account on Twitter is pretty straightforward. As indicated above, a good way to do this is to compare / contrast pages that you like and use your inventory list to identify to-dos. Next, the real work begins. *What will you tweet? Who will care?* Let's reverse engineer some companies and their **tweeting strategies**:

**Kogi BBQ (https://twitter.com/kogibbq)**. Their tweeting strategy is 90% about the location of the taco truck, with a few tweets about "what's cooking" or "insider specials," and the occasional back-and-forth with a hard-core Kogi fan about the joys of Korean BBQ. That's it.

**REI (https://twitter.com/rei)**. Their tweets are largely off-loads to blog posts, YouTube videos, and Instagram photos about the fun of outdoor activities, some participatory contests for hard-core REI fans, headline links to in-depth blog posts on outdoor fun, and about 10% shameless "buy our stuff isn't this a cool product" tweets. Like many retailers, REI uses Twitter as a place to communicate deals, insider information, and special offers to its most devoted customers.

**Woot (https://twitter.com/woot)**. Their tweets are 100% about discounts and bargains, as Woot (owned now by Amazon) is all about discounts and special deals. It's the home shopping network gone Twitter.

**Greenpeace** (**https://twitter.com/greenpeace**). This non-profit tweets photos that inspire about wildlife and nature, links to blog posts about environmental issues, and political calls to action.

**Cato Institute** (**https://twitter.com/catoinstitute**). This political action organization tweets about politics from a conservative perspective, with offlinks to its blog and videos plus the occasional call to action.

**Zak George** (**https://twitter.com/zakgeorge**). A dog trainer and huge YouTube success, Zak George tweets links to his YouTube videos, some links to his Facebook page, and the occasional tweet about a sponsored product.

Throughout, your job is to reverse engineer competitors or companies you admire in terms of their tweeting strategy. What are they tweeting (blog posts, pictures, infographics, videos), and why are they tweeting it (to stay top of mind, sell stuff, get viewers on YouTube). Who is following them and why? What's in it for the followers? How does all this tweeting activity lead ultimately to some sort of sale or business action? Summing up, Twitter is used most commonly, to:

- stay top of mind, pestering and reminding customers to "look at me, look at me!";

- communicate with influencers, superfans, and fans, i.e., people who are passionate (or potentially passionate) about your brand;

- leverage *#hashtags* to reach a wider audience and participate in society-wide discussions; and/or

- reach out to journalists, bloggers, and other influencers.

For your next **TO-DO**, download the **Twitter Tweeting Strategy Worksheet**. For the worksheet, go to **http://jmlinks.com/social2020** (then reenter the code '**social2020**' to register your workbook), and click on the link to the "Twitter Tweeting Strategy Worksheet." You'll answer questions to help you understand what other companies are doing on Twitter, and begin to outline your own tweeting strategy.

## Content is King

As you work on a tweeting strategy, you'll quickly realize you need a lot of content! Remember to create a **content marketing system** of:

- **Your own content**. Twitter is all about off-loads to blog posts, infographics, images, photos, videos, Memes, and other types of your own content. Twitter and blogging go together like peas and carrots, while Twitter and video go together like scotch and soda.

- **Other people's content**. Relevant content in your industry. By curating out the garbage and identifying the cool, fun, interesting stuff, you can use other people's content to help your tweets stay top of mind.

- **Interactive content**. Twitter is perhaps the most interactive social media platform. ""Like" the tweets of others. "Comment" on the tweets of others. "Retweet" them to your followers with comments. @*mention* people constantly. "Tweet to" famous people, superfans, and influencers, even if you don't know them. By interacting with the content of others you can open the door to "real" relationships.

To identify relevant content from other people, I recommend setting up a Feedly account (**http://www.feedly.com/**) and using tools like Buzzsumo (**http://www.buzzsumo.com**), and Google Alerts (**https://www.google.com/alerts**). You can also create Twitter lists by topic and thus pre-organize whom you follow into easy-to-access and content-specific lists. Use a tool like TweetDeck to take this to the next level. Organize your content into topic groups, and then as you find content useful to your target audience, "tweet out" that content. Also, monitor key *#hashtags* in your industry and chime in with relevant tweets (and retweets) on topics that are trending.

Use a tool like Hootsuite to schedule your tweets in advance. Or, inside of TweetDeck (now owned by Twitter), you can use its built-in scheduler.

As for your own content, Twitter is best used by staying on topic and sharing original, useful content such as in-depth blog posts, free eBooks or webinars, infographics and instructographics, videos on YouTube. Twitter is a headline service pointing to the "rest of the story" on your blog, video, or infographic.

## » PROMOTE YOUR TWITTER ACCOUNT AND TWEETS

Once you've set up your Twitter account, and begun to populate it with tweets on a regular basis, you've essentially "set up" your party on Twitter. Now it's time to send out the invitations.

**In and of itself, a Twitter Page will not be self-promoting! You've got to promote it!**

Assuming your Twitter account shares lots of yummy, useful, fun, provocative content that when seen by a user will entice him or her to "follow" you on Twitter, here are some common ways to promote your Twitter account and Tweets:

- **Real World to Social.** Don't forget the real world! If you are a museum store, for example, be sure that the cashiers recommend to people that they "follow" you on Twitter? *Why? Because they'll get insider tips, fun do-it-yourself posts, announcements on upcoming museum and museum store events, etc.* Get your staff to promote Twitter in that important face-to-face interaction. If you're a barbeque truck in Los Angeles, post signs to "follow us on Twitter" on the trucks, and have staff cajole customers to "follow you." *Why follow you on Twitter? To learn where the taco truck is, to get special deals, and to learn what's cooking.* Use the real world to promote your Twitter account, and be ready to explain "why" they should follow you on Twitter. What's in it for them?

- **Cross-Promotion.** Link your website to your Twitter Page, your blog posts to your Twitter Page, your YouTube to your Twitter Page, etc. Notice how big brands like REI do this: one digital property promotes another digital property.

- **Email**. Email your customer list and ask them to follow you on Twitter. Again, you must explain what's in it for them.

- **Twitter Internal**. Interact with other accounts via the @ sign, share their content, comment on timely topics using #hashtags, and reach out to complementary pages to work with you on co-promotion. (See below).

- **Use Twitter Plugins**. Twitter has numerous plugins that allow you to "embed" your Twitter Page on your website, and thereby nurture cross-promotion. To learn more about plugins, visit **http://jmlinks.com/31r**. Among the better ones –

  o **The Tweet Button**. Make it easy for people to tweet your content (e.g., blog posts).

o **The Follow Button**. Make it easy for Web visitors to follow you on Twitter.

- **Leverage your Fans**. People who like your Twitter Page are your best promoters. Do everything you can to get them to retweet you to their own followers. Remember, it's *social* (!) media, and encouraging your customers to share your content is the name of the game. You want to leverage your fans as much as possible to share your content.

# DON'T FORGET THE REAL WORLD AS A TWITTER PROMOTION STRATEGY

### Three Special Ways to Promote via Twitter.

Twitter has three very special ways to promote yourself or your company that are much stronger than on other social media.

### Use #Hashtags to Promote Your Company

The first is the **hashtag**. Because Twitter is all about news, the use of hashtags on trending or controversial topics is bigger on Twitter than on any other social media. Identify trending or important hashtags and include them in your tweets. Use **http://hashtagify.me** to identify hashtags in your industry, and don't forget about major trade shows which often have (and promote) their own hashtags. Then include these hashtags in your tweets, and make sure that your tweets are not only on topic but also offlink to something useful, provocative or important. In that way, they'll discover you via a hashtag and then follow you permanently.

> **VIDEO.** Watch a video tutorial on how to use the "#" sign or "hashtag" on Twitter for marketing purposes at **http://jmlinks.com/16u**.

### Industry Trade Shows and Hashtags

Here's a hashtag use you do not want to miss: industry trade shows. Nearly every industry has THE trade show or a few KEY trade shows. Nowadays, these will have hashtags, such as *#CES2019* for the 2019 Consumer Electronics Show. To see the

*#CES2019* hashtag in action, visit **http://jmlinks.com/31s**. Obviously this show occurs every year and the 2020 hashtag *(#CES2020)* is rather easy to guess in advance.

Pre-identify the hashtags of your own industry trade show(s) as well as subordinate, session or topic hashtags, and start tweeting on those themes before, during and shortly after the show. Attendees know to look for the show hashtags to find out what's cool, exciting, and worth visiting.

### Episodic Use of Twitter for Marketing

For many businesses, simply knowing the hashtag of "the" industry conference and tweeting during the yearly, or twice yearly, trade conference in and of itself will justify using Twitter for marketing:

> *Hey, #CES2020 attendees! Come by our booth at 2:30 pm for a free laser wand give-away.*

Identify the Twitter account of the industry trade show(s), and they'll easily show you the relevant hashtags. Make sure you have a robust Twitter account set up before the big show, and then during the show start tweeting on show-related hashtags. For many businesses, this "trade show" use of Twitter is the most important marketing use of Twitter.

Here's something *devious*. Identify the hashtags for all your industry shows, including the ones you do *not* attend in the "real world," and insert them into your tweets during show time. In this way, you can tweet "to" attendees of a show without actually being there!

### @Someonefamous

The second promotion strategy is what I call **@someonefamous**. The idea here is to reach out and "have a conversation" with someone more famous (with more followers) than you. Think of it like Dr. Phil making it on the Oprah Winfrey show: her audience saw this new "doctor," and some of her fans became his fans. The trick is to find business partners, complementary companies, or other people / companies on Twitter who are influencers and who have more and/or different fan bases than you.

A useful tool to use is Buzzsumo (**http://www.buzzsumo.com/**). Search for your keywords and identify influencers tweeting about those topics. Identifying them is the easy part. The hard part is getting them to engage in a Twitter conversation with you. You have to convince them to have a conversation with you on Twitter, and then once you're talking to their fans... convince their fans to follow you, too.

Once you are lucky enough to start a conversation with someone more famous than you, remember to use the "dot" in front of the "@" sign to correctly broadcast your message. To learn more about this, visit **http://jmlinks.com/2k**.

> **VIDEO.** Watch a video tutorial on how to use the "@" sign or "handle" on Twitter for marketing purposes at **http://jmlinks.com/16y**.

**Pitch Journalists via Twitter**

We've discussed this already, but you want to think of journalists and bloggers on Twitter as a promotion strategy:

> **@journalists**. Identify journalists on Twitter, find their handles, and tweet "to" the journalists, pitching them on story ideas. Journalists love Twitter because it's where stories break first. They listen to their Twitter feeds as businesses, organizations, and individuals "pitch" them on story ideas via Twitter.

Indeed, you can even advertise to select lists of journalists by using username targeting on Twitter. One simple trick is to just search twitter for the word "journalist" plus a keyword like "organic" and then click on "people." Here's a screenshot:

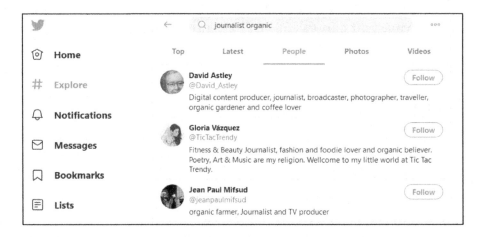

In this way you can quickly build out a targeted list of journalists who cover the organic industry. Follow them, tweet to them, and pitch them on your content. Isn't Twitter amazing?

**Get Retweeted**

The third Twitter promotion strategy is the **retweet**. By posting items that are funny, scandalous, interesting, shocking, outrageous or otherwise highly contagious, you get people to retweet your tweets, thereby (again) allowing their followers to see you, and hopefully, begin to follow you as well. To research what is retweeted in your industry, simply do a Twitter search with the letters "*RT*" in front of your keywords. For an example, visit **http://jmlinks.com/21** to see a search on Twitter of retweets of *#organic* as in "RT organic" searched via Twitter search.

Here's a sample RT:

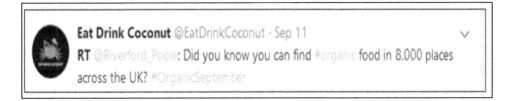

## » ADVERTISE ON TWITTER

Besides these organic promotion methods, there's paid advertising on Twitter. You can promote your tweets as well as create custom advertising campaigns to promote your account and/or clicks to your website. To begin advertising, log in to your account and click on your profile at the left. Then find "Twitter ads." Here's a screenshot:

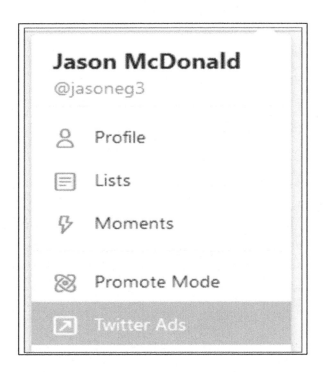

This gets you to the dashboard. You can then set up *Campaigns > Ad Groups > Ads* and target them to audiences. Click to *Tools > Audience Manager* to see Twitter's targeting options. As you create a Campaign, you'll be prompted either to promote your account or an individual tweet. You can then choose demographic targeting. Here's a screenshot showing people who show interest in "organic:"

| KEYWORDS | | |
|---|---|---|
| organic | Add | Exclude |

**BEHAVIORS**

| | | |
|---|---|---|
| Natural & organics – Buyers of natural & organic products. Provided by Datalogix. | Add | Exclude |
| Natural living – People who choose natural and organic alternatives for every item on their l... | Add | Exclude |

FOLLOWER LOOK-ALIKES

| | |
|---|---|
| Organic Consumers, @OrganicConsumer | Add |
| Plum Organics, @PlumOrganics | Add |
| Organic Live Food, @OrganicLiveFood | Add |
| Organic Lifestyle, @OrganicLife | Add |
| Organic Valley, @OrganicValley | Add |
| Planet Organic, @planetorganicuk | Add |
| OrganicEnergy™, @ScheckterEnergy | Add |
| Organic Life, @OrganicLifeMag | Add |
| BluePrint, @BPOrganic | Add |
| Happy Family Organics, @HappyFamily | Add |

CONVERSATION TOPICS

Note that you can target the followers of any account; meaning you can target people who follow your competitor, or people who follow an industry trade show, etc. Twitter also has a new feature called "promote mode" that is based on "artificial intelligence." It promotes your account for $99 / month. To access this feature, log in to your account, click on your icon at the top right, and find "Promote Mode." Here's a screenshot:

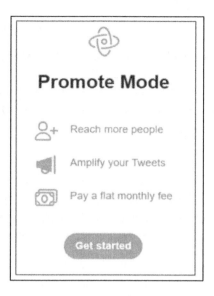

This new mode walks you through a country-specific target and keywords and is an easy way to promote your account.

To learn more about advertising on Twitter visit **http://jmlinks.com/31t** or **https://ads.twitter.com/**. Because journalists and bloggers often follow Twitter intensely for breaking news, one of the smartest strategies is to make an "influencer list" on influencers on Twitter and then advertise your tweets directly to those high-impact Twitterers. To learn more about username and follower targeting on Twitter, visit **http://jmlinks.com/1k**.

## » MEASURE YOUR RESULTS

Measuring the success or failure of your Twitter marketing can be a challenge. Let's look at it from the "bottom up" in terms of items a marketer might want to know or measure vis-a-vis Twitter:

- **Sales or Sales Leads**. Have tweets or Twitter marketing resulted in actual sales leaders (completed feedback forms for a free offer, consultation, eBook, download, etc.) and/or eCommerce sales?

- **Branding / Awareness**. Has Twitter increased our brand awareness and/or improved our brand image?

- **Top of Mind / One Touch to Many**. Has Twitter helped us to stay "top of mind," by reminding potential customers of our company, products, and/or services?

- **Tweet Interactivity**. Have people read our tweets? Have they interacted with our tweets by favoriting them, and/or retweeted our tweets?

- **Twitter Account**. Is our follower count increasing, and if so, by how much and how fast? Where are our followers physically located, and what are their demographic characteristics?

The last of these is the easiest to measure: simply record your Twitter follower count each month, and keep a record of it month-to-month. I generally do this on my *Keyword Worksheet*, where I also track inbound links to my website, and my review count on review media such as Google, Facebook, and Yelp.

## Analytics Inside of Twitter

Inside of Twitter, click on your profile picture on the left of the screen, and then in the pull-down menu at the three dots, click on Analytics. Here's a screenshot:

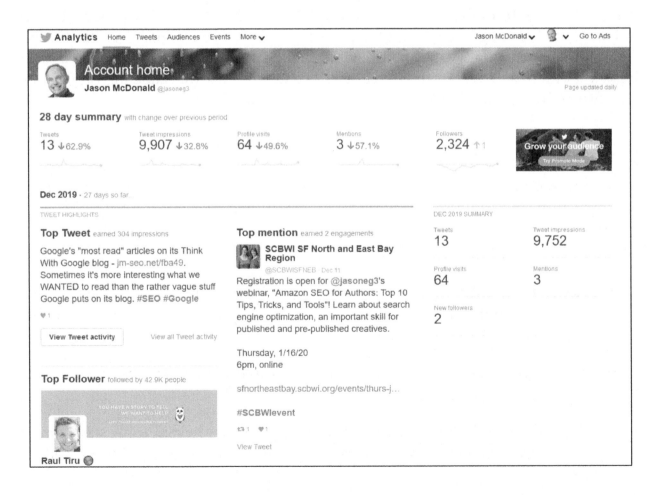

There you can see which tweets gained the most impressions, as well as engagements by Tweet such as clicks, follows, and retweets. Twitter will also tell you whether links you are sharing are getting clicked on and so on and so forth. Twitter also has a feature called **Twitter cards** that bridges your website to/from Twitter activity If you enable Twitter cards on your Website, you get attribution for your Web content plus more data on that inside of Twitter. Learn more at **http://jmlinks.com/31u**.

## Google Analytics

Most of us want to drive traffic from Twitter to our website, or even better to our e-commerce store or to download a free eBook or software package to get a sales lead. Google Analytics will measure how traffic flows from Twitter to your website, and then what happens upon arrival.

Sign up for Google Analytics (**https://analytics.google.com/**) and install the required tracking code. Inside of your Google Analytics account on the left column, drill down by clicking on *Acquisition > Social > Overview*. Then on the right-hand side of the screen, you'll see a list of Social Networks. Find Twitter on that list, and click on that. Google Analytics will tell you what URLs people clicked to from Twitter to your Website, giving you insights into what types of web content people find attractive.

You can also create a Segment to look at only Twitter traffic and its behavior. For information on how to create custom Segments in Google Analytics, go to **http://jmlinks.com/1f**. For the Google help files on Segments go to **http://jmlinks.com/1g**.

In sum, inside of Twitter, you can see how people interact with your Twitter account and tweets. Inside of Google Analytics, you can see where they land on your website and what they do after they arrive.

## »» CHECKLIST: TWITTER ACTION ITEMS

Test your knowledge of Twitter! Take the *Twitter marketing quiz* at **http://jmlinks.com/qztw**. Next, here are your Twitter **Action Items**:

❑ **Research** whether your customers (and competitors) are on Twitter. What are they doing? What interests them, and Why?

❑ Identify a few **customer profiles** that match your *buyer personas*, and determine how active they are.

❑ Identify **companies** to "emulate" or "reverse engineer" who are doing a good job on Twitter.

❑ Set up a **Twitter account** (learn the basics like #hashtags, @mentions, and retweets) and begin posting useful content following the 280 character limit and Twitter lingo.

❑ Brainstorm a **Twitter content marketing strategy** of your own content, the content of others, and interactive content on industry trends and topics. You need a lot of content to succeed at Twitter!

❑ Strategize how to **promote** your Twitter account and tweets, including **advertising** to promote content and grow your followers.

❑ Identify, join, and participate in **relevant #hashtags** on Twitter used by your target customers; do not spam!

❑ Identify **key influencers** (e.g., journalists or bloggers) and note their @*handles*. Where appropriate, tweet to these key influencers when you have highly interesting content or free offers such as eBooks, key news, new product samples, etc.

❑ **Measure** your **KPIs** on Twitter such as the follower growth, likes, comments and retweets of your tweets as well as traffic from Twitter to your website or eCommerce site.

Check out the **free tools**! Go to my *Social Media Marketing Dashboard > Twitter* for my favorite free tools on Twitter. Just visit **http://jmlinks.com/smmdash**.

## ⏵⏵ DELIVERABLE: A TWITTER MARKETING PLAN

Now that we've come to the end of our chapter on Twitter, your **DELIVERABLE** has arrived. Go to **http://jmlinks.com/social2020** (then reenter the code '**social2020**' to register your workbook), and click on the link to the "Twitter Marketing Plan." By filling out this plan, you and your team will establish a vision of what you want to achieve via Twitter.

# 6
# INSTAGRAM

Owned by Facebook, Instagram now boasts 1 billion *daily* users, and *millions upon millions* of photos and videos shared per day. Its "stories" feature, which allows a daily picture / video blog for users, now surpasses 500 million daily users, double that of competitor Snapchat. Instagram is far and away the #1 photo-sharing social network. But, is Instagram for you? Or, more importantly, is Instagram for your business? The trick from a marketing perspective is to not only "fish where the fish are," or rather "share photos where the photo sharers are," but a) to identify and create incredible photo and video content that will engage your customers, and b) to promote your Instagram content to really build your brand and sell more stuff. And with IGTV or "Instagram TV," Instagram is setting its sites on being the YouTube for a new generation in a new, vertical format.

In this Chapter, we'll start with the basics of how to use Instagram, proceed to how to research and identify brands to emulate, and turn to tips, tricks, and techniques to leverage Instagram's free and paid opportunities. Along the way, we'll look behind the scenes to "reverse engineer" companies that do Instagram well. By Chapter's end, you'll have a good idea as to whether Instagram is just a waste of time for you (*because either your customers aren't on it in a meaningful way, or because you can't connect your brand to the fun, family, photos, and fake of Instagram, or both*), or whether Instagram is a social media network that will help you not only photograph, but bring home, the marketing bacon.

**Let's get started!**

**To-do List:**

» Explore Concepts and Brands on Instagram

» Reverse Engineer Instagram Strategies

» Set up Your Business Page on Instagram

» Learn Technical Tips to Using Instagram

» IGTV: Instagram TV, Instagram Stories, and Snapchat

» Inventory Likes and Dislikes on Instagram

» Brainstorm and Plan an Instagram Marketing Strategy

» Promote Your Instagram Account and Posts

» Work with Instagram Influencers

» Measure Your Instagram KPIs

»» Checklist: Instagram Action Items

»» Deliverable: an Instagram Marketing Plan

## » EXPLORE CONCEPTS AND BRANDS ON INSTAGRAM

Instagram is phone-first, meaning it is an app that is meant to be enjoyed on the mobile phone. 99.9% of your users will use Instagram on the phone or tablet, and I doubt that many people even know you can access Instagram on the desktop (although you can). So get out your iPhone or Android Device and visit the Apple App Store or Google Play on your phone. Search for "Instagram App" and download and install the app if you haven't already. For personal use, it's best to use Instagram on your phone, and as a marketer, I recommend that you do so as well so that you experience Instagram how it's meant to be experienced, and how most of your users will experience your own brand.

Use Instagram as a user, first, before producing Instagram content as a marketer, second.

It's probably easier for purposes of marketing research, however, to use Instagram on the desktop. Once you have it installed on your phone with a username and password, just visit **https://www.instagram.com/** and login to your account. You (and your team) can now browse, research, and "reverse engineer" competitors and other brands from your big-screen desktop. For purposes of easy explanation, I recommend you start out by visiting and following Kool-Aid (yes, the tasty beverage you may have enjoyed as a kid) at **http://jmlinks.com/34a** or @*koolaid* as they say in Instagram-speak. Kool-Aid is an easy-to-understand, consumer brand on Instagram.

As we walk step-by-step through Kool-Aid's business profile, I want you to "drink the Instagram Kool-Aid" so to speak, and get the hang of looking behind the scenes at what Kool-Aid (and other brands) are trying to do on Instagram. Instagram is fun! Instagram is a party!

But, calm yourself down, and remember, social media marketing is not just about throwing a fantastic party. It's about throwing **a party with a purpose**, namely to bolster your brand equity among your target audience and, ultimately, to sell more stuff (or more Kool-Aid) as we shall see.

## The Elements of An Instagram Profile

Starting on Kool-Aid's business profile on Instagram, you'll see the following elements:

**Profile Picture.** This is the big smiling red icon that represents the Kool-Aid brand. Notice how it's a smile, and not a frown, because Instagram (like its parent, Facebook, is all about friends, family, fun, photos, and fake). Everyone is having a good time on Instagram, and if they're not, they're supposed to fake it.

**The Timeline.** It may not be officially called a "timeline," but as on a Facebook business Page, any user can click "up" to the account and see the "timeline," a series of posts by the brand (or a friend) to his or her account. These are represented by square boxes. Note in the top right corner of any Instagram post that there is often a video camera icon (indicating a video post), or if the icon is missing, it's just a photo. Unlike other networks, Instagram starts with the photo or video; you can't post something that is text alone.

**Status Stats.** Across the top, you can see whether you are "following" an account, as well as the number of posts, of followers, and of those being followed. Kool-Aid has 27,400 followers, 202 posts, and is following 13 accounts. Like Twitter, this is public knowledge; anyone can pretty much instantly see who follows whom, and then follow the followers of a competitor and interact with them to gain their attention.

**The Bio.** Any profile on Instagram, whether that of a person or of a brand, has a bio and the bio is allowed one (*and only one*) **clickable website link**. This is the place to explain your business value proposition (your answer to the question, why follow you on Instagram?) and use the clickable link to get customers from Instagram and to your website, e-commerce store, or another place to take an action such as buy your stuff. New on Instagram, just below the bio are "Story Highlights," little snippets with clickable links that are excerpts from the company's "Story."

Here's a screenshot of Kool-Aid's brand page on Instagram:

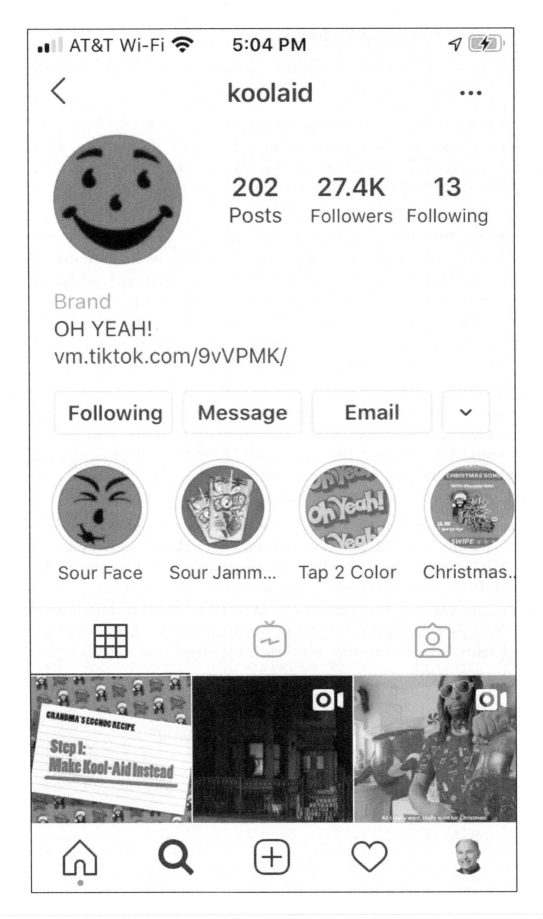

You can see the red smiling Kool-Aid profile picture, that it has 202 posts, nearly 27,400 followers, and is following 13. It's bio just says "Oh yeah!" with a link to its TikTok account. Just below that are the "Story Highlights," which are little video snippets from its larger story with links. The three photos below that are its latest posts, and the video camera icon in the top right indicates that two of the three are videos.

Kool-Aid is not, however, taking advantage of all available features for brand pages. Let's review what Kool-Aid is doing right and what not so right on Instagram. First, it is on Instagram, participating and sharing content. So that's a plus. Second, it is taking advantage of the clickable link in its bio, and this is a big opportunity not to be missed, as it is the ONLY link easily available to all brands on Instagram. That's the link to Kool-Aid's TikTok account, but it could be to its website or e-commerce store. Third, however, a brand can include a *hashtag* in its bio (such as a brand-centric hashtag by which its avid super fans can share their own photos and experiences about the brand), and mentions of partner brands using the "@" symbol. A brand can also include a message button and email link (which Kool-Aid has), and even a new "shop" feature to leverage Instagram for e-commerce. On the negative side, therefore, Kool-Aid is missing a brand hashtag and failing to use the shop feature.

As a contrast, take a look at Rustic Cuff at **https://www.instagram.com/rusticcuff/**. Rustic Cuff is a Tulsa-based boutique producer of custom bracelet jewelry. As with Kool-Aid, here's a screenshot from my iPhone, as not all features are visible on the desktop:

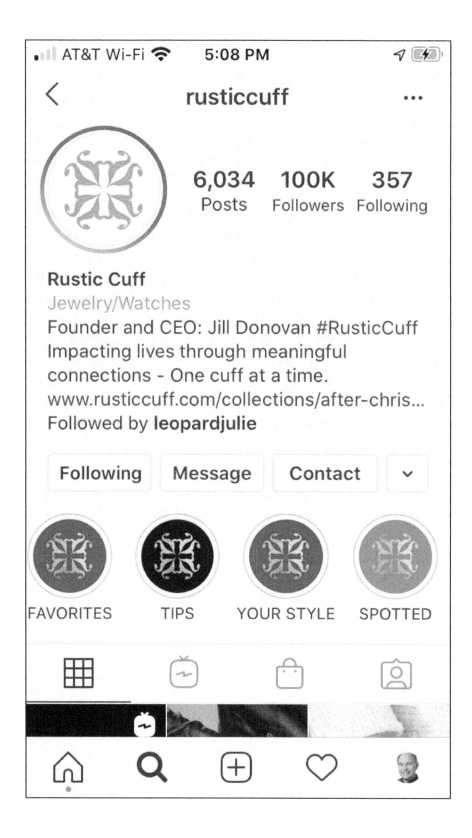

Notice, first of all, the branded hashtag or *#RusticCuff*. Click on this on your phone or on the desktop, and this takes you to posts by both the vendor and its fans around the brand. You can access it at **http://jmlinks.com/45d**. Here's a screenshot:

This means that there are 26,353 posts around the branded hashtag. Many are from Rustic Cuff, but many are from customers, fans, and superfans, too. So a branded hashtag is a big opportunity for your brand and superfans to build community through photo and video sharing to your branded hashtag.

Returning to the Rustic Cuff Instagram account, notice the "shop" button. (Note: you will see this button only on the mobile version, not the desktop. It's the little "shopping bag" icon). This new "Instagram Shop" feature is a direct connection to an e-commerce store. Learn more at **http://jmlinks.com/45e**. Here's a screenshot of what you see after you click the "shop" icon on Rustic Cuff's Instagram page:

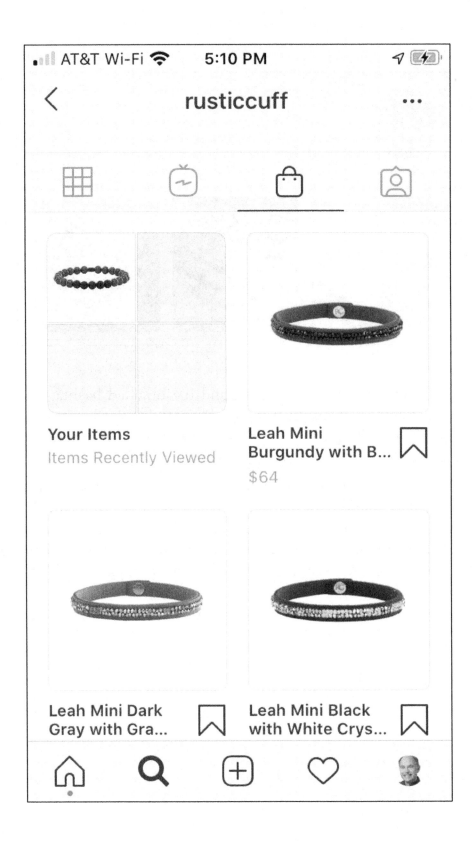

This allows a user to toggle between Rustic Cuff posts that she likes and the e-commerce store and thus purchase them via a direct link from Instagram.

As with all social networks, look at competitors and big brands through the prism not only of a user but of a social media marketer. What do you like? What do you dislike? What features are enabled, such as the clickable contact links, branded hashtags, or the new shop feature? Take this knowledge back to your own Instagram account, and enable what you like, and disable or ignore what you don't.

Once you know a question such as "How do I set up shop tags on Instagram?," you can literally "Google it" to find an answer, visit YouTube for helpful videos, or visit the Instagram help files at **https://help.instagram.com/**. Instagram also has a more advertising-focused resource for businesses at **https://business.instagram.com/**.

### The Elements of an Instagram Post

Returning to *@koolaid*, let's take a look at the elements of an Instagram post. Here's a screenshot of a recent post by the tasty drink maker:

They're posting a co-op marketing effort with *@LilJon* that's a Christmas contest. Notice the reference to "link in Bio."

Here are the elements:

**The Photo (Or Video).** This is, of course, is the primary element on Instagram. This is a photo you upload from your camera or take directly with the Instagram app. You can edit it in Instagram (or use third-party apps), put on filters, etc., but ultimately it's just a photo (yes, a photo that you have done so incredibly artistically and amazingly well that it "goes viral" and gets your users so excited that they like, comment, and share your post to others – but structurally and conceptually, it's just a photo or a video).

**The Caption.** This is what the user inputs about the photo. Kool-Aid's is "We're kicking off December" Notice the use of hashtags and "link in bio" as a way to direct users to places to get more information and join in on the conversation.

**The Comments.** Users can comment on a post, and you can see those here. Many of them include their own *#hashtags* or *@handles* as well. This gets to the social media nature of Instagram; read the comments in detail, and you'll see that they are very "unfiltered." Instagram is all about pop, mass culture, so be prepared. Perhaps not everyone will be as excited about LilJon's co-op relationship with KoolAid as you are.

**The Likes.** Symbolized by the "heart" sign on Instagram, these "likes" function just like a "like" on a Facebook post, indicating that the user "likes" it, or "endorses" it. This post has 536 "likes."

**Other Elements.** On the phone, one can click on the heart icon, the comment icon (to make a comment) as well as a little paper airplane icon (to "send" it to one's friends akin to a "share" on Facebook or Twitter), and a "bookmark" icon to save it to a collection.

**Clickable Action.** This occurs only on paid advertising posts. Normally, a post to Instagram cannot have a clickable item (so most organic posts will say something like "click on the link in my bio for more info"). But advertising posts, can and do have clickable links. As you browse Instagram on your phone, pay attention to the ads, and you'll see blue buttons / clickable actions. Otherwise, most brands will say "click link in bio" to learn more.

You can post about anything to Instagram but the posts by brands that do the best fit the culture of friends, family, fun, and photos. Keep it simple. Keep it fun. And keep it photogenic to succeed on Instagram.

For instance, here's a post by Southwest Airlines (**https://www.instagram.com/southwestair/**) of two married flight attendants on Valentine's Day that got 6,959 likes and hundreds of comments:

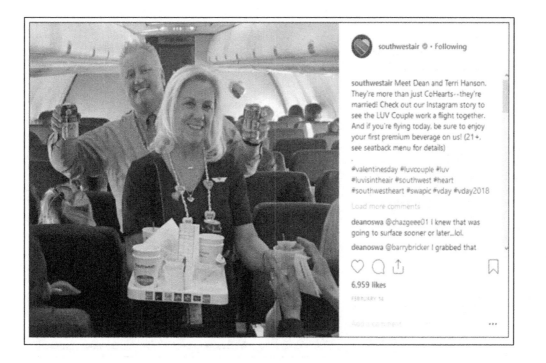

Notice the use of hashtags like *#valentinesday, #luv, #southwest* and *#vday2018* which helped to promote the post across users browsing Instagram on the international day for lovers. If you think about this post as an example of content marketing, you can see that the SouthWest brand is piggybacking on the "friends, family, and fun" sharing that goes on around Valentine's Day by featuring two wonderful employees who are in love. It's building the SouthWest brand as a "fun" company and thus in a subtle way building the company's brand equity. The best brand posts on Instagram work with (and not against) its photogenic culture of friends, family, and friends.

## Searching Instagram

As you get started, an easy way to find posts and brands on Instagram is to use the desktop version. This gives you a big screen, and you and your team can work together to research what's relevant to your brand on Instagram.

Just enter keywords like "organic" or "weddings" into Instagram search, and you can browse posts and thus find persons and brands to follow. If you enter "wedding," for example, it will show you possible accounts to follow in the pull-down. Here's a screenshot:

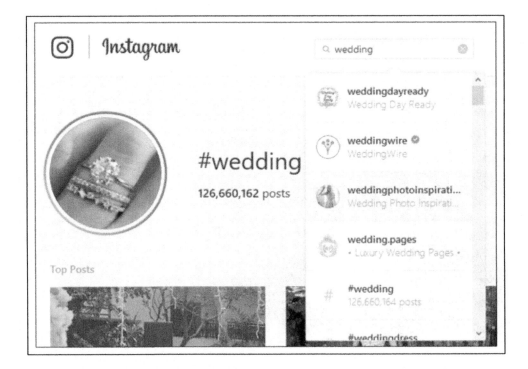

If you put the "#" sign in front, it becomes a hashtag which is more about finding posts than accounts, as in *#weddings*. Try typing in some of your keywords with the # (hashtag) symbol; just remember that hashtags are always made with no spaces, so it's *#valentinesday* not *#valentines day* or *#valentines #day*. As you find posts, click on them and you can see the poster's account at the top; you can click up to check them out or just click "Follow" to follow that account. Here's a screenshot:

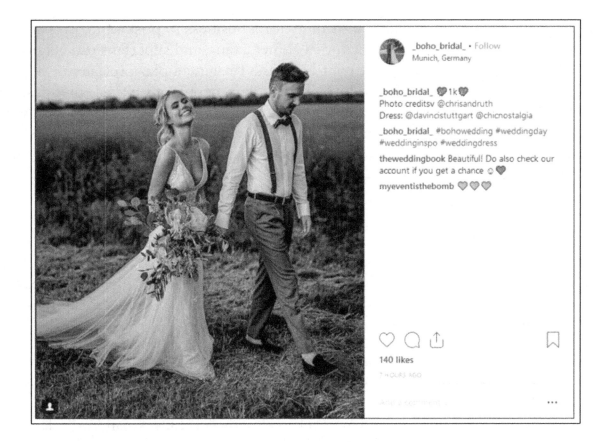

You can also use Google to search Instagram. Just go to Google and type in *site:instagram.com {keyword}* (no space between site: and instagram.com), as for example *site:instagram.com organic* or **http://jmlinks.com/45f**. Using these techniques, identify brands that are either competitors to you, in or near your industry, or just doing a great job on Instagram as marketers. Look for ideas in terms of how they set up their account, and – most importantly – how and what they are posting to Instagram. Which posts are getting the most likes and comments? Which features such as "stories" or "shopping" are enabled and why?

## Instagram Stories

In competition with Snapchat, Instagram has a feature called *Instagram stories*, which is now averaging 500 million daily users (roughly two times as many as Snapchat stories). These are short narrative video clips that tell your story on a day-to-day basis. If someone you are following has a story, their Profile Picture will glow on the phone with a pinkish / red circle around it.). Simply click on their icon, and then you can watch a short video of that person's (or brand's) Instagram story. To learn more about Instagram Stories, read the help file at **http://jmlinks.com/27n**.

You can easily see the marketing opportunity for a business to post a fun, provocative "insider" story to Instagram so that your customers, fans, and superfans can get insider information and fun insights about your business. Imagine a pizza restaurant posting an Instagram story of "how we make our incredible pepperoni pizza," or a fashion designer sharing his daily shaving and man-beauty routine. "Insider stories" are what brand stories are ultimately about on Instagram. Check out your competitors and companies-to-emulate and see what they post to their stories; reverse engineer the marketing message nestled inside a good "story."

**Sample Instagram Business Accounts**

Here are some brands that do Instagram well. Pay attention to their account set up, including branded hashtags, use of the "shop" feature, stories, story highlights, etc., and then to what they're posting not just in terms of photos but in terms of captions and hashtags as well as the user engagement.

**Rustic Cuff** at **https://www.instagram.com/rusticcuff/**. This Tulsa-based retailer of handmade bracelets is one of my hometown favorites, and uses all the major features. It's proof that a relatively small business can really leverage Instagram including the "shop" feature.

**MadeWell** at **https://www.instagram.com/madewell**. Here's the mother ship (for females) of the casual brand. Another excellent example of over-the-top chic materialism on Instagram. "Shop till you drop."

**MadeWellMens** at **https://www.instagram.com/madewellmens**. This casual-chic brand does an excellent job at connecting Instagram to its shopping feature. Pay special attention to how it "tags" product posts to its Instagram shopping tab.

**mDesign** at **https://www.instagram.com/mdesign**. Notice how this brand has the fully enabled "Buy on Instagram" feature so users can seamlessly purchase directly via the app. Click on the "shopping bag" icon and then a product. You'll notice that it says "add to bag" rather than "visit website."

**Foundr Magazine** at **https://www.instagram.com/foundr/**. This magazine uses Instagram as a quote-of-the-day, inspirational message and focuses on entrepreneurs.

**Bass Pro Shops** at **https://www.instagram.com/bassproshops/**. This outdoor retailer shares content around fishing and outdoor sports and does a great job with contests.

**The Pioneer Woman** at https://www.instagram.com/thepioneerwoman/. Another account that's native to my home state of Oklahoma, the Pioneer Woman shares recipes and cooking tips for those who "love butter" and love to cook. Notice how she uses the "Story Highlights" feature to showcase recipes. Yum!

**Museum of Sex** at https://www.instagram.com/museumofsex/. This New York-based museum pushes the envelope of what's allowable on Instagram and promotes itself as a "must-see" destination in New York City. Instagram is very much part of "pop culture," and "sexy" and "Instagram" are a natural. Try the hashtags *#sexy* or *#muscles*, and note that any brand that can leverage our fascination with the body, hedonism, looking good, and being sexy is a great fit for Instagram.

**Banksy** at https://www.instagram.com/banksy/. Banksy is an "underground" artist who uses social media and social sharing to build one of the weirdest brands on the Internet. Check out his movie, "Exit Through the Gift Shop" at **http://jmlinks.com/45g** for a through-the-looking-glass look at art and brand-building.

**Topshop** at https://www.instagram.com/topshop/. This account is all about women's fashion and trends, with lots of social engagement on Instagram. Check out *#topshopstyle* for its brand hashtag and watch how it engages users to share themselves wearing Topshop styles.

**Aeromexico** at https://www.instagram.com/aeromexico/. The Mexican airline, as we shall discuss in a moment, does a pretty good job of leveraging adjacent fun themes of places to go and see in Mexico, as opposed to just the "boring" aspects of air travel.

**Outdoor Voices** at https://www.instagram.com/outdoorvoices. Yet another brand that is lucky enough to have Instagram shopping fully enabled.

The point is to find competitors, similar companies, and brands to emulate. Then "lurk" behind the scenes and "reverse engineer" what they're doing at a technical level with features like branded hashtags, shop tags, Instagram stories, what they're doing at a content level in terms of what they're posting as images, videos, and text captions, and what's getting engagement from their fans (and why).

**The Instagram Game: Followers, Likes, and Engagement**

As on other social media networks, the game on Instagram is to get people to follow your company, and once they follow you, get them to like, comment, and share ("send") your posts to their friends, family, and contacts.

**Engagement** is the key to content marketing on Instagram, so you need to brainstorm fun, provocative photo or video content that engages your users.

# LIKE ALL SOCIAL MEDIA, INSTAGRAM CRAVES ENGAGEMENT

Instagram, like Facebook or Twitter, follows the structure of timeline and newsfeed. What a friend posts to her timeline shows up in my newsfeed. If she posts a photo of herself and her boyfriend having fun at Disneyland, then that photo will show up in my newsfeed, where I can "like," "comment," or "share" it to my own friends. In this way, Instagram is very much *Twitter with pictures*.

**Users have profiles and post pictures / videos to their timelines.** They can also post Instagram stories, which are collections of photos and videos, sort of a "day in the life" of a friend or brand you follow.

**The videos / pictures / stories posted by User A appear in User B's newsfeed if they're connected to each other.** Instagram, like Facebook, also monitors interaction in a quasi-Edgerank fashion, ranking which posts are prominent on the newsfeed as measured by previous interaction among the parties. The more interactive you and an account are, the more likely it is that your followers will see your posts prominently in the newsfeed.

**Businesses can have brand Pages on Instagram**, and when an individual follows a brand (similar to liking the brand's Facebook Page), posts by that brand will appear in the newsfeed of followers if the posts are "engaging" enough as judged by the Instagram algorithm.

**Businesses can enable Instagram shopping** and, if they're big enough, "buy on Instagram." These new features enable brands to integrate social media with shopping directly. Learn more at **http://jmlinks.com/53n**.

**Users can like, comment, or share posts by others to their own followers**. Note one weird technical glitch here on Instagram: unlike on Twitter or Facebook, one person can only share with one other person. Instagram does not have a "one to many" share feature, which limits the ability of posts to "go viral" on Instagram..

## Instagram is Open

Despite being owned by Facebook, Instagram is actually more like Twitter in that it's very **open**. Anyone can quickly set up an account, and a business profile exists independently, not needing to be "sponsored" by a personal profile. Most of the information is public on an account unless that account user changes the default settings to make things private. You don't usually have to wait for an acceptance to follow a brand or a person on Instagram; you just follow as you do on Twitter.

This actually makes Instagram really great for brands to be discovered by new users, and it makes it very easy for you to snoop on your competition's Instagram strategy.

## Business Profiles and Personal Profiles

While there's not a clear distinction between business and personal profiles in terms of the basics, it's best to choose a Business Profile for your business. (Note: just to confuse us, it's called a Business *Page* on Facebook and a Business *Profile* on Instagram).

A Business Profile allows for advertising and also provides reporting. To set up an Instagram account for a business from scratch, however, you must first have a Facebook Page for your business. (To learn how to set up a Facebook Page for your business, visit **http://jmlinks.com/29a**). So, first set up a Business Page on Facebook, and then open up the Instagram App to set up a new Instagram Business Profile.

Note: to set up a business profile on Instagram, you'll have to do this first on your phone by "signing up" as an individual. You can read the official step-by-step guide to setting up a business profile on Instagram at **http://jmlinks.com/28x**. Follow the steps to create a new Business Profile on Instagram.

## Converting a Personal to a Business Profile

You can also convert an existing Personal Profile to a Business Profile if you mistakenly set up your Business Profile as a Personal Profile. (And you can convert back again). However, because a Business Profile on Instagram must be connected to a Business Page on Facebook, be sure that you have first set up a Business Page on Facebook, then follow these steps:

1. On your phone, open the Instagram app, go to your profile and tap the gear icon.

2. Tap Switch to Business Profile.

3. Connect to your Facebook Page.

4. On the Set Up your Business Profile page, review your business contact information and press done.

A Business Profile is recommended as it allows contact buttons such as "email" or "message" near the top of your profile, depending on the contact information you provided. You also get better metrics for a Business Profile. To read the help file, visit **http://jmlinks.com/27k**.

## Managing Multiple Accounts

Fortunately, once you have both a personal Instagram and a business Instagram, you can manage both via one app on your phone. Go to the gear icon, and then scroll down to the very bottom and find "Add Accounts." To read the help file on how to set this up, visit **http://jmlinks.com/27m**. You can manage up to five accounts on Instagram via one phone and one app install. Once you have more than one account on your phone, you can switch between accounts. Here's how:

1. Open the Instagram app on your phone.

2. Click on your photo or logo at the *bottom right* of the app.

3. At the *top middle* of the page, you should see your Userid and a downward chevron or arrow. Click that.

4. This will open up all available accounts, so then click on the account you want to be active in.

To switch back, follow the steps as listed above.

## » REVERSE ENGINEER INSTAGRAM STRATEGIES

We'll return to some of the technical features of Instagram in a moment, but let's look at what's going on on Instagram first. Like any social media network, you want to figure out what people are doing on Instagram, and what brands are trying to do as marketers as well. Like any good party planner, you want to figure out if your target customers are on Instagram, what they're engaged in, and then turn a skeptical eye towards what other companies and brands are doing to "reverse engineer" their marketing strategies.

First up, ponder for a moment what you, your friends, and family are doing on Instagram, leaving aside companies and brands for the moment. If I take a look at myself as well as my friends and family on Instagram, it's pretty clear that 99% of what people are doing on the network is paying attention to friends and family as they have fun in their daily lives, and taking photos (and videos), along with posting these to their Instagram Stories. At its core, Instagram is really just a multiperson scrapbook sharing photos and videos largely of the "fun stuff" in one's life.

But there are two big currents on Instagram. One is friends and family that share photos of their lives (admittedly exaggerating the positive and downplaying the negative). The other is consumer brands like Target, REI, and Gucci as well as consumer personalities like the Kardashians and other influencers who are "all in" when it comes to consumerism, materialism, and hedonism.

Is Instagram fake? Absta-INSTA-lutely. Like Facebook, Instagram is more "life as it should be" than "life as it really is." Instagram tends to be very narcissistic as people post photos of themselves, their families, their friends, and their super cool, amazing, perfect life to "show off" how great their life is (vs. your sad pathetic, boring life and dysfunctional family). Big brands and celebrities are even more so. The Kardashians, for example, are (probably) an example of this sort of Insta-fantasy. Check out Kim at **https://www.instagram.com/kimkardashian/**, or Khloe at **https://www.instagram.com/khloekardashian/**. I love the Kardashians, don't get me wrong. I just don't particularly believe that what they project about their lives is "reality."

Like most of social media, Instagram isn't really about reality. It's about projection and perception. You might disagree with it on a cultural level; you might even think it means we are living in a very shallow consumer culture devoid of meaning. But it is what it is. The marketing point here is that smart brands leverage customer **narcissism** and the **desire to show off**; they encourage customers to "showcase" that they are "living their best life" by using the company's products or services. Instagram is the consumer culture on crack.

## Search by Location

Let's look at some other techniques to browse Instagram and look for marketing opportunities. One good way to see what "real people" are doing on Instagram is to search by location.

Simply go to Instagram and type in a city, such as Pittsburgh, Tulsa, or Houston. To browse Instagram posts on Tulsa, for example, visit **http://jmlinks.com/27p**. Then drill down into a post, and you can snoop into what that person was posting, and how their family, friends, and acquaintances reacted. For example, here's an adorable Dad and daughter post that's been tagged with *#Tulsa*:

You can then click "up" to the person who posted it, in this case, *@biggestrayray* and see what he's posting to his account. (Note how, like Twitter, Instagram is very open — many people have little idea just how public what they do on Instagram is).

You can also find location-based posts by neighborhood or landmarks, which is excellent for a local business in a neighborhood. For example check out *#downtowntulsa* (Downtown Tulsa, Oklahoma), *#brooksidetulsaok* (Tulsa's Brookside neighborhood), or even *#tulsafarmersmarket* for things around Tulsa's best farmers' market. Search for neighborhoods and landmarks in your city or town, and discover through Instagram what people post that's location-specific. Find brands you like (or compete with) and drill into the accounts of people that are interacting with brands.

If you're a local business, the take-aways here are a) use local hashtags or geotags when you post to Instagram, and b) consider advertising on Instagram which can also be geo-targeted. Instagram, while mammoth, also has a very unique local side to it.

## Research the Fans of Your Competitors

You can find a competitor and then literally drill into their fans. The easiest way to do this is on the desktop, though you can do it on the phone app, too. Here's how:

1. Find the Instagram account of a competitor or company you want to research. We'll use Peet's Coffee (**https://www.instagram.com/peetscoffee/**) which is the Bay Area's best coffee chain.

2. Click on followers at the top. This then pops up a list of everyone who follows them. You can literally click "follow" in blue to follow that account, or click on the account name and check them out.

Realize that when you follow someone on Instagram, they often follow you back or at least check you out. It's all very public. So don't be creepy. Plus there is a limit of 300 accounts to follow each day; 7,000 lifetime limit. So if you rapidly follow accounts, you'll get blocked. But as a research tool, this is a great way to investigate who's following a competitor and how fervently. "Follow for follow" is also a promotional tool; within reason, people whom you follow with your brand account will tend to follow you back (or at least check you out). So consider "following" key people who "follow" your competitors.

You can also drill into a competitor's post (vs. their entire account), and see which posts are the most popular as measured by likes and comments. Simply find a competitor, click into one of their more popular posts, and then click over to those people who liked it or commented on it. Here's a screenshot from Peet's Coffee:

If you click on @*missberberry*, you can see her account. If you click on the 547 likes, you can see all the people who liked this post and click over to their accounts, too. Here's a screenshot:

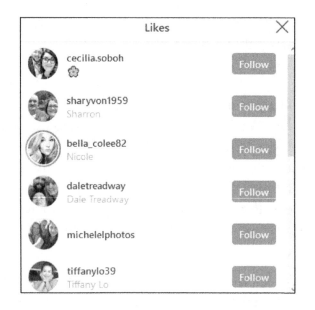

I would not recommend that you follow each and every person who likes a competitor's account or posts. But in terms of research, it gives you a window into your competitor's Instagram strategy, what they post, what gets engagement, and even the types of people who are engaging with their posts. As you browse accounts, you can see how many followers they have and thus get a crude measurement of their clout on the network. Instagram – like Twitter – is extremely public and open.

**Business Strategies on Instagram.**

With some basics under our belt, let's revisit what brands are doing on Instagram. Remember – unlike a person – a brand isn't on Instagram "for fun." Rather, whether it's the camping gear retailer, REI, the Mexican airline, Aeromexico, or Tulsa's Rustic Cuff jeweler, brands have an ultimate **goal** for Instagram: **to sell more stuff**. I think you could argue that this is also true for public personas like the Kardashians, who are more brands than real people if you think about it.

If you work backward from the "ultimate goal" of selling more stuff, you can see that many brands are on Instagram to build "brand equity," that warm and fuzzy feeling that tells you when it's time to book a trip to Mexico, you want to fly Aeromexico airlines, when it's time to go camping, you want to shop for a tent via REI, and when it's time to buy a gift for mom or your girlfriend, a trendy bracelet from Rustic Cuff is a good gift to buy online. Oh, and when it's time to vote for President, *@realdonaldtrump* might be a good place to "make America great again." (Or not, depending on your politics.). And when you look to people to emulate as lifestyle leaders, you look to the Kardashians (Or not, depending on your values).

Instagram is about image and the projection of image. It's about knowing who your target audience is, and who it is not. It's about doing a communicative, visual dance with them via photos and videos.

**Consumer Brands on Instagram**

By far the biggest and most active business accounts on Instagram could be categorized as consumer brands. Take a brand like REI (@REI), for example. (You can browse it on your desktop at **http://jmlinks.com/32u**). REI posts photos of cool people doing cool things outdoors, with its clothing, gear, and accessories taking a backseat to just people having a great time enjoying nature. It's pretty easy to see that REI's Instagram marketing strategy is to share fun photos of its customers wearing or using REI gear and to encourage "user-generated content" from customers by having contests and using hashtags like *#optoutside* (**http://jmlinks.com/27q**). As you scroll through REI's account, you can hover to see the number of "likes" and "comments" as indicated by the heart icon and the comment icon, respectively. Because REI does a great job with its photos, videos, and strategy and because outdoor fun is a photogenic fit to Instagram, it's easy to see that Instagram is a huge and successful part of REI's Internet marketing efforts.

# REVERSE ENGINEER THE BIG BRANDS ON INSTAGRAM

Or take a brand like Whole Foods (@*wholefoods* at **http://jmlinks.com/32v**), another big retailer, but this time of food. Whole Foods shares fun, colorful photos of healthy, organic foods (which, incidentally, you can buy at its many stores…), as well as uses hashtags like *#Foods4Thought* and *#WholeFoodFaves*. Even more interesting, notice that Whole Foods uses the Instagram shopping service Like2b.uy at **http://like2b.uy** (**http://jmlinks.com/32w**)) to integrate its Instagram posts with its blog and website. Here's a screenshot:

If you click on the Like2b.uy link, you'll see photos that "match up" to Whole Food's Instagram posts and you can go from there to the Whole Foods website, blog, eCommerce site, etc.

Like2b.uy (**https://www.curalate.com/solution/like2buy/**) is a workaround against the fact that Instagram allows one, and only one, clickable URL in an account in the bio. Another vendor that allows a way around this functionality is Olapic's Tap-shop platform at **http://jmlinks.com/32z**. The Instagram shop feature (**http://jmlinks.com/45h**) is yet a third option. Rustic Cuff has this feature enabled, so check that out. Refer to my companion *Marketing Almanac* for a complete index to the best Instagram resources, including eCommerce plugins and services.

Consumer brands, in summary, are big on Instagram. For your first **TO-DO**, look deep into your consumer soul and identify some fun consumer brands that you personally like. Find and follow them on Instagram. What you'll see is brands leveraging photogenic product shots as well as photogenic shots of happy customers using their products and services. The truly great marketers on Instagram, like REI, have figured out how to mobilize their customer evangelists to post, like, comment, and share product photos for them.

## Tap into the Narcissism of Your Customers

There's a certain self-serving narcissism in our modern, ego-centric culture in which you post your "amazing" trip to Machu Pichu (1,659,478 posts as of December 2019 at **http://jmlinks.com/27r**), your "incredible" trip to Disney World (11.8 million posts at **http://jmlinks.com/27s**), or your "meaningful" Destination Wedding (8 million posts at **http://jmlinks.com/27t**). The point is that if it's "fun" and it's "photogenic," and especially if people want to "show off" to their friends and family about how much "fun" they're having… it's a perfect fit for Instagram marketing! As a brand, if you can tap into our very human desire to "show off" to our friends how cool, fun, brilliant, smart, incredible, holier-than-thou, moralistic, compassionate, perfect, rich, with it, living-the-life, and any other narcissistic impulse that we share as humans… well, that's the way to market successfully on Instagram. Brand hashtags on Instagram such as *#optoutside*, *#doingthings*, or *#rusticcuff* are examples of how brands leverage consumer narcissism as a marketing strategy on Instagram.

Note also that geographies like Tulsa, Oklahoma, (**http://jmlinks.com/33a**), Niles, California, (**http://jmlinks.com/33b**), or Havana, Cuba, (**http://jmlinks.com/33c**) also have hashtags or technically what are called "location tags." You can even create a location, such as your business address and then promote it to customers for location-tagging. See **http://jmlinks.com/33d**.

# INSTAGRAM TAPS INTO OUR HUMAN DESIRE TO "SHOW OFF"

Airbnb (**http://jmlinks.com/32x**), for example, is a brand that truly does Instagram well, and taps into this "show off" component of the human ego. Who doesn't want to share photos of their fun Airbnb vacation for a little surreptitious gloating vis-à-vis their friends back home, stuck in cubicle hell at work? REI also fits this mold as people "show off" their incredible communions with nature, using REI products.

For a small business, an example of this affinity would be a wedding planner, wedding photographer, or pretty much anything in the wedding industry. Just search Instagram for the hashtag *#wedding,* and you'll find over 170 million posts sharing the fun, faith, and love that is that glorious day (*plus products and services to buy at a convenient wedding superstore near you, act now supplies are limited*). Brainstorm how and why your customers might want to "show off" that they are using your products in a photographic / video way, and you're on the way to real Instagram marketing success.

### Non-fun Brands that Connect to Something Fun

If your brand isn't fun, don't despair. You can connect to something *adjacent* that is truly fun. Take air travel. Let's face it; air travel isn't exactly fun these days. Unlike camping or staying in a fabulous Airbnb location, air travel in and of itself is anything but fun. And it's not very photogenic. What would people take photos of besides the planes? I mean, should you have your customers photograph the crowded and dirty seats, the overhead bins, or those crazy, blue, and loud toilets?

An airline, therefore, has to "look out the window" to find things that truly are fun (such as travel), and connect these adjacent *fun* things to the *non-fun* experience that is air travel.

Check out United Airlines at @*united* on Instagram (**http://jmlinks.com/33e**), or for an airline that does tend to be a bit more fun, I recommend Aeromexico at **http://jmlinks.com/33f**. The point is if your brand is serious or not-fun, brainstorm ways that you can attach it to more fun types of activities, especially ones that are photogenic. This strategy is at the heart of all the airlines on Instagram. But it goes for B2B or more serious consumer brands as well. Consider Sunrun Solar at **http://jmlinks.com/45j**. That brand posts photos of solar panels, as well as outdoor nature-type photos that highlight the synergy between clean energy and a healthful outdoor environment. Here's a screenshot:

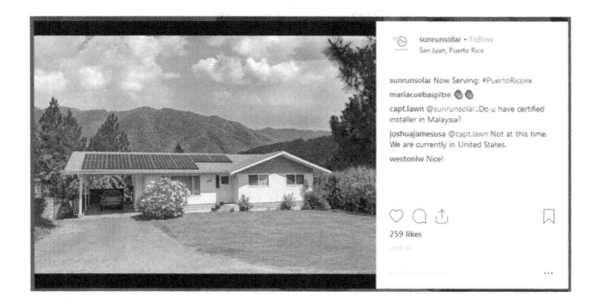

Solar panels in and of themselves are neither fun nor photogenic, so the trick would be to identify photos that ARE fun and photogenic but somehow connect to solar power. Check out the hashtags *#solar* or *#solarpanels*, for instance, for ideas.

**Really Unfun Products or Services: What to do?**

Next, take a look at the big insurers like Geico (**http://jmlinks.com/33h**), Allstate (**http://jmlinks.com/33j**), or Progressive (**http://jmlinks.com/33k**). Insurance is not only "not fun," it's one of the most expensive, mistrusted and obnoxious experiences of a consumer's life. (*The policies can be next to impossible to understand, and as my Dad says, the insurers are great at taking your premiums but not so great at paying out when* *something happens. Regardless of my views on insurance, as an Instagram user, I'm not exactly going to share a photo of me on Instagram going over my life insurance policy!).*

Insurance is boring, unphotogenic, mistrusted, and not exactly something the average consumer would spontaneously share on Instagram. So, what is to be done?

Like the airlines, the insurance companies attempt to attach themselves to something fun and photogenic. Their job is much more difficult because while Aeromexico takes you to Cabo San Lucas or Puerta Vallarta which are fun and photogenic, you probably won't exactly take a picture of your house burning down and caption it, "Wow! I'm glad I have Allstate." I also doubt I'm going to take a photo of myself in my coffin and say, "Wow! I'm glad I have USAA life insurance!" (Though perhaps my wife will take a selfie with me, *#itsfinallyover*).

Accordingly, the insurance companies are worth looking at on Instagram as examples of "out of the box" marketing thinking. An example would be Progressive's hashtag *#parentamorphosis*, which attempts to make fun of the transformation from a hip twenty-something into a boring thirty-something with two kids in tow.

Here's a screenshot:

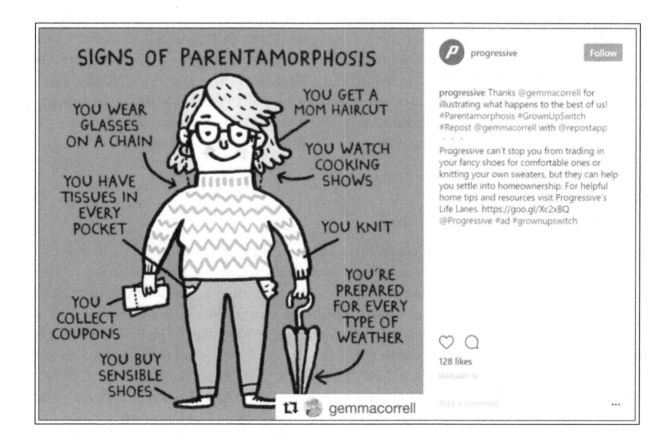

This post garnered 128 likes, which is far from tremendous, but it shows the strategy attempt by one of the country's biggest brands to attach the non-photogenic, non-fun themes of insurance to the fun, photogenic themes of Instagram.

## Gurus and Visual Instruction

If you, or your small business, can explain things to people and if those things can be explained in such a way as to be visually appealing, then an Instagram guru strategy might work. Consider the fitness industry, for example, which posts photos and short videos to Instagram to teach users how to get fit (and occasionally promotes products and services to buy). Check out Certified Fitness, for example, at **http://jmlinks.com/33m** with 9,340 followers and 3252 posts as of December 2019. Inspirational posts are mixed with instructional videos to build a brand that promotes fitness. Or for a bigger brand, check out 24 Hour Fitness at **http://jmlinks.com/33n**. Or check out the 29 million posts to the hashtag *#fishing* and 11.8 million to *#hunting*. These are visual sports or activities that blend a "Gee! Look at the huge fish I caught" narcissism of the users with the visual "how-tos" of vendors and a good dose of selling and brand identity.

Even outside of the purely visual, brands that explain things can find a niche on Instagram. Sue B. Zimmerman is one of the goddesses of Instagram, and she shares tips, tricks, and pretty much the visual story of her life at **http://jmlinks.com/33p**. Dog guru Zak George uses Instagram to share photos of dogs and dog-training tips at **http://jmlinks.com/33q**, as does the much more successful (at least on Instagram), Cesar Millan (**http://jmlinks.com/33r**). All of these "guru strategies" blend insider tips, tricks, and secrets with a personalized view into the life and viewpoints of the guru him or herself.

## Politics, News, and Entertainment

Finally, like Twitter, Instagram has found a place in news and entertainment. Big-time politicians like President Trump use Instagram to showcase a visual magazine of their day-to-day events and achievements. Like him or hate him, don't ignore him: check out Donald Trump on Instagram at **http://jmlinks.com/33s**. And notice the use of specific hashtags such as *#MAGA* and *#TeamTrumpBTS* (**http://jmlinks.com/27y**) to help his fans and followers coalesce with their own user-generated content to help Team Trump. Trump is a "brand" on Instagram, not structurally different from a "brand" like REI or AirBnB. And, if you don't like Trump (and I am certainly not going to tell you my political opinions), check out other politicians like Elizabeth Warren, Joe Biden, or Tulsi Gabbard who are competing with Trump as political brands. The point is that all smart politicians use Twitter these days – all of them.

Notice as well by checking out Trump's posts and hashtags that, well, Instagram, like Twitter, is not totally under the control of Team Trump, so in politics as in everything on social media, be careful with hashtags! People who hate you can also chime in and boy will they! Here's a screenshot of a Trump post to Instagram with comments such as "Do America a favor and resign now:" As on Twitter, he's not in control of the "conversation" around his "claim" to have a 50% approval rating:

But back to news and entertainment, any brand that is visual and news-oriented can do well on Instagram. Consider Nasa at **http://jmlinks.com/33t** with 52 million followers or Al Jazeera at **http://jmlinks.com/33u** with 2.9 million. Any news organization, political candidate, or political cause that can connect its message to the visual centricity of Instagram can succeed. Even the Vatican is online at **http://jmlinks.com/33v**! If you're a nonprofit and especially if your mission is visually oriented, Instagram can be a great place to build a cause and connect with like-minded followers.

## Which Strategy Fits You Best?

The strategic point of all these examples on Instagram is to get you to look deep into your marketing soul and ponder whether:

You're a **fun brand**, in a **fun, photogenic industry** such as travel or jewelry, so Instagram is a natural and easy fit for your online marketing. (Example: @*Airbnb*, @*Disney*, @rusticcuff).

Or

You're a **non-fun brand** adjacent to a **fun, photogenic** industry such as airlines, so Instagram fits only if you attach your "non-fun" brand (air travel) to the photogenic outcome, *travel*. (Example: @*aeromexico*, @*united*).

Or

You're a **non-fun brand** in a **non-fun, non-photogenic industry** such as insurance, so Instagram only works if you attach your non-fun brand to something fun (hence the attempts by @*Progressive* and @*Geico* to make insurance fun or post things that have little to do with insurance but are visually fun, and then (somehow) connect this back to their brand).

This is even true for nonprofits, which should also identify if they are *fun* or *not fun*, *photogenic* or *non-photogenic* for the purposes of their strategy. Your **TO-DO** here is to determine where you fit:

**Fun and photogenic**: use direct photos of the product or service, and encourage user engagement around the direct use of the product or service (*e.g.*, *Disneyland encouraging users to share photos of themselves having fun at Disneyland*).

**Not fun but adjacent to something fun and photogenic**. Use photos of the "result" of the product or service in something that is fun and photogenic (*e.g.*, *encouraging persons who tan in tanning booths to share photos of their sexy, tanned bodies at the beach; check out #tanning on Instagram. Another example is how airlines* (not fun) *use travel* (fun) *to promote themselves on Instagram* (@*SouthWestAir*)).

**Not-fun and non-photogenic**: attach your Instagram marketing to an adjacent or even unrelated theme. An example would be @*Progressive* on Instagram, sharing photos of their employees enjoying summer at Progressive Field Ballpark in Cleveland. *Baseball is fun, the ballpark is fun, and so… insurance is fun…*

## Sentimentality and Aw Shucks on Instagram

Another common strategy is to use quotes and emotion-inspiring photos to attach your brand to something that people will "agree with" because it has a strong emotional component. One of my favorite examples of this is @*Islamic_Teachings* (**http://jmlinks.com/33w**) which shares meaningful quotes about Islam.

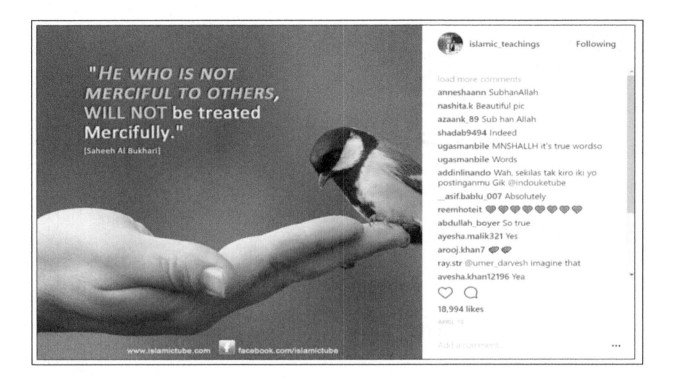

So something serious, *religion*, is connected to something beautiful, *a bird*, with a quotation that provides *food for thought*. It's also something we probably all agree on: we should be kind to each other. *Aw shucks*. This post received 18,994 likes. Foundr magazine uses this type of quote strategy as well at **http://jmlinks.com/33x**. So we have "Fear is the disease. Hustle is the antidote" with 9,045 likes in just 22 hours and hundreds of comments:

We'll return to researching and "reverse engineering" brands on Instagram in a moment, but let's dive back into tips and tricks to manage your Instagram efforts better.

## » SET UP YOUR BUSINESS PAGE (AND LEARN ITS ADVANTAGES)

You want to use Instagram as a business, not as an individual. So when you set up your Instagram account, be sure to set it up as a business. To do so, follow the steps at **http://jmlinks.com/45r**. If you've mistakenly set yourself up as a personal profile, follow the link to "Convert Existing Account" to convert it.

A business account on Instagram comes with many advantages:

1. **Contact Info**. Business profiles have easy-to-find contact information, which allows users to contact you with questions. If you have an e-commerce store, you can also apply for the new "shop" feature to enable links to the new Instagram shopping experience.

2. **Instagram Insights**. Business accounts get data on user activity, while personal accounts do not.

3. **Advertising**. Business accounts can advertise, which is very useful to grow your followers and engagement. Personal accounts can't advertise.

4. **Post from Desktop Apps**. For business users, Instagram is more accessible via the desktop, including desktop software programs like Hootsuite. This makes it easier to manage.

5. **Connection to Facebook**. Because Instagram is owned by Facebook, Instagram Business accounts are connected to Business Facebook accounts, again making management easier.

6. **Instagram Stories with Links**. Businesses that have more than 10,000 followers can have links in their Stories and Story Highlights via the "swipe up" feature, giving you more opportunities to drive traffic from Instagram to your e-commerce store.

7. **Shopping**. Instagram is clearly moving in the direction of being e-commerce and shopping friendly. Businesses can set up a "shop" on Instagram, tag products in photos, and otherwise enable a seamless shopping experience between their Instagram account and their e-commerce store.

The main downsides are fears that having a business profile will make your business look "salesy" to users, and that the organic reach of business profiles will suffer, just as Facebook clobbered the organic reach of business Pages on Facebook. It's likely that at some point, Instagram will REQUIRE businesses to convert, so this risk is there regardless of what you do. You can also try a two-pronged strategy – having a personal profile for the CEO or company spokesperson and a business profile. The former can be more "behind the scenes" and "personal," and the latter more "organizational" and "formal." As always, know your brand and experiment with what will work best for you and your business.

**Advertising on Instagram** is managed via the Facebook platform. You can set up demographic targets using all the techniques on Facebook (see Chapter 3 on Facebook to learn more about Facebook demographic targeting, which also applies to Instagram). Once you have a Business account on Instagram, you can advertise your posts to:

- People who follow your Business Page on Instagram and/or Facebook.

- People you choose through demographic targeting (such as women, aged 18-24, living in Tulsa, who are interested in weddings, etc.). Facebook and Instagram know a lot about their users, and so leveraging this data to target your Instagram posts is really incredible.

- People you choose through the Facebook Pixel, that is people who have hit your website. In this way, you can target likely customers who have "hit" your website when they are on Instagram.

Instagram advertising is a great way to gain more exposure for your posts and grow your followers. Learn more at **http://jmlinks.com/45v**.

## » LEARN TECHNICAL TIPS TO USING INSTAGRAM

We'll assume that you've set up a business profile on Instagram, and done the basics of adding a profile picture, filling out your bio, including a link to your website or eCommerce store. It's a best practice, especially for larger, more consumer-focused brands, to create a company-centric hashtag, so that your fans have a virtual way to "tag" their posts about your product or service. Airbnb does this, for example, simply with the hashtag *#Airbnb*, and Southwest Airlines does it with *#SWApic* to encourage its customers to tag photos about their Southwest trips.

### Learn a Little Photography

Before we dive into technical tips on Instagram, let's take a moment and talk about **photography**. Instagram is all about photos and videos, so it's very worth your while to become a better photographer. You can Google "how to take better iPhone photos" for example, or go to YouTube and look for tutorials on photography. To read a nice, short article on how to take better Instagram photos, visit **http://jmlinks.com/45u**. But spend some time simply learning how to identify photo-friendly subjects, and how to optimize your photos on your camera. The subject and quality of your photos matter a lot.

Indeed, with the rise of IGTV, Instagram is pushing "vertical video" in a bid to undo nearly a century of horizontal video dominating film. Check out Instagram's tips for vertical video at **http://jmlinks.com/45k** as well as success stories at **http://jmlinks.com/45m**.

### Use Instagram Hacks and Techniques

Now, let's dive into some of the technical tips to being a better Instagram user:

**Use Hashtags.** As has already been discussed, hashtags are big on Instagram. In fact, hashtags are more important on Instagram than on Twitter, and a post can often have five, seven or even ten hashtags at the end of it. Use a tool like Hashtagify.me (**http://jmlinks.com/27v**) or Hashtags.org (**http://jmlinks.com/27w**) to identify customer-friendly hashtags for your account bio and posts. Also, just search Instagram for your keywords to identify hashtags that have a lot of volume.

**Tag People.** As on Facebook you can "tag" people, and thereby notify them that they were included on your feed. So, for example, if customer Jane Doe follows your Pizza Parlor, then you can take a picture of her and her friends on her birthday, and tag all of them in the Instagram app. In that way, they all get notified that they were "tagged" and are encouraged to share the post with their own friends via Instagram.

**Shopping / eCommerce.** Instagram does not allow clickable URLs in posts. Therefore, third-party services have emerged such as Olapic Tapshop (**http://jmlinks.com/32z**) or Curalate's Like2Buy (**http://jmlinks.com/32w**) that can cross-connect your account to photos that match up with your posts. If you have an active business account, you can also apply for the new "shop" feature on Instagram at **http://jmlinks.com/45n**. You can even "tag" a product which will create a link to your e-commerce store.

**Link in Bio / Link in Profile.** This phrase is commonly used in a post on Instagram to remind people, "Hey! If you want to buy this or check it out on my blog, the clickable link is in my profile" or "Link in my bio" is another way people reference this idea. Use a service like Link Tree (**http://jmlinks.com/45w**) to have a handy index of referenced links.

**Add Locations.** This is a unique feature of Instagram. When you upload a photo, you can "tag" it to a location such as San Diego or Miami. This improves your chances of showing up in the *Instagram Explore* feature (See: **http://jmlinks.com/27z**), which is where people can go to explore what's up with their friends, connections, and other algorithmically generated accounts and posts. Think of Instagram as an online magazine, and this helps you get into their flippable newsfeed, so to speak.

**Multiple Image Posts.** Instagram now allows more than one photo per post. Some people hate this feature, but others like it. The easiest way to use it is to access your camera roll, and click on "select multiple" to select multiple photos.

**Boomerang.** This is a quick video plugin for Instagram. Simply find it in the Apple Store or on Google Play by searching for *Instagram Boomerang*. This fun app allows you to shoot a quick, looping video and upload it to your Instagram account. You can download Boomerang on both Google Play and the Apple App Store.

**Instagram Live.** As on Facebook and YouTube, you can "go live" on Instagram. Brainstorm fun, live events for your customers and "go live" on Instagram. Learn more at **http://jmlinks.com/45p**.

**Manage Multiple Accounts.** Once you've set up your own personal Instagram account and that of your company, how can you manage both of them? Within Instagram, go to settings (Gear icon on the iPhone), and then scroll to the bottom to "add account." You can also use a third-party desktop app like Hootsuite or Buffer to manage multiple business accounts, including posting from the desktop and scheduling out your posts.

**Instagram Help.** Yes, Virginia, there is help on Instagram! Simply visit **http://jmlinks.com/33y**. You can search by keyword for help on a variety of topics. Instagram for business focuses more on advertising issues but can be found at **http://jmlinks.com/33z**. They also have a very good Instagram for business blog at **http://jmlinks.com/45q**.

## Know the Question, and Find the Answer

Remember that *once you know the question, you can find the answer*. One of the best ways to do this is to simply "Google" your question. Just go to Google and type in something like, "How to schedule Instagram posts," or "How to manage multiple accounts on Instagram," and you can usually find a quick blog post or YouTube video that will answer your query. "Once you know the question," I always say to my Stanford students, "You can find the answer." So spend some time reverse-engineering what users and competitors are doing on Instagram, and then formulate a question for Google along the lines of "how do they do such-and-such." A good tip here is to use the Tools menu on the far right of Google and select "Past Year" so as to get recent, up-to-date answers. Here's a screenshot:

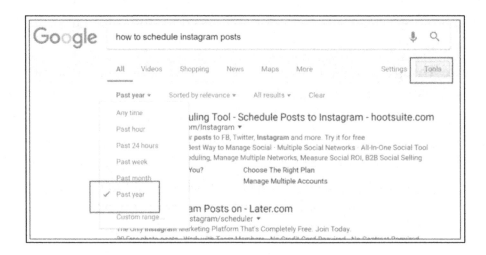

## » INVENTORY LIKES AND DISLIKES ON INSTAGRAM

Now that you have the basics of Instagram down, as a user, and you've taken a look at some of the big brands like REI, Airbnb, or Aeromexico that are doing Instagram well, it's time to do your own inventory as a company. Your goal is to identify companies that are doing Instagram well, and "reverse engineer" what you like or dislike about their Instagram marketing strategy. Remember: you don't only want to find and follow companies in your industry or niche because many of them may not be that savvy.

In fact, I recommend that you distinguish among and identify three distinct company types. That is, you need to:

1. Find companies *in your niche or industry* such as competitors.

2. Find companies *in similar niches or industries* (e.g., B2B companies if your B2B, B2G companies if your B2G, etc.)

3. Find some *big brands* that you and your team agree you like.

To start your research, download the "Instagram Research Worksheet." For the worksheet, go to **http://jmlinks.com/social2020** (then enter the code '**social2020**' to register your workbook), and click on the link to the "Instagram Research Worksheet." Along the way, pay special attention to the "people" on Instagram, and whether (and how) they are interacting with the brands you identify above.

### Finding Companies on Instagram

To identify companies on Instagram, start with your keywords and social media themes. Let's take a few hypothetical examples, such as a plumber, a wedding photographer, and a B2B company that sells business insurance. So we'd have keywords such as:

**Plumber**. *Plumbing, plumber, home improvement, DIY, toilet repair.*

**Wedding Photographer**: *weddings, marriage, photography, bridal.*

**Business insurance**. *Insurance, business insurance, small business, risk management.*

Here are the methods to search Instagram by keyword, looking for accounts to follow and reverse engineer:

**Method #1: Instagram Search.** Go to Instagram, either on the desktop or on your phone. Type your keywords into the search box. Then look at the posts that come back, and click up to the account holders, or look at the comments and likes, and click over to those people who are interacting with the posts. Make a list of those accounts that fit your target.

**Method #2: Google Search.** Use Google. Go to Google.com, and enter *site:Instagram.com* plus your keywords, as in *site:Instagram.com "business insurance"* (There's no space between *site:* and *Instagram.com*, and use quotation marks around keyword phrases). To see an example, visit **http://jmlinks.com/28c**. Next, scroll down the list, and Google will identify accounts on Instagram that have those keywords.

**Method #3: Use a Geotag**. Type in a city name such as *Tulsa* (**http://jmlinks.com/28g**) into the Instagram search box. This is a good way to see the posts across a wide range of industries and topics so that you don't get "boxed in" to seeing just posts in your industry.

**Method #4: Instagram Explore.** Instagram Explore works best if you first configure your personal Instagram account for a few weeks, and be sure to follow competitors and others in your industry. Then, open up your Instagram App, and click the "Magnifying Glass" icon on the bottom. Instagram will suggest photos and accounts to you, based on your interests and behavior. By following competitors and paying attention to things "as if" you were a customer, you can get Instagram to find interesting companies to "reverse engineer." Across the top, you can also swipe by category for suggestions. Here's a screenshot:

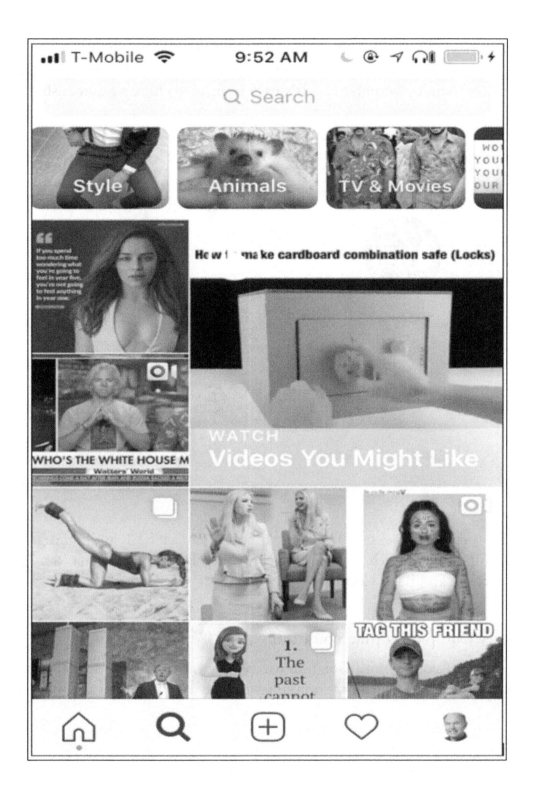

So if you clicked on "Style," you'd see posts on that topic and can then click up to follow a person or brand that might be relevant for your marketing research. You can also access *Instagram Explore* on the desktop or at **https://www.instagram.com/explore/**.

**Method #5. Explore Account Suggestions.** You can also find one brand you like, and then click on the downward arrow to the right of "message" in the app to see "similar" companies. It's easy to miss, so here's a screenshot:

In this way, you can find one brand such as REI and then find similar or competitive brands to follow such as in this case Patagonia, the National Park Service, and Back Country.

## Inventory Companies that You Find

For example, if you search Instagram for *toilet repair* (**http://jmlinks.com/28a**), you'll find posts by people and a few companies on the topic. I found this post, for example:

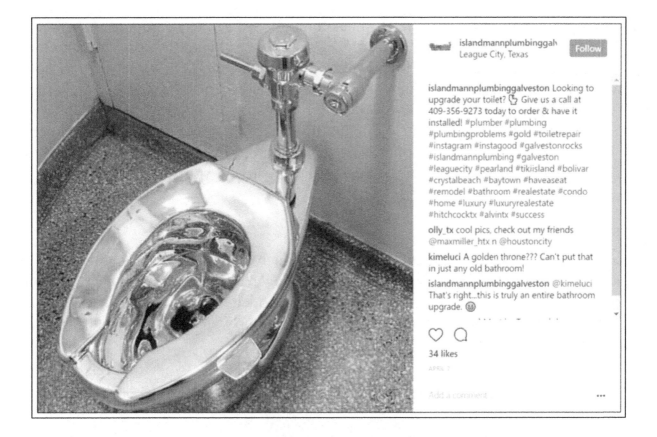

*Toilet repair* on Instagram, who knew?

Notice that the post was made by *@Islandmanplumbinggalveston* (**http://jmlinks.com/28b**). So, click on the name of the account, and then you can start to "reverse engineer" this account and its posts. Take some notes as you and your team discuss what you like, and what you don't like, about *@Islandmanplumbinggalveston* and its posting strategy.

> **Profile Picture**. IslandMann's is a red, white, and blue logo. Do you like it, or would it be better if it were a plumber, perhaps the owner?
>
> **Bio**. IslandMann's bio says ⚒🔧Island Mann Plumbing 🚿🚽 IMP #Plumber Team serving #Brazoria, #Galveston & South Harris Counties 🏠Whole house #repiping and Start #saving buy & install your #TanklessHeaters 🛁 www.islandmannplumbing.com
>
> **Followers**. Note that it has 47 posts, 170 followers, and 233 following. This doesn't show a high degree of interactivity, so perhaps Instagram isn't for plumbers?

Take a moment and look up a few other plumbers. You might compare IslandMann with *@theTacticalPlumber* (**http://jmlinks.com/28d**). Compare the profile picture to profile picture, bio to bio, and follower count to follower count. Note, for example, how *@theTacticalPlumber* has branded hashtags (*#PlumbSmarter*, and *#TheTacticalPlumber*). Click on those and see what's going on among its customers. Can your company identify and create a unique branded hashtag for your own customers? Would they care enough to post photos tagged in that way? What about having a contest or customer reward incentive for the best photos posted to your hashtag?

**Posting Strategy**

Next, note the interactivity of individual posts. Which ones stand out as something you – as a user – would take note of on Instagram, and even like, comment, or share? Which ones have the most interactivity? Why? Notice, for example, this post (**http://jmlinks.com/28e**) which is a plumber pushup video, with 183 likes, and 21 comments:

Think deeply about each post. Notice, for example, that this isn't a plumber doing plumbing (*boring*), but it's a kind of sexy guy showing off how strong he is by doing push-ups (*fun*). And then (spoiler alert), as you watch it you realize it's a spoof. It's very similar to posts that "real people" make on Instagram; it's personal, it's funny, and it's photogenic. And notice that it's actually a repost from somewhere else. So this post indicates that *@theTacticalPlumber* is being playful and having fun with Instagram, not just posting boring plumbing stuff.

And yet, it does relate to plumbing, and it does build the company's brand. So what types of posts might you make that would be fun, playful, and photogenic and yet connect to your brand? Don't be boring!

As you look at Instagram accounts that pique your interest, try to "reverse engineer" each company's **posting strategy**. Looking at their posts, are they merely informative, fun, photogenic, or something else? How do they connect to the brand image that the vendor is seeking to project? How frequently are items posted? Look at likes, comments, and shares. Is their posting strategy engaging their users, and why or why not?

## A Different Vendor

Let's do this again with another search and vendor. My search on Google for *site:Instagram.com "business insurance"* led me to *@WeddingInsuranceGroup* (**http://jmlinks.com/28f**). This is a British company that offers insurance for vendors in the wedding industry. They have 283 posts, 518 followers, and are following 1,202. Note that they are an insurer (*boring!*) but they are adjacent to a very Instagram-friendly business, weddings (*fun!*).

Their bio says:

> *The specialist independent insurance broker for wedding and event businesses. We cover niche professions. Visit our site for a quote.*

Scroll down through their posts and attempt to "reverse engineer" what they've posted and why. You'll see a lot of posts with quotations speaking to the fear that the photography or catering equipment might get stolen, something might go terribly wrong, and hence the need for business insurance. But also take a look at how they use hashtags such as *#WeddingWednesday* which reaches out not to just their B2B customers but people actually planning weddings who might be interested in insuring the big event (what if the groom gets cold feet?). Notice the use of single images, carousel images, and even videos. Here's a post that is a collaboration with a vendor they insure, Luxury Classic Jaguars:

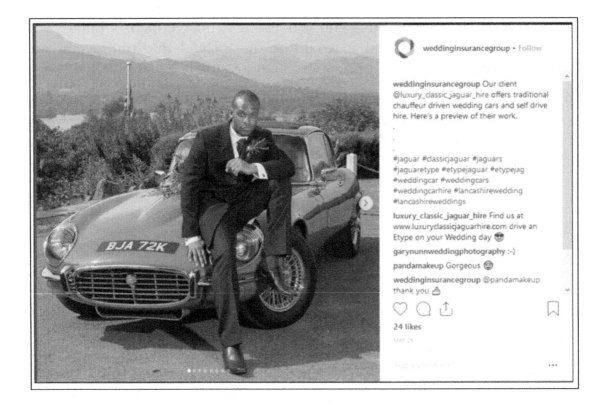

In terms of posting, they have fun images, they use hashtags and emojis, they use "shout-outs" to their partners, and they encourage cross-posting. This is clearly a B2B business that is using Instagram to be visible on a venue that their own customers (Wedding photographers and the like) clearly see as essential. The wedding insurance itself isn't fun, but the way that they connect to the adjacent industry is.

**Wrapping Up Your Research**

For your **TO-DO**, download and complete the **Instagram Research Worksheet**. For the worksheet, go to **http://jmlinks.com/social2020** (then enter the code '**social2020**' to register your workbook), and click on the link to the "Instagram Research Worksheet."

Pay the most attention to **posting strategy**. After all, setting up an Instagram account isn't very difficult. It's what types of photos or videos get posted, how successful they are at generating interactivity, and how all this buzz connects to some business objective that matters. I recommend that you create an editorial calendar for all your social media posts; for Instagram, this would mean planning out what types of photos or videos you are going to shoot, when, where, and how. Like any good party, there should be a lot of systematic planning towards the food and entertainment that needs to be produced on a regular basis! It just looks easy, but that's an illusion.

## » IGTV: INSTAGRAM TV, INSTAGRAM STORIES, AND SNAPCHAT

Instagram, like all the major platforms, is strongly encouraging the move to video. You can post short videos directly to Instagram, and they've launched IGTV which is long-form, vertical video. IGTV is clearly meant to become a direct competitor to YouTube. To access IGTV, simply open the Instagram app on your phone and click the TV-like icon at the top. It looks like this:

As on YouTube, you can search, have "Channels" that you follow, and even find "popular" or trending videos. It's a Brave New World of vertical video, clearly hoping to leapfrog YouTube as a major video platform. You can upload videos directly from your phone, or you can pre-edit them in vertical format and upload via your PC. Learn more at **http://jmlinks.com/45s**.

Instagram Stories, in contrast, are short pictures or videos you upload to your "story" as a brand. Stories are essentially a "day in the life" of an individual or brand, told in photo and video format. They are a direct competitor to **Snapchat** (**https://www.snapchat.com/**). Snapchat, of course, invented many of the aspects "stolen" by Instagram such as stories or filters, and so far it looks like Instagram is going to win out. And don't forget you can just upload video directly to Instagram as a post from your phone.

Instagram is very video-friendly, and the company clearly sees video as its future, so stay tuned. As for Snapchat, visit the Apple App Store or Google Play and download the Snapchat app. For a few good introductions to how to use Snapchat, visit **http://jmlinks.com/28h**, **http://jmlinks.com/28j**, and **http://jmlinks.com/28m**. You can browse the official Snapchat help files at **http://jmlinks.com/28p**.

Discovery and sharing on Snapchat are quite a bit different than on "traditional" social media networks, in that Snapchat is primarily a one-to-one photo messaging app, one in which videos and pictures disappear after twenty-four hours, while the other networks like Instagram are one-to-many. I can have *one* tweet on Twitter, and it's pushed out to many *thousands* of followers, who can all like, comment, and share that tweet. That's not exactly possible on Snapchat. In addition, as a brand, I can have a *stable*, on-going account on Instagram where users can find me, easily, and where things don't disappear after twenty-four hours. On Instagram, I can have a clickable URL in my bio, and on other networks like Twitter or Facebook, I can insert links from a social media post to a desired action such as read my blog post or buy my product on my eCommerce store. Hashtags, search and discovery are all far easier on the traditional social media networks vs. Snapchat. Snapchat, in my humble opinion, is in a bit of a bind because the very features that make it fun for teenagers such as the disappearance of posts, the lack of a stable footprint to one's account, and the one-to-one nature of the medium make it difficult for marketers to use.

# IT'S INSTAGRAM AND SNAPCHAT, NOT INSTAGRAM OR SNAPCHAT

Nonetheless, I'd caution against *either/or* thinking and recommend you do *both/and* thinking. For now, you can certainly ignore Snapchat, but as its features converge with Instagram, it's pretty easy to envision a reality in which you can pretty easily do both Snapchat and Instagram. In fact between snaps (photos) and Snapchat stories (videos), it's already pretty similar to Instagram. The difference is mainly in how information is shared on each network, and who uses it, with Snapchat stuck primarily in the teenage set and females, and Instagram reaching many more people, not just the teenage set and women.

### Snapchat Stories and Instagram Stories

The best opportunity on Snapchat is for you – as a brand – to share an in-depth story for your most passionate followers, or superfans. It's as if your super fans wanted to follow you and your every move on Snapchat "as if" you were just another friend. Because discovery is so haphazard on Snapchat, you'll have to use your offline promotion tactics (think "follow us on Snapchat") to build a user community. I would argue that you can essentially post the same content to your brand's Snapchat story as to its Instagram story, and that many of your other posts would work as well. Just remember that Snapchat is really a messaging, one-to-one service not a social media network, whereas Instagram is a true social media network. It has more reach.

To learn more about Snapchat for business, visit **http://jmlinks.com/28n**.

## » BRAINSTORM AND PLAN AN INSTAGRAM MARKETING STRATEGY

Returning to Instagram, it's time to brainstorm, plan, and execute an Instagram marketing strategy for your company. I'll assume you've researched your customer base and decided they're on Instagram, plus looked at competitors, similar companies, and just brands that "get it," to get a sense of what you like and what you don't like about brand marketing on Instagram. You've completed the *Instagram Research Worksheet*. Now download the *Instagram Posting* and *Instagram Marketing Plan Worksheets*. (For the worksheets, go to **http://jmlinks.com/social2020** (then enter the code '**social2020**' to register your workbook)).

### Instagram Set Up

The *Instagram Research Worksheet* gives you your basics. Identify a profile picture. Write a bio that includes a link to your website. Decide if you want to enable a clickable email link. And decide if you want to use an Instagram-related link service such as Like2b.uy (**http://jmlinks.com/32w**) or Olapic's Tapshop platform at **http://jmlinks.com/32z**. Enable at least one Instagram account for your business, but you'll probably need to manage multiple accounts on your phone. If more than one person will be uploading photos and videos, then have multiple people enable it on their phones. Consider using a third-party app like Hootsuite to manage and schedule your posts.

### Instagram Posting Strategy

What and how should you post? First and foremost, figure out if you are a *fun* company in a *fun / photogenic* industry, where people will want to share photos of themselves directly using your product or service, or you're a *fun or not fun* company in a *fun or not fun* industry, where you'll have to strategize something adjacent to your industry. Are you an Airbnb that's directly fun? Or are you more like an airline like Aeromexico where the experience itself isn't that fun, but there's something adjacent (travel) that is fun? Or are you like Allstate Insurance where your business isn't fun, your industry isn't fun, and it's not really adjacent to anything that's fun, either? So check off:

❑ We're a *fun company in a fun industry*, so we'll post (and get our fans to post) fun photos of them actually using our product or service.

❑ We're a *not fun company adjacent to something fun*, so we'll post (and get our fans to post) fun photos of them using something adjacent to our industry.

❑ We're a *not fun company in a not fun industry*, so we'll really have to think out of the box to use Instagram!

Your **posting strategy** will reflect the reality of how fun and photogenic your products or services truly are.

# ARE YOU A FUN COMPANY, OR A NOT FUN COMPANY?

Next, identify who's going to take what photos / videos, when, where, why, and how. Create an editorial calendar to pre-identify Instagram opportunities such as industry holidays or events (think Cinco de Mayo if you're an avocado company, or Christmas if you're an Irish gift store). Other opportunities might be when customers use your product or service in a photogenic way; think "Kodak Moments" like they used to have in Disneyland. A museum store might have a contest among its customers to share a fun photo of mom or grandma with the kids, buying fun stuff in the store. What are your "Instagram moments" for your business? Think ahead for when there are the best opportunities for Instagram buzz, and write those down in your posting strategy worksheet.

Finally, start posting! Instagram – like all social media – requires that you post a lot of content on a regular basis, and you won't know what works until you start doing it. So get started!

**Instagram Shopping**

Instagram is great for brand-building, but certain types of products or services fit well into its culture for **shopping**. Shopping works best for products or services that are highly visual, and/or those that fit into our consumer culture. Things that are both photogenic and fit into a consumer mentality will do the best.

For example, if you sell **retail items** like dresses, purses, leather goods, etc., **visual services** like wedding photography or birthday party management, or **life experiences** like travel or life-coaching, Instagram shopping should be central to your social media marketing.

Just remember that the infrastructure that *enables* shopping is not the same as the *promotion strategy* that makes potential customers want to engage with your brand. The steps are:

1. **Create Engaging Content.** You must create content that engages your customers, sparks their curiosity, and empowers their imagination.

2. **Promote Your Instagram Content.** Content by itself is insufficient. You need to promote your content to customers through every trick of the trade: real-world to social, cross social as in from Twitter to Instagram, Instagram organic as through the use of hashtags, and even advertising.

3. **Have a Clear Call To Action (CTA).** A strong brand encourages customers to take action. That can be an obvious CTA such as a shopping post with tagged items, or a more subtle CTA such as "link in bio," but regardless you as the marketer need to encourage customers to take the final step: buying your products or services either off or on Instagram.

Your content can encourage excitement and then subtly (or not so subtly) explain that it's "for sale." Here are the three ways that you can enable a shopping experience for your customers via Instagram:

1. **Mention Shopping Opportunities**. A small company or brand might simply mention that customers can "DM" (direct message) them to inquire about purchasing a product or service in a post. Some companies create unique, branded hashtags so users can post and inquire via hashtags. By having a business account, you can also enable the "contact" buttons such as email or messaging. As you post, remind customers that what you're posting is "for sale" and they can DM you for more info or click the "email" button, etc.

2. **Use a Link Service**. You can mention "link in bio" often in your posts, thus directing users to your website or, to be more specific, to a link service like Curalate Like2Buy or LinkTree that can match your posts on a one-to-one basis to items in your e-commerce store.

3. **Enable Instagram Shopping**. If you have an e-commerce store on your website, you can activate the Instagram shopping feature. This is the most direct way to enable e-commerce via Instagram. Note that, if enabled, this allows you to "tag a product" via Instagram. Here's a screenshot of a tagged product post by *@outdoorvoices*:

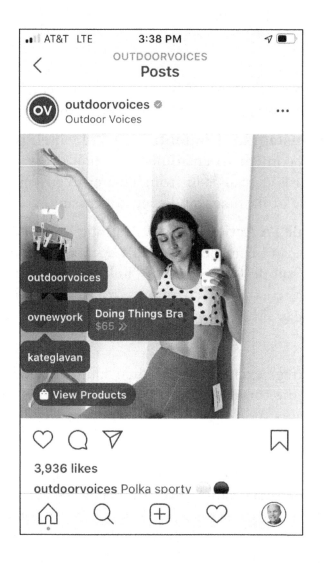

Users can click on "View products" to shop, or click directly on the "Doing Things Bra" and purchase it for $65. Learn more about tagging products at **http://jmlinks.com/53p**.

## » PROMOTE YOUR INSTAGRAM ACCOUNT AND POSTS

The best Instagram account in the world isn't worth a hill of beans if no one sees your posts. Like all "parties" on Social Media, you have to promote your Instagram "party" for it to be successful. First, populate your Instagram account with fun photos even if you have zero or just a few followers. There has to be something there that people want to engage with before you start promoting.

Once you're up and running, here are ideas on how to promote your Instagram account and posts:

**Real World to Social**. For most businesses, this is by far the most important tactic and the cheapest. Simply ask your customers to follow you on Instagram at the point of real contact. A museum gift shop, for example, can install placards at check out that say, "Follow us on Instagram," or even better, a small tablet displaying the store's Instagram account in real-time that people can see and click on as they wait in line. Have the clerks ask people if they're on Instagram, and ask them to follow the shop. "Why follow us?," you ask. Because we share fun photos, have contests, and even communicate special deals and discounts!

**Shout outs and Collabs**. Identify complementary vendors in your niche, and reach out to them for collaborative Instagram marketing. If you're a wedding photographer, reach out to the wedding florist, the wedding venue, the cake maker, the priest, rabbi, or another officiant at the wedding… ask them to "collab" with you and/or give you a "shout out," and reciprocate.

# YOU GOTTA PROMOTE YOUR INSTAGRAM TO BE SUCCESSFUL

**Hashtags**. Instagram is very hashtag-friendly. Be sure to use **geotags** (your location) in your posts, and identify and use relevant hashtags. People use Instagram like a magazine, to discover content that they care about, so deploy hashtags that feed that interest and make sure that the content they will discover is "sticky" so that they follow your account. (Use hashtagify.me (**http://jmlinks.com/27v**)) to find trending hashtags on Twitter and Instagram that are relevant to your brand, and include them in your posts. In addition, identify one or more "branded" hashtags unique to your company to encourage social sharing around your brand. REI does this, for example, with *#optoutside* across all its social media channels.

**Website / Other Social Media**. Be sure that your website links to your Instagram, easily, and cross-promote from your other social accounts (e.g.,

Twitter) to your Instagram. Don't forget to use your customer email list and email newsletters to promote and advertise your Instagram. Use one social media to promote another.

**Interact with Others**. Follow other accounts, and like, share, and comment on posts made by those accounts. Identify your competitors, and look at who follows them. Follow those people, and like, share, and comment on their Instagram accounts. **Warning**: Be aware that if you follow / interact with too many accounts too quickly, you can get banned from Instagram! (See **http://jmlinks.com/28r** for more information). So don't be spammy! More tips on being interactive with your fans –

> **Follow Relevant People.** "Follow for follow" still works on Instagram, so identify and follow industry leaders, the followers of your competitors, etc. This means that if you follow them, they will likely follow you back. Warning: do not overdo this as there is a cap of about 300 follows per day, and a lifetime cap of 7000. Don't spam!

> **@Mention People.** Mention out key influencers, your own users and other people in general in your comments and captions. By "shout outs" to others, you'll get their attention. **Tag** people as well.

> **Like and Comment on the Posts of Others.** Look at your users, and the friends of your users, and like their posts. Ditto for comments. Comment on what others are doing on Instagram.

> **Reshare Your Users' Posts.** Selectively share / or repost some of your users' posts (with their permission). Sharing isn't as easy on Instagram as on Facebook, but you should still do it. For example, you can reach out by email to someone who posts a photo, have them email it to you, post it to your account and include their @handle in your caption.

> **Engage with Your Own Users**. Instagram isn't just about broadcasting to your customers. It's also about interacting with, and engaging with them. Pay attention to who follows you, already, and interact with their comments to your account. Follow them back. Spend at least an hour a day interacting with your customer. Identify and cultivate superfans that might be willing to promote your business. Ask your fans for comments. Post a picture of a draft product or service, and ask users for their opinions. Post a survey question and ask users to chime in in the comments field. Post a photo and ask for a caption; have a caption contest, and give the winner a gift card. Be provocative!

**Advertise on Instagram**. Yes, Instagram has advertising! And yes, you can use it to promote your Instagram business account, as well as offlink to your website or e-commerce store. Since Instagram is owned by Facebook, you manage an Instagram ad through your Facebook account. You need a Facebook Page for your business and need to connect that Page to your Instagram account to be able to advertise. You can read the official help file at **http://jmlinks.com/28w**.

## Instagram Contests

Among the most important Instagram promotion strategies are **contests** and **giveaways**. One easy way to do this is to establish a hashtag for your brand, and then ask users to post a photo on that hashtag as part of the contest or giveaway. You select a winner, based on the posts. For an example, check out *#jorgstyle* which has had a contest based on user photos (**http://jmlinks.com/28s**). Here's a screenshot of the singer Pitbull, who's using the hashtags *#contest, #Pitbull* and *#Mr305* to promote his brand. Yes, you can go to Las Vegas and see him live – just post a picture of you and your Mom. What's more special than a picture of you and your mom honoring Pitbull? (*A selfie of you and your mom at the Pitbull concert in Las Vegas shared to Instagram, of course*).

A quick way to browse contests and look for contest ideas on Instagram is to use the Google *search site:Instagram.com #contests* at **http://jmlinks.com/28t**. Of course, there are vendors such as Gleam.io that will help you manage Instagram contests (**http://jmlinks.com/28u**). Just Google "Instagram Contests" and you can easily find helpful vendors or apps. Read the official Instagram restrictions at **http://jmlinks.com/28v**.

## » WORK WITH INSTAGRAM INFLUENCERS

Instagram is probably the most important social media network these days for so-called **influencers**, though influencers are big on YouTube, too. What's an influencer?

> *An influencer is a person who has a relevant and substantial social media following and is willing to promote your product or service, usually for a fee.*

Here's where it gets tricky. You want to distinguish among:

**Fans and Superfans.** These are people who truly use and like your product or service and are active on Instagram and might promote you "for free" because they basically really love you.

**Paid Promotions / Contests.** This is using giveaways, contests, or other tactics to encourage your fans and superfans to promote you. You either pay them, or they get some type of free stuff in exchange for spreading your message.

**Influencers.** This term has come to mean people who have a very substantial following on Instagram (or YouTube) and who will promote your product or service for a fee. Make sure that they are relevant to your brand; it's not just about quantity, after all, it's about quality and relevance.

It is also possible that people who have a significant following might be willing to collaborate with you and your brand in exchange not for money but just for free stuff, or even because they just truly love your brand, products, and/or services. A hotel chain, for example, might comp a guest to stay at the hotel and in exchange expect photos, videos, and shout-outs about the brand. Or a restaurant might give discounts to people in the restaurant for similar behavior. So you'll have some "influencers" who might promote you for free because they just really love you, some who want free stuff, and still others who want money.

FTC regulations require persons who are getting free stuff and/or being paid to acknowledge a paid relationship in their posts, but this regulation seems to be widely ignored. Instagram also requires the influencer ("paid") posts be identified with the tag "Paid partnership with" your company. See Instagram's requirements at **http://jmlinks.com/45t** and check out posts fulfilling this requirement at **http://jmlinks.com/46g**.

To find influencers, look at your branded hashtags and look for fans and superfans who are already engaged. Follow them back and look at how many followers they have. Reach out to them with offers of free stuff and/or money to promote your brand.

Search Instagram by keyword and look for accounts that are relevant. You can also use services like Buzzsumo to find out what type of content is being shared (and by whom), Hashtagify.me (which tracks Instagram in its paid version), and paid services like Pixlee (**https://www.pixlee.com**). Just Google "influencer marketing Instagram" and you can easily find companies and services that broker the relationship between influencers and brands on the platform.

## » MEASURE YOUR INSTAGRAM KPIS

Although Instagram does not easily allow links to your website, Instagram marketing can still be measured. Define the KPIs (Key Performance Indicators) that will indicate that your Instagram marketing efforts are either building your brand awareness and/or directly selling more stuff.

Establish some KPIs (Key Performance Indicators), such as:

- **Followers**. Measure your follower count each month. It should go up.

- **Engagement**. Measure, for each post, is it getting likes, comments, and shares. Which posts get the most engagement? Why or why not?

- **Action**. You're not in this for your health. Is Instagram –
  - o **Building your brand**? Increasing your brand awareness in a positive way? If so, why? If not, why not, and what can you do to fix it?
  - o **Leading to sales** actions such as completed feedback / inquiry forms or purchases at an eCommerce website? For some brands (e.g., Airbnb, Rusticcuff), Instagram CAN lead to real sales, but for others, this isn't a realistic objective.

Your Instagram strategy – working *backward* – should go from a sale / sales lead to better brand awareness, to a fun, photogenic post by you or a fan, to a strong account on Instagram. To devise your strategy, don't start at a conceptual level with the photo or post; rather, start with what you want, such as either better brand awareness or an actual sale (or both), and work backward.

Don't forget to think about user-generated content (UGC). How can you use contests, hashtags or other prompts to motivate your customer fans to engage with you on Instagram and even create and upload fun content around your brand? Interact with your users and others on Instagram by liking, commenting on, and sharing their posts. Tag people in your photos and videos. Follow individuals, as the "follow for follow" vibe is still very strong on Instagram. Measure whether these outreach efforts are getting resonance, or not, and why.

Finally, on an on-going, monthly basis, measure your Instagram performance vis-a-vis your KPIs and record them as you should be doing for other social media networks like Facebook, LinkedIn, or Twitter. Is your fan base growing? Is your engagement growing? Are you seeing improvements in your brand equity? And are you getting any actual sales performance from your social media efforts? How can you improve?

If you are using links to your website whether just in your bio, or whether to an e-commerce store, or if you're lucky enough to qualify for links in Story Highlights and/or the new Instagram shop feature, measure traffic from Instagram to your website using Google Analytics (**https://analytics.google.com/**). Inside of your Google Analytics account on the left column, drill down by clicking on *Acquisition > Social > Overview*. Then on the right-hand side of the screen, you'll see a list of Social Networks. Find Instagram on that list, and click on that. Google Analytics will tell you what URLs people clicked to from Instagram to your Website, giving you insights into what types of content people find attractive (if you have more than one URL on Instagram as in the Stories Highlights feature or Shop feature).

You can also create a custom **segment** to look at only Instagram traffic and its behavior. For information on how to create custom segments in Google Analytics, go to **http://jmlinks.com/1f**. For the Google help files on segments go to **http://jmlinks.com/1g**.

Measure your Instagram strategy as the Big Picture of why your company is on Instagram in the first place, and your posting strategy as the tactical manifestation of this. Everything needs to work together towards a common goal of bolstering your brand on Instagram and ultimately helping you to sell more stuff.

## »» Checklist: Instagram Action Items

Test your knowledge of Instagram! Take the *Instagram marketing quiz* at **http://jmlinks.com/qzin**. Next, here are your Instagram **Action Items**:

❑ **Research -**

❑ Whether **your customers** are on Instagram. If so, what or who are they interacting with? What turns them on, and why?

❑ Whether **your competitors** are on Instagram. If so, what is their Instagram posting strategy and does it seem to be working as measured by followers and interaction? Why or why not?

❑ Whether **there are similar companies to emulate**. Are there companies (not your competitors) that are doing a good job on Instagram? If so, who are they and what are they doing?

❑ Whether there are relevant **#hashtags** on Instagram or **#geotags** that connect potential customers to themes that make sense for your business.

❑ **Set up** a business profile on Instagram, including –

❑ **Profile Picture**

❑ **Bio Description with link.** Describe your company's value proposition in a fun way, and use a service like Like2Buy if desired.

❑ **Contact Info.** Make sure that your contact information is included in your Business account. If possible sign up for the shop feature.

❑ **Posts.** Begin posting photos and/or videos of your business that fit to the Instagram culture of friends, family, fun, photos, and fake.

❑ **Instagram Stories**. If possible, create a daily Instagram story about your brand. Save stories as "highlights" so that they show under your profile. Once you have 10,000 followers, you can embed links as well. Watch Sue B. Zimmerman's excellent video on "Story Highlights" at **http://jmlinks.com/45x**.

❑ **Instagram Shopping.** If applicable, set up the Shop feature for your e-commerce store or consider using "link in bio" or a link service to link from Instagram to your website.

❑ **Brainstorm** a **content marketing strategy** for Instagram. Are you a "fun company" in a "fun industry," a "not fun company" adjacent to a "fun industry," or a "not fun company" that's not near "anything fun?" Then brainstorm –

❏ **Photos** to take of your business, products, and/or services that "fit" with Instagram.

❏ **Videos** and **Instagram Stories** that "fit."

❏ **UGC** or "User Generated Content." How can you get your fans / customers to not only interact with content you produce but produce content themselves that helps build your brand?

❏ **Interactive Content.** Be interactive on Instagram. Follow your fans back, and follow new people to get their attention. Like and comment on what your fans are saying. Make your brand interactive.

❏ **Promote** your Instagram business profile through strategies like *#hashtags*, follow for follow, cross-connections to other digital properties like your website, Twitter, Facebook, etc., and even consider contests or **advertising** on Instagram.

❏ **Measure** your Instagram results such as increase in followers, increases in post interactivity, traffic to your website and/or eCommerce store.

Check out the **free tools**! Go to my *Social Media Marketing Dashboard > Instagram* for my favorite free tools on Instagram. Just visit **http://jmlinks.com/smmdash**.

## »» DELIVERABLE: AN INSTAGRAM MARKETING PLAN

Your **DELIVERABLE** has arrived. For the worksheet, go to **http://jmlinks.com/social2020** (then enter the code '**social2020**' to register your workbook), and click on the link to the "Instagram Marketing Plan." By filling out this plan, you and your team will establish a vision of what you want to achieve via Instagram marketing, including your KPIs (Key Performance Indicators). Be sure to complete the Instagram research and posting worksheets as well.

# SURVEY OFFER

**CLAIM YOUR $5 REBATE! HERE'S HOW -**

Visit **http://jmlinks.com/survey**.

1. Take a short, simple survey about the book.

2. Indicate whether you want a $5 rebate or want to make a contribution to our scholarship fund.

**WE WILL THEN -**

- Rebate you the $5, or thank you profusely for helping a deserving young marketer.

**~ $5 REBATE OFFER ~**

**~ LIMITED TO ONE PER CUSTOMER ~**

**SUBJECT TO CHANGE WITHOUT NOTICE**

**GOT QUESTIONS? CALL 800-298-4065**

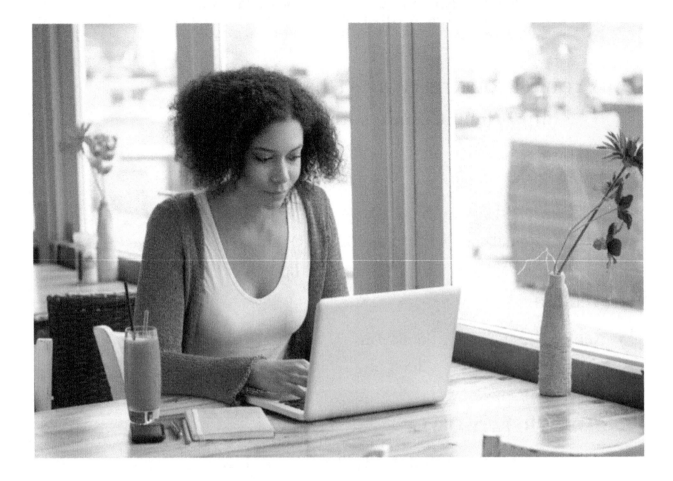

# 7
# YOUTUBE

YouTube, in particular, and video in general, provide a two-for-one punch to your social media marketing. First, video itself can be the "there there," the content that you post on Twitter, Facebook, LinkedIn, etc. People love, watch, and share video as one of the most popular types of content across social media. Nowadays, however, video doesn't just live on YouTube. It lives on Facebook, Instagram, LinkedIn, and even Twitter. TikTok is the new kid on the block, and it's video only. You can even stream "live video" on Facebook, Instagram, and – of course – YouTube. Second, as a social media platform in its own right, YouTube works much like Facebook or Twitter. People "like" (*thumbs up* in YouTube lingo), "comment on," and "share" your videos. They "subscribe" to your channel and get notifications when you release a new video. Video, in short, is both *content itself* and a social media platform *in its own right*, that is, *YouTube*.

In this Chapter, you'll learn the basics of what makes a good video for any platform. As for YouTube, you'll see similarities to Facebook: setting up a channel ("Page") on YouTube, uploading a video ("post") to YouTube, and the fact that people subscribe to your channel ("like" your "Page"). You'll also learn that video brings three very different marketing mechanisms in its role as content. Video can be used as a **supportive medium**, it can be deployed via **SEO** (Search Engine Optimization) to show at the top of Google and/or YouTube searches, and it can be tweaked for **social sharing** or even **viral marketing** across platforms.

**Let's get started!**

**TO-DO LIST:**

» Get What's So Great about Video

» Explore How YouTube Works

» Inventory Companies on YouTube

» Understand the Three Promotional Uses of Video

» Tell Stories through Video

» Set up Your Channel and Upload Videos

» Advertise on YouTube

## » GET WHAT'S SO GREAT ABOUT VIDEO

Video is the fastest-growing form of content on the Internet, and video is the most viral type of content. People love video! But why? In his prescient 1964 book, *Understanding Media*, Marshall McLuhan argued that "the medium is the message." *Understanding Media* is a complex, nuanced book, but suffice it to say that McLuhan was one of the first to realize that people would respond to video in an emotional way. McLuhan wrote his book during the massive cultural transition from the written word in books and newspapers to the video projection of television in the 1950s and 1960s. He understood why advertisers love television because TV puts viewers into an almost hypnotic trance, opening their minds and hearts (as well as their wallets) to the messages of advertising. And McLuhan predicted that television would alter culture and politics, as video heightened emotions and could often overwhelm rationality in human decision-making.

Were McLuhan alive today, the social scientist would not be surprised at the popularity of "cat videos" on the Internet, the fact that trends like the "Harlem Shake" or "Ice Bucket Challenge" are able to "go viral" by leveraging both the power of video and the power of influencers, nor the power of video to create political controversy over events at the US border, the relationship between police and minority communities, the election of Donald Trump, or other powerful political images that seemingly sweep across the culture day in and day out. More recently, authors like Richard Brodie and Susan Blackmore have argued that the Internet accelerates the spread of "memes" or "idea viruses," and that video plays a key role in transmission.

For marketers and business owners, video brings together two key features that exist almost nowhere else in social media:

1. the ability to **leverage emotions** to persuade potential customers to like your brand and buy your stuff; and

2. an increased likelihood of **social sharing** by one user to others.

Video by its very nature is also an ideal medium for "showing" rather than "telling," so it plays well in the "how to" space as for example in popular videos like "how to tie a tie," or "how to get a puppy to stop biting," with 67 million views and 1.5 million views on YouTube, respectively. And in an era in which (unfortunately) the general population is declining in education and intelligence, video is "easy" to understand vs. reading which is "hard." People, not surprisingly, prefer emotion to reason, showing to telling, and viewing to reading. Video hits all three of these trends.

Leaving aside the general decline of Western civilization, video is an incredible tool in your marketing toolbox. Imagine videos about your brand, product, or service that touch on emotions, spur social sharing, explain how to use your product (and its benefits), and are so easy to consume as content that the user need merely sit back, relax, and absorb your marketing message. What's not to like about video?

# VIDEO IS EASY TO CONSUME AND HARD TO PRODUCE

*Production*, that's what not to like. Producing video, as compared with still photos or text posts, is difficult. It requires knowledge of visual storytelling as well as production techniques such as scripts, camera, sound, and editing. Even a short YouTube video is rather difficult to produce and can be intimidating. With some effort and some tools, however, it's increasingly easy to create videos. So don't be intimidated! Rather, embrace and enjoy the video revolution in marketing.

## » EXPLORE HOW YOUTUBE WORKS

Video and YouTube are among the most dramatic, most viral components of the Internet. Who doesn't know the "Harlem Shake" (**http://jmlinks.com/1m**) or the "Ice Bucket Challenge" (**http://jmlinks.com/1n**)? Who hasn't watched "Will it blend?" (**http://jmlinks.com/1o**) or "Dear 16 Year Old Me" (**http://jmlinks.com/1p**)? And who hasn't fallen into the trap of assuming all YouTube is, are silly cat videos, Beyoncé and Jay-Z videos, and inappropriate High School humor? It is, but YouTube is much, much more than that as a marketing opportunity (and as a social phenomenon).

As we shall see, there are three basic ways that videos can help you with social media marketing:

1. **Video as a supporting medium**: acting as the "content" that you "share" via other social media, including your website. (This is true on your website, on YouTube, on Facebook and even on LinkedIn or Twitter).

2. **Video as a discovery mechanism via SEO** (Search Engine Optimization), helping you promote your company, products, or services via YouTube and Google search.

3. **Video as a share / viral promotion tactic**, because people love and share provocative videos, not just on YouTube but via on all social media networks like Facebook, Twitter, LinkedIn or Pinterest.

We should also mention **#4** – video as an *advertising* medium. YouTube presents unique advertising opportunities, and "video ads" are now common on Facebook, Twitter, and LinkedIn.

We'll dive into the details in a moment. But first, log on to YouTube and get your bearings. (For the official YouTube starter guide, go to **http://jmlinks.com/1q**). If you're familiar with Facebook and Twitter, you'll see many similarities right out of the gate:

- Individuals (or brands) have an "account" or "**channel**" on YouTube, set up by registering with an email address and using their Google account to manage their account.

- Individuals (or brands) can **upload videos** to their "channel," and when uploading, give each video a TITLE, a DESCRIPTION, and KEYWORD TAGS as well as designate a VIDEO THUMBNAIL.

- Individuals "**subscribe**" to the channels of other individuals (or brands) on YouTube, and when someone you subscribe to uploads a new video, you get a notification in your YouTube news feed as well as via email that a new video has been posted. A new feature on YouTube is the "bell," located to the right of the "subscribe" button; subscribed users can click it to increase the likelihood of notifications.

- Individuals can **thumbs up / thumbs down videos** (akin to "like" on Facebook of a post), comment, and share the videos via other social media as well as create playlists of videos on YouTube.

- Companies can create **brand channels** on YouTube. Like Twitter or Instagram,

YouTube is very easy and open: anyone can quickly create a channel. Like Twitter or Instagram, YouTube does not really distinguish between the Channel or Account of an individual vs. that of a company. And YouTube really does not authenticate users, so it's super easy to set up a Channel and post videos as either an individual or a company.

For assistance on how to set up a company YouTube channel, visit **http://jmlinks.com/1r**. Your first to-do is thus to either set up a YouTube account as an individual or as a brand, and then start searching for, watching, and interacting with videos. What videos pique your interest? What videos seem relevant to your target customers? Which brands or individuals that are relevant to your company are already on YouTube and what type of video content are they producing that's getting transaction?

## » INVENTORY COMPANIES ON YOUTUBE

After you've signed up for YouTube, your mission is to identify competitors on YouTube as well as brands that interest you in order to make an inventory of your likes and dislikes when it comes to YouTube as a channel for marketing. I'll focus largely on how to use YouTube as a brand, but let's distinguish between these three types of YouTubers:

1. **Pure Users**. These are average people who don't post videos but rather just watch video content. They are "content consumers" and not "content producers." These are your target audiences as a marketer. Like Twitter, YouTube reaches pretty much everyone on the planet. "Riches are in the niches;" so don't be discouraged by the high-profile pop culture elements on YouTube. There are many wonderful niche users and niche usages!

2. **Amateur Content Creators**. These are people who create and upload videos about their lives, likes, habits, or other things, but whose goal isn't to make money or go viral. They are simply using YouTube like they'd use Facebook, TikTok, or Instagram to upload and share content about their lives. Note that an individual can be both a user on YouTube and a creator of content, just as they can be on Twitter or Facebook.

3. **Professional Content Creators or Influencers**. These are individuals who really function as brands. An example would be PewDiePie with over 102 million subscribers on YouTube (**http://jmlinks.com/44d**). PewDiePie's real name is Felix Arvid Ulf Kjellberg, and this Swedish national was named by Time magazine as one of 2016's most influential people. This type of content creator

generally makes money off of Google ads placed on YouTube and/or brand endorsements. Think of this type as akin to "Oprah" on YouTube, where a single individual IS the brand and money is made by product tie-ins and advertising. Patreon (**https://www.patreon.com/**) and YouTube subscriptions are new ways for YouTube creators to make money by directly charging users for video access. In some cases, they're open to accepting money to promote your products as an "influencer."

4. **Brands**. These are companies on YouTube as opposed to individuals who are uploading content and have a marketing agenda of either a) supporting their other social media channels with video content, b) ranking on Google and/or YouTube search and/or c) getting shares by users or even going viral with their brand message. An example would be the Always feminine products' Channel at **http://jmlinks.com/44e**.

As you get started with YouTube, start to contemplate whether your business is best served by a brand Channel or by an individual Channel (such as the company CEO or lead celebrity), or perhaps both. Perhaps working with influencers would be higher ROI, or perhaps merely using YouTube as an advertising venue would be best. Regardless, as marketers, realize that you are producing video for the marketing purpose of building your brand and/or selling more stuff, either directly or indirectly. You're not producing video for video's sake any more than you might be producing art for art's sake. We're talking video as marketing, not video as art.

## How to Browse YouTube for Videos and Channels

To get started, you need to explore what individuals or brands are out there that represent competitors, companies to emulate, or just uses of YouTube that you can see might advance your marketing agenda. How do you find Channels and videos?

One obvious way to make your shortlist of companies to follow is to simply visit their websites, and look for a link from their website to their YouTube channel. A big brand like REI, Target, or Geico, for example, will usually have the YouTube icon somewhere on their website, often in top right or on the bottom footer. Simply be signed in to your personal YouTube account, click on their link to YouTube, and then once you land on their channel, click the red "subscribe" button. Click the "bell" if you want to ensure notifications. Here's a screenshot:

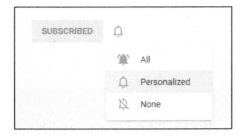

A second way to find companies to subscribe to is to **browse YouTube**. When you are logged in to your YouTube account, simply click on "Browse channels" located on the left-hand side of the screen or in the middle of the screen. This is a bit confusing because once you are an active YouTube user, YouTube hides some of these links, so here are some direct links to click when you are logged in to your YouTube account:

Browse Channels at **http://jmlinks.com/44f**.

YouTube Live at **http://jmlinks.com/44g**.

YouTube Trending at **http://jmlinks.com/44h**.

Channels are especially interesting. On each category, you can click on the category name (e.g., *Film and Entertainment*), and drill down to channels in that category. Identify channels that interest you and hit the "subscribe" button. As you subscribe to channels, they will begin to appear on your home screen on the left column under "Subscriptions."

To unsubscribe, just click on "Manage subscriptions" and/or go to the channel and hit the now-gray "Subscribed" button. Notice as well that after you subscribe when a Channel posts a new video it will show in your "news feed" under recommended or under the Channel itself. In this way, YouTube is like Facebook or Twitter in that once someone establishes a social media connection, the news feed of the one pushes content when the timeline of the other has something new. As a marketer, you want to drive folks to subscribe to your channel and to hit the "bell" so that they receive your notifications.

## How to Search YouTube

Most of the action on YouTube really occurs at the level of the video, and not the channel, however. By this, I mean that most of the high video counts, sharing, and even videos discovered via search occur via individual videos and not channels. You need to be a good searcher to understand YouTube!

**VIDEO.** Watch a video tutorial on how to search YouTube at **http://jmlinks.com/17a.**

To search YouTube directly, simply type keywords that matter to your company into the search bar at the top of the screen. For example type, *organic food*, to find YouTube videos on *organic food*. Here's a screenshot:

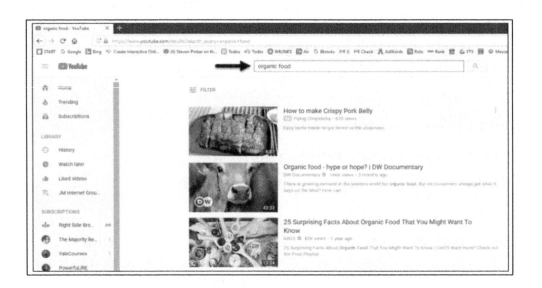

Like the Google search engine, YouTube will return a list of the most relevant videos. Simply click on a video to watch it, and then click "up" to the channel to learn more about the channel that produced it. Or you can just hit the red "Subscribe" button directly to subscribe to the channel. Here's a screenshot:

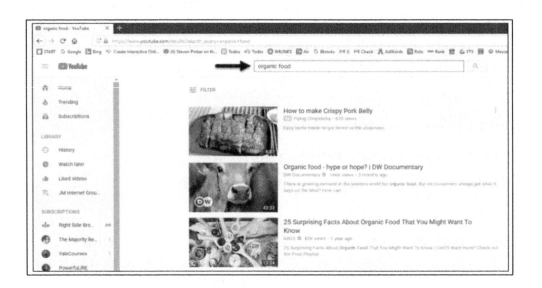

You can also thumb up / thumb down a video, comment on it (using your Google account), and share it. If you click on the share icon below a video, YouTube gives you all the social icons plus a link to "Embed," which provides the HTML code you need to embed a video on your own website or blog.

# SEARCH YOUTUBE BY KEYWORDS TO FIND RELEVANT VIDEOS AND CHANNELS

Going back to search, type "organic food" into the search bar. Next, on the top left, click on *Filter*, which opens up a set of parameters by which you can narrow your search. Here's a screenshot:

| ⇄ FILTER | | | | |
|---|---|---|---|---|
| **UPLOAD DATE** | **TYPE** | **DURATION** | **FEATURES** | **SORT BY** |
| Last hour | Video | Short (< 4 minutes) | Live | **Relevance** |
| Today | Channel | Long (> 20 minutes) | 4K | Upload date |
| This week | Playlist | | HD | View count |
| This month | Movie | | Subtitles/CC | Rating |
| This year | Show | | Creative Commons | |
| | | | 360° | |
| | | | VR180 | |
| | | | 3D | |
| | | | HDR | |
| | | | Location | |
| | | | Purchased | |

Click *Upload date > This year*, which will turn on *filter #1* (videos of the last year), then re-click *Filter*, and then click *Sort by > View Count*, which will turn on *filter #2* (most popular). In this way, you can find the most popular videos by view count vs. a time period (one year). You can also do this by week or month.

You can also use Filter to search for Channels by keyword. Enter your keyword such as "organic food," and then under Type select "Channel." This is a quick and easy way to find the most popular channels by keyword. Note that as on the Google search engine, a search for "Organic Food" (with quotes) is different than a search for *Organic Food* (without quotes). Play around with your keywords and social media themes to identify the most popular Channels in your niche.

Next, click around at the various videos, and identify what sorts of topics you find people producing and watching in your industry. Pay attention to the thumbs up / thumbs down count, and comments per video. Like a good party planner, you are looking to identify the types of entertainment that attract and engage your guests.

With respect to an individual video, pay attention to the total views, thumbs up / thumbs down, and comments. Here's a screenshot of data for the video, "Is Organic Food Worse for You?" at **http://jmlinks.com/53t**:

This means that this video had 1.8 million views, 36,000 thumbs-up, and 2,400 thumbs down. If you scroll down to comments, you can see the **comments** count (4,265 as of December 2019), and you read through them. You can also see the date a video was published. In this way, you can see how "popular" a video is on YouTube and how "interactive" it is vis-à-vis the user base.

Two good tools to get more data are *TubeBuddy* (**http://jmlinks.com/53r**) and *vidIQ* (**http://jmlinks.com/53s**). Each has a free and a premium version. Here's a screenshot of data from vidIQ for this video:

The plugin will also give you data for the channel as a whole, plus "hidden" tags added to the video and the rank, if applicable, for those keywords. Here's a screenshot:

In this way, as you start your YouTube research, you can find channels and videos of competitors and companies-to-emulate and then drill into specific videos to see data about user engagement and the hidden optimization added to the video by the creator. Then, on your own videos, you can use this feature to see how well an individual video is performing.

**Search Google for Videos**

Another way to find interesting videos by keywords is to search Google. First, type your keywords into Google, and then click the *more > videos* button. Here's a screenshot:

You can also use the button "Tools" on the far right to filter these results by videos of the last year, or by source (e.g., CNN.com or YouTube.com), but unlike on YouTube itself, you can't filter by view count.

By browsing, searching YouTube directly, or searching Google for videos, your objective is to identify channels and videos that have high view counts as well as high thumbs up / thumbs down, and comments. What do people like? Why do they interact with it? How can this knowledge be applied to videos relevant to your company? Your goals or questions are:

- Are your potential **customers** on YouTube, and if so, what types of videos are they watching? Which relevant videos have the highest view counts? What keywords or themes seem to be the most popular? Why?

- Are **individuals** ("content creators") and/or **companies** similar to yours on YouTube, and if so, what kinds of videos are they producing? Look out for competitors and companies-to-emulate.

- What types of videos are gaining the most **interactions** as measured by thumbs up / thumbs down, comments, shares, and subscriptions to the channel?

For your first **TO-DO**, download the **YouTube Research Worksheet**. For the worksheet, go to **http://jmlinks.com/social2020** (then reenter the code '**social2020**' to register your workbook), and click on the link to the "YouTube Research Worksheet." You'll answer questions as to whether your potential customers are on YouTube, identify brands to follow, and inventory what you like and dislike about their YouTube channels and individual videos.

## » UNDERSTAND THE THREE PROMOTIONAL USES OF VIDEO

While YouTube does have channels, subscriptions, and social spread just as other social media, the lion's share of activity comes directly from the videos themselves. Thus, it is very important to understand the three promotional uses of video.

### YouTube Noise: Pop Culture

Before we turn to those uses of video, however, let's pause for a moment and consider the tremendous noise caused on YouTube by pop culture. When you innocently log in to your YouTube account, you will be bombarded by a) music videos, b) ridiculous college humor / professional / silly videos, c) movie trailers, d) crazy trending news and so on and so forth. This is the dominant use of YouTube in terms of views, but just as cable TV has hundreds of channels, and you can drill down to very specific, and very useful channels and programs (think, for example, about cooking or fishing shows on cable TV, that are not high volume but are very high value to people who really care about cooking or fishing). So, before your boss freaks about and dismisses YouTube because of the crazy videos on cats and the videos by pop culture media icons, remember that for most of us marketers the value of YouTube is in the **niches** that matter to us: the niches that create and contain content that our customers care about. They exist; you just have to find them!

> **Quantity** is about video views count.
>
> **Quality** is about whether your videos are reaching your target customers and leading to brand awareness, email sign-ups, sales leads, or even sales.

# YOUTUBE'S RICHES ARE IN THE NICHES

With that in mind, let's investigate the three basic uses of YouTube.

## #1 Use of YouTube: Supportive Use of Video

If a picture is worth a thousand words, a video is worth ten thousand. If you are selling a complex product or service, creating and hosting explanatory videos can really help your sales process. Let's face it. Today's busy consumer doesn't really want to read a lot of text! They like videos because videos convey a lot of information quickly and easily, and videos convey emotional content.

Let's assume, for example, that you are a personal injury attorney in San Francisco. People are going to search for you via Google with keyword searches like "Personal Injury Attorneys SF," or "Auto Accident Attorney Bay Area." Then, they're going to land on your website, see a lot of intimidating text, and want to learn more about you as an attorney. Are you smart? Are you nice? Are you someone that they can trust?

In the old, pre-video days, they'd have to call you on the phone and come in for a quick interview. Then, they'd get in the car with their spouse, and have a little chat: *did you like her? Did she seem smart? Could we trust her with our case?* It would be all about "emotional intelligence," and "gut feeling."

Video allows you to post a quick introduction to you and/or your firm on your website, and start that process of "emotional intelligence" in just a few clicks of the mouse. In a very non-threatening way, videos give you the opportunity to pitch to a potential customer.

Here are some examples of this "supportive" use of video from the personal injury lawyer community. These videos that are not meant to "go viral," but rather to "support" the content of a website:

> **Farar & Lewis (https://www.fararlawgroup.com/).** Notice the introductory video in the center of the homepage at **http://jmlinks.com/53u**.
>
> **Walkup Law (http://www.walkuplawoffice.com/).** Again, notice the video in the center of the homepage. Note that this one is not hosted on YouTube but rather on their own website.

The hosting location, however, is not very important. What's important is that in a complex industry such as legal services, these companies are using video to "support" the content of their website, and provide potential customers and "easy" way to acquire some "emotional intelligence" about the law firm.

> *A **supportive** video explains what your company offers, using a friendly, visual video format to communicate emotional trust.*

Another area that uses videos in a supportive way is the technology industry. Take a look at the Analog Devices channel (**http://jmlinks.com/13b**). Watch a sample video from their participation at the *Embedded World Trade Show* at **http://jmlinks.com/1t**. Essentially, they are taking a video recorder to the trade show and recording the "dog and pony show" that each product marketing engineer gives to a prospect who walks up to the trade show booth. The dance goes like this:

- *Hi, what does Analog Devices have new and exciting for engineers that you're exhibiting here at the Embedded World Tradeshow?*

- *Oh, hi there, my name is John Doe, Product Marketing Manager at Analog Devices of the super widget. Let me walk you through what we're exhibiting.*

- *Thank you. (Mentally: oh that's interesting, that fits what I need, he seems like a nice guy, and they seem like a great company... I'll follow up on doing business together after the show).*

By posting these videos to YouTube, Analog Devices creates linkable, shareable **content**, that it can post to its Facebook, Twitter, LinkedIn, and even website pages. It can also email these videos out to prospective clients who inquire but were unable to attend the industry trade show. They are using video to **support** their marketing efforts, and none of these videos are designed to "go viral" like a cat video or Beyoncé's latest over-the-top music video. That's not their purpose.

> Analog Devices' use of YouTube is all about **quality**: using YouTube to reach highly qualified, target customers not to create massive view counts.

A third way to see the supportive use of video is to go to Facebook and look at brands you admire. You'll often see them sharing video content. Use a tool like Buzzsumo (**http://www.buzzsumo.com/**), enter your keywords, and look for videos that are being shared on social media. In most cases, these videos are functioning to "support" the social media marketing: like blog posts, videos can be simply content that you share.

Buzzsumo is $99 / month, but it's worth trying it for just a month to see what YouTube content is popular. To do so, log in to Buzzsumo, select "Web," then type the following into the search bar:

It's a good idea to use quotes around a phrase. Here's a screenshot of a Buzzsumo search for youtube.com "organic food" showing that #1 most popular YouTube video in the last year:

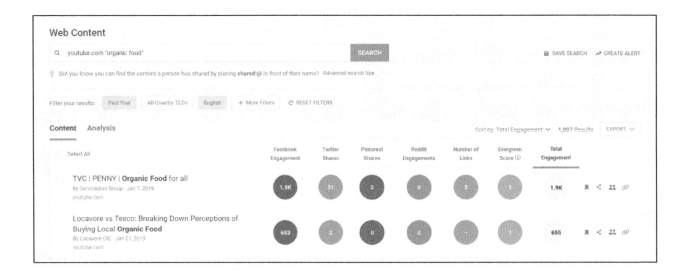

This shows that the video "Organic Food for all" had 1.9K shares on Facebook. You can search by Facebook, Twitter, or Links, to see the share measurement of any video. You can also click into Twitter and see who shared it.

> **Tip**. Look for videos in your industry with high share counts, thumbs up, comments, and shares as indicated on YouTube itself at the video level and via third-party tools like Buzzsumo. Even if your goal is only to use video to support your website, you want to research what type of content engages your customers and produce accordingly.

If you sell something complex, something that people use "emotional intelligence" to evaluate, video allows you the opportunity to share that information quickly and easily.

## Showing Rather than Telling

If you have "how to" content that is best explained visually, videos can be fantastic for your social media marketing. Any type of content that is better explained by "showing" than by "writing" is an excellent candidate for video. You can also, of course, use video for "after the sale" events such explanations to commonly asked technical support questions.

The **supportive** use of video, with free hosting of those videos on YouTube and a universal player, is an opportunity not to be missed!

## #2 Use of YouTube: Search Discovery or SEO Use of Video

YouTube is the number two search engine, behind Google and far ahead of Bing. One of the heaviest uses of YouTube is for "how to" searches. Simply go to YouTube and start typing "how to" and you'll see a list of common YouTube searches.

Here's a screenshot:

```
how to

how to tie a tie
how to get the mammoth skin in fortnite
how to draw
how to make slime
how to wrap a gift
how to basic
how to connect ps4 controller to iphone
how to crip walk
how to train your dragon homecoming
how to get woolly mammoth fortnite
                                    Report search predictions
```

You can also type other words more relevant to your company like "How to grow" or "How to put on," etc. to see more specific "how to" searches relevant to your industry. If your company has any type of "how to" content, especially "how to" content that is best explained in a visual way, you can SEO-optimize YouTube videos to show up for search.

Let's say, for example, that you sell pet food. People who have new puppies are often curious about how to potty train their new puppy. So they'll Google or search via YouTube "How to potty train a puppy." Presto! You now have an idea for an informative video, and in that video, you can embed mentions, and links to your website for more information and products to buy. Or let's say that you sell makeup. People are dying to know the best way to put on mascara. So they search "How to put on Mascara." Here's a screenshot of common "how to" searches with makeup:

```
how to put on

how to put on fake eyelashes
how to put on eyeliner
how to put on makeup for beginners
how to put on makeup
how to put on eyeshadow
how to put on a tampon
how to put on a tie
how to put on lipstick
how to put on a wig
how to put on mascara
```

So your first step is to do some keyword research. What types of searches are people making on YouTube that are relevant to your product or service? Use "YouTube autocomplete" by simply typing keywords into YouTube and paying attention to what people enter (this is driven, largely, by keyword search volume). Use a tool like Ubersuggest or Answer the Public, which pull "suggestions" from Google for keyword discovery. If you have a Google Ads account, use Google's Keyword Planner tool to identify high volume, high-value keyword searches on Google (which generally also translate to YouTube). Check out my Dashboard at **http://jmlinks.com/smmdash** > *keywords* for more free tools to research keywords.

A video channel that is 100% built around "how to" searches is *Zak George's Dog Training rEvolution* at 2.2 million subscribers at **http://jmlinks.com/13c**. Notice how each of his videos is optimized for searches that puppy and dog owners do to learn "how to" train their dogs. Here's Zak's video in the #1 spot for "how to potty train a puppy":

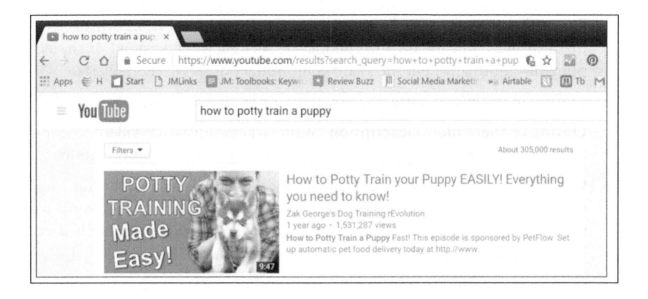

In a similar way, if your company, service, or product touches on something that customers are eager to learn "how to" do, then create videos on these topics and optimize them for relevant keywords. Zak's Channel is a good example of an SEO-focused YouTube marketing strategy.

### Branded Keywords: Your Competitor Names

As for keywords, also pay attention to very specific branded searches. If a competitor has a hard-to-use product, and you know that people search YouTube for that product, you can include that product name in your video headline, to snag viewers who are searching for the product. Identify adjacent, branded search terms and snag that traffic to your own videos. For example, YouTube searches such as "Netgear router set up" or "How to use a Black and Decker drill" are ripe for this type of adjacent keyword optimization.

> **VIDEO.** Watch a video tutorial on the three uses of YouTube (supportive, SEO, and sharing / viral) at **http://jmlinks.com/16z**.

### Optimize Your Video via SEO for YouTube

Once you've identified keywords that people search on Google and/or YouTube, looking for video content, it's time to optimize your video using the tactics of Search Engine Optimization or SEO. Here's what to do:

1. **Create Your Video**. Obviously, you have to create a short, informative video that explains "how to" do what people are looking to understand. It should be primarily informative but showcase your product or service nonetheless.

2. **Optimize the Video Title**. Write a keyword-heavy video title.

3. **Optimize the Video Description**. Write a keyword-heavy video description and include a link in *http://* format to your website for more information.

4. **Optimize the Video Transcript**. YouTube pays attention to what you "say" in the video via voice recognition software, so be sure to "say" the keywords when you are presenting. For example, "In this video, I am going to explain how to tie a tie." If possible, upload subtitles or closed captions to the video.

5. **Optimize the Video Tags**. When you upload the video, be sure to use no more than five keyword-relevant tags.

**Tip.** It's a best practice to have your keyword-heavy content ready to go upon upload, as the first indexing by YouTube is the strongest. Don't upload first in a temporary version, and come back later to optimize.

Here's a screenshot of Zak's "How to Potty Train Your Puppy" video:

Notice how the video title and video description both contain the exact phrase "How to Potty Train * Puppy." It's obvious that the video regurgitates to YouTube the target keyword phrase.

**Learn "How To" Optimize a YouTube Video**

Take a look at the following "how to" searches, and browse the top-ranked videos to confirm how they optimize their video titles and descriptions:

- How to Put on Eyeliner at **http://jmlinks.com/1w**

- How to stop a puppy from chewing on a leash at **http://jmlinks.com/1x**

- Living wills and advanced directives at **http://jmlinks.com/1y**.

It's easy to optimize the video headline, description, and tags (not visible to the user). That's your first step.

Next, you need to think about **interactivity**. In rewarding videos with top search positions, YouTube pays a lot of attention to how many views a video has and how interactive a video is, similar to the way that Facebook rewards posts that have high Edgerank. You want users to "interact" with your video: thumbs up / thumbs down, comment, share, and embed. How do you get high video counts and high engagement?

- **Ask.** In your video, ask users to "subscribe to your channel," or "thumbs up" if you like the video, or "enter questions in the comments below." You can drive interactivity simply by asking for it.

- **Cards and End Screens.** "Cards" (see **http://jmlinks.com/31z**) are clickable popups in a video that can lead to actions such as links to your website. "End screens" (see **http://jmlinks.com/31y**) allow you to recommend other videos, playlists, and a call to subscribe to your channel at the end of a video.

Here's a screenshot of the "i" information link that pops up in the top right of a video:

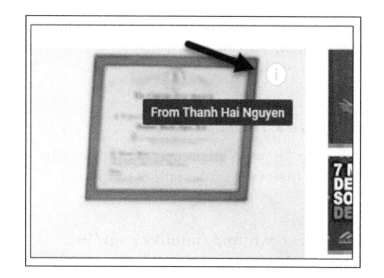

And here's a screenshot of the video card that pops up after a user clicks the "i" link.

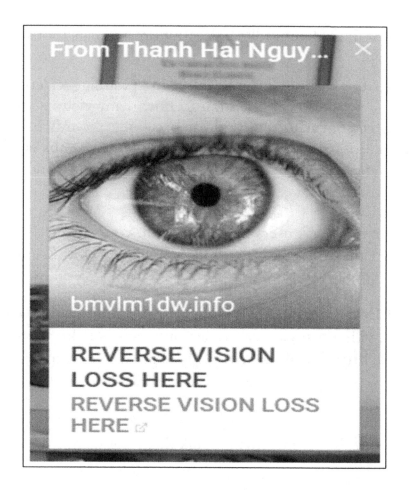

That link is then clickable to his website. To see it in action, watch my video on the "Mozon Local SEO Conference" at **http://jmlinks.com/32a** and click on the "i" on the top right of the screen. If you pay attention while watching the video, you'll see that when the YouTube card first appears it "pops out": a message.

You can create clickable links to other videos as well as to the subscribe feature, and you can create messages to users that ask for interactivity. For the official YouTube help article on creating a custom subscribe button for your videos visit **http://jmlinks.com/32b**. You can watch a video tutorial on cards and ends screens at **http://jmlinks.com/53v**.

Finally, it's increasingly clear that YouTube rewards videos that have long "watch times," meaning people actually stick around and watch all or most of the video. So as you create video content pay attention to the watch time data (available in *Creator Studio* on your YouTube Channel). YouTube wants "sticky" content – content that people want to watch, continue to watch, thumbs up, write comments, and share. Quality, as measured by user **engagement**, is thus job #1 for success on YouTube.

Because YouTube rewards videos with high view counts and engagement, promoting your video is a key part of success on the SEO path. Have an external **promotion strategy** ready for every video as soon as you upload it. Since YouTube pays attention to the **view count** (*higher is better*) as well as interactivity, use your other social networks to promote your video. Post your video on Facebook, Twitter, LinkedIn, etc., email your video link out to your email link. Even consider advertising the video upon launch on YouTube (**http://jmlinks.com/13d**), to drive the view count up as well as the interactions. "Embeds" of your video (when your video is embedded or linked to from an external website) and links to your video from external websites are also important signals to help drive a video to the top of search. The more views of your video, the more embeds of your video across the Web, the more links to your video, the higher it will rank in relevant YouTube and Google searches.

# CREATE A VIRTUOUS CIRCLE: THE MORE A VIDEO IS VIEWED, THE MORE IT SHOWS IN SEARCH

The on page text optimization of the video, interactivity, and external promotion all drive a video to the top of YouTube. Once on the top of YouTube search, a **virtuous circle** can kick in: the more a video shows at the top of YouTube search, the more people watch it, the more they watch it, the higher the view count and interactivity, which drives it higher on search and so on and so forth.

### #3 Use of YouTube: Sharing and Viral Videos

Videos are one of the most shared content across social media. We've all seen compelling videos, and shared them across Facebook, Twitter, or LinkedIn. Videos are highly shareable! Why? Largely because video can convey **emotional content** in a much easier way than can text or images. And emotion drives sharing: funny, shocking, provocative, outrageous – any of the big human emotions are the ultimate driver of sharing across social media.

# VIDEOS GET SHARED BECAUSE OF EMOTIONAL CONTENT

If you have a product or service that people do not heavily search for, then you can attempt to leverage the share path via YouTube. How? First and foremost, identify a logical **emotion** to drive the shares. *Utility* is one emotion, in the sense that people will share a video that is useful with friends or family. For example, a video on "how to make your Facebook completely private" (**http://jmlinks.com/1z**) has over 8 million views. So creating something so useful that people share it with friends and family is one way to leverage YouTube sharing to promote your product.

But utility is the weakest of human emotions. **Fear, anger, outrage, humor** – all of these emotions are much, much stronger than mere utility!

For most businesses, the best emotion to tap is **humor**, because humor can encourage sharing without having negative side effects on your brand image. One business that has really leveraged YouTube sharing is Blendtec Blenders (**http://www.blendtec.com/**). Their YouTube channel, entitled, "Will it blend" (**http://jmlinks.com/36v**) is all about taking crazy items and blending them in their powerful blenders: being humorous and yet showcasing their product. One of my favorite viral videos produced by Blendtec concerns Justin Bieber, with over 3.7 million views. Watch it at **http://jmlinks.com/2a**.

If you can connect your product to something insanely funny, then you can use humor as the "fuel" to drive social sharing of your product or service. Just remember it has to be insanely funny. Fun examples are "Girls don't poop" (**http://jmlinks.com/2b**), This Unicorn Changed the Way I Poop (**http://jmlinks.com/44k**), or "The man your man could smell like" (**http://jmlinks.com/2c**). For the latter, I recommend you read the Wikipedia discussion at **http://jmlinks.com/2d**, where you'll learn that "behind the scenes" an immense amount of work and promotion went on to make the video "go viral."

## Going Viral

To "go viral," a video must be so highly shared that one person shares it with two, and the two share it with four and so on and so forth. For a video to go viral, it must have a strong emotional pull, and to get started, must usually have strong external promotion including advertising.

*It takes a match to ignite a forest fire, after all.*

**Humor** is one emotion that can start viral sharing. Another is **sentimentality**. Especially for non-profits, videos that tug on the emotions can be used to encourage social sharing. Examples of this strategy are "Dear 16 Year Old Me" (**http://jmlinks.com/1p**), "Dear Future Mom" (**http://jmlinks.com/2e**), and "Always #LikeAGirl" (**http://jmlinks.com/36s**) These videos feature real people, sharing authentic emotional stories about a social cause or problem. People share them to "support" the cause. The "Ice bucket challenge" and "It gets better" are other examples of this use of "showing support" to promote a cause.

Finally, I want to draw your attention to Mike Tompkins (**http://jmlinks.com/13e**) as an example of a marketer who leverages viral sharing via YouTube. Tompkins produces "covers" of pop songs on YouTube, such as his first video on Miley Cyrus "Party in the USA" (**http://jmlinks.com/2f**). The strategy is to "piggyback" on popular YouTube searches for "branded content" (e.g., "Party in the USA" or "Party in the USA cover") and then "hijack" users to his own wonderful videos. Then, users "subscribe" to his channel, and he has a promotional vehicle combining YouTube search and viral sharing because his videos are strong and innovative enough to be shareable in their own right.

*It's not search OR share on YouTube: it's search AND share.*

Indeed a video such as Tompkins' "Starships" (**http://jmlinks.com/2g**) is leveraging search, share, and the use of influencers (the cast of Pitch Perfect) to promote it and get it to "go viral"). Similarly, the "It gets better project" (**http://jmlinks.com/36t**) is leveraging influencers, sentimentality, user-generated content, and a "cause" that many people agree with to get its videos to "go viral" and spread its message.

**Always #LikeAGirl**

Let's return to one of my favorite viral videos, "Always #LikeAGirl." This is an excellent example of a viral video that has an ulterior marketing motive. Always (the feminine product manufacturer) commissioned a video about stereotypes, and cleverly entitled it, "Always *#LikeAGirl*" (**http://jmlinks.com/32c**). (Note the insertion of their brand name and the #hashtag – clever marketing, no?) Please take a moment and watch this incredibly powerful and thought-provoking video; as a consumer. I guarantee it will make you think deeply about the societal messages we embed into young girls. As a father of two girls, it certainly made me think.

But then, "reverse engineer" this video as a marketer. If Always had created a video about tampons or pads, it wouldn't have exactly been an award-winning, viral video. Pretty boring and not exactly a topic people would share. So clearly, Always brainstormed a message that blended into its corporate brand, touched on women's issues, and had the potential to go viral by being emotional and counterintuitive. The brand message (*buy Always products*) takes a back seat to the socially conscious message about our prejudices concerning what it means to run "like a girl."

> In an effective **viral video** for a corporate brand, the brand message isn't in the *foreground*. It's in the *background*.

As a marketer, the task is to "reverse engineer" these efforts at sharing and virality and determine if there is a path to viral marketing that *fits your company*. Again, for most for-profit companies, the best emotion is humor, while for many non-profits, sentimentality and causes that people actively support are good mechanisms to spur social sharing. If you can identify a potential concept for a viral video for your company, product, or service, I recommend you watch this YouTube video on "Why Storyboard?" at **http://jmlinks.com/53w**. Before you invest blood, sweat, tears, and budget in an attempt to "go viral," first storyboard your video and test market it.

Here's one final thought. Don't be intimidated by "viral videos." You and your company might not be able to make an over-the-top viral video with view counts in the hundreds of thousands. However, think about the reasons why a user might share your video. Is it funny? Is it humorous? Does it touch on a sentimental emotion? Even if your video doesn't "go viral," you can engineer in emotional touchpoints and calls-to-action to encourage a viewer to share it with friends and family, thus expanding your reach. It's not ultimately *supportive vs. SEO vs. viral* in terms of video production; it can be *both / and*.

## Which of the Three YouTube Strategies Will Work for You?

To summarize, identify which of the following strategies on YouTube are most relevant for your company:

**Supportive.** Create and upload videos that support your website and other social media. This is largely using YouTube as a hosting platform as opposed to a promotional system.

**Search / SEO.** To the extent that people search for keywords near your product or service, you can optimize your videos for discovery by search.

**Share / Viral.** To the extent that your videos have emotional content, you can encourage discovery by social sharing and even virality.

Remember that in all cases you usually need to use external promotion tactics such as sharing your videos on Facebook, Twitter, and LinkedIn, reaching out to influencers who will help promote your videos, and even advertising on YouTube to extend the reach of your videos.

## » TELL STORIES THROUGH VIDEO

Humans love stories. From our prehistoric roots around campfires to today's multimedia digital environment, we've been wired to respond to narrative. Who said what to whom? What happened next? Why are you telling me this? And, above all, where's the emotional thrill in what you're telling me? In the beginning was the Word, and we're all wired to respond to it.

Video, whether on YouTube, Facebook, Instagram, or elsewhere, is an ideal storytelling medium. Look back at some of the videos, I've mentioned above such as the Always "Like a Girl" video or the Blendtec blend of Justin Bieber. Notice how they follow the elements of story from hook to rising action to climax to *denouement*, the French word for the falling action. Indeed, whatever video you are working on should follow the elements of story as described by many, including "Ron Popeil," the so-called father of the infomercial.

*It slices, it dices, but wait there's more.*

Popeil and others have identified these elements to an engaging story of any type:

1. **The hook**. Capture their attention with an ear- and eye-grabbing first scene. Shakespeare started many of his plays with an explosion, a few witches, or a fight scene in order to capture the audience's attention, and so should you.

2. **The problem.** Here, especially when you're selling something, you need a statement of the problem. It can be simple as, "Your puppy won't stop biting the leash," or as complicated as "The multitudinous ways in which girls can put on eyeliner." But there needs to be a problem or challenge that the viewer wants to solve, or at least learn about.

3. **The solution**. Here's where you (and your product or service) come in. You have the solution to the problem, and you ask the viewer to allow you to explain how.

4. **The Soft CTA**. You implicitly or perhaps even explicitly, begin to explain to the user your call to action. It can obviously be for them to "buy your stuff," but in some way or another you start to lay the groundwork for them to "want" what "you have."

5. **Credibility**. Why are you an expert? What's so great about your product or service? A problem calls for a solution, but why is your solution so great and why should the viewer believe you?

6. **The Hard CTA**. Here's the hard call to action, so tell the viewer to "act now" while "supplies last" or perhaps offer a coupon or discount code that expires in 24 hours. You want to motivate them to "pick up that phone" or "click that button!"

7. **The Gush**. This concept comes from Derral Eves (**https://derraleves.com/**) a prominent YouTuber and teacher of everything YouTube. Eves uses "The Gush" to signify that final, often humorous, kickback that comes after the hard call to action. The camera returns, and we see something funny or intriguing to make us laugh and help us retain the message.

Go back and re-watch the Squatty Potty infomercial on YouTube, "This Unicorn Changed the Way I Poop," at **http://jmlinks.com/44k**. As you watch it, notice how it goes through the seven phases above. Notice as well how it uses outrageous humor and funny, sort of disgusting graphics, to hold your attention and motivate you to share this video with your friends and family if only for the reason that it's funny. It's a great example of an infomercial on YouTube and with 37 million views, 110K thumbs up,

5,500 thumbs down, and hundreds of comments, this video has leveraged YouTube's algorithm to help make the Squatty Potty a household word.

This video and all successful videos on YouTube tell a story.

Storytelling isn't easy, but it isn't exactly rocket science either. Storyboarding is a step-by-step methodology to help you plan and organize the production of your videos. Check out an excellent video on how to storyboard by YouTubers Mary Doodles and Whitney Lee Milam at **http://jmlinks.com/44n**. While you're there, check out the cornucopia of videos about how to do YouTube successfully at the official *YouTube Creators' Channel* at **http://jmlinks.com/44p**. Then, take your own product or service, and brainstorm a "story" around it perhaps in a straightforward infomercial format, or perhaps in some type of question and answer format that will appeal to your target customers. Remember: social media is a party and not a prison, so a good story has to be compelling and engaging, or they'll simply stop watching. Search YouTube by keywords that matter to you and "reverse engineer" the stories inherent in the successful videos that fit your niche and delight your target audience.

## Live Video is a Story, Too

Even if you're going to do live video on YouTube, you want to think in terms of a story. Imagine you were going to give a live theater or stand up performance for comedy. You might be very spontaneous, but you'll still have an idea of your hook, the script you'd want to follow, and even the call-to-action you might want from your audience. Even live video is a form of storytelling. You can "go live" either on the YouTube app for your phone, or via the desktop – just click the camera icon at the top right and then "Go Live." Here's a screenshot:

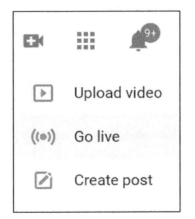

If you click "create post," you can now post messages to YouTube that will show to your followers when they log in to YouTube. In this way, YouTube is trying to become a bit more like Facebook or LinkedIn. You can upload a video, create a poll, or upload an image. Learn more at **http://jmlinks.com/53z**.

### Write Your (Draft) Story and Get Technical

So your to-do here is to create a draft story. Then, your next to-do is the technical aspects of shooting the video. You'll need a script, actors, a set, and an outline of the scenes. The technical aspects of video production are outside the scope of this book, but just realize that a few Google searches can help you with everything from how to write a short script or storyboard, to the best video cameras, microphones and other technical things you'll need. You can also look for local videographers to come to your place of business and help you shoot one or more videos. Just be aware that, in my experience, those who excel at the art of telling stories (a.k.a., writers) are not necessarily the same people who excel at the technical skills of shooting or editing video (a.k.a., photographers). They possess two different skill sets. Finally, you'll need to either edit your video yourself using software such as Windows Movie Maker, Apple iMovie, or more sophisticated software products like Camtasia. YouTube even has its own built-in editor accessible after you upload your video at **https://www.youtube.com/edit**.

The end result should be a short, emotion-packed, engaging video that focuses on your solution to the desire or problem your customers have. It may have the goal of supporting your website or other social media channels, of showing up high on YouTube or Google searches, or "going viral" or at least "getting shared." But regardless of which of the three YouTube goals your video is focusing on, it must tell a good story.

Finally, once you upload your video, you'll want to optimize the Video Title, description and link to more information, plus both cards and end screens, which I'll explain in a moment.

### » SET UP YOUR CHANNEL AND UPLOAD VIDEOS

After you've made an inventory of YouTube channels and videos that interest you from a marketing perspective, you're ready to set up your own YouTube channel. Assuming you haven't done this already, the best way to do this is from your Google or Gmail account. Here are the steps:

1. **Login to your Google account** (either via Gmail or an email address for which you have created a Google account).

2. **Go to YouTube** by typing **https://www.youtube.com/** in the browser address bar, or using the Google pull-down menu to go to YouTube.

3. Go to your Channel List at **http://jmlinks.com/31w.**

4. Click on "Create a new channel."

(For the official YouTube help article on how to create a channel, visit **http://jmlinks.com/12z**). At that point, you will be "inside" your new YouTube channel. (If you already have a channel, simply log in to YouTube.) Make sure to keep the email address and password in a safe and secure place, as you need this each time to log in to your Channel.

On the top right of the screen, click on your profile picture, and then **YouTube Studio**. Here's a screenshot:

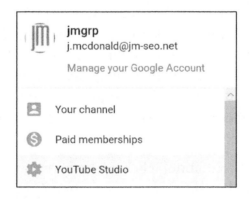

That gets you into *YouTube Studio*, but note that as of this writing YouTube is transitioning between the "old" *Creator Studio Classic* and the "new" *YouTube Studio*. To toggle between them, use the menu at the bottom left of the screen. Some of the features have not yet been migrated. So let's start with "Creator Studio Classic."

Inside of "Creator Studio Classic," first set up your community settings. This controls who can comment on your videos. Go to *Community > Community Settings*, where you can manage the ability of users to post comments on your video. Under "blocked words," for example, you can forbid the use of certain words, as well as ban users who have not behaved well from interacting with your channel. You can also use YouTube filters to control comments and block possibly spammy content from auto-posting (where you then approve or disapprove it).

Next, click up to "Channel." Here you can set features such as the following.

**Monetization**. This allows you to make money off of YouTube advertising. Unless your view counts run into the millions, I do not recommend turning on monetization.

**Upload Defaults**. You can set the defaults such as the category, license, and video tags. This is useful if you are going to upload a lot of videos.

**Branding**. You can add a watermark or brand label to your videos across your channel.

**Advanced**. Here you manage issues such as your linkage to a Google Ads account. Most importantly, enter your website as an "associated website" as this will begin the process to allow you to insert clickable links into video cards. You can also enter your Google Analytics ID here for better data in Google Analytics. And, obviously, allow your Channel to be shown as a recommendation for promotion purposes.

We'll return to some of the "Classic" settings in a moment at the video level. So, let's toggle back to "YouTube Studio" and update the look and feel of your Channel. To change your *profile picture*, go back to the initial view of YouTube Studio, and click Your Channel icon in the top right. It can be a little hard to toggle between the YouTube Studio settings and the "View Channel" settings, so sometimes just log all the way out and start over at YouTube.com. Or, you can often see the settings on the far right column, under your brand icon.

Once you've made it to Your Channel, click on your picture on the top left, hover over it, and click on your Channel cover or icon to change your Channel background image or icon. You can also upload *channel art*, which is similar to Facebook cover photos, by clicking on the large photo in the middle. Fill out your Channel "*About > Description*" section with keyword-heavy but short content explaining what your Channel is about, and why folks should subscribe to it. Here, you can also create backlinks to your website, and other social media sites. If things are not clickable, find the "Customize Channel" link and then click back into this or that element.

One of the more important things to do is to create an "Unsubscribed Trailer." Create a video that explains what your Channel offers and – most importantly – why a user should subscribe. Click into "Customize Channel" and then "Home." Under Home find the link for "For returning subscribers." Click "Feature Content" and select your video. Learn more from the official help file at **http://jmlinks.com/31x**.

Remember that there are three distinct areas to set up: *Your Channel look and feel, YouTube Studio*, and *Creator Studio Classic*. If you can't find what you want on one of them, look to the others. There's no rhyme or reason to how YouTube has organized any of this. Don't ask why; YouTube, like its parent, Google, basically sucks at user interface design, so the best strategy is to just click on everything and explore what can be changed and how. I'll confess it is mind-boggling how with all that money and all those smart people they can make such a mess of it, but they have. *Deal with it.* One trick I use is to open three tabs in my browser so I can have all three elements viewable as I "hunt for Red October" to find a feature I want to change. Help is available at the top right under the "Question Mark" or at **https://support.google.com/youtube**.

## Monetization

One of the big questions in setting up a YouTube Channel is whether or not to allow monetization. Monetization merely means that YouTube will be able to place ads on your videos. For most businesses, I strongly advise against allowing advertising or monetization on your channel, as your goal once you have a customer viewing your videos is for them to buy your product or service, not to go off and buy someone else's. Why be paid pennies by YouTube for ad clicks, when you can make dollars by selling customers on your own product or service?

Furthermore, unless your view count is in the millions, you'll earn next to nothing via YouTube monetization. (The only practical reason to monetize a video is if you absolutely insist on using copyright-protected music; for that sort of music to be allowed, you must allow advertising on your video via monetization).

## Channel Optimization for SEO

YouTube is the No. 2 search engine, ahead of Bing (but behind its parent, Google). As I have already explained, you should optimize each and every video for YouTube SEO by having a keyword-heavy video title, description, and tags. You should do the same with your channel. Place keywords in your channel keywords field. To enter your channel keywords, click on *YouTube Studio > Settings > Channel* keywords. Here's a screenshot:

On the Advanced tab, you can also link your YouTube account to your AdWords account, as well as to your Google Analytics account for metrics purposes. Don't forget to associate your YouTube account with your website as well. To do this, fill in your website *http://* address in the "Associated website" field and follow the verification instructions. You can learn more about link your website to your YouTube channel at **http://jmlinks.com/53x**. At the end of this process you should have fully set up your Channel.

**Upload Videos**

To upload a video, click back to your profile picture, then select the video icon at the top right. Then click the "Upload video" text. Select a video to upload, and start uploading.

Input a:

- **Video Title**: Write a keyword-heavy but catchy video title.

- **Description**. Write a keyword-heavy but catchy video description. Include an *http://www.yourcompany.com* link to your website. Be sure to use the http:// prefix, as that makes it "clickable" to your website.

- **Tags**. Identify no more than five relevant keywords tags for your video.

- **Public**: set the video to *public* (anyone can see), *unlisted* (only people with the link can view), or *private* (restricted access).

- **Custom thumbnail**. Upload a custom video thumbnail, which will appear in YouTube search. Or, YouTube will automatically create three options for you.

Custom thumbnails are worthy of attention. Your video thumbnail will show in YouTube search and alongside other videos or at the end of a video. They are your "teaser" or "hook" to get a user to click through and begin watching the video. They need to function like ads. The best thumbnails include photos of people (you, your CEO, or someone key to the company come to mind) plus some very big and bold text. Try a search on YouTube for your keywords and evaluate which videos have a lot of views and interaction and look at their thumbnails. Learn more about custom thumbnails from *YouTube Creator Academy* at **http://jmlinks.com/44q**. I strongly recommend that you create custom thumbnails for each and every video.

## » ENABLE CLICKABLE LINKS IN YOUR VIDEO

Be sure to include a clickable link in your video description, preferably right after the first sentence, and in the format of **http://www.yourwebsite.com/**. It MUST be in the *http://* format to be clickable! You can then reference the link for "more information" in your short video ad, such as telling the viewer, "Click on the link in the video description to learn more!"

Here's a screenshot from the famous Dollar Shave Club video's description, showing the clickable link from the video description to their website:

That link - **http://dlrshv.es/b3FELr** - gets the user to the Dollar Shave website with just one easy, click, so you gotta have one in your video!

**Create Cards and End Screens in Your Video**

"Cards" and "End Screens" on YouTube are yet another way to drive traffic from your video to your website. Cards are clickable links in the video itself. "End screens" occur at the end of a video and are also clickable links. In order to create YouTube cards or end screens that link to your website, however, you must link your YouTube account to your website, and you must join the YouTube Partners Program. (See **http://jmlinks.com/49u**). This requires more than 1,000 subscribers, so it will not be available if you have a brand-new account.

To add a "card" to your video:

- Click on your logo on the top right of YouTube, when you are logged into your Channel.
- Click on Creator Studio, and then click on Video Manager on the left-hand menu. (Note: you may see "YouTube Studio" which is in beta roll out as of this writing; in that case, click to the bottom and return to "Creator Studio Classic.").
- Find your video and click edit.

# "CARDS" ARE CLICKABLE LINKS IN A VIDEO

Click on "Cards" to enable YouTube's "Cards" feature, and insert text, an image, and a link to your website URL.

> **VIDEO.** You can read the official Google help file on YouTube cards at **http://jmlinks.com/27h**.

Cards appear in the top right of a YouTube video and "pop out" when they appear. Users can click on them to learn more and then click from the card to your website. Here's a screenshot showing the card in the top right corner:

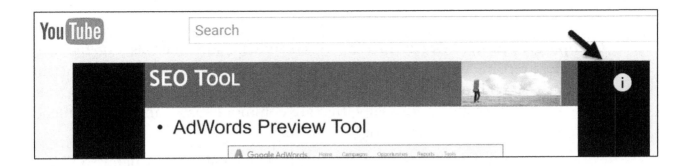

Just remember as you set up videos and/or video ads on YouTube to be on the lookout for where it will allow you to put clickable links: in the video description, in cards, in call-to-action overlays, and in the new call to action extension. All options are not always available, so just be aware that you may or may not see them. To learn more about cards and end screens, visit **http://jmlinks.com/53y** for the official YouTube explanation.

For your second **To-do**, download the **YouTube Setup Worksheet**. For the worksheet, go to **http://jmlinks.com/social2020** (then reenter the code '**social2020**' to register your workbook), and click on the link to the "YouTube Setup Worksheet." You'll answer and outline the basic setup issues for your YouTube channel.

## » ADVERTISE ON YOUTUBE

YouTube offers robust advertising options. You can use advertising to expand the reach of your YouTube videos especially for persons in "search mode" on YouTube by keyword or those who are easy to target demographically such as persons who love to fish, people who want to try out cosmetics, or perhaps religious people who want to watch Christian videos. You can use YouTube advertising to boost your video view count and engagement and in that way, YouTube advertising can work to support your organic YouTube efforts. (See **http://jmlinks.com/32f** for the official guide to YouTube advertising).

To create a video campaign, you'll need a Google Ads account, preferably linked to your YouTube account. Although you can place text and graphic ads on YouTube, we'll assume you have a video you want to promote through advertising. With that video in hand, here are your steps.

If you already have a *Campaign > Ad Group* on YouTube, you can skip this section. If not, to create a video campaign, log in to Google Ads, and click the blue circle. Select *Video* as the campaign type. Select one of the three options – *Product and brand consideration, Brand awareness and reach*, or *Without a goal*. The first two give you step-by-step instructions, while the third option is totally do-it-yourself. Follow the steps to define:

**Campaign Name.** Give it an easy-to-remember name such as *Cat Boarding: YouTube.* I recommend you put YouTube at the end so you can see at an instant that this is a YouTube Campaign and not a Search or Display Campaign. Note there are two formats on YouTube that are commonly used, and I recommend you create separate campaigns for each format.

> **Instream Ads.** These are video ads that generally appear before a video. The user is forced to watch up to five seconds and then he or she can click into the ad or click "skip." Name your Campaign something like *Cat Boarding: YouTube – Instream.*
>
> > **In-stream Ads** occur in what YouTube calls the **TrueView** ad format, meaning you pay, if and only if, a person clicks thru on your ad, watches more than 30 seconds, or half of the video ad (whichever is lesser). There is also what are called a TrueView for action or TrueView for Shopping, which are format subtypes that allows a prominent Call to Action (CTA). To learn more, visit **http://jmlinks.com/49v**.
>
> **Video Discovery Ads.** These are video ads that appear when a user pro-actively searches YouTube by keyword. These are similar to ads on Google.com. Name your Campaign something like *Cat Boarding: YouTube – Discovery.* Here, you pay when someone clicks on your ad.
>
> **Other Formats.** YouTube also offers other formats such as Outstream Ads (on partner sites), Non-skippable in-stream ads (ads that the user cannot skip), and Bumper ads (short six-second ads that are non-skippable), but these are generally used only by very large advertisers who want to use YouTube like television for branding purposes. See **http://jmlinks.com/49w** to learn about all available formats.

**Budget.** Set up a daily budget. Just as on regular Google Ads, you specify a maximum spend per day.

**Networks.** Here, you need to make an important choice –

> **YouTube search results.** Use this option to show your video when someone pro-actively searches on YouTube. (*Must be used in combination with the next option*).
>
> **YouTube videos.** Use this option more when people are in "browse" mode to show your video before, after, or along videos as people browse. (*Must be used in combination with the first option*).

**Video Partners in the Display Network.** I <u>do not recommend</u> this option, so uncheck it. Here you have the same problem with click fraud and nefarious sites as on the Google Display Network.

**Ad Group.** Create an Ad Group, again reflecting your product or service (keyword) organization such as *Cat Boarding, Cat Grooming,* or *Cat Toys* and name it appropriately as for example *Cat Boarding: YouTube Discovery – Keywords,* or *Cat Boarding: YouTube Instream – Remarketing.*

**Bidding.** Set a bid per view. Note that on YouTube you pay by the *video view,* not by the click. YouTube uses what they call "TrueView" pricing meaning you pay if, and only if, the user watches your video for at least thirty seconds or to the end of the video, or if it's a search ad if they click on the video and/or an action. See **http://jmlinks.com/41g** for a full explanation.

**Targeting.** Leave these options blank for now, as we will discuss in detail. These are marked as *People who you want to reach* and *Content where you want your ads to show.*

**Create your video ad.** Enter the exact URL of the video you want to promote here. Select a format such as *In-stream ad* or *bumper ad* ("browse mode") or *video discovery* ("search mode") ad. Write a headline and description. Select a landing page; I recommend that you use *Your YouTube channel page.*

Again, similarly to regular Google Ads, Google stupidly makes you go through every step even if you are not ready. Once a *Campaign > Ad Group* is created, however, you can then insert new Ad Groups and Ads much more easily, adjust targeting, etc. Just go through the steps to create your first *Campaign > Ad Group > Ad* and then it will be much easier to manage. What's stupid about this is you only have to do this the very first time, and then from then on, it's much easier to manage.

At the end of this process you should have your first *Campaign > Ad Group > Ad.* Pause it so that it doesn't start running until you are completely ready.

### Location Targeting in YouTube

You can geotarget on YouTube. For example, Jason's Cat Boarding Emporium could target people watching "cat videos" who also live in San Francisco. Or a pet store could target people watching videos on dog and puppy training who live in Oakland, Berkeley, or El Cerrito, California.

# LOCATION TARGETING WORKS IN YOUTUBE

Geotargeting makes it easy to get your ads right to people near your local business and is one of the most exciting features in YouTube advertising. Accordingly, select your Geotarget (e.g., United States, or drill down to a specific city or state). You do this by being at the Campaign level and selecting *Locations* on the left. For example, since I am only interested in people who live in San Francisco and have cats, I could target cat videos on YouTube but by setting the geotarget to San Francisco, only people who are physically in San Francisco would see my ads. This is a fantastic feature to YouTube advertising as you can have your cake and eat it too – meaning target very broad video types (e.g., "cat videos") but to very narrow locations (e.g., "San Francisco").

## Mobile Bid Adjustment

You can also control your mobile bid adjustment in YouTube, if you do / do not want to run on phones and/or tablets. Once you've created a Campaign, click on *Devices* on the left and configure your device targeting by setting bid adjustments up or down. An example here might be a probate attorney who would figure that the most serious people would be watching her videos on their computers, and so she would set a bid adjustment of negative 100% for mobile. If you think there is a strong pattern between mobile vs. desktop vs. tablet, this is yet another useful YouTube targeting refinement.

## Target Your Ad: Video Targeting

Now that you've inputted your ad to YouTube, it's time to dive into targeting options. Targeting "lives" at the Ad Group level, just as in regular Google Ads. Click into your Ad Group on YouTube, and you'll see targeting options on the left. As with the Display Network, it's a best practice not to mix and match targeting options (though you can in some situations). Let's review targeting options.

> **Keywords.** Here, similar to the Display Network, enter **keywords** that you think someone might be searching on YouTube and/or that might describe similar or adjacent videos. **This is the most common and most powerful way to target your videos.** In our *Cat Boarding* example, we'd enter keywords like *cats, cat boarding, cat care, kittens*, etc. Google has taken away a lot of YouTube targeting features, so I wouldn't worry about plus signs, quote marks, etc., just enter keywords and remember that, as on the Display Network, the targeting is pretty loose on YouTube. Note that Google uses how they search not only on YouTube but on Google for keyword-based targeting.

**Audiences.** Here you will see *Search | Browse | Ideas* at the top. Click into *Browse*, and you should see:

> **Who They Are.** This is demographic targeting based on attributes such as Parental Status, Marital Status, Education, and Homeownership.

> **What their interests and habits are.** These are "affinities," such as whether they're into Banking & Finance, Beauty & Wellness, Food & Dining, etc.

> **What they are actively researching or planning.** This refers to "in-market audiences," such as people who are "in the market" to buy a house or a car. If relevant to you, this is one of the best targeting options.

> **How they have interacted with your business.** This leverages your remarketing audience. So, for example, you can "tag" people who visit your website and then show them your video ad as they browse YouTube videos. You can also expand to "retargeting" using Google AI to expand to people "similar" to those who have already hit your website.

> **Combined Audiences.** This is a new feature that allows you to use "And" statements to combine any of the above features.

**Demographics.** You can see the age, gender, parental status, and household income of the people who have viewed your YouTube advertising.

**Topics** This is very similar to audiences and attempts to target people based on things that interest them like games, health, fitness, etc.

**Placements.** This is unique on YouTube. You can find videos or channels that allow advertising and then copy / paste their URLs here. However, if a channel or video is not "monetized" (meaning that the owner does not allow YouTube to place ads), this is all in vain. Double-check to see if you see ads on any relevant placements. Google doesn't enable clickable links here, so open up a new browser window and search YouTube by Channel or Video name to find out if it allows advertising. If you see ads, it does. If you don't, it doesn't.

### Evaluate Your YouTube Advertising Performance

Once your ads are up and running on YouTube, evaluating the performance is similar to the rest of the Display Network. Click into an Ad Group. Then, along the left column, click:

**Keywords** to browse the keywords the triggered your video ads. As elsewhere on Google Ads, you can create "negative keywords" to block your ad.

**Audiences** to learn characteristics about the audiences reached.

**Demographics** to see age information (if available).

**Topics** to see topics.

**Placements** and then *Where ads showed* to see which videos / channels ran your ad. As on the Display Network, you can block your ad from placements.

You can also go into Google Analytics to view clicks coming from YouTube to evaluate what happens "after the click." To do this, create a Segment by clicking on the *Segments* tab in Google Analytics, and then *Custom*, and source as *YouTube.com*.

And within your YouTube Channel, you can click into *Creator Studio > Analytics* to browse information about your videos.

> **VIDEO.** Watch a video on how to set up Segments in Google Analytics at **http://jmlinks.com/25p.**

Returning back to your YouTube Channel (not Google Ads, and not Google Analytics), you can go to *Creator Studio > Analytics* and then drill down into an individual video to see key performance indicators such as watch time, view duration, views, geographies, genders, traffic sources, and playback locations. In summary, there is really a wealth of information in Google Ads, Analytics, and YouTube about what happens with your videos!

## » EXPLORE FACEBOOK, LINKEDIN, AND INSTAGRAM VIDEO

Video is more than YouTube, of course. A video can live on your website, for example. Or, you can place so-called "native" video on Facebook, Instagram, and LinkedIn, not to mention short video on Twitter. As you work on your video marketing strategy, therefore, don't miss opportunities on the other platforms.

I will now review each platform but before I do that, let's talk about some commonalities – across platforms.

1. Video is the fastest-growing content type across all social media platforms.

2. Each platform (Facebook, Instagram / IGTV, Twitter, YouTube / Google, TikTok) tends to favor "native" video, that is video hosted on its platform.

3. All platforms, including YouTube, have video as a "share" path, wherein consumers share videos with each other, but YouTube alone dominates the "search" path as when a consumer is pro-actively searching for a video explaining "how to tie a tie."

4. Videos that get shared, across all platforms, tend to have emotional, shocking, counterintuitive, etc., content. The more emotional, the more counterintuitive, the more shocking a video is, the better it does.

5. All platforms reward videos that spur engagement as measured by views, comments, shares and "watch time."

The three big differences between YouTube and the offer platforms are thus a) that only YouTube has videos that really respond to user pro-active search queries, b) only YouTube has an easy-to-use repository format so you can have a Channel as a place to permanently store your videos, and c) only YouTube offers an easy "embed" code so that you can embed your videos on your website. Some of these features exist on Facebook, Instagram, or LinkedIn (such as embed code) but they are so hard to manage that you're better off using YouTube for those purposes.

## Facebook Video

Facebook is keen to become the #2 player in video, but the way that video works on Facebook leverages only the "supportive" and "share/viral" use of video. Don't think of Facebook video as an *alternative* to YouTube but rather as a *complement*.

Conceptually, there are two marketing paths to video success on Facebook:

> **Supportive**. Upload your video directly to Facebook as a "native" video. This use of video on Facebook "supports" your marketing message by providing content for you to post and share on Facebook. Facebook favors "native video" in its algorithm vs. non-native videos hosted on YouTube, so if reach on Facebook is your goal, native is the way to go.

> **Share / viral**. A video on Facebook can be shared or even go viral. As with YouTube, it's emotional videos that get a lot of shares or go viral on Facebook. Again, because Facebook favors its own videos, you will get better organic traction with a native video. In addition, you can advertise the video via Facebook advertising. Facebook live video also has a heavier reach as promoted

by the Facebook algorithm. (Learn more about Facebook live at **http://jmlinks.com/36w,** and YouTube live at **http://jmlinks.com/36x**).

Facebook, unlike YouTube, isn't a very good storage repository for video, nor does it have the SEO / discovery use of video. (You can have a video tab on your Facebook Page but there is no cross-Channel discovery on Facebook, and the organic reach of videos is pretty poor). Accordingly, you might think of launching your video simultaneously on Facebook AND YouTube, but then in the long term, nurturing only the YouTube version as an "evergreen" video.

To upload a video to Facebook, you first need to have a business Page. You obviously also need a video to upload, generally in the MP4 format. Once you have set up a business Page and have a video you want to upload to Facebook, then simply go to that Page either on the desktop or on the mobile phone and look for the "upload video" icon. Here's a screenshot from the desktop:

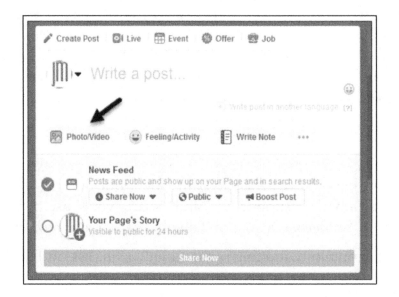

For an example, check out the Antiques Roadshow videos on Facebook at **http://jmlinks.com/44v**. Notice how they've enabled the "video" tab on their Facebook Page.

Facebook also has a rather new feature called "Facebook Watch" at **https://www.facebook.com/watch**. As on YouTube, users can follow a Facebook Page to be alerted when new videos are uploaded. This is an attempt at direct competition with YouTube. A business Page on Facebook can thus host videos on Facebook, which show up on its video tab, and on the "watch" page. The problem is that the organic reach of Facebook is poor compared to organic reach and discovery on YouTube, and few users even know about Facebook watch, so it is not much of a destination website in the way that YouTube clearly is.

Facebook is also encouraging "creators," that is individuals who post videos that are heavily shared or even go viral, to move to Facebook via its new "Creator" page type. You can learn more about the Facebook creator program at **http://jmlinks.com/44w**.

All in all, the main opportunities on Facebook for video are really the "supportive" or "share / viral" use of video. To succeed on Facebook, you need to budget some advertising dollars to promote your videos, or they won't be seen by many people.

### Instagram Video

Instagram, of course, is owned by Facebook. So it's not surprising that many of the opportunities are the same. Instagram favors native videos in its algorithm as well, and Instagram has launched Instagram TV or IGTV. The main difference is that Instagram videos must be in the vertical format, not horizontal. Learn more about Instagram video at and Instagram TV at **http://jmlinks.com/44x**. Learn more about the vertical video format on Instagram at **http://jmlinks.com/44y**.

As on Facebook, the main reach is either people who already follow you on Instagram or videos that "go viral" due to lots of social sharing. It isn't yet much of a competitor to YouTube for long-term video hosting or discovery. Note as well that on both Instagram and Facebook, brands can have "stories" which are daily video summary of events and highlights. Learn more about Facebook stories at **http://jmlinks.com/44z** and Instagram stories at **http://jmlinks.com/45a**.

### LinkedIn Video

LinkedIn is the latest social platform to embrace video. Obviously, the personality of LinkedIn is more serious, professional, B2B type marketing, so the videos that will do well on LinkedIn are going to fit its unique culture. The structure and set up is very similar to Facebook, so LinkedIn isn't much of a stable repository for video but rather a network for distributing video to your existing users. Video will show in their news feeds and, if a video is controversial, emotional, or counterintuitive enough, the video has the chance to "go viral" and get shared by people on LinkedIn.

LinkedIn seems to favor "native video" over YouTube-based video, so – again – you're better off uploading video directly to the platform.

Once you have a video in MP4 format, simply log in to your LinkedIn personal profile or your LinkedIn company page. Simply click on the "video" link and upload your video. Here's a screenshot:

To learn more about native video on LinkedIn, visit **http://jmlinks.com/45b**.

## » MEASURE YOUR RESULTS

Owned by Google, YouTube provides very good metrics on both your channel and your videos. From inside your YouTube account, click on *YouTube Studio > Analytics*. Next, you can drill down to any video, and investigate:

**Views.** Total views and views over time.

**Estimated Minutes Watched.** Total minutes watched.

**Engagement.** Variables such as likes, dislikes, comments, shares, videos in playlists, and subscribers generated by the video.

**Demographics.** Your top countries and gender distribution.

**Traffic Sources.** How people found your video. Click into "top traffic sources" to view the actual search keywords, "external" to view referrer websites, "suggested videos" to view related videos that generated traffic. If you click "YouTube Search," it will show you which keywords users inputted to find your video. If you click "Suggested videos," you can see which videos preceded yours and thus you became a "suggested video" to that one.

YouTube is very keen on watch time, so click on "Average View Duration," and YouTube will show you your video, and the user spikes or drop-offs as you watch the video. This is a very useful way to learn what's working and what's not in terms of user engagement.

## Google Analytics

For many of us, we want to drive traffic from YouTube to our website, even to our e-commerce store or to download a free eBook or software package to get a sales lead. Sign up for Google Analytics (**https://analytics.google.com/**) and install the required tracking code. Inside of your Google Analytics account on the left column, drill down by clicking on *Acquisition > Social > Overview*. Then on the right-hand side of the screen, you'll see the word "Social." Click on that, and then find YouTube on the list, and YouTube to your Website, giving you insights into what types of video people find attractive.

You can also create a custom Segment to look at only YouTube traffic and its behavior. For information on how to create custom Segments in Google Analytics, go to **http://jmlinks.com/1f**. For the Google help files on Segments go to **http://jmlinks.com/1g**.

In sum, inside of YouTube, you can see how people interact with your channel and videos. Inside of Google Analytics, you can see where they land on your website and what they do after they arrive.

## »» CHECKLIST: YOUTUBE ACTION ITEMS

Test your knowledge of YouTube! Take the *YouTube marketing quiz* at **http://jmlinks.com/qzyt**. Next, here are your YouTube **Action Items**:

❑ **Research** whether your customers (and competitors) are on YouTube. Start with keyword searches on YouTube. What videos seem to be engaging? Which videos generate the most interaction, including shares? Why?

    ❑ **Brainstorm** for your company / industry, which type(s) of videos make the most sense: ❑ supportive ❑ search / discovery and/or ❑ viral / sharing.

    ❑ Consider **Facebook, Instagram,** and **LinkedIn** as alternatives for video. This might be that these alternatives are better venues where your customers "hand out," or it might be that live video is better for you on Facebook or Instagram. Don't think either YouTube or other networks but rather posting video to all of them.

❑ Set up your **company channel.** If you see opportunities on YouTube, set up your company channel, including profile picture, cover photo, the "about" section, and at least one video explaining what you do and who should care.

❑ If you have more than one video, consider an "**Channel trailer**" that answers the question of why they should subscribe to your channel.

❑ **Promote** your **video**(s) through SEO (Search), cross-promotion on your other social channels, the real world, and even advertising on YouTube.

❑ **Measure** your **results** in ways such as video views, thumbs up / down, comments as well as the growth of your Channel subscribers. Use YouTube cards or call-to-action overlays to send traffic from YouTube to your website, and measure conversions such as sales that originate in YouTube.

Check out the **free tools**! Go to my *Social Media Marketing Dashboard > YouTube* for my favorite free tools on YouTube. Just visit **http://jmlinks.com/smmdash**.

### »» DELIVERABLE: A YOUTUBE MARKETING PLAN

Now that we've come to the end of our chapter on YouTube, your **DELIVERABLE** has arrived. Go to **http://jmlinks.com/social2020** (then reenter the code '**social2020**' to register your workbook), and click on the link to the "YouTube Marketing Plan." By filling out this plan, you and your team will establish a vision of what you want to achieve via YouTube.

# 8
# PINTEREST

Some social media platforms like Facebook, YouTube, and LinkedIn are broad, reaching many people with many diverse interests. Others are narrow, reaching only specific people (demographic groups like *young folks* or *women*, for example) or specific usages (e.g., *finding a plumber, commenting on the news*, etc.). Yelp, Tumblr, Instagram, Twitter, and Pinterest fall into this latter category. They are very strong in certain niches, but not so strong as truly mass platforms. If your specific customer segment or usage case is active on one of these media in particular, it can work spectacularly well. If not, then all your hard work bombs out into oblivion.

Pinterest is such a platform: incredibly strong in **online shopping, do-it-yourself** (DIY) and the **female demographic**, and all but absent from nearly everything else.

Shoppers use Pinterest to browse the Internet and "pin" items they might want to buy onto "boards." Do-it-yourselfers use Pinterest to share ideas on how to build this or that, knit this or that, or construct this or that. And women, always a heavy shopping and craftsy demographic, use Pinterest as a "buying / idea platform" and as a great platform for do-it-yourself crafting and recipe-sharing.

Pinterest, in short, is *the* network for consumer retail, *the* network for craftsy do-it-yourself including recipes, and *the* network for women (or not to be sexist, the network for anyone who loves to browse and shop).

**Let's get started!**

**TO-DO LIST:**
>> Explore How Pinterest Works
>> Search Pinterest and Identify Stuff to Follow
>> Inventory Companies on Pinterest
>> Set up and Optimize Your Account
>> Brainstorm and Execute a Pinning Strategy

» Promote Your Pinterest Account, Boards, and Pins

» Measure Your Results

»» Checklist: Pinterest Action Items

»» Deliverable: A Pinterest Marketing Plan

## » EXPLORE HOW PINTEREST WORKS

For a basic introduction to Pinterest, check out the official guide at **http://jmlinks.com/36z**. Next, in terms of marketing opportunities, the best way to understand Pinterest is to grasp the concept of an **idea board**. Imagine a virtual corkboard in the Internet cloud to which you (and others) could "pin" sticky notes, photos, videos, and other content around a theme.

Let's use the example of someone planning out her ideal dorm room for freshman year at college. First, she signs up for Pinterest and creates a profile. Compared with Facebook, Pinterest is very basic. Not a lot of information is displayed in a Pinterest profile, pretty much just a profile picture and a very brief description. Next, she should download and install the Pinterest button (see **http://jmlinks.com/54a**) as well as the Pinterest app (available for both Android and iOS). Once installed, she can now surf the Web (or use the Pinterest app for iPhone or Android) and "pin" interesting items to "boards" that she sets up.

For example, she'd set up a board called "my dream college room" or even more specific boards like "my dream bathroom supplies," or "my dream desk." Let's say she goes to Amazon and finds an amazing desk light. She can "pin" this desk light to her "dream desk" board. People who follow her (or this board) on Pinterest, thus see this desk light in their Pinterest news feed, whereupon they can comment on it and (*gasp!*) even buy it for her. And of course, she would pin not just one desk light, but several possible desk lights, several pencil holders, several ink pads, a few art posters for above her desk, and on and on. It's as if she's building a collage of desk possibilities, from which she can select the perfect accessories. As she creates idea boards for her dream desk, dream closet, dream door room, and dream bathroom supplies, she can invite her friends, her Mom, or her sorority sisters to collaborate by commenting and pinning to the boards as well.

Another example would be a person like myself that is crazy for dogs. I love dog photos, tips on how to get your dog to behave, dog toys that you buy on Amazon or elsewhere, tips on dog snacks, DIY dog toys, etc. I love dogs! Especially I love Labradors! So I can create boards to help myself follow what's out there in the "dog world," and then follow persons who have more time than I do who share their own passion for dogs, dog toys, dog tips, Labs, black Labs, Lab puppies are the cutest dogs, etc. And if a person likes dogs but also, for example, likes football (which doesn't interest me), I can follow only his "dog toy" board and not his "I love Raider football" board. Pinterest makes it easy for me to share, learn about, follow, comment, love, like and engage with other dog lovers wherever they may be in a visual way and interact with folks who share my passion for dogs but not other passions that I have, or that they have. It's a really awesome system and unique in social media (*although Google+ had a similar concept which it stole from Pinterest, but Google+ is now thankfully dead, so Pinterest is essentially unique*).

Pinterest, in short, is a **visual bookmarking** and **idea board** system, one that can be social as well, and one that makes online shopping as easy as discover, click, and buy. People also use it before purchase in the real world, as a social scrapbook to group together products and services they might want to buy at a brick and mortar store. And do-it-yourselfers use it to share ideas about how to build this or that, how to cook this or that, etc.

# THE ESSENCE OF PINTEREST IS THE IDEA BOARD

The structure of Pinterest in a nutshell is:

**Individual profile**: me, Jason as a person, or Wells Fargo as a brand.

**A board**: collections of items from the Web on topics like my "dream dorm room," "dog toys to possibly buy," "do-it-yourself Christmas decorations," or "recipes for summer parties."

**Pins**: I can "pin" things I find on the Web such as blog posts, videos, images, or products to buy to my "boards" as a collection of ideas, things to buy. I can also upload items directly.

**Search**. I can browse Pinterest, search Pinterest, or search the Web for interesting things to "pin" to my boards.

**Collaboration**: I can invite others to comment on my board or pins, and to pin items to my boards directly. I can also pin things to their boards.

**Social**: I have a news feed, wherein Pinterest shows me the pins of people, brands, and boards I follow as well as suggestions based on my (revealed) interests. People can also follow my boards and me, and like, comment, and reshare items that I am pinning. Through collaborative boards, we can pin and share ideas together.

To get the hang of Pinterest, create your personal and/or business profile, create some boards, download the "Pin it" button, and start playing with the Pinterest app or using it on the desktop. Using Pinterest is the best way to begin to understand how to market on Pinterest. For example, to view a Pinterest search for "dream college dorm rooms," visit **http://jmlinks.com/2o**. To visit some sample idea boards, visit **http://jmlinks.com/13f**. Here's a screenshot of a search for "dream college room":

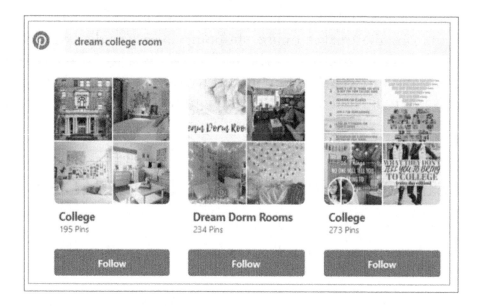

Notice how people use Pinterest as a **visual bookmarking system** of ideas (largely, but not exclusively, of stuff to buy or make), and how others can comment on, and even contribute to these boards in a collaborative fashion.

Accordingly, there are two basic marketing opportunities on Pinterest:

> **Direct**. Get your items "pinned" to the boards of others, or have them show up in relevant Pinterest searches. This is a direct buy path: customers "discover" your pins and then buy the product or service referenced by them. (These can also be links to blog posts or videos).
>
> **Indirect**. Create "idea boards" of your own that are relevant to your product or service. This is more indirect, in the sense that customers find your boards interesting or helpful, and then "follow" your boards, thus learning about your products or services that have been "pinned" to your boards as well.

Once you understand the idea of visual bookmarking or "idea boards," then you've "got" Pinterest. Once you grasp the idea of being a "helpful vendor" with "helpful boards" that identify fun, lively things to do, buy, or make, and you grasp the idea of encouraging your customers to "pin" your products to their boards, you've "got" the idea of marketing via Pinterest.

For example, when I find a post on Pinterest about a DIY dog toy, I can then pin it to my board of DIY dog toys. Here's an example:

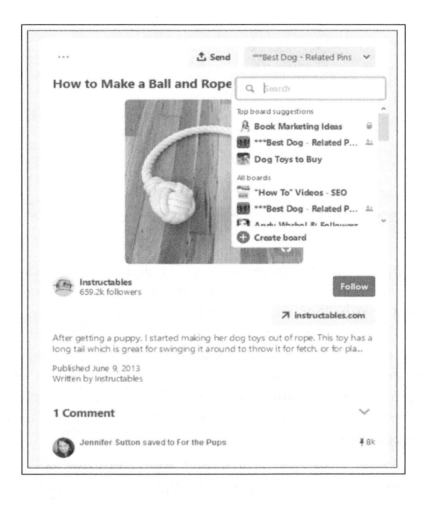

At the top right, you can see Pinterest prompting me to save it to one of my boards such as my "Best Dog-Related Stuff" board. Then notice at the bottom left, how it indicates Jennifer Sutton saved this Pin as well to her own board titled, "For the pups." I can then click over to her or her board and discover a fellow dog lover to follow on Pinterest. In this interactive way, people browse stuff on Pinterest, save it to their own boards, and discover folks with similar interests.

Using the Pinterest button, you can also surf the Web and pin items you find to your boards. So, for example, I can go to Amazon, find a dog toy that interests me, and pin it to my board. Here's an example of this:

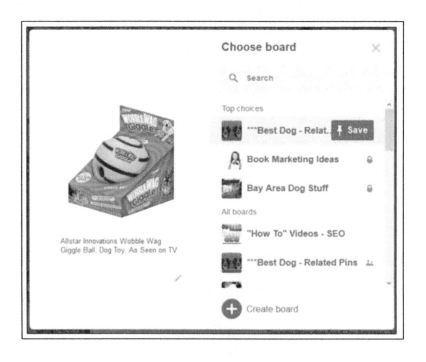

In this way, Pinterest is very "outward-looking." You as a brand should do everything you possibly can to encourage people to pin FROM your website or e-commerce store TO their Pinterest boards. Pinterest offers a free "save from your website" button that enables this feature on your website or e-commerce store easily; learn more at **http://jmlinks.com/46p**. Obviously, you need a visually appealing, highly shoppable type of site (preferably an e-commerce one) for this to work well. Another feature is so-called "rich pins" which transmit data in real-time from your e-commerce store to your pins on Pinterest (such as price, colors, and other options). Learn more at **http://jmlinks.com/46q**.

In this way, Pinterest is unique as a **social bookmarking system**. People find interesting stuff on the Web and pin it to their Pinterest boards. Others connected to them then follow and/or engage with that content, giving Pinterest a unique niche in the interaction between the Web and social media content, in e-commerce, and in visual content such as DIY (do-it-yourself).

**Your Pinterest News Feed**

As on other social media, people can "follow" other people or brands (or just their boards) and when that person, brand, or board has a new pin, that new pin shows in their news feed. In addition, notifications are generated when someone likes, comments, or repins one of your pins (or boards, or account).

Once you've done some basic research and identified persons / companies, boards, and hashtags to follow, when you log in to Pinterest you'll see their new pins in your news feed. This is the same structure as on Facebook. If I follow you, and you post a pin, then it shows in my news feed (and vice-versa if you follow me back). You can also click on "Following" on the top right when you log in to see the newest pins from folks you follow Here's a screenshot:

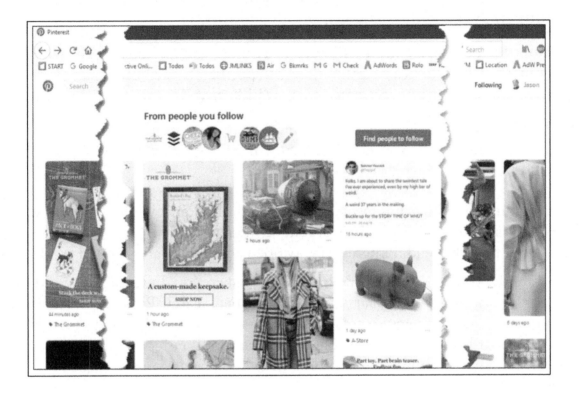

You can then click on the "Find people to follow" to access yet another way to find hew folks or boards to follow on Pinterest.

Now, flip this around. As a brand, you want to create pins and boards that people want to follow. This means that there has to be a "there there," that there has to be interesting and compelling content that people actually want to learn about. You have to position your brand as a "helpful expert" producing either original content and/or curating the content of others that's engaging. Content is king on Pinterest as it is on all the social media networks!

## » SEARCH PINTEREST AND IDENTIFY STUFF TO FOLLOW

You can search Pinterest directly by keyword, or by clicking on the categories button, one can browse Pinterest by categories. Let's review how to do each. As you search Pinterest you're looking for:

- **Individuals**. These can be power Pinterest folks who are really active on the platform. These are superfans and other "brand advocates."

- **Companies or brands to follow**. These might be direct competitors, companies in your industry, or just big brands that seem to be doing a great job at Pinterest like Target (**https://www.pinterest.com/target/**) or Martha Stewart Living (**https://www.pinterest.com/marthastewart/**).

- **Boards**. This is unique to Pinterest. You can either follow ALL of Target's content, or you can drill into a specific board such as Kids Toys (**https://www.pinterest.com/target/kids-toys/**).

- **Hashtags**. Like Twitter and Instagram, Pinterest is very hashtag-friendly. Identify and write down hashtags that matter to your company.

Once you find something interesting, just click the red and white "follow" to either follow that company, person, or board. Like Instagram or Twitter, there is no required acceptance at the other end. Pinterest is very open and public, and primed for discovery.

If, for example, you were an organic baby food maker, you'd identify keyword themes like *organic, organic food, organic baby food*, etc., and then search Pinterest for companies, people, boards, and hashtags to follow. So search by keyword and start to find pins, people, and boards that you like or that are relevant to your company. When you find an interesting pin, you can then save it to a board you create on the fly or have already created.

For example, I have a board called "Best Dog-Related Pins" and I can save interesting pins to that board. Here's a screenshot:

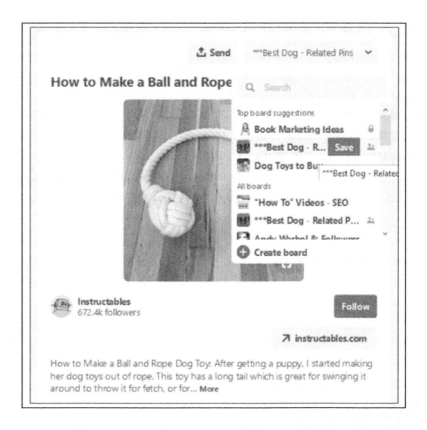

If a pin has a lot of engagement, you can also click down into the comments and find who pinned this pin to which board. For example, Bob Spangler saved this pin to his board "Garden 2":

You can also see that Natural Living Ideas has 55.6 thousand followers and that "Garden 2" has 7,000 followers itself.

In this way, you can search by keyword and find the most popular pins, boards, and people to follow. Pinterest is a search engine, in a sense, as well as a social media platform. With the basics in hand, let's review the available methods to discover pins, people or brands, or boards to follow.

**Method #1. Keyword Search.** Simply type into Pinterest one of your keyword themes such as "organic gardening" and then search **all pins** (the universe of all pins on the topic), **product pins** (these are specific products to buy), **people** (this is both real people and brands or companies on Pinterest), and **boards** (these are idea boards on the topic). Here's a screenshot showing the pull-down menu at the far right:

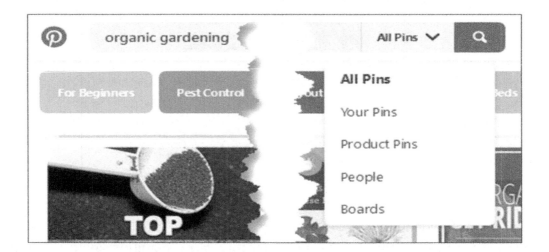

Search each category and begin to follow people / brands and/or boards that are relevant to your company. Look for engagement as measured by repins and comments. For example, here's a "quote" pin by Muhammed Ali, "If your dreams don't scare you, they aren't big enough," and here's a screenshot showing the comments and repins:

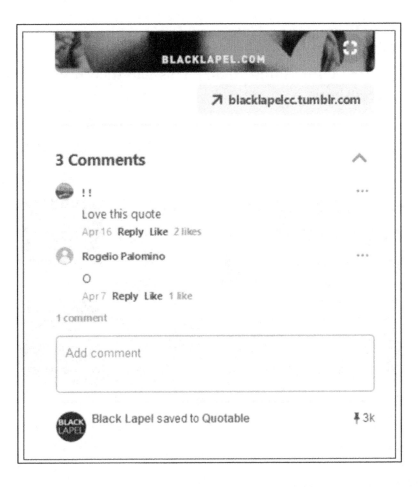

When you simply type a keyword into Pinterest search, you can also just pay attention to the suggestions that occur just beneath it. Here's a screenshot for "organic:"

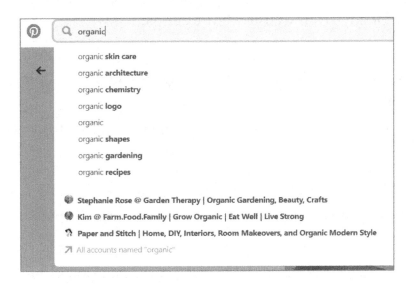

**Method #2. Browse Pinterest by Category.** Pinterest has sort of hidden this feature, so type this URL into your browser to access it: **https://www.pinterest.com/categories/**. This will then bring up a category index of Pins. Here's a screenshot:

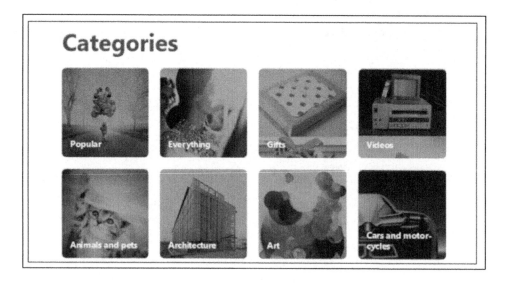

You can then click into a category and see pins as well as subcategories. For "Animals and pets," for example, you get suggestions like "Dogs and puppies" or "Cats and kittens." Click on these, and you get more suggestions and subcategories.

**Method #3. Browse by URL.** This is a little geeky, but it's a great way to see which URLs have the most traction on Pinterest as a competitor or a big brand. To do this, you create a very special type of URL, type this into your browser, and see what pins are being pinned for any given website. For example,

> **https://www.pinterest.com/source/nytimes.com/ = pins from the New York Times**
>
> **https://www.pinterest.com/source/rei.com** = pins from REI.com

You can do this for your own website, as in

> **https://www.pinterest.com/source/jm-seo.org/** = pins from JM-seo.org.

Simply replace *jm-seo.org* in the string above with your own domain, and then copy/paste the complete URL into the address bar of your browser. Do this for your company on a regular basis (bookmark the URL), and you can see what customers and potential customers are pinning from your website; within Pinterest analytics, you can verify ownership of your website and get even more details on your own site.

**Method #4. Use Google.** Finally, you can go to Google and enter *site:pinterest.com {keyword}* as in *site:pinterest.com "organic food"* or **http://jmlinks.com/46n**. You can use the Tools menu at the top right to select past year, past month, or even past 24 hours to see trending and new topics on Pinterest.

At the end of this process, you should have built up a list of persons or companies, boards, and hashtags to follow on Pinterest. Note that hashtags are only clickable on the phone, and then only in the Pin description.

## » INVENTORY COMPANIES ON PINTEREST

The best way to decide whether Pinterest has any value to your marketing is to **research** other companies on Pinterest and observe how their fans interact with them on the platform. First, you need to understand how to find companies on Pinterest. Second, you should make a list of companies (and boards) to follow on Pinterest (and follow them with your personal profile). Note: it's important to realize that you can and should follow BOTH companies AND boards, as one company (e.g., Whole Foods) can have multiple boards (best soups, ideas for grilling, salad concepts, etc.). Third, you need to know how to determine what customers are doing on Pinterest, and fourth, you must assess whether any of this has potential value for your company's marketing strategy.

> **VIDEO.** Watch a video tutorial on Pinterest marketing basics at **http://jmlinks.com/17c**.

Remember that you're not really or necessarily a true Pinterest user. You're a brand researching what's going on, and figuring out if Pinterest is for you, and if so, what content strategy will work the best. You are more interested in how competitors and other companies use Pinterest as a marketing vehicle in *your* industry. To find companies in your industry, look at the pins returned for your searches as listed above and at the bottom look for URL's that sound corporate or pins that indicate "promoted pins."

For instance, if you are in the dog toy industry, you might end up at any of these companies' Pinterest pages:

> **Waggo Pet (https://www.pinterest.com/WaggoPet/)** - Lifestyle brand and purveyor of design-driven, happy-centric goodies for home and pet. You'll see

that they have a board called "ETC" focused on dogs at **https://www.pinterest.com/WaggoPet/etc/**.

**Collar Planet Online** (**https://www.pinterest.com/collarplanet/**) - specializes in unique Martingale Collars, Pet Jewelry, Jeweled and Leather Dog Collars and Leashes. Large assortment of dog costumes, dog clothes and more!

**Swanky Pet** (**https://www.pinterest.com/swankypet/**) - Stylish dog collars and more! All items are made-to-order --- let them know what to make for you!

A quick way to find companies after a search is to hit CTRL+F on your keyboard (COMMAND F on Mac) and type in "promoted." That will highlight the promoted (company) pins. These are pins that are being advertised and consequently will originate from companies as opposed to individuals. When you click on these, you'll go to their websites. But you can then put their name back on Pinterest to find their brand pages. The reality is that brands that are advertising are also putting a lot of effort into organic on Pinterest as well.

# IDENTIFY COMPANIES WHO DO PINTEREST MARKETING WELL, AND REVERSE ENGINEER THEM

As you research companies via your keywords, look for companies with many followers and whose boards / pins show a great deal of interaction: many pins, likes, repins, and comments. Pinterest, after all, is a *social* medium, and your goal is to identify companies that "get" Pinterest well enough to build large, engaged follower communities.

Not surprisingly, since Pinterest is so successful in consumer retail, many of your large retailers have the most sophisticated marketing efforts on Pinterest. Identify a few consumer retailers you like, follow them on Pinterest, and "reverse engineer" their marketing strategies. Here are some of my favorites:

**Target** at **https://www.pinterest.com/target/**.

**Martha Stewart Living** at **https://www.pinterest.com/marthastewart/**

**Chobani** at **https://www.pinterest.com/chobani/**.

**Birchbox** at **https://www.pinterest.com/birchbox/**.

**Everyday Health** at https://www.pinterest.com/everydayhealth/.

**Free People** at https://www.pinterest.com/freepeople/.

**Intel** at https://www.pinterest.com/intel/.

**Amazon** at https://www.pinterest.com/amazon/

While we're looking at retailers, here's a neat trick to explore Pinterest by pin. First, do a search for your keyword (e.g., "T-shirts"). Next, find a pin that sparks your interest – especially one that is a product photo. Click on the pin. Finally, in the bottom left-hand corner click on the *rounded square icon*, and Pinterest will do a "visual" search for similar products. Here's a screenshot:

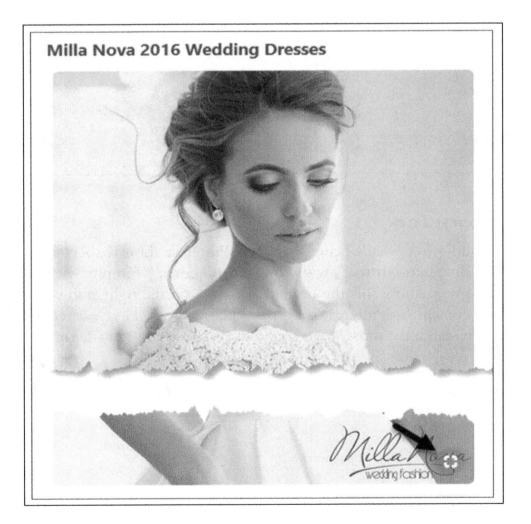

Once you click, you then get visually similar results with suggestions along the top. Here's the screenshot of that:

## Another Pinterest Trick

Another method to see what's being shared on Pinterest about a specific domain is to use a tool like Buzzsumo (**http://www.buzzsumo.com/**). Simply type in the domain of interest into Buzzsumo, sort the Pinterest column on the right, and you can see the most popular content on Pinterest for a particular domain. Here's a screenshot using Buzzsumo to research the most shared content from Marthastewart.com:

**Web Content**

| Q marthastewart.com | | | | SEARCH |

Narrow your results by using the negative operator to exclude non relevant terms, for example: **skincare -beauty** Advanced search tip

Filter your results: | Past Year | All Country TLDs | English | + More Filters | ↻ RESET FILTERS

**Content**  Analysis

☐ Select All

| | Facebook Engagement | Twitter Shares | Pinterest Shares |
| --- | --- | --- | --- |
| **Cat Hammock**<br>By Chloe Mackintosh - Mar 14, 2019<br>marthastewart.com | 16.5K | 14 | 16K |
| **Why Lever Knitting Is Called the Fastest Method in the World**<br>By Roxanna Coldiron - Feb 19, 2019<br>marthastewart.com | 2.8K | 10 | 8.1K |

Don't be afraid to "follow" companies via Pinterest (even your competitors). In fact, I strongly encourage it: by "following" companies you actually "like," you'll experience them marketing to you, and you can then reverse engineer this for your own company.

For your first **TO-DO**, download the **Pinterest Research Worksheet**. For the worksheet, go to **http://jmlinks.com/social2020** (then reenter the code '**social2020**' to register your workbook), and click on the link to the "Pinterest Research Worksheet." You'll answer questions as to whether your potential customers are on Pinterest, identify brands to follow, and inventory what you like and dislike about their Pinterest set up and marketing strategy.

## » SET UP AND OPTIMIZE YOUR PINTEREST ACCOUNT

Now that you've got the basics of Pinterest down, it's time to set up or optimize your Pinterest page. Remember, people have "profiles," and businesses have "accounts" on Pinterest, often also called "Pages." You'll generally want a business account, or Page, on Pinterest. To set one up for the first time, go to *Pinterest for Business* at **https://business.pinterest.com/**. You can also convert a "profile" to a business "account" if you mistakenly joined as an individual at **https://business.pinterest.com/** and click on the "Join now" text and then "Switch to a business" or go to **http://jmlinks.com/32h**.

Since you are joining as a business, be sure to claim or verify your website. Follow the instructions at **http://jmlinks.com/46r**. This will give you better analytics and mark pins that link to your domain with your profile picture.

Once you've joined, you have only a very basic set up – your profile picture, username (URL), "about you," location, and website. That's it. Once you've filled out this information, you're set up on Pinterest as a business.

Next, set up some boards by clicking on the "Create a Board" on the left of the screen. Here's a screenshot:

When you create a board, give it a name, a description, a category, a map or location (useful if you are a local business). Be sure to include keywords as this is critical for discovery in Pinterest search, but don't be spammy. Write in natural English yet include your keywords. If you're just building out the board, you can also temporarily make it *secret* and then change it to *public* at a later date.

## Ask for Collaborators

Pinterest boards can be collaborative, meaning you can have more than one "manager," and you can even invite customers or others to help pin stuff to your boards. If your company has superfans, this is a great way to engage with them. If you want to make a board collaborative, you identify "collaborators" by typing in their names or email addresses. Pinterest will then invite them to start pinning items to your board. The easiest way to start pinning items to your board is to download the "Pinterest button" onto your browser. You can also manually copy URL's over to pin an item. With the concept that a board is an "idea board," start identifying and pinning items from the Web such as blog posts, images or photos, and yes, even products from your eCommerce store to your new board.

## Board Strategy

Social media is a *party*, not a *prison*, and so it goes with your Pinterest boards. Your boards should attract people to follow them by providing something useful, something visual, something fun. Ask these questions. What is the board "about"? Who will want to "follow" it, Pin stuff from it (or to it), comment, share, and click from the board to your products? Take a board like "Gifts for Dog Lovers" at **http://jmlinks.com/3a** vs. the board "Dog Gifs" at **http://jmlinks.com/3b**. The purpose of the former is to identify fun dog gifts to BUY, while the purpose of the latter is to share funny pictures of dogs and build the brand image of *BarkPost* (**http://barkpost.com/**), a New York-based blog on dogs that also sells dog-related products. Both are legitimate social media marketing users of Pinterest – the former is just a more direct plea to "buy our stuff," whereas the latter is more a "look at this cool stuff" (and by the way check out all the cool stuff we sell).

*Hard sell* or *soft sell*: both work on Pinterest.

In sum, it is incredibly important to brainstorm your boards! The questions are:

- **What is this board about?** What ideas does it collect, how does it function as a useful "idea-generator" on a particular topic?

- **Who will be interested in this board?** What value are you providing as the board-creator and board-curator by having this board? A board on dog toy ideas "saves time" for people who a) love dogs and want toys and/or b) need to buy a gift for a person who loves dogs and wants toys. Your value is curating "in" the cool stuff, and curating "out" the dumb stuff. A board that collects funny pictures of dogs is meant to give viewers a quick and easy way to get a few laughs during their busy day, and a board that collects do-it-yourself ideas for cheap dog toys helps dog lovers save money, and have fun, by building their own dog toys. Who will be interested is a function of what the board is about.

- **What will you pin to this board, and where does that content live?** Is it stuff from your eCommerce store? Stuff on Amazon? Blog posts, or how to articles? Items from your own blog? YouTube video? Content is king, on Pinterest, as on all social media.

For your second **TO-DO**, download the **Pinterest Setup Worksheet**. For the worksheet, go to **http://jmlinks.com/social2020** (then reenter the code '**social2020**' to register your workbook), and click on the link to the "Pinterest Setup Worksheet." You'll answer and outline the basic setup issues for your Pinterest business account (page) and boards.

Content is king, and queen, and jack. Now that you've set up your Pinterest Page, you need to think about posting (or rather pinning). Turn back to your Content Marketing plan, and remember you'll need both other people's content and your own content to pin:

- **Photographs and Images**. Pinterest is very visual, and you'll need to systematically identify photographs and images that fit with your brand message and ideally encourage likes, comments, and repins (shares).

- **Blog Post and Content Summaries**. To the extent that you have an active blog and are posting items that fit with the common uses of Pinterest, pin your blog posts to Pinterest.

  o Note that the first or "featured" image will become the shareable image. Choose striking, fun images for your pins, even if what you are pinning is just a blog post!

- **Quotes**. People love quotes, and taking memorable quotes and pasting them on graphics is a win/win.

- **Infographics and Instructographics**. Factoids, how to articles, especially ones that are fun, do-it-yourself articles, lists or collections of tips or products, are excellent for Pinterest. Anything that helps a person organize ideas about products or services to buy or make will work well on Pinterest.

- **Items to Buy**. Yes! You can (and should) pin items to buy on your Pinterest boards. Unlike most other social media users, Pinterest users are "in" the shopping mode in many ways, so tastefully pinning cool items that can be bought is not just expected but encouraged.

Indeed, Pinterest realizes that buying is a logical way to monetize the site, and so they have announced "Shopping on Pinterest" at **http://jmlinks.com/32j**. You can also read about *buyable pins* at **http://jmlinks.com/3d**. Another option here is so-called *rich pins*, which are dynamically updated pins from your eCommerce store. Learn about them at **http://jmlinks.com/3e**.

Clearly, Pinterest will help you shamelessly promote, link to, and sell your stuff via Pinterest! In this sense, it is unique among social media in being so unabashedly pro-e-commerce.

## » PROMOTE YOUR PINTEREST PAGE, BOARD, AND PINS

Once you've set up your Pinterest business account, and begun to populate it with boards and pins on a regular basis, you've essentially "set up" the party. Now it's time to send out the invitations. In and of itself, neither a Pinterest Page nor a Pinterest board will be self-promoting!

# MAKE YOUR BOARDS USEFUL, FUN, AND MESMERIZING FOR YOUR USERS

Remember: social media is a **party**. You must have yummy yummy food and entertainment for people to show up, and stick around. Thus, as you promote your Pinterest Page, always keep front and center "what's in it for them" – what will they get by "following" your Pinterest page and/or Pinterest boards, and checking them out on a regular basis?

Assuming your Page and/or boards have lots of useful, provocative content, here are some common ways to promote your Pinterest account and boards:

- **Real World to Social.** Don't forget the real world! If you are a museum store, for example, be sure that the cashiers recommend to people that they "follow" your Pinterest Page and/or boards? *Why? Because they'll get insider tips, fun do-it-yourself posts, announcements on upcoming museum and museum store events, selected items from your online museum store, etc. Oh, and we'll share collections of do-it-yourself tips as well as gift ideas for that hard-to-buy-for someone in your life.*

- **Cross-Promotion.** Link your website to your Pinterest Page, your blog posts to your Pinterest Page, your Twitter to your Pinterest Page, etc. Notice how big brands like REI do this: one digital property promotes another digital property.

- **Email.** Email your customer list and ask them to "follow" your Page or boards. Be specific: you can drill down to specific **subgroups** and match their interests with **specific boards**. Again, you must have a reason why they'll follow it: what's in it for them? Have a contest, give away something for free, or otherwise motivate them to click from the email to your Page, and then "follow" your page or board.

- **Pinterest Internal**. Interact with other Pages, Pins, and Boards, repin their content, comment on timely topics using #hashtags, and reach out to complementary Pages to work with you on co-promotion.

- **Pinterest SEO / Search**. People use Pinterest to generate ideas, especially before shopping for something big like a wedding or a dorm room, and therefore search is very big on Pinterest. Research your keywords and name your boards and pins after those keywords, and include keywords in your description. As you get likes, pins, and repins, the Pinterest algorithm will reward your pins with higher placement in Pinterest search results.

- **Use Pinterest Plugins**. Pinterest has numerous plugins that allow you to "embed" your Pinterest items on your website, and allow users to easily "pin" your eCommerce or blog posts to their own boards. Get them at **http://jmlinks.com/13g**. In this way, your blog can promote your Pinterest Page, your eCommerce site can promote your Pinterest Page, and your Pinterest Page can promote your eCommerce store and/or blog. Similarly, your YouTube videos can promote your Pinterest Page, and your Pinterest Page can promote your YouTube Videos. And the same goes, of course, for your Pinterest boards.

- **Leverage your Fans**. People who like your Page are your best promoters. Remember, it's *social* (!) media, and encouraging your customers to share your content is the name of the game. You want to leverage your fans as much as possible to share your content. Asking key influencers to participate in a board is a great way to both build content and encourage publicity.

# ENCOURAGE YOUR FANS TO CONTRIBUTE TO YOUR BOARDS, AND SHARE YOUR CONTENT

Here are some specific items worth mentioning:

**Group boards.** Group boards allow you to collaborate with your employees and customers on Pinterest. Check them out at **http://jmlinks.com/54b**. Brainstorm a collaborative project between you and your customers, and use Pinterest as a means to cooperate online.

**Rich Pins and "Buyable" Pins.** These two mechanisms link your eCommerce store to/from Pinterest. They are not promotion mechanisms per se, but they make the buying process as easy as possible. Check out the links at **http://jmlinks.com/3d** and **http://jmlinks.com/3e** to learn more about these cross-linking strategies.

**Hashtags.** Like Twitter and Instagram, Pinterest has hashtags which are ways that people can communicate on a theme. Anything marked with a *#hashtag* is clickable in a pin. Here's a screenshot of a pin with the hashtag *#weddingdresses* highlighted:

And here's what happens if you click on that link: **http://jmlinks.com/13h**. It generates a search on Pinterest for *wedding dress*. So the long and short of it is that by including hashtags in your pins, you become more findable in Pinterest search whether directly or by the search engine function. Identify relevant hashtags and include them in your best pins.

**Search.** Throughout, remember that search is very important on Pinterest. Make sure that you know your keywords, and that you weave these keywords into the titles and descriptions of your pins and boards. People use Pinterest as a "search engine" to find interesting products and ideas, similar to how people use Yelp to identify fun restaurants and great plumbers.

*Search, and therefore search optimization, should be a major part of your Pinterest promotion strategy.*

**Advertise.** Advertising is increasingly important to success on Pinterest. I've mentioned *rich pins* and *buyable pins*, which are integrations between your online store and Pinterest. "Promoted pins" function much the same way as "promoted posts" on Facebook: you identify a pin to promote, and by advertising, Pinterest pushes these pins to the top of the news feed and search functions on the site. Learn more at **https://ads.pinterest.com/**.

## » MEASURE YOUR RESULTS

Once you set up a business account and boards on Pinterest, Pinterest gives you decent metrics on how popular they are. To find them, click on the "analytics" link on the left of the Pinterest web page when you're logged in as a business account. Here's a screenshot:

That will transport you to **https://analytics.pinterest.com/**. You can also confirm your website and Pinterest will show you what people are pinning from your website or blog. (Note: analytics are only available for corporate accounts, not personal profiles).

## Google Analytics

For many of us, we want to drive traffic from Pinterest to our website, even to our e-commerce store or to download a free eBook or software package to get a sales lead. Sign up for Google Analytics (**https://analytics.google.com/**) and install the required tracking code. Inside of your Google Analytics account on the left column, drill down by clicking on *Acquisition > Social > Overview*. Then on the right-hand side of the screen, you'll see a list of Social Networks. Find Pinterest on that list, and click on that. Google Analytics will tell you what URLs people clicked to from Pinterest to your Website, giving you insights into what types of web content people find attractive.

You can also create a custom Segment to look at only Pinterest traffic and its behavior. For information on how to create custom Segments in Google Analytics, go to **http://jmlinks.com/1f**. For the Google help files on Segments go to **http://jmlinks.com/1g**.

In sum, inside of Pinterest, you can see how people interact with your Page and posts. Inside of Google Analytics, you can see where they land on your website and what they do after they arrive. This includes eCommerce, as Google Analytics is very well integrated with eCommerce. You can learn not only if Pinterest is sending traffic to your website but also whether that traffic is converting to inquiries, downloads, and eCommerce sales.

## >>> Checklist: Pinterest Action Items

Test your knowledge of Pinterest! Take the *Pinterest marketing quiz* at **http://jmlinks.com/qzpi**. Next, here are your Pinterest **Action Items**:

☐ **Research** whether your customers (and competitors) are on Pinterest. What are they doing? Why? Be sure to distinguish among individual accounts, business accounts, pins, boards, and hashtags. Be sure to understand how to both search and browse Pinterest.

☐ **Set up** a **business account** on Pinterest as well as one or two boards that represent customer interests.

☐ **Brainstorm** a **content strategy** for Pinterest at both the board and pin level. Be systematic and diligent about pinning. Be interactive, including asking your superfans to participate in your boards.

☐ If appropriate, enable **rich pins** and/or **buyable pins** for your eCommerce store.

☐ **Promote your pins** both on Pinterest by strategies like #hashtags and SEO, and off of Pinterest by real-world to Pinterest promotion, cross-promotion, etc. Consider **advertising** if Pinterest is a strong "yes" for you and you have the budget.

☐ **Measure** your results on Pinterest at the pin, board, and account level (are you getting interactivity from real customers?) and whether activity is translating into better brand awareness and even eCommerce sales.

Check out the **free tools**! Go to my *Social Media Marketing Dashboard > Pinterest* for my favorite free tools on Pinterest. Just visit **http://jmlinks.com/smmdash**.

## >>> Deliverable: A Pinterest Marketing Plan

Now that we've come to the end of our chapter on Pinterest, your **DELIVERABLE** has arrived. For the worksheet, go to **http://jmlinks.com/social2020** (then reenter the code '**social2020**' to register your workbook), and click on the link to the "Pinterest Marketing Plan." By filling out this plan, you and your team will establish a vision of what you want to achieve via Pinterest.

# SURVEY OFFER

**CLAIM YOUR $5 REBATE! HERE'S HOW -**

Visit **http://jmlinks.com/survey**.

1. Take a short, simple survey about the book.

2. Indicate whether you want a $5 rebate or want to make a contribution to our scholarship fund.

**WE WILL THEN -**

- Rebate you the $5, or thank you profusely for helping a deserving young marketer.

~ **$5 REBATE OFFER** ~

~ **LIMITED TO ONE PER CUSTOMER** ~

**SUBJECT TO CHANGE WITHOUT NOTICE**

**GOT QUESTIONS? CALL 800-298-4065**

# 9
# LOCAL SEO & REVIEW MARKETING

Let's suppose you have a restaurant, or you're a local plumber, dentist, CPA, or divorce attorney or any of the thousands of local businesses that service customers in their day-to-day life. Before the advent of social media sites like Yelp, Google, YP.com, Airbnb, TripAdvisor, and their kind, consumers might have gone to the physical yellow pages or perhaps visited your website after a Google search. You were in charge of your marketing message; *your customers couldn't really "talk back."*

The "Review Revolution" led by Yelp and since followed by Google, YP.com, Airbnb, TripAdvisor, Angie's List, Amazon, Facebook, and other sites, dramatically changed the local landscape. A happy customer can leave a **positive** review about your business, and a not-so-happy customer can leave a scathingly **negative** review.

> *Reviews, in short, allow consumers to talk back: the good, the bad, and the ugly. And the just plain crazy.*

Moreover, it's not just that customers leave reviews. It's that customers read reviews, indeed that they rely on reviews when making judgments about which businesses to patronize. If they see five star or four-star reviews on Google or Yelp, they may reach out to your business with a phone call or email inquiry, or visit your restaurant, bar, or coffee shop. If they see two-star or negative reviews on Yelp, Google, or other local review sites, they may skip over you and go to competitors who have better online reviews.

> *Online reviews, in short, can make, or break, your local business.*

Using Yelp and Google as models, this Chapter explores the "Review Revolution." While the focus will be primarily on *local* businesses, it's a fact that the "review revolution" impacts any business in which customers Google the business name plus "reviews" prior to making a purchase, which is pretty much all businesses.

**Let's get started!**

**TO-DO LIST:**

» Explore How Review Sites Work

» Inventory Companies on Yelp, Google, or Other Relevant Sites

» Claim and Optimize Your Listings

» SEO Your Local Website

» Cultivate Positive Reviews

» Monitor and Improve Your Online Reputation

» Measure your Results

»» Checklist: Review Action Items

»» Deliverable: A Local SEO Marketing Plan

## » EXPLORE HOW REVIEW SITES WORK

Imagine it's 1994, ten years prior to Yelp's founding, and you have a local Italian restaurant in Los Angeles, California. One day you are lucky enough to be visited by the review critic for the *Los Angeles Times*. You recognize her from her picture in the paper, and you realize that she can make – or break – your new Italian eatery. You do your best not to let her know you recognize who she is, and you do your utmost to ensure that she has a positive experience at your restaurant. One week later, your hopes and prayers are answered: a positive restaurant review in the local newspaper. Business booms.

Alternatively, if she had written a critical review of your restaurant, business would not have *boomed*. It would have *busted*. **The restaurant critic, in short, had an immense amount of power over local restaurants.** However, if a) you were a small restaurant, you had minimal chance of ever getting reviewed, and b) if you were a divorce attorney, plumber, massage therapist, CPA, or many other types of local businesses, there were essentially no reviewers available. For those types of businesses, there were essentially no reviews at all.

Enter the **Review Revolution**. In October 2004, Yelp (**http://www.yelp.com**) was founded. Consumers could now review not just local restaurants but plumbers, dentists, massage therapists, and thousands of other types of local businesses. The Review

Revolution was like any other mass revolution: the masses burst open the doors of the castle, turned over the table and chairs, and even executed the "ruling class." *It was a bit bloody. It was a bit noisy. And it was a bit unpleasant.* If, for example, you were the *Los Angeles Times* restaurant critic, your absolute power over restaurants was broken. The Review Revolution brought democracy to local reviews. Now anyone could review anything. Say "bye-bye" to the review aristocracy, and "hello" to review by the masses. And this didn't just happen on Yelp. It happened to books on Amazon, to apps on the Apple App Store and Google Play, to music on those digital platforms, to movies on the IMDB archive, and on and on.

But here's the rub. Like the French Revolution, the Review Revolution brought the masses into the ecosystem. It has not been very organized or coherent; online reviews run the gamut from informative to ridiculous, from true to faked. Whereas the big reviewers of the *Los Angeles Times, San Francisco Chronicle,* and *New York Times* were educated and civilized (though they could be brutal in their reviews), the new review class can be rough and tumble. Anyone – and I do mean anyone – can write a review: good, bad, or ugly. And let's not forget: *just plain crazy.* To be frank, we are still living in this unsettled Review Revolution, and like the French Revolution, there is no going back: the old system is dead.

# UNDERSTAND THE REVIEW REVOLUTION

If you're reading this Chapter, you've probably already grasped that online reviews can make or break your local business performance. Many, if not all, potential customers consult online review sites like TripAdvisor, Airbnb, Yelp, or Google before engaging with local businesses. If they see *positive* reviews, they are primed for a *positive* experience. If they see *negative* reviews, they are so *negatively* primed that they may avoid any contact whatsoever with your business. Reviews now impact all types of local businesses; nearly every local business is being reviewed online 24/7 365. And products are being reviewed on Amazon, employers are being reviewed on Glassdoor.com, and nearly every business (even B2B businesses) are being reviewed via Google "reputational searches," that is, when prospects simply Google your company name plus the word "reviews," as for example, "Geico reviews" or "Zoho reviews" on Google.

## The Review Ecosystem

Reviews are a fact of life, but how do reviews work? Let's step back for a moment and ponder the **review ecosystem**. With Yelp as the most important independent local review site, we will use Yelp as our model and recognize that what's true for Yelp is generally true for all review sites because they all follow the same social media rules of engagement. (Most of this also applies to reviews on Google, which is far and away the #1 site for consumer reviews online.)

Here's how review sites work:

1. **Businesses have listings**. Business listings are created *without the permission or participation of the business owner* and exist whether or not the business owner has claimed, optimized, or participated in the review ecosystem. *You as the business owner do not have the right to "delete" your listing on a review site!* It's like a business Page on Facebook, to the extent that your business has an online "Page" on Yelp, Tripadvisor, Healthgrades, etc. But unlike on Facebook, you are not in control!

2. **Customers write reviews**. Registered Yelp users (or Google users, or Airbnb users, or Glassdoor users, etc.) are able to write reviews about any business they choose. *If your business is not listed, users can even create a listing for your business and then review it.* These reviews may be good or bad, extremely positive or so negatively scathing as to infuriate you as the business owner. The Yelpers are basically in control, not the businesses.

3. **Customer reviewers also establish reputations**. The more reviews a customer writes, the older his or her profile as a reviewer on Yelp, the more friends on Yelp, the more thumbs up or thumbs down to their reviews, the stronger their profile gets. Yelp has filters to filter out "fake" or "weak" reviews from showing entirely. The stronger the customer profile, the higher their reviews rise on the pages of those businesses that they have reviewed. Your business and the Yelpers are both simultaneously establishing a reputation, and that reputation impacts whether your information (your listing, their review) shows prominently on Yelp. (Remember: the same is true for Google, TripAdvisor, Airbnb, and even Amazon).

4. **Businesses establish a reputation**. As your business is reviewed on Yelp, the more positive reviews it has, the more customers see it prominently in the search results, and the more come to visit it (especially first-time customers). But the more negative reviews you have, the less you're seen in search, and the fewer customers you get. This is called a "virtuous circle" and a "vicious circle."

5. **Prospective customers read reviews**. Potential customers visit sites like Yelp, CitySearch, TripAdvisor, Google, and search for businesses via keywords. They find businesses of interest and read the reviews. Generally speaking, people believe reviews especially if there are a lot of them, and even if they do not know

the reviewer personally (which they generally don't). This is called "stranger marketing." Reviews thus function as a "trust indicator":

   a. **Positive reviews** incrementally help your business to get new customers;

   b. **Negative reviews**, however, can have a disproportionately devastating impact on your business.

6. **Businesses claim their local listings**. Businesses have the right to claim and optimize their listings. By claiming its listing on a site like Yelp, a business can "optimize" it by improving the business description with accurate keywords, uploading photos, responding to reviews, and in some cases as on Google posting social updates. While businesses cannot delete their listings nor their negative reviews, they can participate in the new social media ecosystem of reviews.

Another major point to grasp is the **"virtuous circles"** and **"vicious circles"** of review marketing: the *more* positive reviews you have, the *more* likely you are to rank at the top of new customer searches (and thus get *more* customers and *more* positive reviews), while the *fewer* reviews you have and/or the *more negative* reviews you have, the *less* likely you are to rank at the top of new customer searches (and thus get more customers). And yet still another key point: the official policy of all the review sites is that you, as a business, should just passively do nothing and not even so much as ask for reviews.

For an overview to Yelp by Yelp, visit **http://www.yelp-support.com/**. For your first **TO-DO**, sign up for a Yelp account (as a consumer, not a business) if you do not already have one. Next, go to Yelp (**http://www.yelp.com/**) to explore some of the following categories in your local city by typing these keywords into the Yelp search box:

*Sushi Restaurants*

*Jazz*

*Plumbers*

*Divorce Attorneys*

*DUI Attorneys*

*Bail Bonds*

Let's take Bail Bonds, for example. Here's a screenshot of a search for "bail bonds" near San Francisco, CA:

Use the clickable links below to do the search:

- Here's a search for "Bail Bonds" near San Francisco, CA at **http://jmlinks.com/4i**.

- And here's one of the top search results: *Le Bail Bonds* at **http://jmlinks.com/32k**. (There's something so classy about being bailed out of jail by the French).

Here are some things to notice about the *Le Bail Bonds* listing.

First, scroll down about halfway and look for "From the business" in red. It starts with "We have multiple offices." This is the **business listing**, as edited and submitted by the business. This indicates that this business has claimed their listing. (You'll also see a blue "Claimed" checkmark next to the business name). Note the inclusion of relevant keywords, the types of search queries users might type into Yelp. Here's a screenshot:

**From the business**                                              ✕

**Specialties**

We have multiple offices located throughout the Bay Area!

The #1 Bail Bonds Company in the Bay Area

Specializing in 1275 holds!

Has your loved one found out the hard way about the law?
Let our bail bonds office help! Our mission is to provide
professional , informative , and dedicated service. We're
here to answer any questions or concerns you may have
about bail anywhere in California .

Le Bail Bonds offers fast efficient service 24 hours a day,
seven days a week. We specialize in short term payment
plans on your bail fees . We have specially trained bail
agents to help get your loved ones out of jail quickly.

We service anywhere in California!

**History**

[ Close ]                                                      ⚑

Second, notice the **photos** at the top of the listing at **http://jmlinks.com/32m**. Click on the photos, and notice how they are "keyword-heavy," including the phrase "bail bonds" and the location "San Francisco." These can be submitted either by the business or by users. So, if you don't submit photos, your users might (and they might be favorable, or unfavorable, to your business).

Third, read some of the **reviews**. Notice that for any individual reviewer, Yelp indicates how many friends they have on Yelp and how many reviews they have written. For example, here is a screenshot of a review by Leslie L of San Jose, California:

Fourth, click on a **reviewer photo**, and you'll go up to their **Yelp profile**. For example, click on "Leslie L" and that will get you up to her profile at **http://jmlinks.com/46s**. You can see that Leslie has 2 friends, has written 16 reviews, and uploaded 5 photos:

Read her reviews and make a guess as to how "real" and how "unsolicited" her reviews are. Some reviews and the reviewers who wrote them will look very legitimate, and others might look solicited, paid, or even faked. You'll soon realize that Yelp, like all the review-based sites, is a hodgepodge of unsolicited and solicited reviews, real and fake reviews, and so on and so forth. To the untrained eye, it can be hard to tell which reviews are truly real and which ones are fake; all the review systems are plagued by fake or paid reviews, even if the average customer is not that aware of this problem.

For example, here's a screenshot of a suspicious review:

Notice how Chloe D, has *zero* friends, has written only *one* review, lives in *Manhattan* and yet reviewed a *San Francisco* Bail Bonds. Is this a real review? A solicited review? Or a faked review?

Fifth, return to Le Bail Bond's company page on Yelp, and scroll to the very bottom and click on "reviews that are not currently recommended." Yelp has a filter that attempts to filter out "fake" reviews and filter in "real reviews." As of November, 2019, you can see that Yelp has filtered out 128 reviews which its algorithm feels are fake and/or solicited. For example, here's a filtered review by David A who has 0 friends and only 1 review:

Read some of the other "non-recommended" reviews and attempt to guess which ones are truly real and which ones might be fake. Do you think Yelp is doing a good, or bad job, with its filter? How do the reviews shown prominently compare or contrast with the reviews at the bottom, or the reviews that are hidden?

You should quickly realize that the reviews that "stick" tend to be from people with robust profiles, extensive reviews, and a relatively long history on the review site. Their reviews also tend to be beefy and specific, with a lot of content that describes a real experience. The reviews that get filtered out tend to be from people with sparse profiles, few or just one review, and a short history on the review site. The content of the reviews tends to be generic or sparse as well. This isn't always the case, but this is the general pattern. The artificial intelligence inherent in these review algorithms, in short, is getting better and better at giving top billing to real reviews and filtering out fake reviews. Far from perfect, yes, but that's the trend.

Now, before you go crazy and start soliciting reviews, keep reading. It's more complicated than this, but you should begin to see that review marketing – like all of marketing – is a **game** of being pro-active and not passive.

**Compare Yelp to Other Review Sites**

Reviews do not exist only on Yelp, however. Take any review site (Google, Airbnb, Avvo, Healthgrades, Amazon) and do the same exercise.

For instance, check out some reviews on Amazon, as a contrast to Yelp, by clicking on **http://jmlinks.com/4m** and **http://jmlinks.com/4n**. For example, here's a screenshot of the #1 ranking *garage door remote* on Amazon showing it has 868 customer reviews:

And here's a screenshot of one of the "customer profiles" of a reviewer of the product:

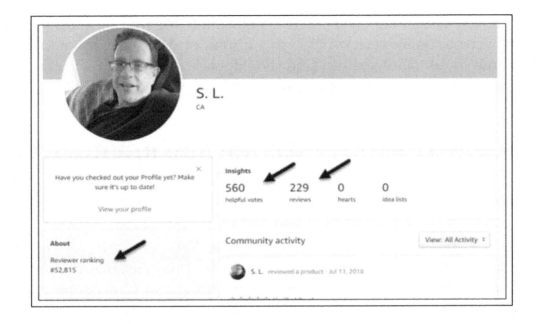

Notice some facts:

- The #1 organic result for "garage door remote" on Amazon has 868 reviews, and 270 answered questions.

- The #1 organic result for "garage door clicker" is titled, "Chamberlain Group KLIK3U-BK Clicker Universal 2-Button Garage Door Opener Remote with Visor Clip, Black" – lots of keywords "stuffed" into the product title.

- The customers who are reviewing it are being scored by how robust their profiles are, how many reviews they have written, the age of their profiles, helpful votes by others, etc., and probably (in terms of Amazon) whether they have purchased a lot or not many products on Amazon.

What's unique about Amazon is that – unlike Yelp or Google – Amazon has data on purchases, that is, Amazon knows whether or not the reviewer actually purchased the product. These are called "verified purchase" reviews on Amazon. This type of data on purchases is available on review sites like Airbnb as well, and is something that distinguishes that class from sites such as Google or Yelp that do not really have purchase behavior.

So as you audit and identify the review sites that matter to you look for differences and similarities to the general patterns. This can impact how you play the game as for example on Amazon where you need to encourage people who actually purchased your product to write reviews as compared with non-purchasers.

Is the new review system fair? Is it a better opportunity for your business than in 1994 when there were no online reviews? Whether it's fair or not, good or not, is a different issue than how you as a business can (and should) play the game of reviews to win. You do not make the review world; you simply live in it.

# LIFE IS NOT FAIR. NEITHER ARE REVIEWS. GET OVER IT.

None of this is perfect, and I am not singling out Yelp, Amazon, or Google. I am drawing your attention to the Review Revolution and the fact that it is not just real people spontaneously reviewing businesses but rather a mix of people writing real spontaneous reviews, people writing solicited (yet real) reviews, and even fake people writing fake reviews.

## Users Believe Reviews

Users believe online reviews! According to a BrightLocal study, fully 92% of consumers now read online reviews (vs. 88% in 2014), and 68% say positive reviews make them trust a local business more (vs. 72% in 2014). You can read the full study at **http://jmlinks.com/5b**. Another excellent book on the social aspects of the Review Revolution is Bill Tancer's, *Everyone's a Critic*, at **http://jmlinks.com/37b**.

## Unhappy Small Business Owners

In my face-to-face classes on social media, review sites are among the most controversial. Yelp, in particular, is literally hated by many small businesspeople because a) they have received what they think are unfair negative reviews on Yelp, and b) Yelp has a reputation for strong-arming businesses into paid advertising. (Yelp disputes this charge, though rumors have dogged the company for years – see **http://jmlinks.com/37c**).

Here's why local businesses often get quite emotional about sites like Yelp:

1. Often times, the only reviews they have about their business are negative reviews, which they feel are inaccurate or unfair.

2. They do not understand how to claim or optimize their listings, nor how to respond to reviews.

3. They do not realize that generally, if they do nothing, they are going to get negative reviews disproportionately.

4. They do not realize that there is a small yet very vocal minority of "haters" on reviews sites that troll businesses and write scathing and bitter negative reviews.

5. They do not understand how reviews work and how to influence reviews in their favor.

Moreover, many small business owners do not step back and compare 2019 with 1994. Then, only the rich, famous, connected, or lucky got reviews in the local papers. Getting reviewed was like winning the lottery: great if it happened in a positive way, but not something upon which you could build a marketing strategy. Today, however, any business can get reviews, and consumers can read those reviews online. The reality is that the Review Revolution created an enormous **positive marketing opportunity** for your business.

Let me repeat that:

*The Review Revolution created an enormous positive marketing opportunity for your business!*

You can either be bitter and angry that your business has negative reviews, or you can be positive, learn the game, and start to leverage the unbelievable fact that – today – even "boring" businesses like plumbers, divorce lawyers, or CPAs can get reviews and use review marketing to market their businesses.

**Who Writes Reviews?**

Let's talk about who writes reviews. Let's get real. Let's assume you are a local plumber. I have a clogged toilet. I go online and find your business. You come out, you fix my toilet, and you give me a bill for $300. You did a good job, and I am happy with the service.

Will I go online to Yelp and write a review? It's doubtful. Unlike my relationship with a local French restaurant, I am not "proud" that I have a leaky toilet, and I got it fixed. While I will likely go on Facebook and share a selfie of me and my wife at the local French restaurant, and likely go on Yelp and write a positive review to "showcase" how wealthy I am, and what a great husband I am, I am not "excited" that you provided me with excellent service with respect to my waste removal system in my bathroom, otherwise known as my toilet. No selfies to Facebook, hopefully, no Snapchat of me on my newly fixed toilet, no positive review to Yelp.

*My toilet has been fixed. I'm happy. Done. Over. End. Writing a review is the last thing on my mind.*

Now, let's say you come out for my toilet repair, and you do NOT do what I consider a good job. Perhaps you crack my tile floor, or perhaps you get dirty water on my rug, or perhaps I just don't like you, or perhaps I find your fee of $300 unreasonable.

*I'm mad. I hate you. I pay the bill. I'm angry, and I want revenge.*

I think to myself, "I'll show you." I go online and vent my anger in a Yelp review. I explain to fellow Yelpers (and the world) how terrible you are, how they should never use your business, etc. etc. I do this to "let off steam" as well as to "feel good about myself" that I am "doing the world a favor" by righting the wrong of your terrible business. I want you to go out of business. I want you to fail. That's justice to me, the unhappy customer.

(Don't believe this happens? To read reviews of the "worst food of my life" on Yelp, visit **http://jmlinks.com/4z**). You'll see a lot of unhappy, bitter, nasty people on Yelp, and that's just for food.

Here are the **dirty little secrets** of the review ecosystem (with the possible exception of entertainment venues like restaurants, bars, museums, etc.):

- Consumers **believe** online reviews when making a purchase decision.

- However, outside of "fun" industries like restaurants and entertainment, the **most likely customer to leave an unsolicited review is the unhappy customer.** The very unhappy customer is very likely spontaneously to write a nasty review about your business!

- Outside of "fun" industries, **happy customers are NOT likely to write reviews**. They are not pre-motivated to share their experience with your plumbing company, your CPA firm, your DUI attorney services on Yelp without a nudge from you. Outside of "fun" industries, you must solicit reviews from happy customers to succeed.

Two other customer segments are likely to leave reviews.

- **Review geeks / extreme Yelpers** – which would be people like myself, digitally connected, and participatory in the Yelp (or Google, TripAdvisor) ecosystems. Review geeks are not necessarily primed to leave positive or negative reviews. They just tend to review frequently. As Yelp has evolved, more and more people ARE leaving reviews spontaneously about local services, which is a good thing.

- The **hostile minority** - these are unhappy campers who, because of sites like Yelp, now have a way to vent their rage at nearly everything. These "unhappy campers" tend to leave unhappy review after unhappy review: bitter and negative, they tend to hate everything and leave a destructive trail of negative reviews in their wake. Unfortunately, without any fault on its part, Yelp enabled the very unhappy, bitter people of the world to spread their negativity by venting against businesses. Don't believe me? Try some Yelp searches, look for negative reviews, and click "up" to the profiles of the reviewers. In just a few minutes, I guarantee that you will find some very negative, pathetic, sad little people.

## UNHAPPY CUSTOMERS OFTEN WRITE REVIEWS

Contrast what you see with "non-fun" businesses, with what you see around "fun" businesses like restaurants, bars, or coffee shops. Here, Yelp (and other review sites) leverages the *social media narcissism* so present in our society. Similar to what you see on Facebook, people like to "showcase" their positive achievements. *Look at me! I went to fancy restaurant X, I went out to dinner, I went to this amazing museum, ate at this exclusive diner, drank at this cool bar, smoked cigars as this cool cigar bar, etc.*

For businesses outside of restaurants and the like, the takeaway here is to realize the following:

*If you do nothing, the most likely reviews you will get will be negative reviews.*

And another truth. In more and more industries, your competitors are pro-actively soliciting reviews and pretty much getting away with it. So if you are passive, you might have ten positive reviews and a couple negative ones, but you'll be competing against a pro-active business that has forty positive reviews and just a couple negatives. It's an arms race to get positive reviews.

## Don't Shoot the Messenger

Now, don't shoot the messenger. Every business will get at least a few negative reviews, sooner or later. If you have just a couple, that's OK and normal (compare yourself to other, similar businesses to establish a baseline). But if you're getting negative review after negative review after negative review, you don't have a Yelp or online review problem, you have a business problem. Don't shoot the messenger; the Review Revolution gives you a new window on how actual customers feel about your product, service, or front-line, customer-facing employees.

## Official Policy

Now, let's return to the Review Revolution, and look at the problem from the perspective of a business owner in some "non-fun" line of business such as plumbers, CPAs or accountants, divorce attorneys, or roofing companies. You're unlikely to get positive reviews unless you do something pro-active. But what's the official policy on reviews?

The official policies of Yelp, Google, TripAdvisor, and the like is that you – as the business owner – are not allowed to solicit reviews in any way, shape, or fashion. Yelp, for example, advises business owners:

> *Don't ask customers, mailing list subscribers, friends, family, or anyone else to review your business.* (Source: **http://jmlinks.com/4g**).

TripAdvisor's explanation is one of the most detailed, and you should read it at **http://jmlinks.com/4h**. It's informative and contradictory in that, like all the review platforms, it ignores the fact that the most likely reviews come from unhappy customers and/or the bitter minority of weirdos on the Internet.

Even Amazon has changed its once more lenient policy to one in which it is now taboo to give away free products yet require a review (**http://jmlinks.com/37d**). Amazon states, "In order to preserve the integrity of Community content, content and activities consisting of advertising, promotion, or solicitation (whether direct or indirect) is not allowed, including… Offering compensation or requesting compensation (including free or discounted products) in exchange for creating, modifying, or posting content."

## The Review Dilemma

So here's the **review dilemma**:

- *On the one hand,* if you do nothing, you are very likely to receive negative reviews from unhappy customers and not so likely to receive positive reviews from happy customers (true in all cases, except perhaps entertainment-type industries), but

- *On the other hand,* the official terms of service forbid you from soliciting reviews from customers.

*Damned if you do, damned if you don't.*

The reality of the Review Revolution is that in most cases and certainly in competitive industries like divorce law, DUI cases, plumbers, roofers, etc., most successful companies are pro-actively soliciting reviews. This does not mean that they are faking or buying reviews; it only means that they are nudging, cajoling, begging, emotionally incentivizing, and otherwise motivating happy customers to go online and take the time to write positive reviews around their business.

*Is this fair? No.*

*Is this in accord with the terms of service? No.*

*Is it the reality? Yes.*

*Is it the public reality? No. Yelp, Google, TripAdvisor, Amazon, and all the other companies do their best to police reviews, but the reality is that the fact that reviews are heavily manipulated by vendors is an open secret.*

But wait a second.

*Is life fair? No.*

*Was it likely that your plumbing company would have been reviewed in the paper in 1995? No. Your small restaurant? No.*

*Even though the posted speed limit on the highway is 60 mph, do most cars actually go 60 mph? No.*

The Review Revolution has given you an enormous, positive opportunity to reach new customers, just like the Interstate Highway System gives you the opportunity to travel cross-country at 65 to 80 mph even though the posted speed limit may be 75 mph (in the West) and 60 mph (in the East).

*Don't be the fastest car on the road. Don't be the red Mazda Miata going 95 mph in front of the cop. Just be in the fast car group, just not the fastest, most egregious car.*

For now, just understand that **positive reviews are the key to success**, that soliciting reviews is technically against the terms of service, and begin to realize that you are going to have to create a strategy to solicit positive reviews, despite the posted terms of service.

Let's turn, first, to identifying companies to emulate on the various review sites. I'll return after that to dealing with the problem of soliciting reviews without getting into trouble.

## » INVENTORY COMPANIES ON YELP, GOOGLE, OR OTHER RELEVANT SITES

If you are a local business, it will be pretty obvious that reviews matter. Even if you are a national business, however, you should realize that online reviews still matter. (This is because many people will Google your company name plus "reviews" to check out your reputation before completing an important purchase).

Your first step, therefore, is to identify which review sites matter to your business. Your second step is to browse similar businesses on those sites and conduct an inventory of what you like and dislike about their listings, realizing that unlike on Facebook, listings on review sites generally occur with or without the permission of the business. Actual control is much more limited. Your third step is to claim and optimize your listings, and your final step is to create a pro-active system to solicit positive reviews in such a way that you don't get in trouble with the review platforms.

Among the most important review sites are:

Yelp (**http://www.yelp.com/**) – the largest local review site with great strength in restaurants, more popular in "Blue" states like New York or California than in "Red" states like Florida or Texas.

Google (**http://www.google.com/**). Accessibly by doing Google searches on relevant keywords. In some cases, you'll need to first find a company, and then Google its name to find its Google page (more below).

Facebook (**https://www.facebook.com**). Rather new to the review ecosystem, Facebook is beefing up its reviews of local businesses. See **http://jmlinks.com/37e** for Facebook's help file on business reviews.

TripAdvisor (**http://www.tripadvisor.com/**). The leading travel review site.

YP (**http://www.yp.com/**). The traditional yellow pages gone digital.

VRBO (**http://www.vrbo.com/**) – a site for identifying short-term vacation rentals.

Airbnb (**http://www.airbnb.com/**) – the leading site for vacation rentals.

Amazon (**http://www.amazon.com/**) – earth's largest retailer, with reviews on billions of products.

Glassdoor (**http://www.glassdoor.com/**) – reviews about businesses from the perspective of employees.

Facebook is a special and growing case of reviews. Consumers don't pro-actively search Facebook (yet) for reviews, but they are beginning to leave them. So Facebook reviews generally function only as "trust" indicators, and/or encourage eWOM (electronic word of mouth). To enable Facebook reviews (now called "recommendations") for your business, see **http://jmlinks.com/32p**.

# IDENTIFY COMPANIES WHO DO REVIEW MARKETING WELL, AND REVERSE ENGINEER THEM

The easiest way to find logical review sites for your company is as follows:

1. Identify the **keywords** by which prospective customers might search for you. For example, if you are a Sushi restaurant in San Francisco, those keywords might

be words such as "Sushi," "Sushi Bar," "Japanese Restaurant," "Japanese Caterers," etc.

2. **Google** those keywords and note which review sites come up.

    a. Also try Google searches by keyword plus words like "directory" or "reviews" as for example, "family law attorney directory" or "family law attorney reviews."

3. Click over to the review sites, and **make a list** of them.

4. Go over to each review site, re-input your search query keywords, and begin to browse company listings on the review sites you have identified.

For example, take "vacation rentals Lake Tahoe" and search it on Google (**http://jmlinks.com/4p**). Also try "directory of vacation rentals." Then, browse the search results, and you'll see sites such as:

> **https://www.flipkey.com/**
>
> **http://www.homeaway.com/**
>
> **http://www.vrbo.com/**
>
> **http://www.tripadvisor.com/**
>
> **http://www.vacationrentals.com/**
>
> **https://www.airbnb.com/**

In this case, you then find out if you already have a listing on each site, if so claim it, and if not create one, and then optimize it. You then begin to solicit positive reviews on each of the most important sites.

You can also check out Bright Local's list of best citations by category at **http://jmlinks.com/46t** as well as Moz's at **http://jmlinks.com/46u**. These capture the most common places to be listed, but I recommend that you also pro-actively search Google for "directories" by keyword, as well as browse your competitors to identify industry-relevant sites.

By using this techniques, you can quickly make a list of the key review sites that are most relevant to your company.

## Google is the Most Important Review Site

Among listing and review sites, "Google My Business" (GMB) (**https://www.google.com/business**) is the most important by far. First and foremost, it's owned and operated by Google and has clear priority on Google search. Having a strong presence via your listing on GMB is the No. 1 way for your business to show on local-related Google searches. It doesn't take much to look forward and realize that if local matters to you and your customers use Google, you'll need to optimize your Google My Business listing! Even if local does not matter to you, try searching for your company name plus "reviews," and your Google My Business listing and reviews will often show up in position #1, but take note of what does show up and begin to claim and optimize other listings as well.

Return to Google, let's just be honest upfront. Google has done a **terrible** job of managing the Google My Business program. They are constantly changing the format, rules, structure, set up – enough to drive a social media marketer insane!

As of November 2019, here's the current set up:

> **Consumers simply browse Google.** Consumers simply go to Google, type in keywords such as "Pizza," "Italian restaurants," or "Family Law Attorneys" and see companies show up in the "snack pack," which is the three listings showing (usually but not always with stars). Here's a screenshot:

**Consumers need a Google account to post reviews.** Consumers can post reviews to Google via their Google account. Anyone, however, can read a review.

**Consumers rate businesses.** Consumers rate businesses on a five-star system and can leave detailed reviews (good, bad, ugly) on the system, whether or not the business likes it.

**Businesses can "claim" their Google listings at Google My Businesses.** To "claim" their listings, businesses go to Google My Business at **https://www.google.com/business,** and they can add a description (now invisible to consumers), photos (visible on Google), and respond to reviews.

**Businesses can post announcements to their Google My Business Listing.** Google now allows a local business to make a post to its business, which will show up when someone Google's the business name as well as often (but not always) when someone does a relevant search on Google, and your business wins a placement on Google Maps. See **http://jmlinks.com/37f** for information on this new opportunity.

Google reviews are critical to success at local SEO. Here's why:

1. **Reviews drive your company to the top of Google.** The *more* reviews you have on the Google system, the *higher* you show on Google searches for local keywords.

2. **Consumers read and rely on Google reviews**, even if they don't understand where they came from or how to write them. The reality is that while *few* consumers *write* reviews, *many* if not most people *believe* them.

**Inventory Companies and Their Local Listings**

As you browse local review sites, identify relevant companies and make a list of their listings on Yelp, Google, or other sites that are relevant. Make a note of:

- Does their **listing** appear **claimed**?

- **Photos**: cover photos and profile pictures. Do you like what you see? Why or why not?

- **Reviews**. How many reviews do they have? Are they mostly positive or mostly negative? Click on the reviewers. Do they seem "real"? Unsolicited? Solicited? Faked? Are vendors responding to reviews? Try to reverse engineer how they might be soliciting or encouraging reviews.

- **Questions and Answers**. Google now allows customers to ask questions and vendors to give answers. Do you see this feature in use in your industry?

- **About Tab**. Check out their about tab, or listing. Read it. Do you like how it's written? Does it include relevant keywords?

For your second **TO-DO**, download the **Review Research Worksheet**. For the worksheet, go to **http://jmlinks.com/social2020** (then reenter the code '**social2020**' to register your workbook), and click on the link to the "Reviews Research Worksheet." You'll answer questions as to whether your potential customers are using reviews, which review sites are important, and inventory what you like and dislike about their review marketing set up and marketing strategy.

## » CLAIM AND OPTIMIZE YOUR LISTINGS

Now that you've identified which local review sites matter, it's time to claim and optimize your listings. All of the sites work in essentially the same way, although there are differences in the details. The basic steps are:

1. Identify the local review site for which you want to "claim" your company listing.

2. Find your listing on the site.

3. Follow the instructions to "claim" it, usually by phone or postcard verification.

4. Optimize your listing description by writing keyword-heavy text, uploading photographs, and populating your listing with your hours of operation and other details.

5. Make sure that your website links back to your listing, and your listing links to your website.

6. Make sure that the business name, address, and phone number are the same on both the listing site and your website (be consistent).

**To do this for Yelp:**

1. Go to **http://biz.yelp.com/**

2. Enter your business name, and address and hit **Get Started** in red.

3. Follow the instructions to claim your business, usually by phone verification.

4. Once you have claimed your listing:

   a. Click on Business Information on the left; re-write your description to contain logical keywords that potential customers might search for, including synonyms (*pizza, Italian restaurant, catering*, for example).

   b. Choose relevant categories from the list provided.

   c. Enter your basic information, hours, specialties (business information), history, and "meet the business owner" with an eye to logical keywords.

   d. Click on photos on the left, and upload nice photos.

5. Make sure that the address and phone on Yelp are the SAME as the address and phone on your website.

6. Make sure that your website links to your Yelp listing (usually in the footer), and that your Yelp listing links to your website.

**VIDEO.** Watch a video tutorial on how to claim and optimize your business on Yelp at **http://jmlinks.com/16x**.

**To do this for Google:**

1. Sign in to your Google account or Gmail (if you use Gmail).

2. Go to **https://www.google.com/business**

3. Click on the green "Start Now" link on the top right. Or, if you don't see that, click on the blue "Add location" button at the top right.

4. Follow the instructions to claim your business, usually by postcard verification, and sometimes (if you're lucky) by phone verification.

   a. When you get the postcard, enter the PIN as indicated in the instructions.

   b. This will verify your listing and give you control.

   c. DO NOT LOSE THE LOGIN EMAIL AND PASSWORD, as it is very hard to reclaim a listing!

5. Optimize your business description by clicking on "info" on the left column. Using the "pencil" icon then edit each option.

   a. **Business name**

   b. **Address**. Enter your correct local address, and make sure it matches the address on your website exactly.

   c. **Categories**. This is very important – choose highly relevant categories, and fewer are better than more, so be as specific as possible though you must use Google's pre-set categories.

   d. **Hours of operation**.

   e. **Phone number**. Do not use an 800 number – use a local number, one that also exists on your website.

   f. **Website**.

   g. **Description**. Write a short, keyword-heavy description of your business.

6. Click on "photos" on the left to change your profile picture, and cover photos, as well as add interior and/or exterior photos.

**VIDEO.** Watch a video tutorial on how to claim and optimize your business on Google at **http://jmlinks.com/17d**.

**VIDEO.** Watch a video tutorial on why Yelp matters for both SEO and social media marketing at **http://jmlinks.com/17e**. Note that Yelp drives reviews on the Bing Search Engine. For example, check out this Bing search for *Pizza* at **http://jmlinks.com/37h**.

Other local listings like YP.com or Citysearch follow similar procedures. To find all of your "second-tier" listings, you can go to Yext (**http://www.yext.com/**) and enter your business name and phone number in the box in about the middle of the page. Then click on the "scan now" blue button on the right. Here's a screenshot:

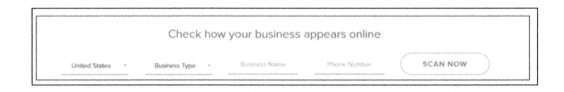

For free, Yext will identify all your local listings. You can then click over to each and claim and optimize each. Or, if you have budget, you can subscribe to Yext, and they will do this for all local listings, including Yelp but **excluding** Google. A competitive service to Yext is MOZ Local at **http://jmlinks.com/37g**. Whitespark at **https://whitespark.ca** is yet another one. Yext is the most expensive and fastest. The other two are slower and less expensive. My preference would be Whitespark as it seems to be the cheapest, and they do the most meticulous job, "by hand," while the other two are automated.

**Citation Consistency and Google Local Searches**

To show up on Google search, it is important that ALL review sites and your website have the SAME company name, the SAME phone number, and SAME physical address. Make sure that your company name, phone number, and physical address appear on your website, usually in the footer. (This is called *NAP* (*Name, Address, Phone*) consistency).

"Citations" refer to the external listings on review websites that confirm (to Google and Bing) that your business has a certain phone number and physical address. This is used by the search engines to filter local search results by their proximity to the searcher or the geographic terms used in the search query.

Using a service like Yext, MOZ, or Whitespark allows you to claim, optimize, and make consistent this information across hundreds of review sites. This consistency is a big help to showing at the top of local searches on Google or Bing / Yahoo. Regardless of how you do it, try to get NAP consistency between your website, the two most important local review sites (Google and Yelp), and then the 2nd tier sites using a service like Yext, MOZ, or Whitespark (or doing that manually if you're a glutton for punishment).

## Organize and Claim Your Local Listings

For your third **TO-DO**, make a spreadsheet of ALL relevant local review sites. Go to each, and claim / optimize your local listings. Be sure to note your login and password!

- CLAIM YOUR GOOGLE AND YELP WITH A PERMANENT CORPORATE EMAIL (NOT AN EMPLOYEE EMAIL) such as **local@yourcompany.com** or **marketing@yourcompany.com**. If not that, create a Gmail to use for all your local listings.

- **DO NOT LOSE YOUR GOOGLE AND YELP LOGIN AND PASSWORDS!**

**Lost password retrieval** on Yelp and Google is a **disaster**! Neither system has a good password retrieval function; on Yelp in particular, if your password is lost, God help you. Do not lose your passwords! Write them down somewhere where you will be able to find them in a few years.

## ›› SEO YOUR LOCAL WEBSITE

SEO or *Search Engine Optimization,* of course, is the art and science of structuring your website so that it ranks well on Google searches. *Local* is an area that crosses both SEO and social media marketing. While you are working on your review marketing efforts, let's review the SEO of your website to make sure that your website SEO and your local review efforts are in harmony:

- **Optimize Your Home Page**. Make sure that your Home Page, especially the TITLE tag contains your keywords and your city. If you are a Miami plumber, make sure that both the word "Miami" and the word "plumber" appears in the visible text of your homepage. Make sure that there is visible content on your homepage that includes your target keywords and every city in which you have an office. If you have multiple locations, create landing pages for each one and link each landing page to the local listings for that city. A few vendors that do a good job of this are PetFood Express (**http://petfoodexpress.com/**) and Home Depot (**https://www.homedepot.com/**). Notice how each has a "store finder" section of the website, and each local store has a local landing page on the primary website.

- **Create a Consistent NAP**. Include a consistent NAP (Name / Address / Phone Number) on your website that matches the NAP on your Yelp, Google, and other local review sites.

- **Cross-link** from your website to your Google and Yelp listings.

- Make sure that all your listings, especially Google and Yelp, **link back** directly to your website.

## Optimize Your Contact Us Page

Even if you have only one location, be sure to have an "about us" or "contact us" page on your website as an optimized page for that city and target keywords. Optimize that page for your target home city by including the city name and keywords in your TITLE tag, plus visible content. Also, on that page, include an embedded Google map, which you can generate by searching for your company on Google, clicking up to the maps tab, and then click the share tab. Next, click on "embed map" to get the HTML code to embed a Google map on your website. Here's a screenshot:

Finally, use the microdata / schema.org system to embed the appropriate JSON-LD schema markup on your website. You can also use the Google "Structured Data Markup Helper" at **http://jmlinks.com/46v** for this function. J.D. Flynn has also created an online tool that will guide you through creating JSON-LD data for you at **http://jmlinks.com/32q**.

## Engage in Local Link Building

As we learned in previous Chapters, Google pays a lot of attention to inbound links to your website. The more (and better) links you have to your website, the higher you tend to rank on Google. What's true at the *national* level is also true at the *local* level.

Google is not stupid. Google is not locally unaware. Google knows all (Remember: just Google "Is Google God?"). Google knows that the local Chamber of Commerce is local to your community, that the local Animal Welfare Nonprofit is local to your community, and that the local Mommy Blogger works just down the street from you. To this end, you want to look for **local links** and get them. Nonprofits are a simple example. Do a Google search for your city plus nonprofit, and then reach out to those nonprofits with sponsorships. In exchange for a sponsorship, require a weblink back FROM the local nonprofit TO your website. For example, try the Google search site:*.org Tulsa "link to your website" at **http://jmlinks.com/51y**. (Replace "Tulsa" with your city, or if there are too few results replace "Tulsa" with your state as in "Oklahoma"). In just a few seconds, you can generate a link of nearby local nonprofits that will provide links to your website. Then visit each nonprofit website and find out whom you have to pay and what you have to do to "sponsor" it and get a local link.

Another example would be to join local **organizations** or **associations** and make sure that your profile (or that of your CEO or manager) includes a link back to your local listing. Just a few quick searches, and you can quickly find nonprofits, associations, organizations, and other local entities that have websites that will link to your business.

For example, if you search for "Car Dealerships Tulsa," you'll see Jim Glover Chevrolet of Tulsa at Position #2 in organic search. An analysis of JimGloverChevy.com in the AHREFs tool indicates these type of "local" links to JimGloveryChevy.com:

**http://www.darrylstarbird.com/links.html** - Darryl Starbird's National Rod and Custom Car Hall of Fame Museum (in Tulsa)

**https://fitfirstresponders.org/partners/** - a Tulsa-based nonprofit supporting firefighters

**https://cuttinghorsecentral.com/listings/view.phtml/Trainers/14/Wesley-Galyean** - a Texas-based horse marketplace

**http://oklahoma.in24.us/chevrolet-dealers.htm** - an Oklahoma-based directory listing service.

http://moreclaremore.com/2015/10/09/volunteers-drive-zipperq4-in-claremore-to-a-record-year/ - a Claremore, Oklahoma, news article

In other words, you can see that this "local" business has "local" links to it, and – accordingly – Google rewards it with a high position on local Tulsa-based searches for car dealers.

**VIDEO.** Watch a video tutorial on local SEO at **http://jmlinks.com/46w**.

## » CULTIVATE POSITIVE REVIEWS

Returning to the social media and review aspects of local, we'll assume you've claimed and optimized the relevant listing services for your local business. Most often this will be at least Google and Yelp, and in specific industries, it might include TripAdvisor, VRBO, or Airbnb. If you sell products, it might be your product listings and uploads on Amazon. Or it might be on Glassdoor.com.

At this point, you have two options:

1. Wait **passively** for positive customer reviews, and hope that the positive reviews will outpace the negative reviews (according to the official policy of Yelp, Google, etc.).

2. Be **pro-active** and try to encourage your happy customers to post reviews.

Which do you think the winners in local search and social media are doing?

## Legal Disclaimer

*You are responsible for everything you do in terms of your Internet marketing. Nothing I am writing here should be construed as required or recommended advice. Legally, I am recommending that you do nothing (option #1).*

*Take responsibility for your own actions as a marketer, and act on your own risk!*

## Soliciting Reviews

That said, here is the reality. If you wait passively for reviews (unless you are in the a very fun industry like restaurants, coffee shops, or bars), the most likely scenarios will be a) no reviews, or b) bad reviews, or at least a preponderance of bad reviews. You, the business owner or marketer can, however, fight back against this dynamic. Here are some strategies to solicit positive reviews about your business:

**Face to Face**. This is the most powerful way to get positive reviews. The employee who is "face to face" with the customer builds rapport with the customer. A scenario might be:

*Technician: "OK, I've fixed your toilet. Let's run through it together, and verify it's in working order.*

*Client: Yes, it's great. Thank you so much!*

*Technician: You're welcome. Hey, if you have a moment, could you do us a HUGE FAVOR and write a review on Google or Yelp about your experience?*

*Client: Yes.*

- If the client knows how to do this, just give him or her a card with a direct link to the review site location.

- If the client does not know how to do this, give him or her a card with step-by-step instructions.

**Phone Reminders**. Either at the time of service or shortly thereafter, call the customer to see "how it went," and if they're happy, ask them to write a review online.

**Paper Reminders**. Either at the time of service or shortly thereafter, mail a physical postcard thanking the client for their business and asking them to write a review on Yelp, Google, etc.

**Email Reminders**. Either at the time of service, or shortly thereafter, send an email thanking the client for their business and asking them to write a review online.

The reality is that face-to-face is, by far, the strongest way to motivate customers to write reviews, phone contact the next strongest, and so on and so forth.

**Help Customers Write Reviews**

Many customers may not understand how to write a review, so a step-by-step instruction sheet would be helpful. Use a URL shortener like **http://bit.ly**, or **http://tinyurl.com** to shorten the link to your local review listing page.

**Google: Generate a REVIEW US URL on Google**

Google, as I have explained earlier, is really a mess. To find a short, easy link to your customer reviews on Google, follow these steps.

1. Go to the GradeUS Google review generator tool at **http://jmlinks.com/13j**.

2. Enter your business name and city or postal code, and press the blue "Get Google Review Links."

3. Select your company from the list it provides, and hit "Continue."

4. Click on the link for "Open in Search Results" and highlight the huge URL string it gives you from Google.

5. Copy this URL string.

6. Go to **http://tinyurl.com/** and paste this URL into the box "Enter a long URL to make it tiny."

    a. If you like "customize" your URL to make it easy to remember / or just cool.

    b. Here's an example: **http://tinyurl.com/revjasonseo**.

*Alternatively –*

1. Go to Google at **https://www.google.com/** and enter your company name plus a keyword and/or your city.

2. Click on the "blue" Google reviews link (you MUST have at least ONE Google Review to use this method!).

3. Highlight the huge URL Google gives you in the top of the browser.

4. Copy this URL string.

5. Go to **http://tinyurl.com/** and paste this URL into the box "Enter a long URL to make it tiny."

a. If you like "customize" your URL to make it easy to remember / or just cool.

b. Here's an example: **http://tinyurl.com/revjasonseo**.

You can write this in an email or on a printed sheet of paper. Here's an example of an email I might send to my clients:

Greetings!

Thank you so much for the opportunity to serve your Internet marketing and consulting needs. As the owner of the *Jason McDonald SEO Consulting Agency*, I truly appreciate your business!

If you have a moment, I would REALLY appreciate an honest review on one of the local listing sites. Here are the instructions:

Google.

1. Sign in to your Google and/or Gmail account at **https://www.google.com/**.

2. Go to **http://tinyurl.com/revjasonseo**.

3. Click on the white "Write a review."

4. Write your review

Yelp:

1. Sign in to your Yelp account at **http://www.yelp.com/**.

2. Go to **http://bit.ly/jason-yelp**.

3. Click on the red "write a review" button

4. Write your review

Thank you,

Jason McDonald

# TO GET POSITIVE REVIEWS, ASK HAPPY CUSTOMERS TO REVIEW YOU

WhiteSpark, which is a leading local review tool company, offers a free tool to help you create nice-looking Web pages and handouts to encourage reviews at **http://jmlinks.com/4t**. In addition, a few paid services are emerging that "pre-survey" your customers. Essentially, they first ask your customer if they liked your company and its product or service. If yes, then that customer is prompted to write a review. If no, then the customer is given a longer detailed survey and that survey is sent to you the business owner; the customer is NOT prompted to write a review. One such service is ReviewBuzz (**http://www.reviewbuzz.com**). Others are GatherUp (**https://gatherup.com/**) and ReviewInc (**http://www.reviewinc.com**).

Note, however, that recently Yelp in particular began to crack down on these services, blocking reviews that originate via their pre-surveys. The "nerd word" for this is called, "review gating." Even Google has now clarified that they are against review gating (See **http://jmlinks.com/47w**). All of this gets you back to the "damned if you do, damned if you don't" conundrums of review marketing, and it reinforces the importance of you, as a small business owner or marketers, taking matters into your own hands and doing your utmost to ask happy campers, and only happy campers, to "do you a favor" and write you a review online. Automating this process is more likely to trigger penalties as opposed to doing it customer-by-customer, face-to-face.


## Be Judicious. Understand "Plausible Deniability"

Understand that according to the official policy, even a mild handout asking for an "honest review" is a violation of the terms of service of most of the review providers! Therefore, I do NOT recommend that you post these publicly on your website. Be judicious: give them out in printed or email format, and only to those happy customers who have been pre-selected by your staff.

Obviously, if a client is unhappy and you cannot fix it to make them happy: DO NOT ASK THEM FOR A REVIEW.

In fact, a common strategy is to manually use "review gating" as follows:

- **Conduct a survey** of customers after they use your service asking them a) if they are happy, b) if they would write a review, and c) if they know how. This could be done formally (an email survey on a site like SurveyMonkey (**http://www.surveymonkey.com**)) or informally just be pre-asking the customer face-to-face, over the phone, or via email. You can also use Jotform and "conditional logic" to set up this type of pre-survey on your website (See **http://jmlinks.com/37j**).

- **If they ARE happy**, then ask them nicely to **write a review**.

- **If they are NOT happy**, either a) make them happy, or b) do **NOT** ask them for a review.

In this way, you avoid motivating unhappy customers to review you online. Indeed, if you are in a sensitive industry (e.g., Bail Bonds, apartment rentals) in which many customers are not happy, I do not recommend you even publicize to your clients face-to-face or in the real world that you are on the review sites. If many of your customers will be negative, then do not make it "easy" for them to give you a negative review!

## Paying for Reviews

Let's face it. Review marketing is the "contact sport" of social media marketing. In certain industries (e.g., DUI attorneys, private detectives, breast augmentation services), many reviews are solicited if not faked and sometimes incentivized with monetary payments.

Should you pay for reviews? Generally speaking, I would not pay for reviews. (I am talking about real clients not completely faked reviews). Some companies do incentivize by giving $25 Starbucks or Amazon gift cards once a review is published; however, if this becomes known to a Yelp or a Google you wrong a very strong risk of being severely penalized.

*Offering monetary incentives to get reviews is a dangerous strategy, so be forewarned.*

Yelp will even mark your listing with an aggressive naughty notice if you are busted paying for reviews. You can browse real examples of this on Yelp at **http://jmlinks.com/4u**. First and foremost, therefore, if you choose to "go to the dark side" and offer payments, I would not publicize it! And: **I AM NOT RECOMMENDING THAT YOU DO THIS**. I am just pointing out that it is done.

Also, note that not only is "paying for reviews" likely to bring down the wrath of Yelp, you can also bring down the wrath of Yelp by offering to pay a negative reviewer to take down their review. Yelp even now explicitly forbids spiffing employees when they successfully get a review. Anytime you are offering money in exchange for a Yelp behavior, then you run that risk – so be forewarned about just how uptight Yelp is about reviews and payments! (Google and other sites have similar policies).

### Incentivize Employees

A better way to increase your positive review count is to offer your employees an incentive, rather than the customer, for reviews published online. Assume, for example, that you are a local pizza joint. Offer your employees a $25.00 bonus EACH after each positive review on Yelp. Or if you are a roofing company, give the technician a handout explaining how to write a review online, and give him a $25.00 bonus EACH TIME a customer posts a review. In that way, you motivate your front-line employees to be customer-friendly, and when there is a positive customer experience, to politely ask the customer to write an honest review on Yelp, Google, etc.

**Motivate your employees to ask for reviews!**

I would not put any pro-active review solicitation strategy in writing on the Internet, just as I would not call the California Highway Patrol and inform them that, in general, I go five miles faster than the posted speed limit while driving the highways and byways of the Golden State.

*Let sleeping dogs lie.*

But just as going 65 mph in a 60 mph zone is unlikely to cause a police action, polite nudges to encourage real reviews from real customers are unlikely to be a big problem. If you do it, just keep it private, and <u>do so at your own risk</u>.

### Don't Overthink It. Just Ask for Reviews from Real Customers

In my experience, if most businesses would simply *ask* a few clients for reviews, they would get them. Yes, you'll ask ten clients to get one review. But you'll get that one review. The real problem is to motivate employees to ask and ask and ask and ask to get that one review to go live on Yelp, Google, or other review sites.

Recognize, understand, and accept that you will ask ten people to get just one review. That's just how it is: customers are self-centered and lazy (but we love them).

Getting positive reviews is hard work. It's not done in a day. Slow and steady will win the race. Just create a culture at your business of great customer service and an awareness of that "special moment" when a customer is happy to ask for a positive, honest review.

# JUST ASK. IT'S SO SIMPLE. JUST ASK.

Do anything and everything honestly and ethically possible to encourage your best customers to "spread the word" by writing reviews about your business online. After just a few positive reviews, you will be amazed at what they do for your business.

## Responding to Negative Reviews

Negative reviews will happen. As the business owner, you may feel as if someone walked up to your newborn baby sleeping calmly in her stroller and said to you:

*Your baby is ugly. Your baby stinks. I hate your baby. I had a bad experience with your baby, and I am going to tell the world how much the baby that you are working for blood, sweat, and tears is terrible.*

Here's an example:

> **Lupita L.**
> **Los Angeles, CA**
> 75 friends
> 95 reviews
>
> ⭐️☆☆☆☆  3/22/2016
>
> 1 check-in
>
> If I could, I would give this truck a 00!!! Worst tacos in the world! Do yourself a favor don't come. Meat was awful. Mulitas had no cheese. To top it off, a large group arrived after me and their food was served b4 my tacos so I had to wait forever. I don't understand how some people give them 4 & 5 stars.

You're human. You're close to your business. It is like your baby. Your first reaction will be **ANGER**.

Resist the temptation to respond in kind. Do not go online and argue with the negative consumer. Do not insult them. Do not use unprofessional language. *When you wrestle with a pig, the pig gets dirty, and the pig likes it.*

Instead:

- **Calm down**. Wait at least 24 hours before doing anything. Sleep on it.

- **Have someone else deal with negative reviews**: an outside consultant or employee who is not emotionally involved. Let a calm head prevail, and it probably will not be the head of the business owner.

- **Try to fix the problem**. If at all possible, reason with the person (you can usually contact them via Yelp, Google, etc.), and see if you can fix the problem. In some cases, you can, and then you can politely ask them to change the review.

- **Respond**. State your side of the situation in a positive, professional manner while acknowledging the right of the reviewer to her own opinion.

Remember: every business will get a few negative reviews, but if your business has more than the average… you may have a "business" problem and not a "review" problem.

**Don't shoot the (review) messenger.**

## Do Not Validate the Bad Review

Please note that if you have a negative review on a site like Yelp, Google, Amazon, etc., and the reviewer has a **weak profile** (e.g., *this is their first review, few friends, etc.*), if you respond to it, you are *validating* that review and making it *more likely* to appear high in your profile. Generally speaking, therefore, I recommend waiting at least a month before responding to a negative review by someone with a weak profile. There is a strong chance it will be filtered out as fake (especially on Yelp). But if after a month, it is still there, then consider a response.

**Responding to Reviews**

To **respond to a negative review**, do as follows. First and foremost, take the high ground. You can log into your business account / profile and respond to negative reviews. This is one of the benefits of claiming your business profile. But be positive and professional. Acknowledge their right to their opinion, but be firm as to your right to state your opinion as well. Second, state your side of the situation but realize you are NOT talking to the unhappy customer. You are talking to the person reading your reviews and deciding whether to reach out to you for a possible business engagement. Explain your side of the story. Often times, negative reviews come from nasty, unhappy people (which you can politely point out as for example, by asking the reader to click on the reviewer's name and see all their other negative reviews to realize that this is just a negative person). Or, the person wasn't a good fit for your business (so explain why). Or the person is being plain crazy. For example, I have had plastic surgeons condemned on Yelp because their waiting room was too hot, or other clients condemned because they didn't respond to an email. Finally, if the review is fake (i.e., by a competitor) or obscene or racist, you can complain to Yelp, Google, etc., and in some cases, they will remove the reviews. (To do this, log in to a personal account on Yelp, and right-click on the offensive review. You can then flag it and complain).

To read Yelp's official guide to responding to reviews, visit **http://jmlinks.com/5e**. To read Google's, visit **http://jmlinks.com/5f**. To read TripAdvisor's, visit **http://jmlinks.com/5g**. For whatever review site that matters to your business, you can usually search their help files for advice on how to respond to reviews. However, remember that the official policies are often very naive about how the game is truly played.

# SWAMP NEGATIVE REVIEWS WITH POSITIVE REVIEWS

A better strategy is to ignore the bad reviews and focus on soliciting positive reviews to "swamp" the negative reviews in an ocean of positivity. Again, in no way shape or form, am I advising you to be dishonest or solicit fake reviews. I am simply advising you to ask happy customers to just take a few minutes and tell their happy stories. If you proactively solicit positive, real reviews, you can drown out or swamp the negative reviews with a preponderance of positive reviews. In short, getting positive real reviews is the best way to respond to negative reviews.

*You don't ask; you don't get.*

For your fourth **To-do**, download the **Review Solicitation Worksheet**. For the worksheet, go to **http://jmlinks.com/social2020** (then reenter the code '**social2020**' to register your workbook), and click on the link to the "Reviews Solicitation Worksheet." You'll create a strategy to encourage positive reviews about your company.

## » Monitor and Improve Your Online Reputation

**Reputation management** is a new buzzword about protecting one's online reputation, whether for an individual or a business. To understand reputation management, first back up and consider the sales funnel, often explained as *AIDA: Awareness, Interest, Desire, and Action.* Prospective customers go through distinct phases as they consider solutions for their problems, needs, or desires:

> **Awareness.** An **awareness** of the problem and the beginning of Internet searches and social media outreach to friends, family, and colleagues about the problem, need, or desire and possible solutions. In this phase, searches are often "educational" in nature as in "how to cater a wedding" or "wedding ideas."

> **Interest.** As a customer becomes aware of available market solutions, they develop an **interest** in vendor offerings and even may make a shortlist. At this stage, and the next, they move closer to an "action," i.e., a purchase or engagement with a vendor solution. Searches at this point become "best wedding caterers" or "Boston catering companies," etc.

> **Desire.** Interest shifts towards **desire** and the customer begins to narrow down his or her shortlist. At this point, searches become *reputational* in nature. They may search a business name PLUS words like *reviews* or *complaints*. If your business were named Gina's Italian Kitchen, for example, they might search Google for "Gina's Italian Kitchen Reviews" or "Complaints against Gina's Italian Kitchen," or "Gina's Italian Kitchen Wedding Catering Reviews." **Reviews** is the operative word; if he or she finds *positive* reviews, that confirms your business is a good choice, whereas if he or she finds *negative* reviews, they may take you out of the consideration set entirely.

> **Action.** A choice is made to purchase the service or engage with your business. Upon completion, the customer may decide to leave her own review about your business for others.

*Reputation management*, in short, is monitoring and protecting your online **branded** and **reputational** searches. To be frank, it is also about attempting to upgrade positive reviews and positive brand mentions so that your online brand image shines.

To understand the search patterns, you can use the example of my company, The JM Internet Group. For example –

a "branded" search is: "JM Internet Group"

a "reputational" search is "JM Internet Group Reviews"

Review sites such as Yelp, CitySearch, Google, etc., as well as ones specific to your industry, can have an extremely positive – or extremely negative – impact on your online reputation. Indeed, branded searches on Google (searches for your company name, or your company name plus 'reviews') often return Google profiles and reviews directly on the right side of the page. For example, here's a screenshot of the search "Mecca Coffee Company" on Google:

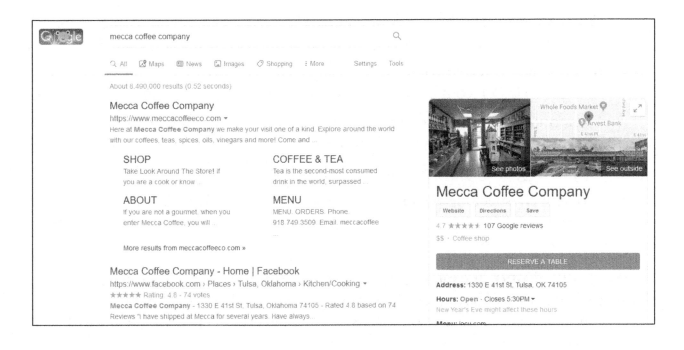

You can try the search at **http://jmlinks.com/32n**. Notice the primacy of reviews and the highlighted Google listing information plus review count on the far right. Scroll down the page and notice how Google identifies reviews on sites like Facebook, Yelp, and even Beeradvocate. Someone interested in going to the Mecca Coffee Company in Tulsa is likely to search for the company by name or perhaps for "Mecca Coffee

Company Reviews." This is even more true for high-value searches like probate attorneys, roofing companies, or kitchen remodeling contractors.

## GOOGLE YOUR COMPANY NAME PLUS REVIEWS AND MONITOR YOUR ONLINE REPUTATION

In addition to identifying, claiming, and optimizing your business listings on relevant review sites, you should also monitor your business on these sites. Usually, the act of claiming your listing in and of itself will generate an email anytime someone reviews your company. Paid services such as ReviewPush (**https://www.reviewpush.com/**), Free Review Monitoring (**https://freereviewmonitoring.com/**), and ReviewTrackers (**http://www.reviewtrackers.com/**) are sophisticated alert systems so that you always know whenever a new review is published about your business.

The reality is that you need to monitor your business reputation at least monthly, if not even more frequently. This means:

1. Doing Google searches for your company name as well as your company name plus "reviews;" and

2. Identifying the key customer review sites that matter for your business, such as Google, Yelp, YP.com, Avvo, etc. (this will vary by industry); and

3. Monitoring your review count, average star score, and whether you are getting more positive reviews each week or month;

4. Responding to negative reviews as needed; and, of course –

5. Pro-actively soliciting positive reviews on the key review sites to bolster your reputation.

For your fifth **TO-DO**, at a minimum, set up a monthly checkup of your listings on the major review sites you have identified. Note in a spreadsheet how many reviews you have, how many are 5, 4, 3, 2, or 1 stars. If you have budget, consider using a paid monitoring service.

## » MEASURE YOUR RESULTS

Let's sum up the bottom line. Reviews impact your business in two important ways:

- as a positive (or negative) "trust indicator" that you are a trustworthy business partner; and

- as a signal to search engines and review sites that you should rank high on searches for relevant keywords.

# MONITOR YOUR REVIEWS

Measurement of reviews, therefore, is focused on these two variables. On your keyword worksheet, I recommend that you create a tab called "local." Then every month, create a line item (for example, March 2020), and note down for your business:

The review site, number of reviews you have, and cumulative star rating.

Secondly, try searches for your strategic keywords on Yelp, Google, and/or on other relevant review sites (e.g., Airbnb, TripAdvisor, etc.), create a line item for each month, and indicate your position on those searches. For example, Andolino's Pizzeria was measured as No. 2 for the Google Search "pizza Tulsa" as seen in this screenshot on September 26, 2018:

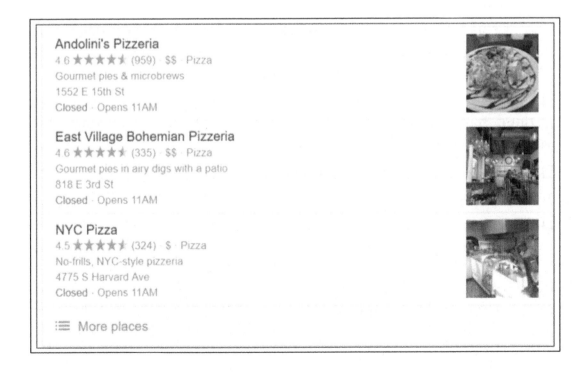

This would be recorded as Andolini's ranking #1 in the Google local pack, and having 959 reviews with a 4.5 star score. In other words, the restaurant is in good shape on both review sites. If it had dipped to a lower position on Yelp, for instance, then a to-do would be to encourage more Yelp reviews.

The two major aspects of monitoring your reviews, therefore are 1) your review count on each review site, and 2) your position on keyword searches on those sites. To the extent possible, you can then accelerate your efforts for a lagging site and relax a bit for a site for which you rank well and have positive reviews. (Note to monitor your rank, you can use the Fat Rank plugin for Chrome to monitor your rank on Google searches at **http://jmlinks.com/25w** or graduate to a paid rank measurement service such as AHREFS.com, MOZ.com, or SERPS.com.

## »» CHECKLIST: REVIEW ACTION ITEMS

Test your knowledge of the Review Revolution! Take the *Review marketing quiz* at **http://jmlinks.com/qzrv**. Next, here are your review **Action Items**:

❑ **Research** whether your customers (and competitors) utilize reviews. Which sites seem to matter for reviews, and why?

❑ Identify a few ***customer profiles*** that match your *buyer personas*, and determine how active they are as reviewers.

❑ Identify **companies** or **products** to "reverse engineer" who is doing a good job on various review sites both in terms of their search rank and their review volume and aggregate star ratings.

❑ Set up or claim **business listings** (e.g., claim your Google My Business account, Yelp account, Airbnb listings, etc.). Be sure to write down the passwords and keep them safe!

❑ **Optimize** your **business listings** by writing keyword-heavy copy into the business or product description, and uploading relevant photos.

❑ **SEO** your website for local search by including city names and keywords on your homepage, plus launch city-specific landing pages especially for those cities in which you have a physical location. Be sure to include your physical address and phone number so that it's easy for Google to see where you are located in the physical world. Include JSON-LD markup language / Schema markup language using the Google Webmaster's Structured Data Mark up Helper at **http://jmlinks.com/46x**.

❑ **Engage in Local Link-building.** Don't forget that, as part of your link-building strategy, you should look for **local link opportunities**. Join local associations, organizations, etc, and work with local nonprofits and business colleagues to get local links to your website.

❑ **Optimize** your **NAP consistency** by having a consistent name, address, and phone on your website and on all relevant listing sites. Consider using a service like Moz Local, Yext, or Whitespark to claim and optimize your secondary listings.

❑ Create a **review solicitation strategy** that you are comfortable with. This may be as simple as simply requiring employees to "ask" for a review after each job, or as complex as a pre-survey that has a review follow up.

> ❑ Pay attention to your company's branded searches on Google and whether review sites are showing up as part of a **reputation management** strategy.

> ❑ **Respond** to **negative reviews**, but be polite and take the high ground.

❑ Measure your **KPIs** (Key Performance Indicators) such as total reviews and aggregate star ratings each month.

Check out the **free tools**! Go to my *SEO Dashboard > Local SEO / SMM* for my favorite free tools on local and review marketing. Just visit **http://jmlinks.com/seodash**.

## »» DELIVERABLE: LOCAL SEO MARKETING PLAN

Now that we've come to the end of our Chapter on local reviews, your **DELIVERABLE** has arrived. For your final **TO-DO**, download the **Yelp / Local Marketing Plan Worksheet**. For the worksheet, go to **http://jmlinks.com/social2020** (then reenter the code '**social2020**' to register your workbook), and click on the link to the "Yelp / Local Review Marketing Worksheet." By filling out this plan, you and your team will establish a vision of what you want to achieve via local reviews.

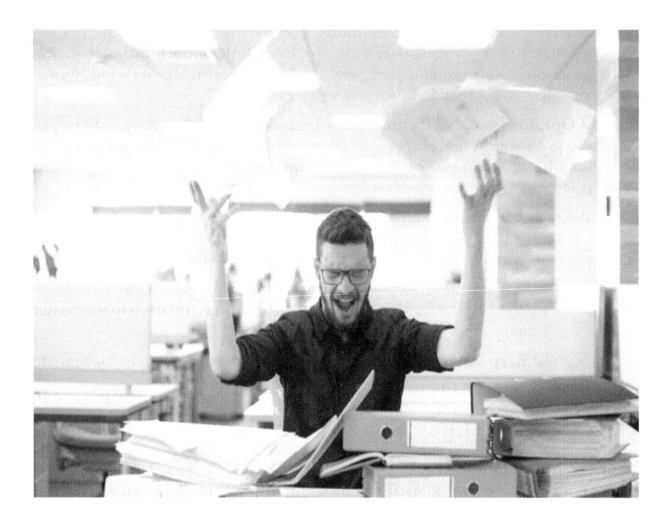

# 10
# EMAIL MARKETING

Email marketing is the "Rodney Dangerfield" of social media marketing. Dangerfield, of course, was an American stand-up comedian with a rather campy, self-deprecating style. He'd say, "Take my wife," and then pause, and say, "No, take my wife – *really*, please take my wife." Another famous Dangerfield quip was that he "Don't get no respect." Of course, he was one of the most successful comedians of his day. Like Dangerfield, email marketing doesn't seem to get "any respect." Yet, like Dangerfield, email marketing is far more effective than its trashy brand image implies.

In this Chapter, we'll explore the basics of email marketing, and we'll connect email marketing both forwards and backward to other social media channels. You can drive email signups, for example, from Facebook, and you can use your email list to drive social media events such as video views on YouTube, Facebook, or LinkedIn. And you can use email marketing to drive e-commerce events. What's not to like?

**Let's get started!**

## To-do List:

» Respect the Intimacy of Email

» Master the Steps to Success at Email Marketing

» Use Your List Forwards and Backwards

»» Checklist: Email Action Items

»» Deliverable: an Email Marketing Plan

## » Respect the Intimacy of Email

Customers may follow you on Twitter, like you on Facebook, or watch you on YouTube. It's not a big deal to "follow" someone on social. It's like meeting up for coffee. But getting customers to give you their email address – well, that's another story. And getting them to give their "real" email addresses, not the one used for spam or junk, that's yet one story more. Getting customers to "opt-in" to subscribe to your email alerts is more than just a cheap date. It's intimate. An email sign up is like a wedding night – they really love you, and they trust you enough to give you access to their email inbox. Those who sign up for your email list are likely to be superfans and micro-influencers, folks who are really "into" you, your brand or "into" the industry, sector, or topic that you represent.

Think about that for a moment.

*The person who is most likely to be willing to give you intimate access to their email inbox is exactly the person who is most likely to be a superfan.*

And superfans are key to influencer marketing, social shares, and promotion across the entire social media marketing universe. You'd be crazy not to use email marketing. Crazy.

Email marketing is the best way to communicate with your superfans. Better than Facebook, better than Twitter, better than LinkedIn. I'd even argue it's better than your own company trade show because email marketing is available 24/7, and you can communicate with superfans throughout the year. Email, when done well, combines "interrupt" marketing with "permission" marketing. When done well, email means that people want to get your communication and can't wait to be "interrupted" to hear your latest message.

Email is awesome!

But people hate email marketing. It's perceived as spammy and trashy.

Why? That's easy. Because it's so *valuable* and because it's so *vulnerable*, email is heavily abused by spam and spammers. If you think about it, however, you'll realize that the *outrage* against spam and spammers is just the flip side of the *intimacy* of email. People are outraged about spam because spam is, to be blunt, a kind of digital assault. It's a forced interruption into an intimate space, which is why spam is so nasty and terrible, and spammers are just awful, horrible human beings. Spammers and robocallers should be confined to a special circle of Hell.

Flip this around, and you'll see that if you can honestly gain customer permission and earn customer trust, then having a consensual email relationship can be great for both you and your customers. You need their trust and permission. For a great read on this topic, check out Seth Godin's *Permission Marketing* (**http://jmlinks.com/43a**).

## Email is Owned Media

Indeed, email can be considered "owned" media vs. "rented" media. While you build out your Facebook or Instagram following, grow your connections on LinkedIn, or encourage views of your YouTube channel, you are ultimately not in control. Each platform creates its own rules, and has its own algorithm. Indeed, years ago brands built out their Facebook Pages and enjoyed tremendous organic reach, for free. But nowadays, Facebook has taken away or at least severely curtailed organic reach on the platform. You don't own your Facebook follower list; you rent it. The same is true across all the other platforms: no matter how great they are, today, there is no guarantee that they won't dramatically change organic reach and the terms of service, tomorrow.

# EMAIL IS OWNED (BY YOU)

Email in contrast is something you own. While you may use a provider like AWeber or Constant Contact, **you own your list**. You configure it, and you send out the email blasts. There is no algorithm to worry about, other than the spam-fighting algorithm of all the email providers like Yahoo, Outlook, or Gmail. Because you own your list as opposed to renting it, your email list is arguably a much more valuable digital asset than the number of your Facebook Page followers or views of your YouTube Channel.

Email can even be used *forward* and *backward* with your other social media marketing assets (as I will explain in a moment), making it a prime catalyst to effective digital marketing. Email can be used to encourage reviews on Yelp, Google, or even Amazon.

## » MASTER THE STEPS TO SUCCESS AT EMAIL MARKETING

How do you use email successfully? First of all, identify what's in it for your audience. Why would a customer sign up for your email list? What's in it for him? Is it a free eBook? A detailed tutorial? Perhaps insider information, special discounts, or free offers? The "reason for subscribing," the reason why they want to receive and read your email list, is the anchor to your email marketing strategy. Start with something free, something compelling, and something non-threatening.

For example, Souplantation / Sweet Tomatoes (**https://souplantation.com/**) has a very easy-to-understand prompt for their list. Sign up and get free coupons and discounts. Here's a screenshot:

And here's their October eLetter with what's cooking and of course special coupons for me:

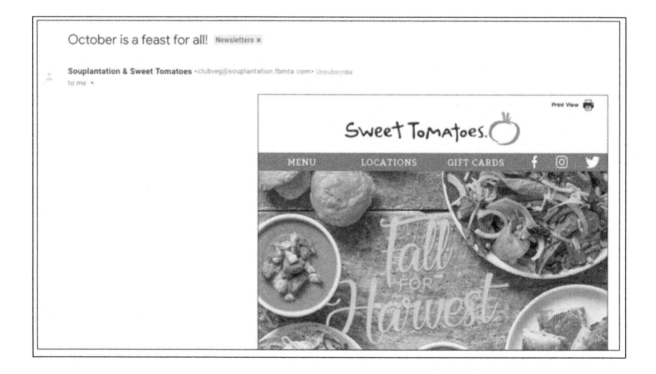

For something more intellectual, I subscribe to the Author's Guild eLetter which shares information relevant to authors. Here's their October eLetter:

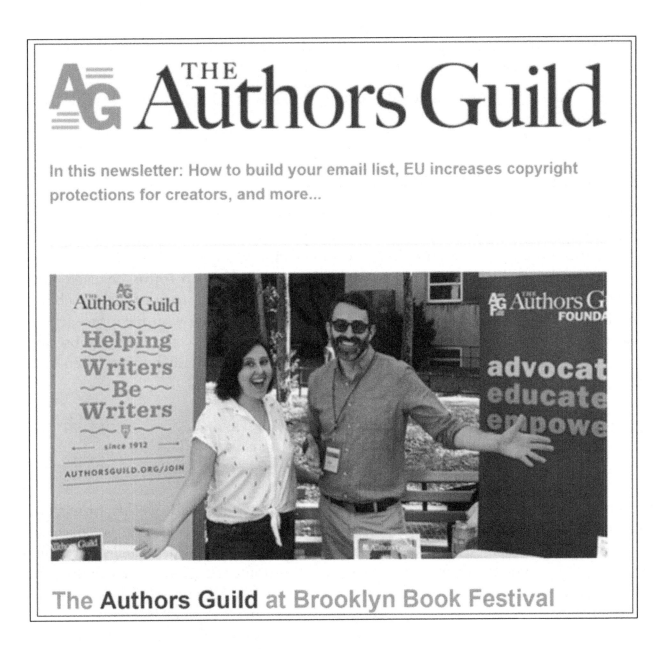

The **Authors Guild** at Brooklyn Book Festival

In both cases, the website promotes sign-ups, and the eLetters have a clear value proposition for the user. You sign up, and you get something. And you keep getting something each month of value, "for free."

As is true for all social media, your "posts" to email (that is the e-blasts that you send out and the content within that email newsletter or other blast) should thus be 80% or more "fun, fun, fun," and 20% or less "buy my stuff." The reason for subscribing needs to always be some type of "carrot," some type of content or offer that's very yummy and on-going, and then each blast needs to be configured to be a type of "sub carrot" as it were. Yes, you can send out an e-blast that is very much "buy my stuff," but the total email marketing package to subscribers needs to be 80% or more "fun, fun, fun," and only 20% or less "buy my stuff."

Always: make it clear that you won't spam them. Don't frighten them away with "hard sells." Don't abuse the trust relationship.

## Technical Issues with Email Marketing

Next, there are the technical issues of email – choosing an email provider like AWeber, MailChimp, or Constant Contact, for example. To be honest, there aren't great differences among them. All provide very good technical support. And all provide a lot of good technical help as to how to build lists, create sign up forms, manage email blasts, unsubscribes, etc. I recommend you use a formal email provider as the technical mechanics of getting your email to recipients, even recipients who have pro-actively subscribed to your list, are not easy. Email faces "spam filters" and even a subscriber who has pro-actively subscribed to your list may not see your email or may even mark it as spam.

*Getting email reliably delivered is no easy feat, so use a paid service.*

There is the actual sending of the emails. Will it be done on a daily, weekly, or monthly basis? Will it be an email newsletter of one size fits all? Will it be more narrowly customized? Or will it be a **DRIP** campaign? (Drip marketing is the strategy of sending "drips," or pre-written emails automatically via a computer program. Amazon does this all the time – a few days after you make a purchase, you're sent a "please review us" email, for example, and a few days after you browse Amazon, you'll be sent a "you may also like" email. DRIP campaigns can also be set up with eBooks and other free tutorials as the first offer, and then plugs for paid services coming next.) The mechanics have to do with the sign-up, sending, and measurement of email messages and email marketing. You can also segment your list into sublists so that people who like dogs get specific messaging, people who like cats get another set of messages, and people who like iguanas get their own specific content. The more personalized and the more customized you can make your emails, the better.

## Promote Your List

Third, there's the issue of promotion. How will potential customers and existing customers find out about your list? What will get them excited about signing up? What are the mechanics of signing up? What are the mechanics of unsubscribing, so that they feel "safe" subscribing to your list in the first place? To grow your list, you want to make sure it's a prominent action on your website, easy to find on your social profiles, and a desired action on many of your posts. If you launch a new, free eBook or webinar, for example, you can use this reasons as a way to drive subscribers. Or, for instance, after a webinar is successfully completed, you can require folks to sign up for your email list to get the recording, and so on and so forth.

## » USE YOUR LIST FORWARDS AND BACKWARDS

Email, like all of social media, is not an end in itself but rather a means to an end, that is a way to build your brand and ultimately sell more stuff. As you work on email marketing, a good way to think about your list is to think forward and backward. As for "forwards," I mean thinking of email along the customer journey or sales funnel as an intermediate step between the coldness of just learning about your brand on Facebook and the hotness of actually making a purchase on your e-commerce store (or becoming an active sales lead via a feedback form).

For example:

1. A customer learns about your brand on Facebook through a post.

2. He signs up to "like" your Facebook Page.

3. Over time, through posts via Facebook, he learns you have an email list with even more interesting content – perhaps content reserved for superfans, perhaps special deals or offers, perhaps inside information on the brand, etc.

4. He signs up for your email list.

5. You then feed him information on your brand, consisting of 80% or more "fun, fun, fun" content and 20% or less "buy my stuff" information.

6. He then ultimately clicks from one of your "buy my stuff" posts to your e-commerce store and makes a purchase.

Facebook is less intimate than email, and email is less intimate than becoming a paid subscriber. You are using email in a "forwards" direction to move customers along the customer journey or sales funnel from Facebook to email to a sales lead to a sale.

## Using Email in a Backward Direction

Email can also be used in a backward direction? How so? Having read this far in the Workbook, you should know that *reviews* matter a lot on Yelp, Google, and Amazon, and that *video views* matter a lot on YouTube, Facebook, Twitter, and LinkedIn. Because email is more intimate than true social media, you can leverage the enthusiasm of your superfans on your email list to grow your social media following and reach. Let's say you've launched a new video on YouTube, you can then:

1. Announce via your email list that you have a beefy, new video on YouTube on topic such-and-such.

2. You can ask your email list fans to watch the video, thumb it up, comment on it, and even share it.

In this way, email can increase the view count and engagement of a video on YouTube, and because the YouTube algorithm pays attention to the velocity of engagement, using email at a strategic moment can help propel a video to the top of YouTube search and shares. The same goes for videos on Facebook, Twitter, and LinkedIn. All platforms reward views, engagement, and velocity – again, meaning that you can use email to prime the pump.

As for reviews, you can offer bonus content for books (as I do) or merely use email to push out requests for reviews on Google, Yelp, and other local platforms. Not surprisingly, paid services like GatherUp and Reviewbuzz rely heavily on email (and text messages) to juice reviews.

In summary, email is not an end in itself, but rather a means to an end, and email can fit into pretty much any phase of the customer journey, moving forward or backward.

Email is awesome!

### »» CHECKLIST: EMAIL ACTION ITEMS

Here are your email **Action Items**:

❏ **Research** -

❏ Whether **your customers** might be interested in signing up for an email newsletter or email notification. Why or why not?

❏ Whether **competitors** and their email marketing efforts. Sign up for their email lists in "stealth mode" and monitor how they use email to marketing.

❏ Whether **there are similar companies to emulate**. Look beyond your own industry, and sign up for the email lists of leading companies that use email well.

❏ **Set up** an email account on one of the big providers such as Aweber, Constant Contact, or Mailchimp and begin building your list.

❏ **Identify a "carrot" for your list.** Brainstorm why people will want to sign up for your list and create a "carrot" (the big reason) and then as you create message, ensure that each message or at least most messages have "carrots."

❏ **Begin sending emails.** Start with content that people will want to get in their email inbox and then brainstorm a –

❏ **Forward path** – that is getting people to subscribe to your list, in the first place, and then using email as an intermediate step between awareness and a desired action such as an e-commerce purchase or a sales inquiry.

❏ **Backward path** – that is, using email to support other social media efforts such as reviews on review sites or video views.

❏ **Measure** your email success via subscriber growth, click-throughs, and unsubscribes to your list.

Check out the **free tools**! Go to my *Social Media Marketing Dashboard > Email* for my favorite free tools on email marketing. Just visit **http://jmlinks.com/smmdash**.

## »» DELIVERABLE: AN EMAIL MARKETING PLAN

Your **DELIVERABLE** has arrived. For the worksheet, go to **http://jmlinks.com/social2020** (then enter the code '**social2020**' to register your workbook), and click on the link to the "Email Marketing Plan." By filling out this plan, you and your team will establish a vision of what you want to achieve via email marketing, including your KPIs (Key Performance Indicators)

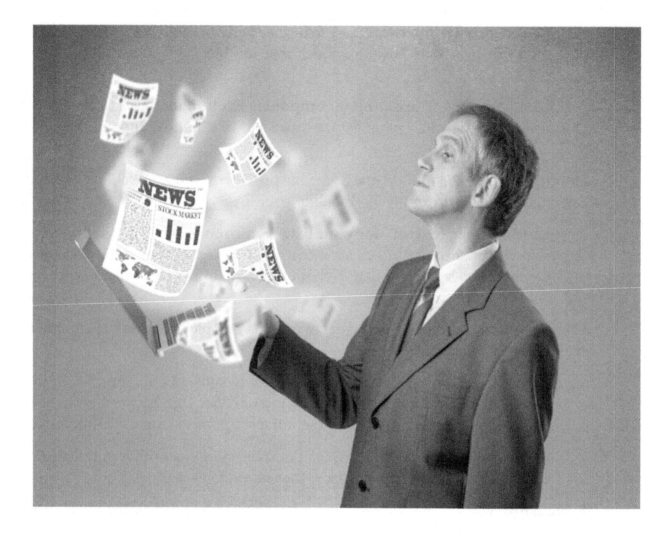

# 11
# EPILOGUE

There's always something new! That's what makes social media fun, isn't it? Come on, admit it: you can't wait for the next new thing. (*Just kidding, you probably can wait, but it won't wait for you*). I guarantee there will be a next new thing, and I guarantee that they will hype it in such a way that you just "gotta" be doing it.

As we end our journey through the world of social media marketing, I want to point out some of the newer opportunities (ones which do not yet have substantial traction for small businesses) and give you a conceptual framework to think about and evaluate them.

Finally, I want to motivate you to "just do it" and "never stop learning."

**Let's get started!**

## To-Do List:

» New Kids on the Block

» Just Do It

» Never Stop Learning

»» Deliverable: a Social Media Marketing Plan

» A Final Favor

## » NEW KIDS ON THE BLOCK

There seems to always be a "new" new thing in Social Media. At the time of this writing, I'd award the "new kid on the block" award to TikTok (**https://www.tiktok.com/**). It's the darling of teenagers and has revitalized short, quirky videos. TikTok shows, among other things, that there is room in social media for innovation. The big providers like YouTube, Facebook, and Instagram failed to capitalize on the hunger for authentic, silly, and – let's admit it – *narcissistic* videos. You can download the TikTok app for both Android and iOS, and check out this new player in the video space. Another "fun fact" is that TikTok is owned by the Chinese, so there are constant rumors about its privacy policies and snooping. But teenagers (mine included) don't seem to care. Will it succeed? Who knows, but I would argue that the same rules of video that apply to marketing on YouTube will ultimately apply to TikTok. Create great, engaging content that "builds your brand" and ultimately "sells more stuff," but in a soft-sell kind of way.

Snapchat (**https://www.snapchat.com/**) is yet another relative newcomer. What's interesting is that Snapchat isn't really a social media app; it's a *messaging* app with ads. So far the main opportunities for brands are in the "stories" feature (organically) and via advertising. It's not clear if Snapchat will survive the competitive onslaught from Instagram, which seems to constantly steal its features. It is clear that Snapchat's model of being more "private" messaging than "social media" is something that Mark Zuckerberg in particular is keen to imitate. Watch for both Facebook and Instagram to trend towards being closed vs. being openness. Twitter, in contrast, seems to be going the other direction.

Yet another one to watch is Medium (**https://medium.com/**), which seems to be the up and coming place for long-form content. And still another one – the growth of podcasting.

For most small to medium businesses, wherever you see opportunities, use them! What is critical for one company may be irrelevant to another, and not just a network (e.g., Snapchat) but a feature (such as "Stories"). It's not one size fits all. And watch out for backlashes as well. I predict oversaturation soon for "influencer marketing" and a backlash against the rather dirty trend of influencers being paid to promote things without really being honest about this fact with their audiences. Privacy is yet another backlash in the works, both from governments (such as CCPA in California or COPPA at the federal level) and from users (who are sick and tired of their data being sold).

Here are my recommendations:

- **Keep your eye out for** new social media platforms that might be relevant to your business like TikTok, Snapchat, Instagram, or Medium.

- **Sign up for a user account**, and find the business help files or "how to advertise" information. Begin your research.

- **Research** whether your potential customers are "on" this social media and – if so – figure out what they are doing.

- Keep an eye out for **competitors** or **big brands. Reverse engineer** what they are doing in terms of marketing, and translate their actions into doable items for your own company.

- **Brainstorm** how you and your company can participate in an authentic way and yet still have a marketing objective. Is it possible to use TikTok, Snapchat, or Instagram Stories to interact with potential customers? How or how not?

- Start slowly, **learn by doing**, and don't be too heavy-handed.


In most cases, you'll see many similarities between the "new" social media like TikTok, Snapchat or Instagram and the "old" social media like Facebook or Twitter. Snapchat, for example, is beginning to overtake Twitter as a place for real-time or instantaneous communication, as well as a way for brands to offer exclusive information, coupons, or deals to their most avid fans. The fact that a "snap" disappears over time isn't really that different from a tweet. Instagram, in turn, isn't that different from photo-sharing on Facebook (it's really just the photo element of Facebook), plus some similarities to Twitter. Remember Flickr? It was really just Instagram before its time. TikTok? It's just Periscope reimagined.

Indeed, once you see how Snapchat and Instagram are "going after" Twitter, it makes a lot of sense why Twitter has earned the dubious title of the "troubled" social media. I have also to commentate that, sadly, it looks like Facebook (which owns Instagram) has largely succeeded in stealing Snapchat's thunder by shamelessly copying innovations like stories. So watch out for these competitive battles with an eye to who wins, and who loses. Facebook seems to be having its own time of troubles, battled by being perceived as stodgy by the young set, loose with privacy on all fronts, and hated by the political class. I envy Zuckerberg his money but not his headaches.

But beyond TikTok, Snapchat, and Instagram, you may find social media like Tumblr (**https://www.tumblr.com/**) or even ones overseas. (China, in particular, has its own unique set of social media platforms). New ones will no doubt pop up, but the structural realities of social media make them all the members of the same genus if not the same species.

Along the way, keep your eye on the established social media platforms like Facebook, LinkedIn, Twitter, and YouTube as they are also innovating and adding new features. Facebook's move to native video, for example, has opened up new marketing possibilities for "native" video on the platform. Facebook Live, and YouTube Live are other examples of new opportunities "within" a platform as opposed to on a totally new platform. I am also very excited about LinkedIn as a blogging platform for B2B. IGTV? Yes please. As an information strategy, identify the official blogs for the media most relevant to your company and follow them. I use Feedly (**https://feedly.com/**) as an easy aggregator for official and unofficial blogs that cover social media. Check out the dashboard (**http://jmlinks.com/smmdash**) > *Social Media Conferences and Social Media Publications* for my favorite resources to stay informed.

## » JUST DO IT

Voltaire said, "The perfect is the enemy of the good," and today's Nike corporation said, "Just do it!" before it, too, got embroiled in controversy. In both cases, the thought is to "learn by doing," to not be afraid to be bold, and to just "get started."

- Don't be intimidated!

- Do some research, make a plan, and get started!

- Just do it!

Many companies get stuck in "analysis paralysis," always researching and never doing. Don't be one of them! Others get stuck in "doing with no strategy," as in tweeting 24/7 when none of their customers are on Twitter.

Do it! But keep your eyes and ears open to strategy, tactics, and results. If it isn't working, try something else. Don't be afraid to try, and fail. (Good advice even for Nike).

Everyone – including myself- is just learning how to "do" social media marketing. Don't be intimidated. There are no real experts. Just fools like me who pretend to know what we're doing.

So just do it, please. *(And email me your ideas, thoughts, suggestions, and questions. I learn more from my students than from anyone else).*

## » NEVER STOP LEARNING

If you haven't already, download my *Marketing Alamanac,* and turn to the Chapter on publications and conferences. Read the social media blogs (I'm partial to the *Social Media Examiner* (**http://www.socialmediaexaminer.com/**)). If possible, try to attend the yearly trade show, *Social Media Marketing World,* which is really a fantastic learning opportunity for those who have already mastered "the basics."

Never stop learning!

## »» DELIVERABLE: OUTLINE A SOCIAL MEDIA MARKETING PLAN

Now that we've come to the end of the book go back to the "Party On" chapter. If you haven't already completed it, your **DELIVERABLE** has arrived. For the worksheet, go to **https://www.jm-seo.org/workbooks** (click on *Social Media Marketing Workbook 2018*, enter the code '**social2020**' to register your workbook), and click on the link to the "Social Media Marketing Plan Big Picture Worksheet." By filling out this plan, you and your team will establish a vision of what to do at the top level, and then by filling out the plans and worksheets for individual media like Twitter, Facebook, or Instagram, you'll know what to do for each individual medium. So get started, and in the immortal words of Garth Algar of the movie Wayne's World, "Party On!"

## » A FINAL FAVOR

If you've read this far, well, I'm impressed. I feel like at this point I should give you the ultimate secret to social media and life in general. I think it's some combination of "never stop learning," "be humble," and most of all "be kind to other people." We're all God's children and if we could just learn to see that in everyone we meet… well, the Earth would be a lot nicer. But I digress.

I hope you've enjoyed this journey with me, and if the Spirit moves you, I would really appreciate a short, honest review of the *Social Media Marketing Workbook* on Amazon. Simply fire up your browser, go to Amazon.com, and search for the book. (You can also click on **http://jmlinks.com/smm**). Click on "customer reviews" and then on "Write a customer review."

Thanks in advance.

# SURVEY OFFER

**CLAIM YOUR $5 REBATE! HERE'S HOW -**

Visit **http://jmlinks.com/survey**.

1. Take a short, simple survey about the book.

2. Indicate whether you want a $5 rebate or want to make a contribution to our scholarship fund.

**WE WILL THEN -**

- Rebate you the $5, or thank you profusely for helping a deserving young marketer.

~ **$5 REBATE OFFER** ~

~ **LIMITED TO ONE PER CUSTOMER** ~

**SUBJECT TO CHANGE WITHOUT NOTICE**

**GOT QUESTIONS? CALL 800-298-4065**

Made in the USA
Monee, IL
21 July 2020